Childhood and Growing Up

Childhood and Growing Up

Theory and Practice

Noushad Husain

SHIPRA

ISBN: 978-81-7541-860-8

First Published in India in 2016

Childhood and Growing Up: Theory and Practice

Published by:
SHIPRA PUBLICATIONS
LG 18-19, Pankaj Central Market, I.P. Ext.
Patparganj, Delhi-110092, India
Tel: 91-11-2223 5152, 2223 6152
E-mail: info@shiprapublication.com
www.shiprapublication.com

The Author Gratefully Acknowledges
His Indebtedness to

God

For His Mercy

Dedicated to My Beloved Son

Arsh Husain

"A Child is like a butterfly in the wind.
Some can fly higher than others,
But each one flies the best it can.
Why compare one against the other?
Each one is different.
Each one is special.
Each one is beautiful."

Preface

The present book entitled as "Childhood and Growing Up" provides the insight into the important changes and notable differences that take place during the development of the children and adolescents. The subject matter of the book deals with the complete concepts of childhood to adolescence and also defines the numerous aspects of child growth and development, which includes physical, mental, social, emotional, cognitive and language development. It describes the principles, facts and details of intelligence and personality development of persons which are presented by various Child Psychologists.

This book is prepared to serve the educational purposes of students, teachers, teacher-educators, student-teachers, parents etc. for developing a better understanding about the growth and development of the children. I hope that after reading the present book, the readers will be able to better understand the different stages of adolescents and their corresponding characteristics, problems and requirements. The teachers will take care all the children and treat them equally.

This book is based on latest Curriculum Framework-2014 developed by NCTE and has 38 important chapters. The chapter 1 deals with introduction to psychology. The chapter 2 and chapter 3 talked about educational psychology and methods of educational psychology respectively. The chapter-4 deals with the principles and different stages of child growth and development. Under this chapter, the growth and development patterns of children are discusses. The knowledge about heredity and environment is discusses in chapter 5. Chapter 6 deals with the concept of individual differences. The next chapter 7 discusses about the development of adolescent and explains in detail the different developmental characteristics of adolescents. The next chapters, namely, chapter 8, chapter 9, chapter 10, chapter 11, chapter 12 and chapter 13 are written especially for explaining the development of adolescents, namely––Motor, Intellectual or Cognitive, Language, Moral and Psychosocial, Emotional and Social. Chapter 14 deals with the meaning and types of parenting styles or child rearing practices.

The objective of writing chapter 15 is to explain the methods to understand children's and adolescent's behavior to the teachers. Chaapter 16 explains in details the concepts of learning and its associated concepts. Chapter 17, chapter 18, chapter 19 and chapter 20 help the readers to understand the learning from behaviourist, cognitivist, constructivist and humanist point of view. Chapter 21 discusses different learning theories with its educational implications. The concept of transfer of learning has been explained in chapter 22. Chapter 23 talked about motivation and chapter 24 explains the discovery learning theory of Jerome Bruner. Chapter 25 and chapter 26 explain in details the concepts of 'children in marginalized environment' and 'deprivation and deprived children'. Chapter 27, chapter 28 and chapter 29 talked about 'thinking', 'concept formation' and 'decision making' respectively. Intelligence and its important theories with its educational implications are explained in chapter 30. Chapter 31 talked about the types of personality. Chapter 32 explains in details the concept, nature, characteristics of creativity. Impact of media on growing children and adolescents has been discussed in chapte 33. Chapter 34, chapter 35 and chapter 36 deal with 'mental health and mental hygiene', 'life skills and ARSH skills' and 'stress and its management' respectively. The meaning of games, group dynamics, conflict and negotiation are explained in chapter 37. The last chapter of the book namely 'Play and Child Development' discusses the importance of play in child's growth and development.

First of all, I thank a lot of my indebtedness to 'God for His Mercy', because without the mercy of God, the present book could not be completed. God gave me a direction, knowledge, support and patience to write this book.

I would like to take this opportunity to thanks my father Mr. Zakir Husain and Mother Mrs. Aiysha Begum, who are always a source of inspiration for my academic work. I would also like to thanks my wife Razda Khan and my beloved son Arsh Husain because without the help and support of my family members this would not have been possible.

The author is grateful to the various authors, writers and editors of the books and journals or any other type of published work for preparing the manuscript of this book. I would like to show my gratitude towards all those authors and publishers, whose works have been consulted, quoted and abstracted to make, the book up-to-date and useful.

With great pleasure, I want to express my grateful appreciation to my beloved son Arsh Husain for inspiring me to write this wonderful book.

In the end, I am thankful to Mr. D. Kumar, Shipra Publications for the meticulous processing of the manuscript and give the book a nice look.

Dr. Noushad Husain

Contents

Chapter-1
Introduction to Psychology

WHAT IS PSYCHOLOGY?

The word, *'Psychology'* is derived from two Greek words, *'Psyche'* and *'Logos'*. *'Psyche'* means *'soul'* and *'Logos'* means *'science'*. Thus psychology was first defined as the *'science of soul'*. The different meanings of psychology are:

Psychology as the Science of Soul

In ancient days, the Greek philosophers like Plato and Aristotle interpreted Psychology as the "science of the soul" and studied it as a branch of Philosophy. But, soul is something metaphysical. It cannot be seen, observed and touched and we cannot make scientific experiments on soul.

Psychology as the Science of the Mind

It was the German philosopher Emmanuel Kant who defined Psychology as the "science of the mind". William James (1892) defined psychology as the science of mental processes. But, the word 'mind' is also quite ambiguous as there was confusion regarding the nature and functions of mind.

Psychology as the Science of Consciousness

Modern psychologists defined psychology as the "Science of Consciousness". James Sully (1884) defined psychology as the "Science of the Inner World". Wilhelm Wundt (1892) defined psychology as the science which studies the "internal experiences". But there are three levels of consciousness – conscious, subconscious and the unconscious and so this definition also was not accepted by some.

Psychology as the Science of Behaviour

At the beginning of the 20th century, when psychologists attempted to develop psychology into a pure science, it came to be defined as the "science of behaviour". The term behaviour was popularized by J.B. Watson. Other exponents are William McDugall and W.B. Pillsbury. According to R.S. Woodworth, *"First Psychology lost its soul, then it lost its mind, then lost its consciousness. It still has behaviour of a sort."*

DEFINITIONS OF PSYCHOLOGY

1. B.F. Skinner defined, *"Psychology is the science of behaviour and experience."*
2. Crow and Crow, *"Psychology is the study of human behaviour and human relationships."*

3. William Mc Dougall, *"Psychology is the science which aims to give us better understanding and control of the behaviour of the organism as a whole."*
4. Kurt Koffka, *"Psychology is the scientific study of the behaviour of living creatures in their contact with the outer world."*
5. According to Woodworth – *"Psychology is the science of the activities of individual in relation to the environment."*
6. Watson – *"Psychology is the positive science of behaviour."*
7. Cruze – *"Psychology is the science of human behaviour and experience."*
8. Guilford – *"Psychology is the science of mental activity of an organism."*
9. According to Charles E. Skinner- *"Psychology deals with the responses to any and every kind of situation that life presents. By responses or behaviour is meant all forms of processes, adjustments, activities, and experiences of the organism."*
10. William James (1892) defined psychology as the *"science of mental processes"*.
11. According to James Sully (1884) – *"Psychology as the Science of the Inner World."*
12. Wilhelm Wundt (1892) – *"Psychology as the science which studies the "internal experiences."*
13. W.B. Pillsbury (1911) and J.B. Watson (1912) – *"Psychology as the science of behaviour."*
14. B.F. Skinner – *"Psychology should, therefore, be defined as a science of behaviour and experiences on human beings"*

NATURE OF PSYCHOLOGY

In simple words, psychology is a systematic and scientific study of mental processes, experiences and behaviours - both overt and covert. The word *'psychology'* has its origin in two Greek words *'psyche'* and *'logos'*. The word *'psyche'* in Greek language refers to *'spirit'* or *'soul'* and the word *'logos'* refers to *'discourse'* or *'study'*. During earlier times it was considered as a discipline which deals with the study of soul. In India the study of such questions was the main concern during Vedic and Upanishadic period. Various aspects of mental processes were analyzed. Subsequently the schools of Yoga, Samkhya, Vedant, Nyaya, Buddhism, and Jainism provided detailed accounts of mind, mental processes and methods to control mind. In modern period it started at Calcutta University in 1916 with establishment of the Department of Psychology.

In the western world, the formal beginning of psychology as an independent discipline goes back to 1879 when Wilhelm Wundt established the first experimental laboratory at the University of Leipzig, in Germany. Since then the growth of psychology has covered a long journey. Today it is one of the very popular subjects among social sciences. It studies all the shades of experiences, mental processes and behaviours. A comprehensive analysis of all these aspects provides a scientific understanding of human nature. The three fold nature of psychology is as shown in Figure 1.1.

1. Study of Experience

Psychologists study a variety of human experiences which are mainly personal or private in nature. They may range from experiences of dream, conscious experiences at different stages of life and experiences when the consciousness is altered through meditation or use of psychedelic drugs. The study of such experiences helps the psychologist to understand the personal world of the individual.

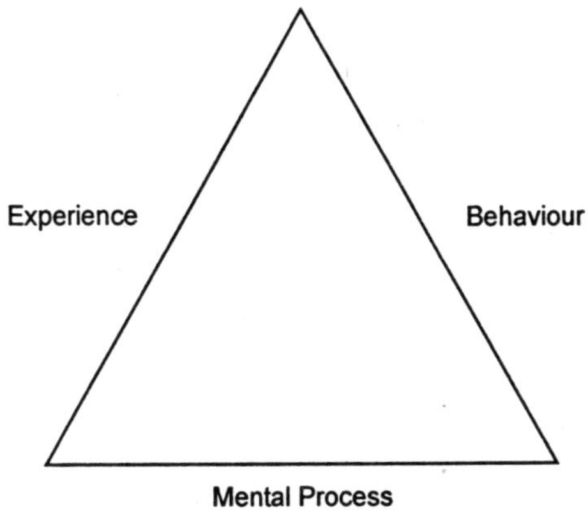

Figure 1.1: Aspects of the Subject Matter of Psychology

2. Study of Mental Processes

Psychology as the study of mental processes tries to investigate the activities happening in the brain which are primarily non physiological in nature. These mental processes include perception, learning, remembering and thinking. These are internal mental activities which are not directly observed but inferred from the behavioural activities of the person. For example, we can say that somebody is thinking if he or she displays certain activities related to finding solution to a mathematical problem assigned to him or her.

3. Study of Behaviour

The range of behaviours studied in psychology is very broad. It includes simple reflexes (e.g. eye blinking), common response patterns such as talking to friends, verbal reports about feelings and internal states and complex behaviours such as handling computers, playing piano and addressing a crowd. These behaviours are either observed directly through naked eyes or are measured through instruments. They are generally exhibited verbally or nonverbally (e.g. facial expression) when an individual reacts to a stimulus in a given situation.

Thus, in psychology the main unit of investigation is the individual human being and his or her experiences, mental processes and behaviours.

SCOPE OF PSYCHOLOGY

Psychology signifies the scientific study of the human mind and mental states, and of human and animal behaviour. It seeks to predict and control the behaviours while finding out the causes through observation and reasoning process. The sole purpose of psychology is to know and understand why people behave the way they do. The domain of psychology has, in course of time, emerged as one of the important disciplines while widening its scopes and being applicable to different fields of human endeavors, such as, employment, industries, education, personality development and being one of its popular branches, to the treatment of mental and emotional problems. A few of its branches may be outlined are as follow:

Organizational Psychology

This branch of psychology is also known as Industrial or occupational Psychology. It is meant to improve the efficiency and effectiveness of business organizations while solving the organizational problems. It seeks to identify the leadership styles, organizational conflicts and the psychological characteristics of the workplace so that there may be considerable improvement in the functioning state of a business. Not only it's concerned with business development but also the effectiveness and efficiency in terms of employees' performance. The psychologist or the consultants of this branch are in great demands as they contribute greatly to the total organizational development.

Social Psychology

While dealing with the social behaviour on the one hand, it is meant to help the people in solving their social problems on the other. It is focused on how the role of society and its culture influence in the development of one's personality. This field of psychology is interested to identify the social situations and the attitudes of the people towards them so as to help the people in altering and improving their attitudes while trying to reduce tensions and making them better human beings.

Clinical Psychology

This area of psychology is much popular among other braches. It deals with mental, emotional and abnormal behaviour of the people. It seeks to help the people come out of their mental disorders. Its practice involves psychological assessment and psychotherapy while various training programmes and personality and intelligence tests are conducted under this branch of Psychology for the treatment of mental problems. Mostly, the psychologist of this field work with psychiatrists.

Counseling Psychology

Counseling psychologists are concerned with the problems of every day life, concerning academic, social, emotional, occupational and organizational. They acquire reasonable knowledge of their field and help their clients to overcome situations causing everyday stress.

They are employed in colleges, universities and hospitals. Though the distinction between Clinical psychologist and the counseling psychologist may be difficult but primarily the area of counseling psychologist involves similar methods as those of clinical psychologist's.

Educational Psychology

It deals with educational processes and practices and is focused on how individual learns through educational settings. It is concerned with teaching methodologies and processes. It is helpful to the students in the achievement of merits while providing required services and guidance to the physically handicapped students. The psychologist of this branch are appointed in schools and colleges.

Whatever area of psychology one belongs to, the ultimate objective is to know about human nature while helping out the individuals in various problems and becoming better human beings. Psychology seeks to understand and predict and control the behaviour that the behaviour may ultimately be such that lets one live peacefully.

BRANCHES/FIELDS OF PSYCHOLOGY

During its journey of more than a hundred years, psychology as a field of enquiry has grown in many directions. In contemporary times a number of specialized fields with focused area of application have developed. The emergence of different fields in psychology indicates the importance and relevance of these areas in our daily life.

Psychology studies and explains the behaviour of entire living organisms. The term *'behaviour'* includes the cognitive, Conative and affective, conscious, subconscious or unconscious, implicit or explicit. It also includes the behaviour of people from infancy to old age, the normal as well as abnormal.

It is very difficult to understand all these aspects of behaviour in one sphere. Hence, in order to make it convenient to study, understand and access the behaviour at different fields of life, psychology is divided into different branches. These branches/fields of psychology are broadly divided into two categories viz., pure and applied.

I. Pure Branches of Psychology

Pure branches provide the theoretical frame work of the subject. These branches deal with formulation of principles, theories and suggest different methods for the assessment of behaviour. The pure branches also suggest certain techniques for the modification of problematic behaviour. The important pure branches of psychology are:

General Psychology

This branch deals with the fundamental rules, principles and theories of psychology in relation to the study of behaviour of normal adult human beings. It explains various psychological processes like sensations, perceptions, emotions, learning, intelligence, personality, etc.

Physiological Psychology

This branch describes the biological basis of behaviour. There is a close relationship between body and mind; the functions of each other are mutually influenced. The functioning of the brain, nervous system, endocrine glands and their relation to cognitive, Conative and affective behaviour is explained in this branch of psychology.

Cognitive Psychology

It deals with acquisition, storage, transformation and application of information the individual uses to understand and interpret events happening around him/her.

Developmental Psychology

Human life passes through various stages of development from conception to old age. This branch explains the growth and development of various processes in relation to behaviour. This field is concerned with the study of various physical and psychological factors which influence the systematic changes which the individual experiences across the different stages of life.

Child Psychology

Childhood extends from 2 to 12 years. This is a crucial period in the life. Future life depends upon development during childhood. Growth and development will be rapid during this stage. Child psychology deals with these aspects.

Animal Psychology

This branch deals with behaviour of animals. Many psychological experiments are conducted to know the functioning of mind in animals. Animals like rats, dogs, chimpanzees, pigeons, guinea pigs, cats are some of the animals used for experimentation.

Findings of these experiments are many times generalized to human behaviour also.

Abnormal Psychology

Today the life is complex. The individual is facing a lot of competition and experiencing conflicts. Constant pressures in life are leading to psychological abnormalities. Abnormal psychology deals with various kinds of mental disorders, their symptoms and causes.

This branch of psychology tries to describe, assess, predict and control those categories of behaviours which are considered as unusual and non-normative. It also deals with various categories of psychological disorders which affect the mental health of the individual. It assesses abnormality in the individual through standardized psycho-diagnostic tools and suggests problem specific treatment.

Social Psychology

Human being is a social animal. Naturally the behaviour of an individual is influenced by society and in turn influences the society. Social psychology deals with interrelationships of people among themselves, likes and dislikes of people, attitudes and interests, the prejudices and social distances people have, group behaviour, group cohesiveness, group conflicts, etc.

Parapsychology

Some of the psychological experiences are beyond the reach of 5 sense organs. That is why they are called extra sensory perceptions (ESP) or sixth sense.

Some of the phenomena studied in ESP are as follows:

Clairvoyance: This is referred to as television, which is seeing the distant things mentally. We perceive at times some situations or things without the help of our eyes. In total – seeing things which happen beyond our visual field through mind is called clairvoyance.

Telepathy: Transformations of emotions from one person to another person who is in a far of place. For example, a person who is in death bed remembering his close relative may be experienced by the concerned person who is far away from him.

Psychokinesis: Moving the objects without direct contact through power of mind is called Psychokinesis. For example, in Mahabharata, Shakuni could move dice with his power of mind.

Precognition: Knowing the future happenings well in advance. At times people will gain the knowledge of future called precognition. For example, some accident or disaster that may take place after sometime will be known before time.

Reincarnation: This is otherwise called rebirth. There are some instances reported where people remember their previous life details.

Contacting Souls

There are some reports that the souls of dead people are contacted through people called Mediums. These Mediums use a plate called Planchette or Ouija board and establish contact with souls.

II. Applied Branches of Psychology

Applied branches deal with the application of psychological principles and techniques for approaching the problems in different fields of life. The main applied branches of psychology areas follows:

Educational Psychology

This field of psychology is mainly concerned with academic performance. It studies the role of various factors which influence learning processes in classroom setting. It focuses on assessing the aptitude, skills and intellectual potential of the students and evaluating their performance. An educational psychologist also helps students to overcome learning difficulties.

This is the most important field where psychological principles are applied. In the field of education 'learner' is the focal point. Other aspects like management, teachers, teaching and learning aids are all meant for learners. Learners differ in their abilities; hence they need different approaches of teaching, learning material, etc. This branch addresses to the problems and improvement in teaching and learning processes.

Clinical Psychology

This branch deals with the therapeutic aspect of mental disorders. There are many types of mental illness requiring varied types of therapies like chemotherapy, psychotherapy, recreational and occupational therapies, behaviour therapy, etc. Clinical psychology is primarily concerned with diagnosis and treatment of various psychological disorders. A clinical psychologist is trained in psychotherapeutic techniques which are used to treat people suffering from psychological disorders. They are employed in hospitals and clinics dealing with mental health problems.

Industrial Psychology

Human beings are different from machines. They will have many problems in their work place like adjustment, safety, security, health, financial and such other problems. Both the management and workers need to cooperate in dealing with such problems. Industrial psychology seeks application of psychological principles, theories and techniques for the study of all these problems and the industrial environment.

Counselling Psychology

Mental disorders may not be completely and easily cured just by drugs and other physical therapies. In addition to other therapies, these patients need counselling also. Counselling is a process in which an interaction takes place between a trained counselor and a client. This branch also helps people to overcome adjustment problems. The counseling psychologist deals with mild problems pertaining to adjustment in social and emotional life, and provides specialized services to deal with marital problems, stress oriented problems and career choice.

Environmental Psychology

This field is concerned with the study of interaction between physical environment and human behaviour. It studies the impact of noise, heat, humidity, pollution and crowding on human performance. It also focuses on the impact of physical environment on psychological health of individuals.

Health Psychology

This field focuses on the impact of various psychological factors (e.g. stress) on the onset progress and treatment of illness. It also deals with various life style diseases such as hypertension, coronary heart disease, cancer and diabetes.

Organizational Psychology

This field is concerned with application of psychological principles and models to study the selection and performance of employees in organizational settings. It also studies the concepts of leadership, motivation, job satisfaction and performance appraisal.

Emerging Fields of Psychology

In addition to the fields mentioned above, a number of new areas have emerged. Some of these branches/fields of psychology are sports psychology, military psychology, aviation psychology, forensic psychology, peace psychology, neuropsychology, political psychology, legal psychology/criminal psychology, political psychology, feminist psychology, positive psychology etc. In this way, psychology has broadened its scope today and gaining more and more importance. It may be expected that in days to come, there cannot be any field of life without the application of psychological principles. Particularly in the field of medicine, for doctors and nurses the knowledge of psychology is very useful and also essential.

BASIC PSYCHOLOGICAL PROCESS

While studying behaviour, it is one of the most important tasks for psychologists to understand the processes which collectively influence a particular behaviour. These psychological processes are

Sensation: It refers to our awareness about various stimuli which we encounter in different modalities such as vision, hearing, touch and taste.

Attention: During attention we selectively focus on a particular stimulus among many stimuli available to us. For instance while listening to a lecture in the classroom we attend to the words pronounced by the teacher and, try to ignore the other stimuli present in the classroom, such as noise made by the fan.

Perception: In the case of perception we process information and make out the meaning of the stimuli available to us. For example, wo look at a pan and recognize it as an object used for writing.

Learning: It helps us acquiring new knowledge and skills through experience and practice. The acquired knowledge and skills further bring a relative change in our behaviour and facilitate our adjustment in varied settings. For example, we learn language, riding a bicycle and applying mathematical skills to solve various problems.

Memory: The information we process and learn is registered and stored in the memory system. Memory also helps us to easily retrieve the stored information when it is required for use. For example, writing the answers in the examination after studying for the paper.

Thinking: In the case of thinking we use our stored knowledge to solve various tasks. We logically establish the relationships among various objects in our mind and take rational decision for a given problem. We also evaluate different events of the environment and accordingly form an opinion.

Chapter-2
Educational Psychology and its Methods

MEANING OF EDUCATIONAL PSYCHOLOGY

Educational psychology is that branch of psychology in which the findings of psychology are applied in the field of education. It is the scientific study of human behaviour in educational situations. According to Charles. E. Skinner, *"Educational psychology deals with the behaviour of human beings in educational situations"*. Crow and Crow said, *"Educational Psychology describes and explains the learning experiences of an individual from birth through old age."* In the words of E.A. Peel, *"Educational Psychology is the science of Education"*.

Education by all means is an attempt to mould and shape the behaviour of the pupil. It aims to produce desirable changes in him for the all-round development of his personality. The essential knowledge and skill to do this job satisfactorily is supplied by Educational Psychology. In the words of E.A. Peel, *"Educational psychology helps the teacher to understand the development of his pupils, the range and limits of their capacities, the processes by which they learn and their social relationships."*

In this way, the work of the Educational Psychologist resembles with that of an Engineer, who is a technical expert. The Engineer supplies all the knowledge and skill essential for the accomplishment of the job satisfactorily, for example, construction of a bridge. In the same way Educational Psychologists, who is a technical expert in the field of Education, supplies all the information, principles and techniques essential for:

- Understanding the behaviour of the pupil in response to educational environment and
- Desired modification of his behaviour to bring an all-round development of his personality.

Thus, Educational Psychology concerned primarily with understanding the processes of teaching and learning that take place within formal environments and developing ways of improving those methods. It covers important topics like learning theories; teaching methods; motivation; cognitive, emotional, and moral development; and parent-child relationships etc. In short, it is the scientific discipline that addresses the questions: *"Why do some students learn more than others?"* and *"What can be done to improve that learning?"*

DEFINITIONS OF EDUCATIONAL PSYCHOLOGY

1. According to Skinner –*"Educational psychology is that branch of*

psychology, which deals with teaching and learning. It takes its meaning from education, social process and from psychology, a behavioural science."

2. Woolfolk (1995) –*"Educational Psychology is the discipline concerned with teaching and learning processes; applies the methods and theories of psychology and has its own as well."*
3. According to Crow and Crow, *"Educational Psychology describes and explains the learning experiences of an individual from birth through old age."*
4. Skinner defines Educational Psychology as *"that branch of Psychology which deals with teaching and learning."*
5. Stephen, *"Educational Psychology is the systematic study of the educational growth and development of a child."*
6. Judd, *"Educational Psychology is the Science which explains the changes that take place in individuals as they pass through the various stages of development."*
7. Peel, *"Educational Psychology is the science of Education."*

Educational psychology is one of the branches of applied psychology concerned with the application of the principles, techniques and other resource of psychology to the solution of the problems confronting the teacher attempting to direct the growth of children toward defined objectives. More specifically, we can say educational psychology is concerned with an understanding of:

- The child - his development, his need and his potentialities
- The learning situation including group dynamics and its effect on learning
- The learning process-its nature and the ways to make it effective. Stated differently, the Central theme of Educational Psychology is Psychology of learning.

NATURE OF EDUCATIONAL PSYCHOLOGY

Its nature is scientific as it has been accepted that it is a Science of Education. We can summarize the nature of Educational Psychology in the following ways:

Educational Psychology is a Science: (Science is a branch of study concerned with observation of facts and establishment of verifiable general laws. Science employs certain objective methods for the collection of data. It has its objectives of understanding, explaining, predicting and control of facts.) Like any other science, educational psychology has also developed objective methods of collection of data. It also aims at understanding, predicting and controlling human behaviour.

Educational Psychology is a Natural Science: An educational psychologist conducts his investigations, gathers his data and reaches his conclusions in exactly the same manner as physicist or the biologist.

Educational Psychology is a Social Science: Like the sociologist, anthropologist, economist or political scientist, the educational psychologist studies human beings and their sociability.

Educational Psychology is a Positive Science: Normative science like Logic or Ethics deals with facts as they ought to be. A positive science deals with facts as they are or as they operate. Educational psychology studies the child's behaviour as it is, not, as it ought to be. So it is a positive science.

Educational Psychology is an Applied Science: It is the application of psychological principles in the field of education. By applying the principles and techniques of psychology, it tries to study the behaviour and experiences of the pupils. As a branch of psychology it is parallel to any other applied psychology. For example, educational psychology draws heavily facts from such areas as developmental psychology, clinical psychology, abnormal psychology and social psychology.

Educational Psychology is a Developing or Growing Science: It is concerned with new and ever new researches. As research findings accumulate, educational psychologists get better insight into the child's nature and behaviour.

W.A. Kelly (1941) listed the nature of Educational Psychology as follows:

- To give a knowledge of the nature of the child.
- To give understanding of the nature, aims and purposes of education.
- To give understanding of the scientific methods and procedures which have been used in arriving at the facts and principles of educational psychology.
- To present the principles and techniques of learning and teaching.
- To give training in methods of measuring abilities and achievement in school subjects.
- To give a knowledge of the growth and development of children.
- To assist in the better adjustment of children and to help them to prevent maladjustment.
- To study the educational significance and control of emotions and
- To give an understanding of the principles and techniques of correct training.

Thus, educational psychology is an applied, positive, social, specific and practical science. While general science deals with behaviour of the individuals in various spheres, educational psychology studies the behaviour of the individual in educational sphere only.

SCOPE OF EDUCATIONAL PSYCHOLOGY

The scope of educational psychology is ever-growing due to constantly researches in this field. The following factors will indicate the scope of educational psychology:

Human Behaviour

It studies human behaviour in the educational context. Psychology is the study of behaviour and education aims at modification of behaviour. Hence the influence of Educational Psychology has to be reflected in all aspects of education.

The Learner

The subject-matter of educational psychology is knitted around the learner. Therefore, the need of knowing the learner and the techniques of knowing him is required. The topics include – the innate abilities and capacities of the individuals, individual differences and their measurements, the overt, covert, conscious as well as unconscious behaviour of the learner, the characteristics of his growth and development and each stage beginning from childhood to adulthood.

Educational Psychology acquaints us with need of knowing the learner and deals with the techniques of knowing him well. Following are the topics studies included in it:-the innate abilities and capabilities of the individual and their measurements, the overt, covert, conscious as well as unconscious behaviour of the learner, the characteristics of his growth and development at each stage beginning from childhood to adulthood.

The Learning Process

After knowing the learner and deciding what learning experiences are to be provided, the emerging problem is to help the learner in acquiring these learning experiences with ease and confidence.

Hence, it deals with the nature of learning and how it takes place and contains the topics such as laws, principles and theories of learning; remembering and forgetting, perceiving, concept formation, thinking, reasoning process, problem solving, transfer of training, ways and means of effective learning etc.

Learning Situation or Environment

It also deals with the environment factors and learning situation which come midway between the learner and the teacher. Topics like classroom climate and group dynamics techniques and aids which facilitate learning, evaluation techniques, and practices, guidance and counseling etc. which help in the smooth functioning of the teaching learning process.

Here we deal with the environmental factors and learning situations which come midway between the learner and the teacher. Topics like classroom climate and group dynamics, techniques and aids that facilitate learning and evaluation, techniques and practices, guidance and counselling etc. for the smooth functioning of the teaching-learning process.

The Learning Experiences

Educational Psychology helps in deciding what learning experiences are desirable, at what stage of the growth and development of the learner, so that these experiences can be acquired with a greater ease and satisfaction.

Individual Differences

It is universally accepted that every individual differs from every other individual. This idea has been brought to light by Educational Psychology.

Growth and Development

It studies the principles governing growth and development. The insight provided by the study will help in scientifically planning and executing learner oriented programmes of education.

Personality and Adjustment

Education has been defined as the all-round development of the personality of an individual. If educational has to fulfil this function all instructional programmes have to be based on the principles governing the nature and development of personality.

Teaching Situation

It suggests the techniques of teaching. It also helps in deciding what learning situation should be provided by the teacher to the learner according to his mental and physical age, his previous knowledge and interest levels. By describing the learner's characteristics, what teaching aids are appropriate for the particular subject can be decided.

Evaluation of Learning Performance

The main objective of education is all-round development of the learner. It includes cognitive, affective and psychomotor aspects of personality. Educational Psychology suggests various tool and techniques for assessment and evaluation such as performance test, oral test and written test. It does not stop at measurement only. After the testing, results of the test are analyzed, causes for poor performance, backwardness in any aspect of development is corrected by guidance and counselling in study habits, examination techniques and learning styles. These are analyzed and the learner is helped so that he can overcome the difficulties.

The Teacher

The teacher is a potent force is any scheme of teaching and learning process. It discusses the role of the teacher. It emphasizes the need of 'knowing thyself' for a teacher to play his role properly in the process of education. His conflicts, motivation, anxiety, adjustment, level of aspiration etc. It throws light on the essential personality traits, interests, aptitudes, the characteristics of effective teaching etc. so as to inspire him for becoming a successful teacher.

Educational Psychology emphasizes the need of knowing the self for a teacher to play his role properly in the process of education. It throws light on the essential personality traits, interests, aptitudes, the characteristics of effective teaching etc., so as to inspire, help teacher handle the stress, conflict and anxiety by giving insight into their own personality.

Guidance and Counselling

Education is nothing by providing guidance and counselling required for the proper development of the child. This is very true, especially in the light of the extremely complex and problematic situation one has to face in the fast growing world. Educational psychology has come to the rescue by developing principles and practical measures helpful for providing effective guidance and counselling.

We can conclude by saying that Educational Psychology is narrower in scope than general psychology. While general psychology deals with the behaviour of the individual in a general way, educational psychology in concerned with the behaviour of the learner in an educational setting.

CHARACTERISTICS OF EDUCATIONAL PSYCHOLOGY

Following are the important characteristics of educational psychology:

- It is an applied branch of fundamental Psychology.
- It combines two fields i.e. education and psychology.
- It is the scientific study of human behaviour in educational situations.
- It is concerned with these factors, principles and techniques which relate to the various aspects of a child's growth and development.
- It is concerned with learning situation and process by which learning can be more efficient and effective.
- Educational Psychology draws heavily from various branches of psychology, biology sociology and anthropology
- Educational Psychology is not as exact as natural sciences since the human behaviour cannot be predicated exactly, because it is dynamic.
- Educational Psychology is a science of education dealing primarily with how, when and what of education.
- It is not a normative a science as it is not concerned with the value of education and does not concern itself with *'what ought to be'*. It only describes what it is; it is an applied positive science.
- While psychology deals with the behaviour of all individuals in all walks of life, Educational Psychology limits its dealing with the behaviour of the pupil in relation to educational environment.
- It does not concern with what and why of education. It gives the necessary knowledge and skill (Technical Guidance) for giving education to the pupil in a satisfactory way.

METHODS OF EDUCATIONAL PSYCHOLOGY

Educational psychology is an important branch of psychology. It is a subject which emphasizes the application of psychological principles in the field of education. It deals with the behaviour of an individual in the educational environment. According to the 'Encyclopedia of Educational Research', *"Educational psychology is the study of the learner and of the learning-teaching process in its various ramifications (branches) directed towards helping the child come to terms with society with a maximum of security and satisfaction"*.

On main objective of educational psychology is to help a teacher to understand his student's behaviour in the educative process. A teacher may face different problems in the classroom as well as outside it. It is important that a teacher understands the significance of individual difference and solves the various problems of the classroom. Therefore, in order to achieve the objective of educational psychology some methods are adopted to collect data to know about a learner's personality.

The first attempt to adopt a method of educational psychology began in the year 1879 by W. Wundt of Germany. In recent years, with the development of technology, researchers have started using new methods of collecting and analyzing data. Some important methods of educational psychology are discussed below:

INTROSPECTION METHOD

Historically introspection is the oldest method of all, which was formerly used in philosophy, and then in psychology to collect data about the conscious experience of the subject. Introspection means to see within one self or self observation. To understand one's own mental health and the state of mind. This method was developed by the structuralists in psychology who defined psychology as the study of conscious experiences of the individual.

Meaning of Introspection

Introspection is a method of self-observation. The word Introspection is made up of two Latin words *'Intro'* meaning *'within'* and *'Spection'* meaning *'looking'*. Therefore introspection implies *'self observation'*, or in other words, to experience one's own mental state i.e., to observe, analyze and report one's own feelings. Hence it is a method where an individual is looking within one self. Angel considered it as *"looking inward"*. In introspection, the individual peeps into his own mental state and observes his own mental processes. Stout considers that *'to introspect'* is to attend to the working of one's own mind in a systematic way.

According to William James, *"Introspective observation is what we have to rely on first and foremost and always. The word intro-spection needs hardly to be defined - it means, of course, looking into our own minds and recording what we there discover. Everyone agrees that through this method one can discover one's own states of consciousness. So far as I know, the existence of such states has never been doubted by any critic, however skeptical in other respects he may have been."*

According to Stout, *"In introspection, we are concerned with the nature of experience itself and with the laws of mental process. The observer in introspection is directed towards the answering of questions of theoretical importance for the advancement of our systematic knowledge of the laws and conditions of mental process." Introspection examines inner behaviour of an individual and an individual knows about his own feelings or thoughts in a particular situation.*

Stages of Introspection

There are three clear stages in introspection:

- During the observation of external object, the person beings to ponder over his own mental state. For example while listening to music, which is to him pleasant or unpleasant, he starts thinking about his own mental state.
- The person begins to question the working of his own mind. He thinks and analyses: Why has he said such and such thing? Why has he talked in a particular manner? And so on.
- He tries to frame the laws and conditions of mental processes: He thinks in terms of improvement of his reasoning or the control of his emotional stages. This stage helps in the advancement of our scientific knowledge.

Merits of Introspection Method

The merits of the introspection method are given below:

- It is the cheapest and most economical method of studying behaviour. We do not need any apparatus or laboratory for its use.
- This method can be used anytime and anywhere. You can introspect while walking, traveling, sitting on a bed and so on.
- It is the easiest method and is readily available to the individual.
- The introspection data is first-hand as the person himself examines his own activities.
- Introspection has generated research which gradually led to the development of more objective methods.
- It is still used in all experimental investigation.
- It is the only method with the help of which an individual can know his emotions and feelings.
- Introspection, as a method, has generated a lot of research and is used in almost all experimental students.
- It is the most economical method and one which enables us to know about the mental state of an individual, i.e. his emotions and feelings.

Limitations of Introspection Methods

The limitations of the introspection method are given below:

- In introspection, one needs to observe or examine one's mental processes carefully in the form of thoughts, feeling and sensation. The state of one's mental processes is continuously changing. Therefore when one concentrates on introspecting a particular phase of one's mental activity that phase passes off. For example when you get angry at something and afterwards sit down to introspect calmly, the state of anger is sure to have passed off and so what you try to observe is not what is happening at that time with yourself but what had happened sometime before.
- The data collected by introspection cannot be verified. An individual may not pass through the same mental state again. There is no independent way of checking the data.
- The data collected by introspection lacks validity and reliability. It is impossible to acquire validity and exactness in self-observation of one's own mental processes.
- The data collected by introspection in highly subjective. It has danger of being biased and influenced by preconceptions of the individual.
- The observer and the observed are the same. Hence there is ample scope for the individual to lie deliberately and hide the facts to mislead others.

OBSERVATION METHOD

We observe so many things in nature. We also observe the action and behaviour of others and form our own notions about these persons. We look at other persons, listen to their talks and try to infer what they mean. We try to infer the characteristics, motivations, feelings and intentions of others on the basis of these observations. So let us study about Observation method employed by psychologists in detail.

With the development of psychology as an objective science of learning behaviour, the method of introspection was replaced by careful observation of human and animal behaviour to collect data by research workers. In introspection we can observe the mental process of ourselves only, but in observation, we observe the mental processes of others. Hence Observation is the most commonly used method for the study of human behaviour.

Meaning of Observation Method

It is one of the oldest and most popular methods of educational psychology. It has replaced the method of introspection of self observation. The observation method is also called *'objective observation'*. According to John Dollard, *"The primary research instrument would seen to be the observing human intelligence trying to make sense out of human experience."* Observation is one of the basic methods which mean that an individual's behaviour (i.e. a person's bodily gestures, facial expression and other bodily actions) is observed. It is accepted by psychologists that an individual's overt behaviour is the result of his internal mental conditions. The observer makes systematic observation through recording in a natural situation. Observation can be both natural and participant. In natural observation the experimenter observes and records the behaviour of the subjects in the natural setting as has been mentioned above; here the subjects are not conscious about their behaviour being observed. In participant observation, the observer becomes a member of the group, gains the confidence of the other group members by building rapport with them, and observes their behaviour. Here also the subjects are not conscious that their behaviour is being observed.

Principles of Observation Method

Certain principles should be followed in the observation method. They are:

- Observation should be made not only of the individual's behaviour but of the whole situation.
- Proper planning of the observation process should be made; objectives must be clear and the proper tools for recording must be kept properly.
- Observer must select the appropriate number of subjects to be observed. Too many will be difficult to manage.
- The time limit of observation must also be fixed. Too long time may make the observer distracted and tired and if it is too short it will not yield the proper information.
- As observation is a systematic process, the observer must have the proper skills and aptitude and the ability to report accurately. Only then will the data be reliable.

Process of Observation

In the process of observation, following four steps are generally required:

Observation of Behaviour

The first step involved in the method of observation is directly perceiving or observing the behaviour of individuals under study. For example, if we want to observe the social behaviour of children we can observe it when they assemble and play.

Recording the Behaviour Observed

The observation should be carefully and immediately noted and recorded. Minimum time should be allowed to pass between happening and recording. It will make the observation more objective.

Analysis and Interpretation of Behaviour

When the notes of behaviour observed are completed, they are analyzed objectively and scientifically in order to interpret the behaviour patterns.

Generalization

On the basis of analysis and interpretation of the data collected with the help of observation method, it is possible to make certain generalization. Social development and behaviour of children have been described by Child Psychologists on the basis of generalization based on analysis and interpretation of the data gathered through the observation method.

Merits of Observation Method

The merits of observation method are:

- This type of observation is a natural and normal way of knowing the external world but also the mind of the subject
- This method is objective in nature and free form personal bias and prejudice.
- Through this method we can observe as many children as we like
- This method is quite suitable for children and abnormal person who cannot be examined through introspection.
- This can be used anytime and anywhere
- Being a record of actual behaviour of the child, it is more reliable and objective than introspection.
- It is an excellent source of information about what actually happens in classroom.
- It is a study of an individual in a natural situation and is therefore more useful than the restricted study in a test situation.

Limitations of Observation Method

The limitations of observation method are as under:

- Observation is useful only for collecting data about overt behaviour which is manifested in a number of activities. This overt behaviour does not provide reliable information regarding the internal mental process. We can only guess about the mental state of the individual on the basis of overt behaviour which may or may not be true. It becomes very difficult to draw any conclusion in case of adults who can hide their actual behaviour in the presence of the observer.
- Subjectivity of interpretation is another limitation of this method. The observer may interpret his sensation of external stimulus on the bias of his past experience. He may be biased in his interpretation. It has also been

found in some studies that strong personal interests tend to make researcher see only those things which he wants to see.

- Observation is subject to two types of errors, sampling error and observer error. The first error occurs because of inadequacies of selecting situation to be observed. The observer error may be due to knowledge and background of the situation to be observed. Because some time the observer is not familiar with the total situation and hence he may commit error.
- There is great scope for personal prejudices and bias of the observer. The observers interest, values can distort observation.
- Records may not be written with hundred percent accuracy as the observations are recorded after the actions are observed. There is some time lag.
- The observer may get only a small sample to study behaviour. It is very difficult to observe everything that the student does or says. As far as possible observation should be made from several events.

INTERVIEW METHOD

Today, for psychological researches, mainly, interview method has become very popular. In this method there is direct face to face contact between the investigator and the subject. Here the interviewer or the investigator asks questions to the subject and records the answers usually without the latter knowing it. In the words of Fred N. Kerlinger, *"The interview is perhaps the ubiquitous method of obtaining information from people. It has been and is still being used in all kinds of practical situations, e.g. the lawyer obtains information from his client, the physician learns about a patient; the administrative officer or professor determines the suitability of students for schools, departments and curricula.*" Only recently, however, interview has been used systematically for scientific purposes, both in the laboratory and in the field. He also said that it is a face to face inter-personal situation in which one person, the interviewer asks a person being interviewed, the respondent, questions designed to obtain answers pertinent to research problems" According to P.V. Young, *"Interviewing is not a simple way to conversation between an interrogator and informant. Gestures, glances, facial expressions and pauses often reveal subtle feelings"*

Merits of the Interview Method

The merits of the interview method are:

- High participation of the subject or respondent. The subject answers the questions in a free manner. Illiterate as well as children provide proper in-depth information as compared to other methods like observation, questionnaire method etc.
- This method is very flexible as it becomes possible for the interviewer to reframe, repeat and rephrase the questions as suitable for the subject.
- The subject's emotions can be studied well. It is often observed that during an interview, the subject may become emotional and get excited, and may express freely his fears, anxieties, and complexes.
- Through the interview method the investigator may get to know the cause

of any behaviour pattern of the subject, the historical background of each incident.

- The data collected through the interview method is reliable. The interviewer analyses and crosschecks the information provided, to find out whether the data is correct or not.
- The interview method can be applied on all types of people- literate or illiterate children and adults and at times also on mentally unbalanced persons.
- In the interview method, the subject and investigator are face to face with each other. Both discuss the problems and during discussion views can be exchanged and this is desirable in order to study every social problem along with the subject's own problems.

Demerits of the Interview Method

The demerits of the interview methods are:

- It is a costly method. It involves a lot of traveling on the part of the interviewer. It is also time consuming as the interviewer has to physically locate a subject.
- A lot of planning is required. The investigator has to provide a number of stimuli to get information from the subject, must make careful observation of the latter's behaviour patterns so the interviewer must remember a number of things at the same time. So the whole process becomes too strenuous.
- The subject may not reveal his true feelings and emotions.
- Sometimes the interviewer may have preconceived notions which may not hold true during interview, but he is reluctant to change his views. P.V. Young said that biased and prior thinking may distort and invalidate the results of the whole interview.
- The interviewer's perception of things may clash with those of the interviewee's. Their beliefs and values may be totally different. So the Investigator must be very proficient and must have proper insight into human nature.
- There can be difficulty in persuading the subject to be interviewed. The subject may tend to be bored during the process and then the data obtained will not be valid

EXPERIMENTAL METHOD

We studied introspection method and observation method used in psychology of learning. But these methods lack scientific objectivity and validity. Experimental method is the most scientific and objective method of studying behaviour. It is the method, which is responsible for assigning the status of Science to Psychology. Let us learn more about this Experimental method.

In 1879, William Wundt established the first psychological laboratory at Leipzing in Germany. Since then, experimental method in psychology has become popular, Experimental method consists of actions performed under pre-arranged or rigidly controlled conditions.

Here the emphasis is on experimentation. Experimentation is where the investigator controls the educative factors to which a group of children are subjected during the period of inquiry and the investigation observes the resulting achievement.

J.W. Best describes, "Experimental research is the description and analysis of what will be, or what will occur under carefully controlled conditions."

Meaning of Experimental Method

It is one of the most important and an objective method of psychology as it is very scientific. It is precise, planned, systematic, or in other words, it is observation under controlled conditions. According to J.W Best, *"Experimental research is the description and analysis of what will be, or what will occur, under carefully controlled conditions"*. In experiments, there is always the attempt to establish certain cause and effect relationships through carefully planned and controlled observation of the subject's behaviour.

Steps in the Experimental Method

The different steps, which are to be followed in conducting a typical experiment are:

Raising a Problem

In any experiment the first steps is to identify a problem. For example it has been observed that the students cheat in the examinations. To stop this, it many recommend strict supervision. But it has also been seen that even when there is strict supervision there is cheating, hence there crops up the problem of cheating under strict supervision or relaxed supervision. This problem may lead to experimentation.

Formulation of a Hypothesis

The next step in experimental method is the formulation of a hypothesis that. Strict supervision may lead to less copying in the examination as compared to the relaxed supervision. This hypothesis is now to be tested by experiment.

Making a Distinction between Independent and Dependent Variables

In the example given above, the cheating behaviour of the students will be dependent variable while the nature of supervision will be the independent variable. It is because by changing the supervision the cheating behaviour is expected change. In the present experiment we manipulate the conditions of supervision in order to discover the ways in which they determine the dependent variable that is the cheating behaviour. We may observe the effect of supervision in the experimental situation and also the effect of relaxed supervision under similar conditions and with the same group of students.

Controlling the Situational Variables

The experiment will not give valid results unless the situational variables are controlled. If the experiment is conducted with different set of students who have been trained in a different manner of have a different value system then the results will be different in comparison to those who have been subjected to experiment earlier. Similarly the other conditions like the person who is supervising the place of supervision etc. have to be controlled. This means that all those conditions, which might affect the dependent variable, are to be controlled. Since, in any experiment there are numerous conditions which are needed to be controlled; it is many a time difficult to do so. Hence we take recourse to various types of experimental designs, which we have described earlier.

Analysis of the Results

Once the experiment is concluded the results are analyzed. In our example we may apply simple percentages to find out in which type of supervision a higher percentage of students have copied. Many a times we apply more sophisticated statistics to analyze the results.

Verification of Hypothesis

The last step in the experimental method is the verification of the hypothesis, which we have earlier framed. The result of the experiment exhibits whether the hypothesis is accepted or refuted. We may find that strict supervision leads to less copying. In that case we may conclude that our hypothesis is accepted. If the results are otherwise then our conclusion will be that the hypothesis is refuted.

Characteristics of Experimental Method

The 'experimental method' has certain characteristics. They are:

- In the experimental method the conditions are always controlled.
- It essentially requires at least two persons, the experimenter and the subject.
- Usually the experimental method is applied on persons in a random order.
- In the experimental method two different types of variables are used – (a) Independent variable like intelligence and (b) dependent variable like home or school environment, other socio-economic conditions etc.

Merits of Experimental Method

Experimental method being most precise and scientific has following merits:

- Experimental method is the most systematic method or getting reliable data.
- Experimental method enables accurate observations due to controlled conditions.
- It allows us to establish cause effect relationship between different phenomena.
- The results obtained are valid and reliable.
- The findings of the experimental method are verifiable by other experiments under identical conditions.
- It helps to protect from the subjective opinions. Hence it provides objective information about the problem.
- It provides adequate information about the problem.
- In experimental method, experiments are conducted under vigorously controlled conditions. The experimenter can control the application and withdrawal of independent variables.

- Experimental method increases ones knowledge or psychological facts in child psychology, social and abnormal psychology.

Demerits of the Experimental Method

Experimental method suffers from various following demerits:

- Experimental method is a costly and time consuming method as it requires a laboratory and apparatus to conduct it properly.
- Experiments are conducted in artificially determined pattern of behaviour. In real life situation it is quite different.
- It needs specialized knowledge and therefore every teacher cannot be expected to conduct the experiment.
- The scope is limited. All problems of psychology cannot be studied by this method as we cannot perform experiments for all the problems that may come up in the diverse subject matter of psychology.
- Accurate measurements, in case of human beings, are never possible.
- It is difficult to always control the independent variable. Therefore it is not possible to create desired conditions in laboratory.
- It is not possible to reach certainty in matters of social science s including educational psychology.
- As human behaviour is changeable, identical behaviour of the same individual not occur even under identical conditions at different times.

CASE STUDY METHOD

The 'Case Study' method deals with the emotional and mental state of an individual. This method is applied to study special behavioural problems of an individual by specially trained teachers, psychologist and psychiatrists. Through this method total information of family background, schooling and also social conditions of the individuals is obtained; hence it can be called a cumulative record which is of great help in understanding the source of an individual's fears, anxiety. worry, or any kind of maladjustment. The main objective of this method is to help the individual adjust better with the environment and gain self confidence to attain higher levels of achievement.

Steps of Case Study Method

Different steps may be used in the case study method. Some of them are mentioned below:

- Basic preliminary information about the subject's name, age, sex, parent's age, education, occupation as well as social status.
- Proper physical check-up of the individual is done to ascertain whether his/her behavioural problem is due to any disease. Only in the absence of any physical ailment can psychological treatment start.
- The subject should be very comfortable with the investigator while the latter takes the information. The investigator (teacher or psychologist) should be friendly and the language of collecting data must be simple so that free and frank responses can be available.
- The investigator must not tire the subject; instead, regular intervals of rest

should be given. The method cannot be applied hastily - it may go on for several weeks or months.

- The behaviour of the individual should be observed in natural setting and working conditions. Doing so will provide correct data which ultimately in most cases, will lead to proper understanding of the root cause of the person's problems.
- Special care must be taken in the post treatment period so that there is no recurrence of the problem. The parents and family members and other associates must take care so that the subject can modify his behaviour and prevent maladjustment.

Limitation of the Cast Study Method

The case- study also has certain limitations. These are:

- The investigator should be technically proficient to handle a case. In most cases, however, the investigators are not found to be experts in this field.
- Sometimes the information may become highly subjective. The subject, parents and other associates may hide certain facts about the subject's behavioural problems and so the data collected may not be reliable and valid.
- There is a possibility of the investigator of becoming involved with the problems of the individual and therefore his diagnosis and counselling or other methods of treatment may not be effective.
- The possibility of errors in understanding the problems as well as treatment is high; therefore utmost care must be taken to minimize the errors.

CLINICAL METHOD

This method is primarily used to collect detailed information on the behaviour problems of maladjusted and deviant cases. The main objective of this method is to study individual case or cases of group to detect and diagnose their specific problems and to suggest therapeutic measures to rehabilitate them in their environment.

It involves the following steps:

- Interview
- Information gathering
- A hypothesis formulate
- Diagnoses are made
- Planned a treatment programme

Chapter-3
Child Growth and Development

The aim of education is to bring about desired changes in the learner. Changes are taking place in an individual due to learning and also due to the natural growth and development. Development of proper attitudes, habits and patterns of behaviour formed during the early years determines to a great extent how successfully an individual adjust himself as he grows older. Since, the task of the teacher is to bring about desirable changes in the growing child, knowledge about growth and development is out most important.

MEANING OF GROWTH AND DEVELOPMENT

The clear meaning of growth and development is as follows:

Meaning of Growth

The terms growth and development are often used interchangeably and regarded as synonymous. Growth is sheer increase in size, height, weight, power etc. It refers to the dimensional augmentation, cellular multiplication, or quantitative changes in size, weight and number. The process of gradual increase of an individual or animal or a seed, germ or root to its full size or maturity is called growth. According to Crow and Crow '*growth refers to structural and physiological changes while development refers to growth as well as change in behaviour*'.

Characteristics of Growth

The main characteristics of growth are given as follows:

- Growth is a complex process
- Growth follows a definite sequence or pattern
- Growth proceeds more rapidly in the early years of life
- Rate of growth is not uniform in different stages and parts
- Growth is not a continuous process. It stops with maturity
- Growth is cumulative in nature
- Growth is influenced by heredity and environment
- The tempo or speed of growth is not even
- There is marked individual difference in growth
- The rate and pattern of growth can be modified by conditions internal and external to the body

Meaning of Development

The term development refers to change in structure, form or shape and improvement in functioning. It does not consist merely of adding inches to one's height or improving one's ability but it is a complex process of integrating many structures and functions. In the words of Hurlock, the term *development means a progressive series of changes that occur in an orderly predictable pattern as a result of maturation and experience.*

Characteristics of Development

The main characteristics of development are as follows:

- Development is the result of maturation and learning
- Development follows a definite and predictable pattern
- Each period of development involves certain hazards
- Certain characteristic traits are associated with each phase of development
- Development is not uniform in al individuals
- Development depends on both heredity and environment
- Development is gradual and it takes time

CORRELATION BETWEEN GROWTH AND DEVELOPMENT

Growth and development are correlated because both occur together. Growth takes place when a child grows taller, his bones, muscles and other parts of the body increase in size. As the child grows his mind and body mature and he is able to function at a higher level. For example; as a child grows in age, the size of his fingers increases in length and in thickness. This is considered as growth. Along with this growth the ability of the child to use his fingers with ease, speed and precision for various purposes also may increase. This change can be considered as development.

COMPARISON BETWEEN GROWTH AND DEVELOPMENT

The difference between growth and development can be seen with the help of the Table 3.1 given below:

Table 3.1: Difference between Growth and Development

Growth	*Development*
Growth is quantitative	Development is qualitative
Growth Is Structural	Development is functional
Growth is observable and measurable	Development is not observable and measurable
Growth is physical and external in nature	Development is internal and can be physical, social, emotional, moral, intellectual etc.
Growth is not a continuous process. It stops with the attainment of maturity	Development is a continuous process. It does not end with maturity
Growth may or may not bring development	Development is possible without growth
Growth refers to changes in the particular aspects of body	Development refers to over all changes resulting in improved functioning of the individual
growth does not depend upon maturation and learning	Development depends upon maturation and learning

PRINCIPLES OF GROWTH AND DEVELOPMENT

Following are the fundamental principles of growth and development:

Development Follows a Pattern or a Sequence

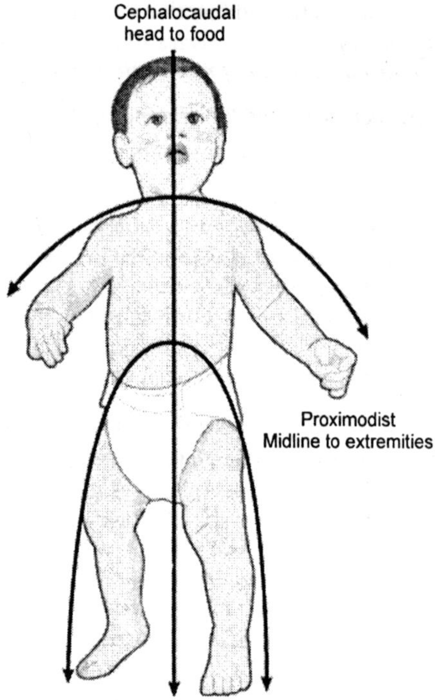

Figure 3.1: Pattern or Sequence of Development in Human

Development tends to proceed from the head downward. This is called the *'cephalocaudal principle'*. According to this principle, the child first gains control of the head, then the arms, then the legs. Infants gain control of head and face movements within the first two months after birth. In the next few months, they are able to lift themselves up using their arms. By 6 to 12 months of age, infants start to gain leg control and may be able to crawl, stand, or walk.

Development also proceeds from the centre of the body outward according to the *'proximodistal principle'*. Accordingly, the spinal cord develops before other parts of the body. The child's arm develops before the hands, and the hands and feet develop before the fingers and toes. Fingers and toes are the last to develop.

Development Proceeds from General to Specific Responses

It moves from a generalized to localized behaviour. The newborn infant moves its whole body at one time instead of moving only one part of it. It makes random kicking with its legs before it can coordinate the leg muscles well enough to crawl or walk.

Development is a Continuous Process

Development does not occur in spurts. Growth continues from the moments of conception until the individual reaches maturity. It takes place at slow regular pace rather than by 'leaps and bounds'. Although development is a continuous process, yet the tempo of growth is not even, during infancy and early years growth moves swiftly and later it slacken.

Different Aspects of Growth Develop at Different Rates

Neither all parts of the body grow at the same rate nor do all aspects of mental growth proceed equally. They reach maturity at different times. Development also depends on maturation. Maturation refers to the sequence of biological changes in children. These orderly changes give children new abilities. Much of the maturation depends on changes in the brain and the nervous system.

These changes assist children to improve their thinking abilities and motor skills. A rich learning environment helps children develop to their potential.

Children must mature to a certain point before they can gain some skills. For instance, the brain of a four-month-old has not matured enough to allow the child to use words. A four-month-old will babble and coo. However, by two years of age, with the help of others, the child will be able to say and understand many words. This is an example of how cognitive development occurs from simple tasks to more tasks that are complex. Likewise, physical skills develop from general to specific movements. For example, think about the way an infant waves its arms and legs. In a young infant, these movements are random. In several months, the infant will likely be able to grab a block with his or her whole hand. In a little more time, the same infant will grasp a block with the thumb and forefinger.

Most Traits are Correlated in Development: Generally, it is seen that the child whose intellectual development is above average is so in health size, sociability and special aptitudes.

Growth is Complex: All of its aspects are closely interrelated. The child's mental development is intimately related to his physical growth and its needs.

Growth is a Product of the Interaction of the Organism and Environment: Among the environmental factors, one can mention nutrition, climate, the conditions in the home, the type of social organization in which individual moves and lives.

There are Wide Individual Differences in Growth: Individual differences in growth are caused by differences in heredity and environment.

Growth is Both Quantitative and Qualitative: These two aspects are inseparable. The child not only grows in 'size'; he grows up or matures in structure and function too.

Development is Predictable: It is possible for us to predict at an early age the range within which the mature development of the child is likely to fall. However, mental development cannot be predicted with the same degree of accuracy.

MEANING OF CHILD GROWTH

Children are not just smaller versions of adults. They have very particular needs and capabilities. One of the major issues in children's education is a lack of knowledge on the part of teachers about how children grow and develop. Good teachers know and understand the many changes that take place from child to adult and structure their learning experiences to best suit the needs of the children.

There are clear stages that children pass through from birth to adult. These stages are the same for boys and girls, but girls generally mature before boys. This is clearly shown in the Figure 3.2.

Physical Growth

Physical growth is obviously important to performance. We will start by looking at how the body changes during development. There are important changes in body size and proportions. These changes affect the way children can perform different skills and activities.

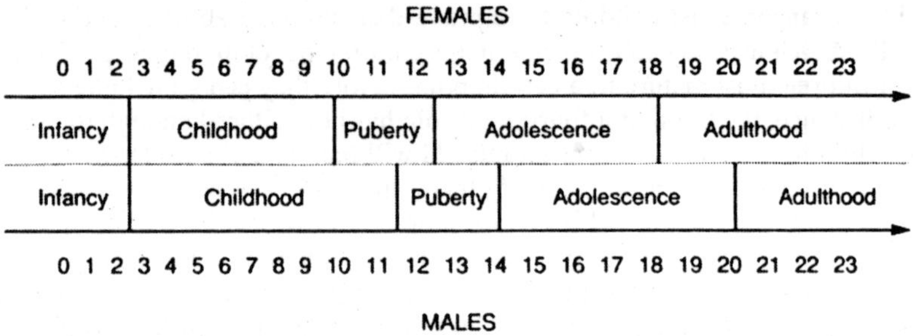

Figure 3.2: Child Growth Stages

Children grow in size at a very fast rate. At birth, infants are only about a quarter of their adult height. This final adult height is usually reached at about twenty years of age.

Characteristic Stages of Growth from Birth to Adult

There are four characteristic stages of growth from birth to adult:

- Rapid growth in infancy and early childhood
- Slow, steady growth in middle childhood
- Rapid growth during puberty
- Gradual slowing down of growth in adolescence until adult height is reached

Both sexes are of a comparable shape and size during infancy and childhood.

Patterns of Growth: Changes in Proportions

The physical proportions of the body at birth are very different from those of the adult. Some body parts grow more than others during development to reach the final adult proportions. The illustration shows the relative size of body parts at different ages.

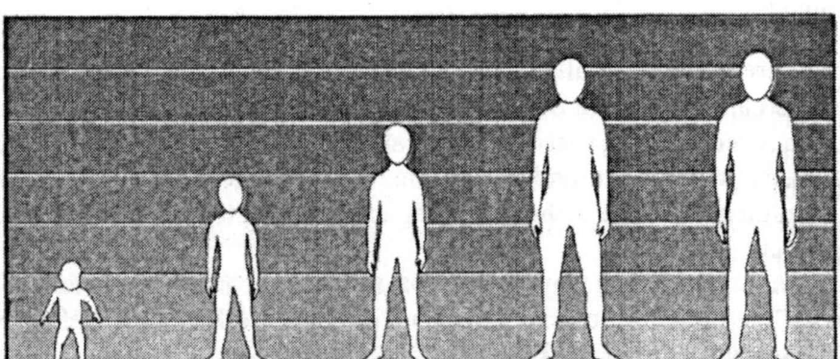

Figure 3.3: Pattern of Growth

The head is proportionally large and the legs proportionally short during childhood. At birth the head is one quarter of the length of the body compared with about one sixth in the adult.

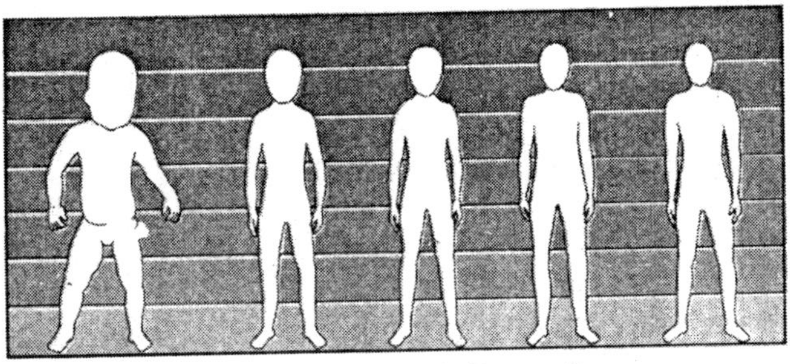

Figure 3.4: Changes in Proportions

The legs are about one third the length of the body at birth and one half in the adult. Because the body proportions change this means that not all of the body segments grow by the same amount.

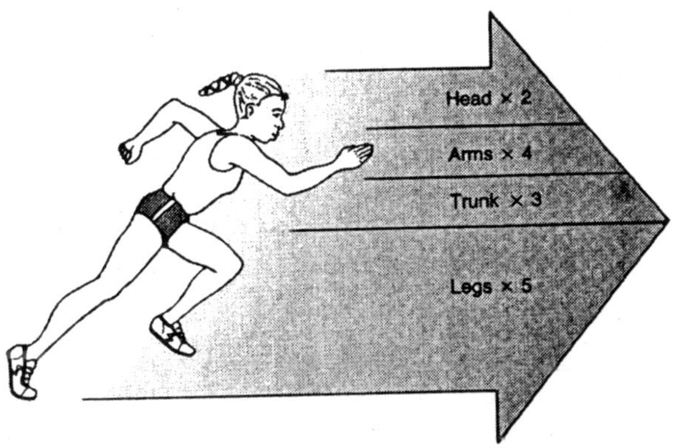

Figure 3.5: Amount of Growth from Birth to Adult

Changes in the size and shape of the body are caused by different segments growing at different times (see Figure 3.6).

These changes in body proportions will have a great influence on how skills will be performed. For example, changes in the relative size of the head in childhood affects the balance of the body during movement and the relative shortness of the legs in the very young limits running ability. At the beginning of puberty children have long arms and legs. They are better suited for running but the rapid growth may make them appear to be clumsy and to have difficulty in coordination.

Growth Spurts

When the rate of growth increases rapidly it is called a growth spurt. The most important growth spurt is the one which occurs at puberty. This spurt produces a rapid increase in both weight and height

The peak of this growth spurt occurs at about age 12 for girls and age 14 for boys. Before this growth spurt there are no important differences between boys and girls in weight and height. During growth spurts most of the child's

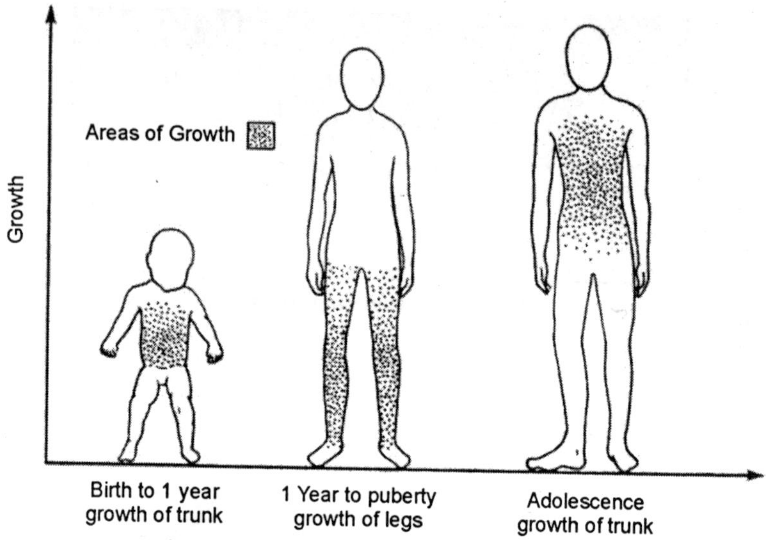

Figure 3.6: Areas of Growth

energy is used for growing. Children will be easily tired and may not be able to keep up their usual volume or intensity of training. Light training will stimulate bodily growth if the child has enough energy.

Early and Late Developers

Each child develops at their own rate and some children develop earlier and some later than the average. For both boys and girls the age at the peak of the major growth spurt frequently occurs up to two years before or after the average age.

	Peak growth		
	Early	*Average*	*Late*
Boys	12	14	16
Girls	10	12	14

Figure 3.7: Age for Peak Times for Growth in Height for Boys and Girls

There can easily be differences of four years in development between children of the same age. Thinking about growth stages and developmental age rather than age alone is perhaps one of the most important considerations when coaching young athletes. Early success may be due entirely to relative size and strength at the time. As other children catch up the early matures may be left behind. On the other hand, the late developers are frequently overlooked if they are judged only on their performances.

Structure of the Body

The changes in size and proportion are the easily observed signs of development. They are the result inside the body of changes to the skeleton. The skeleton of a child is mostly cartilage, which is softer than bone and can bend. The process by which cartilage becomes bone begins very early in life in special growth areas in the bones. These special growth areas are called growth plates.

These growth areas in the bone are the weakest part of the bone. They can be easily injured by a sudden force or a repeated force. Mild forces can stimulate bone growth, but excessive forces can cause damage and have serious long term effects.

Rebounding, repeated vigorous throwing and the use of weights should be avoided during periods of rapid growth. Once the body stops growing the growth regions become bone and are no longer weak areas (Figure 3.9).

Children and Exercise

Children do not tolerate exercise as well as adults. They are much less aware of their real limits. Children do not breathe as slowly or as deeply as adults. The average six year old child breathes in 38 liters of air to get one liter of oxygen. The average 18 year old needs only to breathe 28 liters of air to get one liter of oxygen. This means that the younger the athlete the harder their bodies must work to provide the oxygen their muscles need.

The body has three energy systems. Two of these are anaerobic, without oxygen, and the other is the aerobic system, using oxygen. Before adolescence children get a higher proportion of their energy from the aerobic system than adults do. In general, children are better at steady, extended exercises. Physical changes, during and after puberty will improve their anaerobic abilities. The amount of this improvement will help decide what event or distance is best for a young child.

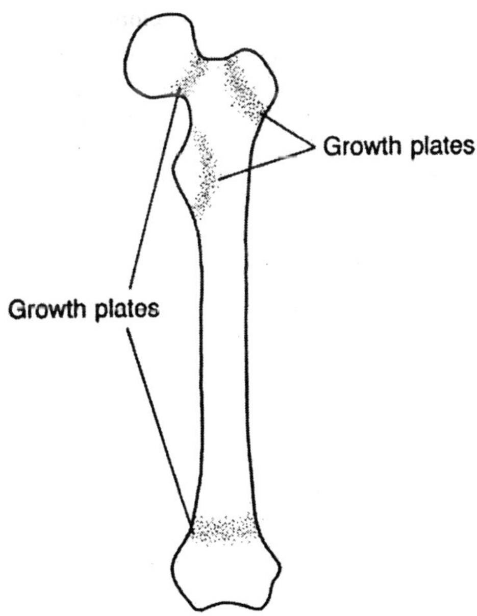

Figure 3.8: Growth Plates of the Thigh Bone—The Femur

Implications of Child Growth for the Teacher and Coach

The following implications will be useful for the teacher and coaches:

- Think about growth stages rather than ages
- Think how changes in physical proportions will affect performance
- Help children understand the changes taking place in their bodies
- Set standards of performance according to developmental age not chronological age
- Group children according to physical development, using height and weight as a guide
- Encourage skill learning for all your athletes, late developers could be very successful later
- Don't use exercises which place excessive force on bone growth regions during periods of maximum growth
- A void weights before adolescence

MEANING OF CHILD DEVELOPMENT

Child development refers to the sequence of physical and emotional changes that occur in a child from birth to the beginning of adulthood. During this process a child progresses from dependency on their parents/guardians to increasing independence. Child development is strongly influenced by genetic factors (the genes passed on from their parents) and events during prenatal life, however is also influenced by environmental facts and learning.

Importance of Child Development

Monitoring child development is important to ensure that children meet their 'developmental milestones'. Although arbitrary time frames that are far from exact, checking that children are roughly 'on track' for their age is helpful in order to detect early on if there are any hiccups in development. This is usually carried out through child/mother services and Paediatricians as infants and toddlers, and later through kindergartens and school term skills assessments.

The earliest possible detection (and treatment if appropriate) of developmental challenges is helpful as it can allow the early intervention to help minimize the impact these developmental hiccups can have on children's skill development and subsequently their confidence, or serve as an indicator of a possible diagnosis.

Developmental milestone checklist/charts are used as a guide as to what is normal for a particular age range and can be use to highlight any areas that a child may be delayed in. However, it is important to be aware that while child development has a predictable sequence. All children are unique in their development and the course in which each child follows to reach each milestone can vary.

Principles of the Development of Children

Human Development involves change. This change occurs at various stages of development and the development pattern at each stage has predictable characteristics. You might have observed that development is a product of maturity and learning. Maturity is mere or less automatic, unfolding biological potential. It is an irreversible sequence and entails biological changes. Such changes are relatively independent of environmental factors as long as environmental factor remain normal.

Categories of Child Development

Categories of child development include:

- Cognitive Development (ability to learn and problem solve)
- Social development (interacting with others)
- Emotional development (Control over his emotions and self-control)
- Speech and Language development (understanding and using language, reading and communicating)
- Physical or Motor development (fine and gross motor skills)
- Spiritual Development (thinking about who we are and how we are in the world)
- Moral Development (development of proper attitudes and behaviours toward other people in society, based on social and cultural norms, rules and laws)
- Sensory Development (Maturing of the five familiar senses: hearing, smell, taste, touch, and vision)

Problems in Child Development

Problems in development can arose due to: genetics, prenatal circumstances, the presence of a specific diagnosis or medical factors, and/or lack of opportunity or exposure to helpful stimuli. Specific assessment by the best fit professional (which may initially be the GP or Paediatrician, and then Occupational Therapist, Speech Pathologist, Psychologist and/or Physiotherapist) can provide clarity about the issues and extent of concern and formulate a plan to overcome the challenge(s). In many cases, as the process of child develop involves multiple skill areas developing at once, there may be benefit in consulting multiple professionals.

Overcoming the developmental challenges is crucial to maximizing the ease and speed of development, minimizing the gap that occur between a child's ability and those of their same ages peers, the confidence of the child as well as frustration that can be encountered by the child's parents and/or care-givers.

FACTORS INFLUENCING GROWTH AND DEVELOPMENT

Right from conception, the beginning of life in a mother's womb, the growth and development of human beings is influenced by a variety of factors categorized broadly as internal and external. They are (1) Internal Factors and (2) External Factors mentioned below:

I. Internal Factors

All those factors which lie within the individual are called internal factors. These includes (1) Heredity, (2) Biological or constitutional, (3) Intelligence, (4) Emotional and (5) Social factors.

Heredity Factors: Heredity is the process of transmitting biological traits from parent to offspring through genes, the basic units of heredity. Heredity also refers to the inherited characteristics of an individual, including traits such as height, eye colour and blood type.

Heredity factors play their part at the time of conception in the mother's womb. What is transferred to the offspring from its immediate parents in the form of genes and chromosomes at this time, constitute the hereditary contribution. This contribution is the real starting point and basis for all the growth and development that takes place later in the life of the child. The height, weight, colour of the eyes and skin, characteristics of the hair, are all decided by these hereditary influences.

The physical structure, nervous system and other things related one's constitutional make-up, body chemistry and physical development are to a great extent decided by hereditary factors. If the hereditary contributions are satisfactory, then with minimum efforts, we get satisfactory results; otherwise we have to make tremendous efforts for achieving desired results or success in terms of child's satisfactory growth and development.

Biological and Constitutional Factors

A child's constitutional make-up, somatic or physical structure, body chemistry etc. influence his growth and development throughout his life.

- A child who is physically week or have internal deformities cannot achieve normal physical and mental growth and development.
- The nervous system which controls the body movement, affects the growth and development of a child in cognitive spheres.
- The endocrine or ductless glands or hormones have important role in growth and development. In case there is over activity (hyperactivity) or under activity (hypo activity) of these glands, it results in serious abnormality in growth and development.
- Defective constitutional make-up like ugly face, short stature and any other deformity of the body may give birth to feelings of inferiority and he may face adjustment problems in the social environment.

Intelligence

Intelligence is considered as a major factor influencing development. Children of high intelligence develop in many aspects faster than that of low intelligence. Even the body movement and behaviour are regulated by his level of intelligence. It affects his social behaviour, moral adjustment and emotional growth. The physical, social, emotional, moral and language development of a child is greatly influenced and controlled by the level of his intelligence.

Emotional Factors

Emotional maturity and adjustability play a vital role in influencing a person's overall growth and development. A child who is found to be overwhelmed by negative emotions like fear, anger, jealousy, etc. is adversely affected in his physical, mental, social, moral and language development. If a person cannot exercise a reasonable control over his emotions, he has to suffer in his terms of growth and development. He may find himself a failure in doing some serious mental activity.

Social Factors

A person's socialization helps him in achieving adjustment and advancement in other aspects of his growth and development. He may learn from his environment, by means of his social nature, which may prove to be a boon to him for his proper growth and development.

II. External Factors

The factors lying outside individual in his environment are collectively called the external factors influencing growth and development. These factors begin their role immediately after a baby is conceived. They are as follows:

Environment in the Womb of Mother

What is available to the child for his nourishment in its mother's womb from the time of conception till his birth is quite important from the angle of his growth and development. A few factors are cited below as examples:

- The physical and mental health of the mother during pregnancy
- Single child or multiple children getting nourished in the womb
- Quality and quantity of nutrition received by the embryo
- Normal and abnormal delivery
- Any damage or accident to the baby in the womb

Environment Available After Birth

Whether a child gets from different conditions and forces of his environment after his birth influence his growth and development in many ways. These are described as follows:

(a) Accidents and Incidents of Life

The growth and development of an individual is greatly influenced by the good and bad incidents and accidents happens in his life time. For example, if a child's nervous system is damaged in an accident, it will hamper his mental development and in turn it will affect his development in other spheres also.

(b) The Quality of Physical Environment, Medical Care and Nourishment

A childes growth and development is greatly influenced by the quality of physical environment and medical care and nourishment available to him for his living and working. These include open space, balanced diet, proper medical care etc.

(c) The Quality of the Facilities and Opportunities Provided by the Social and Cultural Forces

What a child gets from his social and cultural environment influences the entire course of his development. A few are mentioned below:

- Parental and family care received by a child
- Economic and social status of the parents and family
- The quality of schooling received by a child
- The quality of peer group relationships of the child
- The quality of neighbourhood and surrounding environment

THE DEVELOPMENTAL PROCESS

Change is the law of nature. Animate or inanimate objects are all subject to change. Seeds, after germinating in the soil grow as saplings and then as specific plants and trees which in turn flower and produce seeds or fruits for further germination. Similar in the case with birds, animals and human beings who can produce their own kind by the transmission of specific characteristics of the species through sexual union.

In all animals, including human beings, the pre-natal period resembles the time taken by a germinating seed to come out of the soil, which then grows and develops into a full-fledged plant or tree. *The process by which a germinating seed or conceived organism is turned into the mature plant or full-fledged being is collectively termed growth and development.*

The process of growth and development are the medium and means for bringing about changes in the organism. In general, growth and development refers to the changes produced by the interaction produced by one's genetic and environmental factors as well as to the changes in the physical, mental, social, emotional and moral aspects involving one's individuality.

STAGES OF GROWTH AND DEVELOPMENT

Growth, development and behaviour of an individual have variations at different ages. Psychologists have divided the life span of an individual into different stages, each of which has certain common characteristics. Knowledge of various stages of development and its characteristics is essential for the teacher so as to make the teaching learning process effective, appropriate, and meaningful.

Modern education is based on the psychology of the educand. The educand's psychology is conforms to the stage of his development. By knowing the various stages of development through which an individual child is passing, the teacher can know his needs, interests and abilities and can plan his teaching strategy accordingly.

The different stages in the growth and development of an individual can be classified as follows:

Human Stage	Year
1. Pre-natal Stage	From conception to birth
2. Infancy	From birth to 3 years
3. Childhood	From 3 to 12 years (*in strict sense up to the onset of puberty)*
a. Early Childhood	3 to 6 years
b. Later Childhood	6 to 12 years
4. Adolescence	From 12 to 19 years (*from the onset of puberty to the age of maturity)*
5. Adulthood	From 20 to 60 years
6. Old Age	61 years and above

Although each stage is different from the other, we cannot draw a clear cut dividing line between different stages since stage merges with the next and because of the fact that developmental process is a continuous one. A study of the pattern of growth and development exhibited by the individuals provides very useful data for parents and teachers to plan the development and education of the children.

Pre-natal Period

The pre natal period extends from conception to birth, normally it is 280 days. The child's development within the womb is a very important phase of his entire development. During this period the developing organism is dependent upon the mother for the digestion of food, excretion of waste products, external respiration, body temperature etc. Factors like mother's health, food, emotional experiences and certain desires are some of the factors which influence the development during this period. Birth is merely an interruption of the normal development. This interruption is characterized by a change in the environment form that of mother's womb to that of the world outside.

Infancy Period

The first 3 years of the life of a child is the period of infancy. The first two weeks is known as the period of *neonate* or the new-born. The period from the third week to the end of three years is known as *babyhood.* These 3 years of life are of tremendous importance in the progress of the individual. It is at this time that the infant adjusts to the totally new environment outside the mother's body and thus learns to be self-dependent.

Developmental Characteristics during Infancy Period

Physical and Motor Development: Rapid physical growth is marked in these years. Boys showed an increased rate in growth than the girls. The trunk grows faster than the head and the proportion between the two changes. The bodily functions tend to become stable and controlled.

Emotional Development: At birth, for the expression of emotions like pleasure and pain, the baby is able to cry only. Later he can express fear, anger, disgust, etc. The child feels pleasure in the company of his mother and distress in her separation.

Intellectual Development: There is rapid improvement in the structure and function of the sensory organs. Now the child is able to perform all functions of seeing, hearing, tasting, smelling, touching etc. almost as good as a mature individual.

Social and Moral Development: Mother is the first and best friend and socializes of the infant. Other family members are in the next in position. At the end of this period the child begins to establish contact with other infants.

Language Development: Language development of the infant begins from the birth cry. The 10 month old child is able to use one word. By the end of the first year he is able to use 3 or 4 words.

Early Childhood Stage (Pre-School Stage)

Early childhood, extends from 3—6 years, is labeled by the parents as the *problem age* or *toy age;* by the educators as the *pre-school age and by the psychologists as the pre-gang age.* During this stage children are obstinate, disobedient, negativistic and antagonistic. Hence most parents consider early childhood as a problem age. Educationally this is the most important and impressionable age. This stage plays a significant role in the development of character and personality. Exploratory age, questioning age, imitative age etc. are the other names of this period.

Developmental Characteristics of Early Childhood

Physical and Motor Development: Early childhood is a period of slow, steady and uniform physical growth. The average annual increase in height is three inches and in weight is three to five pounds. Eruption and replacement of teeth is a remarkable in this period. Brain has developed 90 per cent of its adult weight. A variety of motor skills like crawling, walking, running, jumping, climbing etc. are also develops in this period.

Emotional Development: Emotions are especially intense during early childhood. The emotional behaviour of the child at this stage is further differentiated into shame, anxiety, envy, hope, disappointment and affection for parents and other members of the family. The most primitive sentiment is his love for his own self. Therefore this stage is called 'Narcissism', auto erotism or self-love. But soon the child extends his sentiments to his parents. According to Sigmund Freud, *Oedipus Complex* and *Electra Complex* are developed in this period. It is certain that, to a great extent, a boy has got great attachment to his mother and the girl to her father.

Intellectual Development: At this stage the child has got varied experiences connected with his immediate environment. He accumulates a heap of knowledge. He understands the basic functional relationship between things and events. He begins to form concepts of physical and social reality. *Ego-centrism* and fantasy are in a high degree at this stage. Gradual development in the perception of size, shape, colour, time; rapid increase in memory, thinking and reasoning, creativity and imagination etc. are also develops in this stage.

Language Development: During the first 8-10 months, the child's only mode of communication is babbling and cooing. The first words are uttered around child's first birth day. Then there is a rapid increase in vocabulary. Words are combined into phrases and sentences, and simple thought are communicated with ease.

Social Development

During early childhood the child acquires the preliminary training and experiences needed to become a member of a group in later childhood. During this stage, children become increasingly aware of their bodies and learn their sexual identities as male and female. This self awareness contributes to the development of their positive and negative self attitudes. During pre-school years children develop new inter-personal and appropriate relationship with others. They learn to share and compete with siblings and peers. The social qualities, such as co-operation, sympathy, social approval, teasing, quarrelling etc. are develops in this period. The important features of socializations during pre-schools years are:

- Feelings of autonomy develops in children
- Social environment expands beyond home

- Child seeks social approval for his actions
- Children of both sexes play together without any discrimination
- They learn to co-operate with others and to make friends on shared interests and similar personality traits

Later Childhood Stage (Primary School Stage)

Later childhood extends from the age of six years to the time individual becomes sexually mature. It spreads from 6 to 12 years. Educationalists call this age as *elementary-school age* and psychologists as *gang age* or *age of conformity.* The period is marked by rather slow and uniform growth. It is in this period, even the nicest child often begins to behave in the most awful way and hence requires proper guidance and counselling. At this stage several functional changes take place in the child. It gradually gains maturity in all physical and mental spheres. As regards sex, it remain dormant, but emerges with great force only at the end of this stage. It is why this stage is called *latency period.*

Developmental Characteristics of Later Childhood

Physical Development: Later childhood is a period of slow and relatively uniform growth until the changes of puberty begins. The growth is slowest for girls between nine and ten years, while boys grow slowest between ten and eleven years. The first teeth are replaced by permanent ones. Bones becomes harder and height and weight increase. Flattening of the forehead, sharpening of the nose and broadening of the chest are other notable changes. The most significant physical change occurring during this period is the lengthening of the limbs.

Motor Development: Motor abilities improve a great deal between sixth and twelfth year. Improving muscle co-ordination helps the child to acquire new skills and improve the already acquired ones. They have a reasonably good mastery over the basic motor skills of sitting, standing, walking and simple finger manipulation. By the age of twelve, muscle co-ordination is almost perfect.

Emotional Development: During this period the child learns to control emotional expression in social situations, especially the unpleasant ones and to use *emotional catharsis* to clear their pent-up emotions. Fear of many common things slowly disappears but fears caused by imaginary stimuli begin in this age. The child experiences more frustration and jealousy is intensified. Desire for acceptance as a member of the gang is developed and he likes to have company of his own sex. A catharsis is an emotional release. This emotional release is linked to a need to release unconscious conflicts. The individual may instead release these feelings in another way, such as through physical activity or another stress relieving activity

Intellectual Development: Primary school stage is the age of intellectual development. The child develops powers of observation, attention, reasoning and abstract thinking. They can focus on more than one aspects of a situation and can globally experience what happens around. His power of perception becomes keen and memory becomes keener. Here he learns the three R's—reading, writing and arithmetic. He is able to read books from which he gathers information and derives pleasure. Rote memory gives place to logical thinking. This is the period of physical and intellectual stability.

Social and Moral Development: This period is marked by greater degree of social awareness. He tires to loosen the control of the family and becomes more increasingly independent of his parents. He becomes an active member of a peer group. Peer group becomes an important agent of socialization during this period. He develops social qualities like co-operation, team spirit etc. to adjust with the social environment. He believes in group loyalty and tries to conform to the rules and values maintained by the group.

Speech and Language Development: During the later childhood, all areas of speech—*pronunciation, vocabulary, comprehension and sentence structure*—improve rapidly. By the age of 9–10, children develop an increasingly complex understanding of syntax. Grammatical errors are slowly eliminated and they talk fluently.

Adolescence Stage (Secondary or Higher Secondary School Stage)

Adolescence is that span of years which boys and girls move from childhood to adulthood mentally, emotionally, socially and physically. It is a period from the onset of puberty to the age of maturity. It is a period of rapid physical and biological changes which may lead to confusions, tensions, frustrations and feelings of insecurity. It is a period of transition when changes of attitude and behaviour are most rapid. Stanley Hall rightly calls it is the *period of stress and strain, storm and strife.* Holling Worth calls this the *period of temporary insanity.* It is because of the restlessness and disturbance due to the nature of development that takes place during this period.

Adolescence experiences create conflicts between himself and society. Change of role in society, shattered relations in home, failure to decide his status in social settings, difficulty in adjusting with the opposite sex, unnecessary restrictions on movement etc. give rise to tensions and worries. During this stage emotions fluctuate very frequently and quickly. He tries to oppose the views of parents and school authorities, but such efforts often fail.

The adolescent lives in an intensely emotional life, in which the rhythm of positive and negative phases of behaviour gets lost. This results in constant alteration between intense excitement and deep depression. All these create a considerable degree of stress and strain in the adolescent.

Adolescent is also known as the *period of transition* because during this period an individual is neither a child nor an adult. During this period the individual's status is vague and there is confusion about the role he is expected to play. He is often looked upon in an ambiguous manner by the elders. Sometimes he is expected to behave as an adult and at other times he is treated as a child. This is the time when the individual is striving to wean himself away from the family in order to become a self sufficient and autonomous person. Some may take the drugs or get addicted to alcohol if their needs are thwarted or denied. Hence Holling Worth calls it a *period of temporary insanity.*

It is a very crucial period when the individual attains maturity physically, intellectually, emotionally, sexually and socially. The growth achieved, the experiences gained, the responsibilities felt and the relationships developed at this stage determine the complete future of the individual.

Developmental Tasks for Birth to Old Age

Havighurst (1953) prepared a developmental model in which he has presented the list of developmental tasks from birth to old age. Every cultural group expects its members to master certain essential skills and acquire certain approved patterns of behaviour at various ages during the life span. Havighurst has labeled them developmental tasks.

According to him a developmental task is *'a task which arises at or about a certain period in the life of the individual, successful achievement of which leads to happiness and to success with later tasks, while failure leads to unhappiness and difficult with later tasks'.*

Although most people would like to master these tasks at the appropriate time, some are unable to do so, while others are ahead of schedule. Though these tasks are applicable to American population, they are generally accepted to be applicable to all. They are as follows:

Developmental Tasks Related to Infancy

This stage covers approximately first two weeks of life. It is the shortest developmental period. It is a time for radical adjustment. The new born infant must make four major adjustments to post natal life viz.

- To temperature changes
- To sucking and swallowing
- To breathing
- To elimination.

Developmental Tasks Related to Babyhood and Early Childhood

The developmental tasks related to this stage are as under:

- Learning to take solid foods
- Learning to walk and talk
- Learning to control the elimination of body wastes
- Learning sex differences and sexual modesty
- Getting ready to read
- Learning to distinguish right and wrong and beginning to develop conscience.

Developmental Tasks Related to Late Childhood

The developmental tasks related to late childhood are as under:

- Learning physical skills necessary for ordinary games
- Building a wholesome attitude toward oneself as a growing organism
- Learning to get along with age-mates
- Beginning to develop appropriate masculine or feminine social roles.
- Developing fundamental skills in reading, writing and calculating.
- Developing concepts necessary for everyday living
- Developing a conscience, a sense of morality, and a scale of values
- Developing attitudes toward social groups and institutions.
- Achieving personal independence.

Developmental Tasks Related to Adolescence

The developmental tasks related to adolescence are as under:

- Achieving new and more mature relations with age-mates of both sexes
- Achieving a masculine or feminine social role
- Accepting one's physic and using one's body effectively
- Desiring, accepting, and achieving socially responsible behaviour
- Achieving emotional independence from parents and other adults
- Preparing for an economic career
- Preparing for marriage and family life
- Acquiring a set of values and an ethical system as a guide to behaviour-developing an ideology.

Developmental Tasks Related to Early Adulthood

The developmental tasks related to early adulthood are as under:

- Getting started in an occupation
- Selecting a mate
- Learning to live with a marriage partner
- Starting a family
- Rearing children
- Managing a home
- Taking on civic responsibility
- Finding a congenial social group.

Developmental Tasks Related to Middle Age

The developmental tasks related to middle age are as under:

- Achieving adult civic and social responsibility
- Assisting teenage children to become responsible and happy adults
- Developing adult leisure-time activities
- Relating oneself to one's spouse as a person
- Accepting and adjusting to the physiological changes of middle age
- Reaching and maintaining satisfactory performance in one's occupational career
- Adjusting to aging parents.

Developmental Tasks Related to Old Age

The developmental tasks related to old age are as under:

- Adjusting to decreasing physical strength and health
- Adjusting to retirement and reduced income
- Adjusting to death of spouse
- Establishing an explicit affiliation with members of one's age group
- Establishing satisfactory physical living arrangements
- Adapting to social roles in a flexible way.

Chapter-4
Heredity and Environment

You ask a question to yourself that why we differ from others and what makes us unique. We are not totally different from others: there are some similarities and common characteristics that are observed among the family members of the same family. Even, some common characteristics among the individuals of same biological race can be observed. What is it that causes such similarities and dissimilarities? The answer usually referred to is heredity, which is a biological inheritance of characteristics transmitted to offspring from parents and forefathers, which makes them resemble in appearance in the same family. Another major factor that determines the individual difference is environmental factor, other than biological inheritance, which includes physical and social/ cultural environment.

Every individual on this earth is different from the other. No one person is fully like other person. Every person differs from the other, either physically or psychologically. Even the twins are no exception to this. They differ in some aspects or other. Particularly when we look at people from psychological point of view these differences are quite obvious. In many instances even the children differ from their parents.

They will have some similarities with some forefathers or grandparents instead of their parents. What makes these differences to exist? What are the causes? The answer to these queries can be traced from two factors, viz., heredity and environment. The basic sources of personality development are heredity and environment.

WHAT IS HEREDITY?

How a child resembles his siblings or parents or grandparents? For this question, the answer usually referred to is heredity, which means that an offspring inherits most of the personality traits from his or her parents and forefathers, which makes him or her resemble like them. Heredity can be defined by Douglas and Holland (1947) as follows: *"One's heredity consists of all the structures, physical characteristics, functions or capacities derived from parents, other ancestry or species."*

Thus, the term heredity can be defined as a biological mechanism, which transfers the genetic traits – physical and psychological – from one generation to another or from parents to offspring.

Heredity refers to the genetic inheritance received by every individual at the time of conception. The origin of every human life can be traced to a single cell called zygote. It is formed by the union of sperm and ovum.

According to Douglas and Holland (1947), *"One's heredity consists of all the structure, physical characteristics or capacities derived from parents, other ancestry or species"*. Life in actual sense begins with the conception, approximately, nine months before birth. Life is the result of the union of these male and female cells. (Sperm and Ovum). Only one sperm (single male cell) is able to establish contact with the ovum (Single female cell) situated in the ovarian duct of the mother and makes if fertile. This process is called fertilization

The fertilized Ovum is technically known as Zygote (structure on a new life). Human life thus starts from a single cell produced by the union of two germ cells (Sperm and Ovum), one from each parent and gradually develops in to a complicated composition of trillions of body cells and yet containing the same genetic material that was inherited at the time of conception.

In other words, In human Zygote there are 23 pairs of chromosomes (23 by father and 23 by mother =46 Chromosomes). There are more than 1000 genes in each chromosome cell. The sperm and ovum will contain 23 pairs of chromosomes out of which one will be sex determining chromosome. Female will have 23 pairs of XX chromosomes. Male will have 22 pairs of XX and 2 single, represented as XY. X chromosome from mother and Y chromosome from father will lead to male offspring, XX from both parents give rise to female. In each chromosome there are innumerable genes.

These genes are the real determiners of hereditary characteristics, which pass on from one generation to the other. At the time of conception, the genes from chromosomes of both the father and the mother fuse together and determine the traits of the offspring to be born.

The physical characteristics such as height, weight, colour of eye and skin, social and intellectual behaviour are determined by heredity. Differences in these characteristics are due to the change in the genes transmitted. Fraternal twins also differ from each other, because they are born out of different genes. However, we find more resemblances in identical twins because they are born out of monozygotic.

The possibility regarding the combination of 23,000 characteristics each from mother and father may help us to understand the reason for uniqueness of each individual. The inheritance of traits at the time of conception makes up the native capital and endowment of an individual that are present with him in the form of sum total of the traits basically present in the fertilized ovum. These are called the heredity factors present in an individual.

Transfer of Genetic Traits from One Generation to Another

Life is actual sense beings with the mechanism of conception, i.e. union of two germ cells – ova and sperm. Each and every germ cell produced by male and female have unique genital code and structure, which determine the individual similarities and dissimilarities. The genetic code bounded with thread-like structure in each cell is called *'chromosomes'*. Each chromosome is made up of very small units called *'genes'*. The composition of genes has been determined in terms of deoxyribonucleic acid (DNA) and ribonucleic acid (RNA). DNA carries the genetic code message from parents to offspring.

Thus, the ancestral stock received from parents at the time of fertilization of the ovum of the mother by the sperm of the father is in the form of chromosomes, genes and their respective classical constituents. The in heritance of traits at the time of conception makes up the native capital and endowment of an individual that are present as sum total of the traits basically presented in the fertilized ovum.

Role of Genes and Chromosomes in Determining Individual Differences

Sex Determination

Hereditary factor begins its influence right from the time of conception of the child through the transmission of chromosomes and genes of its ancestral stock from its immediate parents. In the mechanism of heredity, the number of chromosomes will determine the nature of species, which varies from one species to another. In human beings, the number of chromosomes is 46 or 23 pairs of chromosomes. Out of these, the first 22 pairs of chromosomes are called 'autosomes', which are responsible for deciding and determining the growth and development of most of the characteristics and biological composition of the body. The remaining 23rd pair is the sex chromosome, which determines the sex of the child—either boy child or girl child (See Figure 4.1).

There are two different types of sex chromosomes: X chromosome (usually big in size) and Y chromosome (comparatively smaller than X chromosome). In a male child, one of the sex chromosome is X chromosome (contributed by the mother) and the other is Y (contributed by the father), i.e. XY. In a female child, both the sex chromosomes (one from each parent) are X chromosome, i.e. XX.

During fertilization, the sperm cells contain either X or Y but the female ova contain only X (all the ova have similar structure in 23rd number of chromosome) as shown in Figure 4.1.

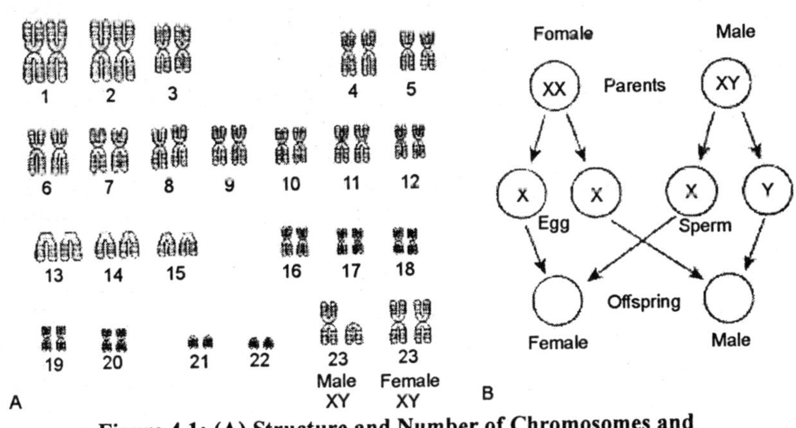

Figure 4.1: (A) Structure and Number of Chromosomes and (B) Determination of Sex

Therefore, a mother's role in the determination of her baby's sex is quite natural. Thus, the father is biologically more accountable for determination of the sex of his child to be born.

Determination of Physical Constitution

Most of the attributes related to our body makeup, its constitution and functioning are well decided and guided by heredity. There are some physical constitutions, such as eye colour, hair texture, skin tone, height, facial structure or outlook and appearance, blood types, fingerprints, etc. Besides, such differences in the physical constitution, structure and body makeup, hereditary factors are also said to be the sole cause of some diseases like tuberculosis, cancer, haemophilia and mental disorders like schizophrenia. These diseases are causes by defect in genes and chromosome and are passed on to subsequent generations.

WHAT IS ENVIRONMENT?

As mentioned earlier, heredity determines the biological traits and characteristics and its role ends with conception. What happens after the conception is determined by environment. Environment refers to any other factor(s) that influences individual growth and development other than heredity factors. To understand the impact of environment, it can be categorized into two types, i.e. internal environment and external environment.

According to Woodworth, *"Environment covers all the outside factors that have acted on the individual since he began life"*. Environment is everything that affect the individual expect genes. Before birth- Environment is at the womb (Physiological and psychological state of the mother, habit, interests). After birth the environment is the physical forces and social or cultural forces.

In simple terms environment means the society, the fields of society and even the whole world. But here, the word environment is restricted to mean the environment within mother's womb and just born, as well as the environment around the individual. Like heredity, environment also has been found to play a very important role in determining the behaviour and personality development of an individual. The environmental influences are those which act upon the organism at the earlier stages of development, i.e., before and also after birth.

Environment includes all the extrinsic forces, influences and conditions which affect the life, nature, behaviour, the growth, development and maturation of living organism (Douglass and Holland). Hence, we can say that environment means all that is found around the individual. The zygote is surrounded by a jelly like substance known as 'cytoplasm'. The cytoplasm is an intracellular environment which influences the development. Though the life begins with single cell, in the process of cell division several new cells are formed and a new internal environment comes into existence.

As the fetus develops the endocrine glands are formed. The hormonal secretion by these glands gives rise to another intracellular environment. Hormones are necessary for normal development, but defects in hormone secretion like over or under secretion may lead to congenital deformities.

The growing embryo is surrounded by amniotic fluid in the uterus which creates another environment. This fluid will provide the necessary warmth and protection against the dangers due to organisms and other chemical effects on fetus.

The fetus is also connected to the mother by the umbilical cord, through which the nourishment is supplied. Sufficient nourishment is necessary from the mother. Otherwise the child will suffer from malnutrition. The defects in mother like drug or alcohol addiction, smoking, malnutrition, diabetes, endocrinal disturbances, small uterus and such other problems cause many problems in child.

The psychological state of mother like over excitement, depression also may cause damaging effect on the child. After nine months, the child is born and enters a new environment which is entirely different. A new life begins in a new environment. This new environment will have a different culture, ideology, values, etc.

The home atmosphere, parental love and affection, association with sibling, neighbours, peers, teachers, etc. will create an entirely different and new atmosphere. This is called social environment. All the social factors stated above shape the personality of the child. There is a long standing controversy regarding the importance of heredity and environment. Supporters of heredity say that the environment cannot change a dog into a goat. On the other hand, the environmentalists are of the opinion that for the development of a plant only seed is not important but also environment like sunlight, manure, water, etc.

Innumerable studies have been conducted on both sides. However, the results indicate that heredity and environment are interdependent forces. Whatever the heredity supplies, the favourable environment brings it out. Personality characteristics attained by heredity are shaped by environment.

Internal Environment

Internal environment approximately influences for the period of 9 months where the foetus gets nourishment in the mother womb indirectly through the mother. Therefore, whatever the mother eats or drinks have an impact on the growth and development of the child. Not only the quality of her diet but also the psychosocial environment. If the mother remains tense, worried, anxious and emotionally upset or mentally perturbed, then it may eventually have an adverse effect on the growth and development of the baby.

Individual differences in children are thus certainly caused by the variations and difference existed in the physical and mental health of their mothers during pregnancy. At the time of delivery also, the environment available to the mother and the child affects the well-being, growth and development of the child. Here, the individual difference may be caused by situations like premature or mature delivery, normal delivery or a caesarean delivery, hygienic or unhygienic conditions and the general atmosphere at the time of delivery.

External Environment

External environment refers to any conditions that influence the child's growth and development, such as physical, social, cultural and psychological environment. This external environment plays major role and imparts long period of influence in determining and modifying the individual's behaviour and result in individual difference. Each and every factor after the birth of child has great influence and develops a unique personality. You may argue that children of the same parents or family have the same environment, then why these children differ in their behaviour? However, if you analyse, the environmental treatment to the individual child differs. Even a mother cannot claim paying equal attention, care and affection to all her children. For example, in most of the Indian homes, male children get more privilege then female children. The same is also true in the case of students beings taught by the same set of teachers in the same classroom set-up. Thus, as reality, it is true that no children receive the same kind of conditions with respect to social, cultural, physical and psychological environment. Hence, individuals are bound to differ significantly from each other in various ways.

CAUSES OF INDIVIDUAL DIFFERENCES

The following are the main causes of individual differences:

Heredity (Nature)

Individuals have various endowments, abilities and capacities provided by heredity, which decide the path of progress and development of an individual. Hereditary also put limits upon individuals' *growth and development* in various dimensions. Hereditary also contribute to sex, intelligence and other specific abilities.

Environment (Nurture)

Environment also plays key role in individual differences. No person from birth to death gets the same environment. Individual differences occur on the basis of simulation received by individual from his or her internal and external environment. This may include family set up, peer group, economic status, education etc.

It is debatable that whether nature or nurture play vital or stronger role in the development of an individual in specific direction. Both are strong contenders in order to distinguish one individual from other.

CONTROVERSY OF NATURE (HEREDITY) VERSUS NURTURE (ENVIRONMENT)

The role of heredity and environment in creating differences and variations among human beings has already been discussed. Now, the question arises that which one of them is more responsible or more important in determining and creating variations and individual differences. The hereditarians claim the heredity is everything. They argued the heredity decides and sets everything about the personality of an individual and consider the environment as just a factor that nourishes the growth and development, but it never changes anything in the basic quality of individual. The environmentalists are of the opinion that heredity does not affect the growth and development of an individual in any way; the individual differences are the product of environmental influence.

American psychologist John Watson, a strong proponent of environmental learning, said "*Give me a dozen healthy infants, well-formed and my own specified world to bring them up in and I'll guarantee to take any one at random and train him to become any type of specialist I might select.... regardless of his talents, penchants, tendencies, abilities, vocations and race of his ancestors"*. He demonstrated that the acquisition of phobia in a child named Albert could be explained by classical conditioning—as a learned behaviour.

There are some twin studies that proved the significant influence of heredity on an individual. In these experiments, the identical twins, who possess the similar genetic materials and are similar in their physical constitution, even though the environment changes for both the individual, but they show similarly in their IQ and other aptitudes, which they possess from the ancestors through heredity. Thus, both hereditarians and environmentalists have tried to collect a fund of experimental evidences in support of their viewpoints. It is hard to make any statement in favour of either heredity of environment in the process of development of an individual and also in the determination of individual differences. Both are equally important and indispensable in their role to determine individual difference.

Chapter-5
Individual Differences

In this world, all natural things—living or nonliving—are created in a unique way, as they have their unique features and characteristics, which differentiate them from one another. These differences and variations become more intense and remarkable as we draw our attention to human beings, who are one of the ultimate creations of the Almighty in the history of evolution. Human beings quite distinctly differ in size, shape, appearance, speed of reaction and innumerable other aspects of their personality makeup and behaviour. These differences in human beings are referred to as *individual differences*.

DEFINITION OF INDIVIDUAL DIFFERENCES

According to the Dictionary of Education, edited by Carter V. Good (1959), *"the term individual difference stands for the variations or deviations among individuals with regard to a single characteristic or a number of characteristics."*

Individual difference stands for those differences that in their totality distinguish one individual from another. Thus, the difference among individuals that distinguish or separate them from one another and make a person a unique individual may be termed *individual difference.*

According to the dictionary of education:

- Individual differences stand for the variation or deviations among individuals in regard to a single characteristic or number of characteristics.
- It is stand for those differences which in their totally distinguish one individual from another. So, we can say that individual differences is the differences among humans that distinguish or separate them from one another and makes one as a single unique individual.

TYPES/AREAS OF INDIVIDUAL DIFFERENCES

Individuals have variety of differences. Some individual differences are natural to humans which, cannot be controlled or changed and some can changed and controlled by human beings living in society. These are the differences which makes humans different in various fields of life. Psychology is academic discipline which studies these differences and prescribes the way of building effective personality of an individual.

Individual differences are observed among the human beings that may be grouped or classified into two broad categories, namely physical or physiological difference and physiological difference. Let us discuss the differences or variations among human beings in the following specific types of varieties:

Physical Differences

The observable differences that are majorly noted among people are the physical differences, such as height, weight, colour of skin, eyes and hair, size of hands and heads, arms, feet, mouth and nose, length of waistline, structure and functioning of internal organs, facial expression, mannerism of speech and walk, hair style and other physical characteristics.

Age Differences

This is visible difference. Age factor determines the characteristics of a person. Age five (5) students and age fifteen (15) students will have variety of differences in terms of height, strength, emotions and cognitive development.

Sex Differences

This is natural one. That is distinction between male and female individuals. This sex differences gives male and female their characteristics relating to body, psychology, mental abilities and cultural or social roles.

Intellectual and Mental Differences

People differ in their intellectual abilities and capabilities like reasoning and thinking, power of imagination, creative expression, concentration, etc. Generally, people are classified based on their intellectual difference as idiot, imbecile, moron, borderline, normal, bright, very superior and genius.

This is the vital areas as far as educational psychology is concerned. Because educational psychology main focus is on mental process and their manipulations in certain directions. Commonly intellectual differences are checked by intelligence quotient (IQ) yard stick. This is clear difference that the IQ ability of one person (male or female) is different from another one. That's why psychologists have done IQ classification as given below:

Sl. No	*I.Q*	*Class*
1.	180/Above	Gifted Person
2.	140 to 170	Genius
3.	120 to 140	Very intelligent
4.	110 to 120	Intelligent
5.	90 to 110	Normal/Average
6.	80 to 90	Dull
7.	70 to 80	Borderline
8.	50 to 70	Feeble minded
9.	25 to 50	Imbecile
10.	0 to 25	Idiot

This information above helps a lot a teacher to know his/her student mental abilities.

Differences in Motor Ability

Wide differences are observed among people based on their motor abilities, such as reaction time, speed of action, hand steadiness, rate of muscular moment, manual dexterity and resistance of fatigue etc.

Emotional Differences

This is also very important factor which gives great distinguish status to a person against others. Those who have control over their emotional feelings, show better learning result as compare to those who are not well emotionally balance. This is one of the vital areas of individual differences where teacher and parents must work hard to produce and bring up sound personality in a student for social role.

It is observed that some people express more positive emotions, whereas, some express negative emotions. Individuals also differ in the manner they express their emotions and manage their emotional behaviour. Some are emotionally stable and nature, while others are emotionally unstable and immature.

Difference in Aptitudes

Variation occurs among the individuals in relation to their specific aptitudes. For example, people are found to have different aptitudes; some are good in mechanical aptitude, while others have scholastic or verbal aptitude.

Difference in Interest

Variation occurs among the individuals in relation to their specific interest and aptitudes. For example, some people have more interest in social interaction and some are happy in solitude. Interest may refer as a motivating force that impels us to attend to a person, a thing or an activity. So, in educational field, differences in interest means, you observe some students like a particular subject, teacher, hobby or profession than other.

Difference in Attitude

Difference in attitude is psyche related to something. Few learners have positive attitude towards a specific topic, subject and profession than other. The role of education in society is to develop a positive attitude.

Difference in Values

Values are the things that are given importance by an individual. Some learners give value to materialist life style, other moral or religious life style etc. So, education must mould the mind of young generation to have a balance values between materialism and spiritualism.

Study Habits

It is clearly observable that some students markedly differ from other students in study habits. Some students are studious and study all the subjects with interest but other may not. Some study in isolation and some in group.

Difference in Psychomotor Skills

Psychomotor skill is related to some skill acquisition. Some students differ in this area also. Some students like football, other cricket etc. Some students easily learn operating a machine and some may not. A wise teacher should diagnose students' psychomotor skills abilities and encourage them in that direction.

Difference in Self Concept

Difference in self concept is the totality of attitudes, judgment and values of an individual relating to his behaviour, abilities and qualities. So, some students have positive self concept than boost their confidence level and perform better against those who have negative self image.

Learning Difference

Individual differences are also found in the field of learning. It is observed in a classroom that some students are very fast learners, some are average and some are slow learners. This difference is observed due to their individual difference in the pattern of studying or depends upon the individual nature of the learner.

Differences in Social and Moral Values

Individuals differ in respect of their social and moral development. Some are found to be more adjusted and have more interpersonal relationships, while others are socially not well adjusted and show more antisocial behaviour. This individual difference is due to their moral and social values.

This area of individual differences means that how an individual is able to adjust to the new changing environment. That adjustment degree varies from individual to individual. The role of environment or nurture is very vital. If, a child gets good environment at school and home, that will help a lot a student to have good adjustment. This social adjustment is a big indicator that makes difference in individual to individual. The more you are socially adjusted to the role, the more you have balanced personality and social life.

Individual differences are natural, which make a person different from another. Now, it is the work of nature-education, training to maximize the good qualities of a student or person and minimize the bad ones in order to have good and peaceful social life for a person. The teacher role in this regard is very vital.

Thus, all the above-discussed aspects distinguish one individual from others, as their personality is unique. There are more dimensions to define the individual difference among the human beings.

ROLE OF HEREDITY IN GENERATING INDIVIDUAL DIFFERENCES

The role of Heredity in generating individual differences is as follows:

Heredity Determining the Sex of the Child

The autosomes (first 22 pair of Chromosomes) are responsible for deciding and determining the growth and development of most of the characteristics and structural composition of our body. Remaining one is the sex chromosome. That will be deciding the gender of the individual (see page 49 also).

- There are two types of sex chromosomes, X and Y
- X + Y= Son, X + X = Daughter (X, Y-Male, X, X-female)
- Father is biologically more accountable for determination of the sex.

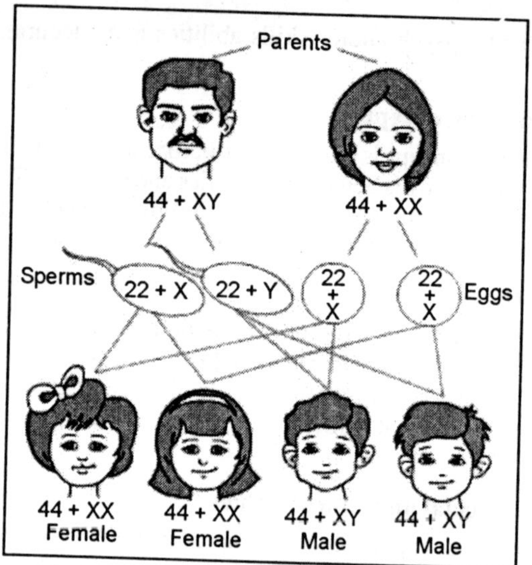

Figure 5.1: Sex Determination of the Child

Heredity Contribute Significantly Towards Physical Constitution

Most of the attributes related to our body make-up, its constitution and functioning are well decided and guided by heredity.

- Ex: hair, facial look, blood type etc.
- Sometimes the role of heredity as a determined of physical condition or bodily make up becomes questionable.

Contribution of Heredity towards the Birth of Twins and the Related Individual Differences

Sometimes two or more ova get fertilized resulting in the birth of two or more offspring's at a time. There are two distinctly different types of twins namely:

- ***Identical twins:*** (Ova Split in to two or more—each part develop in to complete individual). They carry exactly same genes.
- ***Fraternal twins:*** two or more ova may mature simultaneously and get fertilized simultaneously by two or more different sperms.

ROLE OF ENVIRONMENT AS DETERMINANT OF INDIVIDUAL DIFFERENCES

The role of environment in individual differences is as under:

Internal Environment (inside the womb)

Whatever mother eats or drinks have an impact on the growth and development of child. Environment available during pregnancy is quite important for the baby. The mother remains tense, worried, anxious and emotionally upset then it may eventually have an adverse effect on the growth and development of the baby. Environment at the time of delivery will affect the child (Normal delivery or not? hygienic or not?)

External Environment (After Birth)

After birth, physical, sociological, cultural and psychological environment affects the growth and development of an individual.

RELATIVE IMPORTANCE OF HEREDITY AND ENVIRONMENT AS DETERMINES OF INDIVIDUAL DIFFERENCE

- Every phenomenon of life is the product of both. Each is as necessary to the result as the other. Neither can ever be eliminated and neither can ever be isolated.
- Nothing is more certain than that heredity and environment are co-acting influence and that both are essential to achievement.
- As a gift from heredity, we get our working capital but it is the environment which gives us the opportunity to invest it.

EFFECTIVE WAYS FOR TEACHERS/EDUCATORS DEALING WITH INDIVIDUAL DIFFERENCE

The following guidelines can help teachers and educators to cope and deal with individual differences:

Knowledge of Individual Personality: The first step to deal with individual differences is the information about an individual choices, abilities, interest and attitudes. In this regard, help can be taken from various kinds of tests, personal records, family, peer group etc.

Adjustment in Curriculum: Curriculum should be rich of all kinds of subjects and co-curricular activities in order to take into consideration the individual interests and capabilities.

Adjustment of Methods of Teaching: Teachers and Educators are on liberty to adopt the proper teaching methods on the basis of individual differences in order to meet different learning styles of the learners.

Special Programmes or Individualized Instructions: School can arrange special classes for a specific group of learners or individualize coaching can also be adopted for a particular duration.

Grouping of Learners: Learners can also be grouped together on the basis of same individual differences in order to teach them in group to save time and resources.

INDIVIDUAL DIFFERENCES AND EDUCATION

The teacher can make use the knowledge of individual differences in education and teaching. The main features in this connection are the following:

Curriculum: In school, the curriculum should be modified to suit the needs of the dull children. Failure to achieve this, adversely affects the development of this kinds of children

Limited Size of the Class: Keeping in mind the individual differences of the students, it is advisable that if they are to be taught properly, a class should not include more than 20 students. With 50 or more students, it is impossible to teach them keeping in mind their specific requirements.

Method of Education: It is never advisable efficacious to use the same method of education in the case of all the children. It should be varied to suit and conform to their individual differences and mental requirements.

Educational Guidance: Knowing the personal differences between students, the teacher can render them signal service by guiding them in their educational career. It is the teacher, who can tell them the subjects, they must choose to pursue in their higher studies, if they are not to do violence to their natures.

Vocational Guidance: Different professions require some specific physical, mental and personality traits of the individual. Hence, knowing their peculiar mental makeup and their tendencies, the teacher can guide the students in the vocation that they should adopt.

Contribution of School, Family and Community in Education: Knowledge of differences among children determines that education in school is not sufficient since many differences are due to the family and community. Hence, according to the modern educational psychologists, to attain the objective of all round development of individuals, prescribed by modern education, the co-operation of school, family, community and the religious institutions is sought.

Individual Training: Having knowledge of individual differences, now many methods of individual training have been devised. The Dalton plan, Project Method, Winnetka Method, Contract Plan and Activity Programme Methods have been devised for individual training. A brief resume of the various methods is given below:

Dalton Plan: In this method, children are not taught in class rooms. They are given subjects that suit their interests and they are given a project that covers a period of 15 days to a month. Such treatment leads to the development of nautrality, independence, co-operation and sociability etc.

Project Method: In this method, the children are required to do work in natural setting and in the process of this work, they are taught novel things.

Winnetka System: In this method, the student on his own tries to attain a certain definite objective and the teacher offers very little assistance. Later on, through some tests, the extent to which the student has attained his goal is discovered.

Contract Plan: In this method, similar to the Dalton Method, the subjects of study are determined and similar to the Winnetka method, the student's progress is measured through tests. In this manner, it is a synthesis of the Dalton and Winnetka method.

Activity Programme: In this method, keeping in mind the interests of the students, activities are prescribed in order to define the curriculum. These activities are based on democratic principles. This helps to develop democratic notion in the children.

Chapter-6
Development of Adolescent

Adolescence is the period of developmental transition between childhood and adulthood, involving multiple physical, intellectual, personality and social developmental changes. The onset of puberty signals the beginning of adolescence, and puberty now occurs earlier, on average, than in the past. The end of this developmental period is tied more so to social and emotional factors and can be somewhat ambiguous.

IMPORTANCE OF ADOLESCENCE PERIOD

Adolescence period is very important because:

Adolescence is a Period of Transition or Role Confusion

Adolescence is known as the period of transition because during this period an individual is neither a child nor an adult. He has passed through childhood and yet is to become an adult. During this stage the status of the individual is vague and there is confusion about the roles which the individual is expected to play. Sometimes he is expected to behave as an adult and at other times, he is treated as a child.

Adolescence is a Period of Stress and Strain

During adolescence the individual comes under social pressure and faces new conditions for which he received little training during childhood. He experiences conflict between himself and with the society. Change of role in society, unfavourable relations in home, difficulty in adjusting with opposite sex, unnecessary restrictions on movements etc. give rise to tension and worries.

During this stage he tries to oppose the views of parents and school authorities. But he is not always successful and it makes him restless, moody and emotionally disturbed one. As his emotions fluctuate very frequently, a considerable degree of stress and strain is created in the individual. That is why the adolescence is often designated as a period of stress and strain or a period of storm and strife.

Peer Group influence during Adolescence

The most important social development during adolescence is the increased influence of peer group. The adolescent picks up the norms, habits and social qualities of his companion. His interests, attitudes and values are greatly influenced by his peers. Peer group is a very powerful instrument in moulding the social behaviour of the teenagers. As mentioned in an English proverb "*A cheerful friend is like a sunny day spreading brightness all around*".

The peer group the adolescent learns to co-operate, to lead and follow, to think for a common cause and to adjust in the challenging social situation. The peer group satisfies various psychological needs of children like acceptance, affection, approval, belongings, fame, recognition, expression of thought and opinion etc. It is in this peer group the individual continues to formulate and revise his concept of *Self.*

NEEDS AND PROBLEMS OF ADOLESCENCE

An individual's needs and problems influence his development to a great extent. Adolescence is a crucial period in the life of an individual with its characteristic needs and problems of adjustment. Every adolescent has certain needs, the satisfaction of which is essential to his continued physical and others aspects of development. *A need is a tension within an organism which must be satisfied for the well being of the organism.* When a need is satisfied the tension is released and the individual experiences satisfaction. There are certain basic needs which are functioning in every individual. They are broadly classified into *Physiological needs and Psychological needs*.

Primary or Physiological Needs

The fulfillments of physiological needs are inevitable because they are concerned with the very existence of the individual. The need for oxygen, need for water and food, need for rest and sleep, need for sex gratification etc. are the important physiological needs.

Secondary or Socio-Psychological Needs

Needs that are associated with socio-cultural environment of an individual are called secondary needs. They are acquired through social learning and their satisfaction is necessary for the psychological well being of the individual. The important socio-psychological needs are as follows:

Needs for Security: The adolescent needs emotional, social and economic security in addition to physical security. The person who lacks the feeling of security may become maladjusted. The need for social security is associated with man's desire for gregariousness.

Need for Love: Affection or love is one of the most basic psychological needs of the adolescents. Adolescents have a strong desire to love and to be loved. The individual who is not loved will not deep proper attitudes and concepts concerning his own worth. Proper love will strengthen the individuals feeling of security.

Need for Approval: There is a carving for recognition in adolescents. His ego gets satisfaction when he is recognized and approved. The adolescent desire that he should be a centre of attraction for the opposite sex and his abilities, intelligence and capacities should be recognized by others. The teachers should find out the field in which the pupil can shine very well and which help him to earn admiration from others.

Need for Freedom and Independence: Adolescence is a time when the individual is striving to wean himself away from the control of parents and elders. He wants the right to give expression to his feelings, emotions and ideas. He feels annoyed and unpleasant when restriction is imposed on him.

Need for Self-expression and Achievement: Every adolescent has an inherent desire for the expression of his potentialities. He may have a poet, musician, painter etc. hidden within him and he want to get adequate opportunities for the expression of his potentialities. He experiences satisfaction when he succeeded in them and failure makes him depressed and disappointed. Hence the curriculum should be appropriate for every pupil so as to permit achievement for him.

PROBLEMS OF ADOLESCENTS WITH SPECIAL REFERENCE TO INDIAN CONTEXT

Any period of development is likely to be accompanied by many potential difficulties. Adolescence is a period of transition from childhood to adulthood that implies many development changes and associated problems. Some of the outstanding problems of Indian adolescence are the following:

Perplexity with Regard to Somatic Variation: Every adolescent has more or less difficult task of adjusting to somatic variation which may occur in connection with puberty. The follow of blood during menstruation in girls and nocturnal emission in boys creates worries and give birth to so many fears and anxieties. Since ours is a conservative society, youngsters are less informed about the physical changes that are occurring during puberty. Lack of scientific information about sex hygiene and philosophy make them to satisfy with crude and perverted knowledge about sex related matters. It creates guilt feeling and so many complexes in the minds of the children which makes them introverted and secretive.

Problems Related with Intensification of Sex-consciousness: The sudden awakening of sex instinct during adolescence results in intensification of sex consciousness. Adolescents are curious to know about sex related topics and are seeking answers to their innumerable doubts in sexual matters. In our country most of the parents are illiterate and they do not have scientific knowledge of sex problems. Moreover, our social values are different from that of western countries, and hence parents hesitate to discuss sex problems with their children. So the adolescents resort socially unacceptable ways to quench their curiosity and to satisfy their sexual needs. There is also the misguiding of print and electronic media that finally results in sexual maladjustment in adolescents.

Adjustment Difficulties with Parents: Adolescents have a strong for freedom and independence. But often it is obstructed by parental oppositions. In Indian context, parental opposition may extend to such areas as choices of friends, choice of education, recreational interests, dress, life-style, our of going from and coming to the home, mode of behaviour etc. The conflict between parental norms of behaviour and peer group relationships often lead to friction in the relationship and adolescents find it difficult to adjust to the needs and demands of parents. Failure to adjust with the parents may result in revolting against parents and authority.

Childhood-Adulthood Conflict: In our society, the adolescent is considered as neither as a child nor as an adult. He has to depend on his parents and elders for his physical and emotional needs. But at the same time he wants to hold independent views and opinions like an adult. He can very well manage his own affairs and resist any unnecessary interference from the part of elders. He begins to feel ashamed and embarrassed for the protection and care shown by the parents. He is often treated in an ambiguous manner by parents and teachers. Sometimes they expect him to behave as an adult and at other times, they treat him as a child. The poor adolescent is caught between the role of the child and the adult, which push him into confusion and tension.

Adjustment Difficulties with School Discipline: Most of the adolescents face a great problem in adjusting with school discipline. Sometimes schools expects too much from students who must submit to teachers who may be tyrannical sometimes. Schools should not implant habits of unquestioning obedience that inhibits the growth of young people towards true independence.

Adjustment Difficulties with Community: The adolescent is expected to find his place in a society marked by increasing social isolation and rapid technological changes. This changing world make it difficult to anticipate and plan for adolescent life. They have difficulty in adjusting their capacity to the demands of the community. At this critical phase most adolescents react by withdrawing into a non-demanding and non-working world of pleasure and satisfaction.

DEVELOPMENTAL CHARACTERISTICS OF ADOLESCENCE

Young people undergo many different changes as they go through adolescence and increasingly take on adult roles and responsibilities. These changes include physical changes, as well as changes to their thought processes and emotions (cognitive and emotional changes), sense of identity and values (psychological changes), relationships (social changes), and realistic aspirations for the future. All young people are unique and therefore the degree, rate and pace of specific physical, emotional and social changes vary with each young person. Adolescence is characterized by rapid change in several areas:

Physical and Motor Development: Physical development this is often the most obvious set of changes in a young person as they grow and develop their adult physical characteristics. During adolescence the physical growth reaches its peak and body takes its final shape. The growth and functioning of organs reach their upper range and the glands become extremely active. There is a sudden shoot up in height, weight and size. The arms and legs developed up to their final length. The size of the bones and muscles increases up to the greatest possible extent. Along with these somatic changes, motor activity also attains its maximum limit.

The respiratory, circulatory and digestive systems acquire their full development. Brain gets fully developed. Pimples may appear on the face. There occurs change in voice among both sexes. The voice of boys deepens and becomes harsher while the voice of girls becomes shrill and sweet during this period.

During adolescence the individual attains *biological maturation* which is accompanied by the appearance of *secondary sexual characteristics.* There is growth of hair under arms and around genital organs. Boys develop beard and moustaches on their faces and in girls the growth of breast and widening of pelvis are significant physical developments. The girls begin to menstruate monthly and boys have nocturnal emission accompanied by erotic dreams.

Emotional Development

Adolescence is characterized by emotional instability and intensity. It is the period of heightening of all emotions like anxiety, fear, love, anger, etc. It is because of this fact the *adolescence is considered as a period of stress and strain.* Adolescents *are* not consistent in their emotional expression. Their emotions fluctuate very frequently and quickly. Sometimes they appear to be enthusiastic and sometimes moody.

With lots of changes in thinking comes a range of emotions that the young person may not have experienced in the same way previously. While the young person is developing their own self identity it is understandable that in this process they may experience more moodiness, irritability, and frustration, however again, as there skills develop, their ability to manage these fluctuating emotions becomes more advanced. These changes also see the young person developing a greater sense of empathy, shifting from a focus of being self centred to now understanding more about the experiences of others.

Self consciousness, self respect and personal pride will be too strong in adolescents. He is often irritable, easily excited and explode emotionally instead of trying to control his emotions. What he feels, he feels it very strongly and when he reacts, he reacts vigorously. At no stage the individual is so restless and emotionally perturbed and touchy as in adolescence. He is too sensitive, inflammable and moody.

Intellectual Development

The concrete thinking of childhood begins to move to more complex abstract thinking. Skills such as planning, prioritizing, organizing thoughts, suppressing impulses, problem solving and weighing consequences are developing and influencing the decision making process in young people.

Adolescence is a period of great intellectual advancement. In this period functioning of the cognitive system develops in to its maximum level. Intellectual powers like critical thinking, logical thinking and abstract reasoning develop. Span of connection widens depth of understanding increases and functioning of memory sharpens.

The adolescent develops fine imagination. The improper channelization of imagination may lead an adolescent to day-dreaming. Writers, artists, poets, philosophers and inventors are all born in this period. The adolescent learns to reason and seek answer to everything scientifically. Ability to solve problems increases during this period. The areas of interest widen and his love for adventure reaches its climax. All adolescents have one or more hobbies and strong likes and dislikes.

Social Development

The most important characteristics of social development during adolescence is the increased influence of ***peer group***. The individual develops a strong sense of loyalty towards the group. He wants to be accepted by the members of the group which he belongs. The friends as well as the peer group selected by an adolescent shape his behaviour to a great extent. They develop a philosophy of life regarding values, beliefs, activities, conduct etc. with regards to the philosophy of the peer group.

While children generally see the family as an integral part of their life, many young people, while continuing to value the role of support of their family, begin to rely more heavily on the support and guidance provided by their friends. In addition, they may also begin to seek out intimate relationships.

Adolescence is the period of increased social conformity. The individual becomes self-conscious of his place in the society. They want to become his behaviour according norms of the society. They seek social status and look for the approval in the society. They develop a feeling of social responsibility and are highly critical of social evils and injustice. During adolescence, boys and girls express a greater need for independence and strive for total social freedom from their parents. They make friendship with those who conform to their standard and posses the personality trait they like. They do not tolerate the interference of others in selecting friends.

In the beginning of adolescence the individual critically examines the moral code and asks a number of questions to establish his view points. Later he develops the ability to differentiate what is good and what is bad.

Psychological Development

Some of the most significant psychological changes relate to the development of autonomy and independent identity. This often leads to the challenging of decisions and actions that they may have previously accepted, and often the discovering of new boundaries as they work to create their own identity.

Sexual Development

The whole personality structure and behaviour of the adolescent is dominated by sex. During adolescence the individual becomes very conscious of sex. Contrary to the style of behaviour during childhood, the adolescent exhibit sexual trends in companionship. During this period the sexual development goes into three stages.

Stage of Auto-erotism: In the beginning sexual tendency manifests in self-love. Boys and girls fall in love with themselves. Self decoration and admiring before the mirror is a common practice. According to Freud this is the stage of ***narcissism***. [Narcissus, a Greek prince of almost unparalleled beauty, fell in love with himself] Self enjoyment by indulging in *masturbation* is prevalent at this stage.

Stage of Homo-sexuality: During the adolescence boys and girls are attracted to the members of their own sex. Persons of this age can often be seen roaming together, praising each other and finding other modes of expressing their mutual affection.

Stage of Hetero-sexuality: During later adolescence, young men and women are seen attracted towards each other. They are increased to make friendship or even establishing sexual relationships with the members of opposite sex.

PSYCHOLOGICAL CHARACTERISTICS OF ADOLESCENCE

The main psychological characteristics of adolescence are as follows:

- *Self-consciousness* is too much developed in adolescence.

- The adolescent is *intensely emotional*
- An adolescent is essentially a *hero-worshipper*
- Adolescent shows *interest in physical attractiveness* and good grooming
- *Sex-consciousness* becomes too intense at this time. They become interested in opposite sex and in extreme cases *homosexuality* is established.
- *Peer group relationship* is too much intense at this time.
- Adolescence is a period of *day-dreaming.*
- It is the *period of acquiring the attitudes and values* needed for effective participation in society.
- The Adolescent wants to free himself from bondage. There is a *tendency to revolt against authority.*
- Adolescents have strong *desire to achieve self-sufficiency* and make himself quite independent like an adult member of the society.

DEVELOPMENTAL THEORIES

Six primary classes of developmental theories: biological, psychoanalytical, behavioural, cognitive, contextual and structural. These are discussed below:

Biological Theories

Biological theories cast human development as an *unfolding* process. Children proceed through a set sequence of invariant stages of development in roughly the same time. The environment provides opportunities for growth but exerts no direct influence; rather, development is overwhelmingly determined by genetics. A primary proponent was Arnold Gesell, who, together with his colleagues, published age-based norms for growth and behavioural changes. The Gesell norms provide general expectations and may be useful for identifying children who do not fit the age-based expectations (e.g., a child who displays excessive "baby" behaviour in the third grade). At the same time, the wide variation in developmental changes between children means that the norms have limited usefulness. When norms are misused and become criteria for learning readiness, they can retard educational progress. Although growth and behaviour are correlated with cognitive development, they are not valid reasons for assuming that children cannot learn.

Current biological work focuses on the extent that cognitive, behavioural and personality characteristics have genetic predispositions. Thus, the tendency for children to understand counting may be largely inherited and the capacity for language acquisition seems biologically predisposed. A long-standing debate concerns the extent that intelligence is inherited. Researchers continue to explore how genetics and environmental factors interact to influence development.

Psychoanalytic Theories

Psychoanalytic theories emphasize the fulfillment of *needs*, which differ as a function of developmental level. Development is viewed as progressive changes in personality, which emerges as children seek to satisfy their needs. Children pass through a series of stages, each of which is qualitatively different from preceding ones. Children interact with their environments to fulfill needs,

Table 6.1: Types of Developmental Theories

Type	*Key Developmental Processes*
Biological	Individuals proceed through an invariant sequence of stages; stage progression is largely determined by genetics.
Psychoanalytic	Development represents a series of changes in personality brought about by need satisfaction. Stages are qualitatively distinct.
Behavioral	Development represents changes in behaviors produced by conditioning; changes are continuous and quantitative.
Cognitive	Development represents changes in mental structures or processes that occur as individuals take in information and mentally construct understandings.
Contextual	Social and cultural factors affect development; changes in persons or situations interact with and influence other changes.
Structural	Development involves changes in cognitive structures or schemas.

and their successes in resolving conflicts associated with need fulfillment influence personality.

Two well-known psychoanalytic theorists were Sigmund Freud and Erik Erikson. Freud (1966) believed that the basic structure of a child's personality was established during the first five years of life. Erikson (1963), on the other hand, felt that development was a lifelong process and thus postulated developmental stages into old age. Psychoanalytic theories emphasize the role of innate factors in development. Needs are innate, and how they are resolved affects development. The role of learning in development is downplayed in favour of need resolution.

Psychoanalytic theories have their share of problems. As with other stage theories (e.g., Piaget's, stage progression from child to child often is so uneven that using theories to explain development is difficult. Although the needs and conflicts described by psychoanalytic theories are well known to parents, caregivers, and teachers, how they can be resolved successfully is left open. Consequently, how significant others in children's lives can best foster development is unclear. For example, should adults provide for all of children's needs or teach children self-regulation skills so they can begin to satisfy their own needs? Theories that offer clearer predictions about development and especially the role of learning have greater applicability to education.

Behavioural Theories

In contrast to biological and psychoanalytical theories that stress innate factors, behavioural theories—while acknowledging developmental capabilities—postulate that development can be explained by the same principles that explain other behaviours. The major developmental changes occur as a result of *conditioning*. Behavioural theories represent a continuity position: Small changes occur over time. Developmental changes are best viewed in quantitative terms: Children learn to do more in less time. The primary mechanism of learning is shaping of new behaviours through differential reinforcement of successive approximations to the target behaviours.

Behavioural theories do not specify critical periods in development. The capacity for learning continues throughout the life span. They also emphasize that the major changes in behaviour emanate from the environment, which provides the stimuli to which children respond and the reinforcement and punishment as consequences of their actions. Frank's comments in the opening vignette indicate a behavioural view of development. Behavioural theories downplay the role of personal factors associated with learners (e.g., thoughts, emotions) and the interaction between learners and their environments.

Consequently, these theories treat self-regulation largely as the establishment of self-reinforcement contingencies. Behavioural methods often are useful in teaching and learning, but explanations for learning and development based on conditioning are incomplete because they negate the role of personal influences.

Cognitive Theories

Beginning with the work of Piaget in the early 1960s, cognitive theories have gained ascendance in the field of human development. Cognitive theories focus on how children construct their understandings of themselves and of the world about them. Cognitive theories are constructivist; they postulate that understanding is not automatic. Others do not convey information that children process rotely; rather, children take in information and formulate their own knowledge. They are active seekers and processors of information. Cognitive theories are interactional because they explain development in terms of interactions between personal, behavioural, and environmental factors. Prominent cognitive theories are Piaget's, Bruner's, Vygotsky's, information processing and social cognitive theory.

Contextual Theories

These theories highlight the roles played by social and cultural factors. Evidence supporting this perspective comes from cross-cultural comparisons showing wide variability in developmental patterns, as well as from studies demonstrating that even within societies there is considerable variation in development (Meece, 2002). Societal practices clearly play a major role in development.

A well-known contextual model was formulated by Bronfenbrenner (1979), who postulated that the child's social world can be conceptualized as a set of concentric circles with the child at the common point of three intersecting circles: school, peers, and family. Outside of these is a larger circle containing neighbourhood, extended family, community, church, workplace, and mass media. The outermost circle contains such influences as laws, cultural values, political and economic systems, and social customs. The model assumes that changes in one level can affect other levels. Thus, physical changes in children can alter their social groups, which in turn are affected by cultural values. The model is highly interactional and is useful for understanding the complexity of influences on human development and its effects.

Cognitive and contextual theories stress that children are active constructors of knowledge and that development is a continuous process across the life span. Contextual theories emphasize the altered nature of social patterns and how these lead children into different interactions with peers and adults.

Cognitive development occurs largely as a consequence of these interactions. In turn, children's behaviours alter environments. Thus, children may develop new interests that change the peer groups with which they closely associate. Some cognitive theories (e.g., Vygotsky's and social cognitive) also are contextual in nature.

Contextual theories often are vague in their predictions of how changes in some aspects may affect development and vice versa. They also can be very complex, with a host of variables postulated to affect one another. This situation makes it difficult to conduct research. Despite these limitations, contextual theories call our attention to the need to study the many factors that are involved in human development

Structural Theories

As mentioned earlier, an issue in the study of human development is whether it represents changes in cognitive structures or functions. Most contemporary views posit changes in functions, but structural theories have figured prominently in the discipline. Structural theories postulate that development involves changes in cognitive structures, or *schemas.* Information that is learned (i.e., enters the structure) can help to alter the structure. These theories do not equate structures with physical locations in the brain; rather, structures are construed as constellations of capabilities or characteristic means of processing information. Two structural theories with relevance to learning are discussed below:

Chomsky's (1957) Psycholinguistic Theory

Chomsky (1957, 1959) formulated a theory of language acquisition based on a system of *transformational grammar*. According to Chomsky, language can be differentiated into two levels: an overt *surface structure* that involves speech and syntax and a covert *deep structure* that includes meaning. A single deep structure can be represented by multiple surface structures. To illustrate this distinction, assume that Akram is playing basketball with Salman. The meaning as it might be represented as propositions in memory is:

Rhonda .... playing basketball (with) .... Salman

This meaning could be translated in various surface structures (utterances and sentences), such as:

- Akram is playing basketball with Salman.
- Salman is playing basketball with Akram.
- Akram? Playing basketball with Salman.
- Basketball is being played by Rhonda and Salman.

Chomsky's transformational grammar contains a number of rules that people presumably use to transform varying surface structures into the same meaning (deep structure). The deep structures are assumed to be part of the individual's genetic makeup. Language development, then, involves the progressive capability of mapping surface structures onto their corresponding deep structures.

Classical Information Processing Theory (Atkinson & Shiffrin, 1968)

Classical information processing theory provides another structural account of development. The Atkinson and Shiffrin (1968, 1971) model assumes that the computer is a useful metaphor for the operation of the human mind. The computer (with corresponding information processing) components are: input (sensory registers), immediate processing (working memory—WM), storage (long-term memory— LTM), output (response), and programming (executive, control processes).

The analogy between the structures of the mind and the computer is useful. Although the mind's structures do not necessarily correspond to physical locations (i.e., the operations performed may occur in multiple locations), structures are constrained in terms of what they do. Once information enters the system, it is processed in linear fashion (i.e., it follows a set path determined by its content) and little room exists for environmental impact (Zimmerman & Whitehurst, 1979). The operation of the structures is largely preprogrammed.

Developmental change occurs in the capacity and efficiency of processing. Through the use of strategies such as rehearsal and organization, older learners—compared with younger ones—are able to hold more information in WM, relate it better to information in LTM, and have more extensive memory networks. With development, information

IMPORTANT POINTS FOR ADOLESCENTS

What adolescents can do?

- Avoid looking at your parents as the enemy. Chances are that they love you and have your best interests in mind, even if you don't necessarily agree with their way of showing that.
- Try to understand that your parents are human beings, with their own insecurities, needs, and feelings.
- Listen to your parents with an open mind, and try to see situations from their point of view.
- Share your feelings with your parents so that they can understand you better.
- Live up to your responsibilities at home and in school so that your parents will be more inclined to grant you the kind of independence you want and need.
- Bolster your criticisms of family, school, and government with suggestions for practical improvements.
- Be as courteous and considerate to your own parents as you would be to the parents of your friends.

HOW CAN TEACHERS AND PARENTS SUPPORT HEALTHY ADOLESCENT DEVELOPMENT?

The following guidelines may helpful for the parents:

- Give your undivided attention when your children want to talk. Don't read, watch television, or busy yourself with other tasks.
- Listen calmly and concentrate on hearing and understanding your children's point of view.

- Speak to your children as courteously and pleasantly as you would to a stranger. Your tone of voice can set the tone of a conversation.
- Understand your children's feelings—even if you don't always approve of their behaviour. Try not to make judgments. Keep the door open on any subject. Be an "open/approachable" parent.
- Avoid belittling and humiliating your children and laughing at what may seem to you to be naive or foolish questions and statements.
- Encourage your children to "test" new ideas in conversation by not judging their ideas and opinions, but instead by listening and then offering your own views as plainly and honestly as possible. Love and mutual respect can coexist with differing points of view.
- Help your children build self-confidence by encouraging their participation in activities of their choice (not yours).
- Make an effort to commend your children frequently and appropriately. Too often, we take the good things for granted and focus on the bad, but everyone needs to be appreciated.
- Encourage your children to participate in family decision making and to work out family concerns together with you. Understand that your children need to challenge your opinions and your ways of doing things to achieve the separation from you that's essential for their own adult identity.

Chapter-7
Motor Development

Motor development is the development of movement. The ability to move is essential to human development. Many motor skills are necessary for everyday life activities e.g. sitting, walking, running, climbing stairs, picking up objects, using cups, knives and forks, pouring drinks, dressing, holding and using pencils, pens, scissors and using keyboards.

Meaning of Motor Development

Development of the motor ability is an important part of a child's physical development. In motor development, changes in activity can be observed through the physical progress. For example, before acquiring the ability of walking, the child passes through a number of stages. Although individual differences are visible in motor activity, even to the extent of individual styles of walking being very distinctive, the approximate time of the development and appearance of certain motor activities in physical development can be established. In motor activities, the motor control starts with the head, in other words, the child first starts by holding his heads erect and focusing on various objects with his eyes. Following this, the child learns to grip objects and then to crawl and walk on his knees. This is represented in the Figure 7.1 given below:

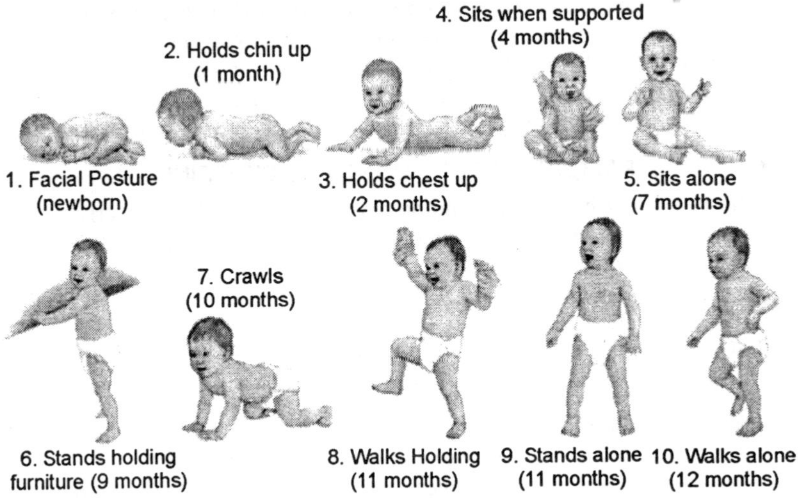

Figure 7.1: Stages of Motor Development of Child in Different Ages

In the child's motor development over the first two periods, the following stages are evident:

Age in Months	*Motor Activity*
1.	Chin high
2.	Raising the chest
3.	Gripping and releasing object
4.	Sitting with some assistance
5.	Lap-sitting and holding objects
6.	Sitting on high chair
7.	Playing with object
8.	Standing with some help
9.	Standing while holding on to furniture
10.	Moving on knees
11.	Raising oneself while holding on to furniture
12.	Walking while holding someone
13.	Climbing stairs
14.	Standing without assistance
15.	Walking alone

For motor development, it is essential that the child be given adequate freedom. If the child is always carried and is not allowed to move around, its motor development is likely to be retarded. The child should have adequate space to play in. If it is left to its own devices on the floor, it will be seen moving its legs and feet.

DEFINITIONS OF MOTOR DEVELOPMENT

1. According to Adolph, Weise, and Marin (2003) - *"Motor development refers to changes in children's ability to control their body's movements, from infants' first spontaneous waving and kicking movements to the adaptive control of reaching, locomotion, and complex sport skills".*
2. *"Motor development refers to the development of a child's bones, muscles and ability to move around and manipulate his or her environment."*

PATTERNS OF CRAWLING AND CREEPING

The beginning of a child's motor development is with the activities of creeping and crawling. Different children exhibit different patterns of these activities. The following Figure 7.2 illustrated the various physical positions that are adopted by the child in developing from the crawling and creeping to the walking stage. These physical positions have been illustrated in the following order:

1. Motion of new born's crawling.
2. Less motion in the hind part, while it tries to raise the head.
3. Control on the movements of head and shoulders improves.
4. There is considerable development in the upper part, while the hip remains on the floor.

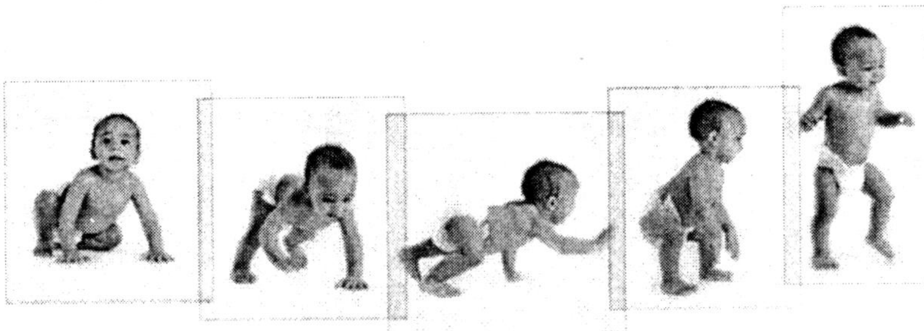

Figure 7.2: Crawling and Creeping Positions of the Baby Child

5. Contradiction between the motion of the head and shoulder, and the hips, with the result that rising of hips leads to lowering of head and shoulders.
6. Motions of rocking in which the hip bone is kept above the ground.
7. Complementary movements of creeping. In starting movement, some children creep on the stomach, others move on all fours, while still others propel themselves by swinging their hips along the surface. Different children start creeping and crawling in different ages. Generally, the child who beings his crawling early also walks erect in shorter time. Although motor activity develop along with general progress of the child, but in encouraging the child to walk wooden or other scooters or rollers can be used. This can induce him to learning walking earlier.

SECTIONS OF MOTOR DEVELOPMENT

Motor development can be further divided into two sections:

Gross Motor Development

Gross motor skills are large movements of the body including sitting, walking, running and climbing stairs. Gross motor development includes the attainment of skills such as rolling over, sitting up, crawling, walking, and running. Gross motor behaviour enables infants to move and thereby attain different and varied perspectives on the environment. Behaviours such as pulling to stand and climbing present children with new learning opportunities. When infants push a toy stroller or shopping cart, they are also engaging in processes related to cognitive development, such as imitation. The gross motor behaviours involved in active outdoor play with other children are related to children's development of social skills and an understanding of social rules. It also includes eye-hand coordination skills such as ball skills (throwing, catching, and kicking). Table 7.1 shows the developmental stages of gross motor development:

Fine Motor Development

Fine motor skills involve the small movements of the fingers and hands. They include picking up objects, using cups, knives and forks, pouring drinks, dressing, holding and using pencils, pens, scissors and keyboards. Through touching, grasping, and manual manipulation, infants experience a sense of agency and learn about the features of people, objects, and the environment. Fine motor development is related to the ability to draw, write, and participate

Table 7.1: Stages of Gross Motor Development

Age	*Developmental Milestones*	*Possible Implications if Milestones not Achieved*
0-6 months	• Rolls over front to back and back to front • Sits with support and then independently	• Poor muscle development for locomotion • Delayed ability to play independently
6-12 months	• Crawls forwards on belly • Assumes a seated position unaided • Creeps on hands and knees • Transitions into different positions: sitting, all fours, lying on tummy • Pulls self to stand • Walks while holding onto furniture • Takes 2-3 steps without support • Rolls a ball in imitation of an adult	• Delayed sensory development due to decreased ability to explore the environment • Poor muscle development • Delayed play skills
18 months	• Sits, crawls, walks • Still has wide gait but walking/running is less clumsy • Pushes against a ball (does not actually kick it)	• Delayed play skills • Difficulty interacting with the environment due to delayed ability to mobilise effectively • Poor muscle development
2 years	• Walks smoothly and turns corners • Begins running • Is able to pull or carry a toy while walking • Climbs onto/down from furniture without assistance • Walks up and down steps with support • Picks up toys from the floor without falling over	• Poor muscle development for running and jumping • Delayed ability to play independently and interact with the environment • Decreased ability to interact socially
3 years	• Imitates standing on one foot • Imitates simple bilateral movements of limbs (e.g., arms up together) • Climbs jungle gym and ladders • Pedals on tricycle • Walks up/down stairs alternating feet • Jumps in place with two feet together • Able to walk on tip toes • Catches using body	• Decreased opportunities for social interaction • Poor development of body awareness and movement planning skills • Difficulties using playground equipment • Difficulties or lack of confidence interacting with other children in active environments (e.g. play cafes, playgrounds)

(Contd.)

Age	*Developmental Milestones*	*Possible Implications if Milestones not Achieved*
4 years	• Stands on one foot for up to 5 seconds • Kicks a ball forwards • Throws a ball overarm • Catches a ball that has been bounced • Runs around obstacles • Able to walk on a line • Able to hop on one foot • Jumps over an object and lands with both feet together	• Lack of confidence in movement based activities • Difficulties using playground equipment • Difficulties or lack of confidence interacting with other children in active environments (e.g. play cafes, playgrounds)
5 years	• Able to walk up stairs while holding an object • Walks backward toe-heel • Jumps forward 10 times without falling • Skips forwards after demonstration • Hangs from a bar for at least 5 seconds • Steps forward with leg on same side as throwing arm when throwing a ball • Catches a small ball using hands only	• May result in poor self-esteem when comparing self to peers • Lack of confidence in movement based activities • Difficulties participating in sporting activities • Difficulties playing with moving toys such as bikes and scooters
6 years	• Runs lightly on toes • Able to walk on a balance beam • Able to skip using a skipping rope • Can cover 2 metres hopping • Demonstrates mature throwing and catching patterns • Mature jumping	• Difficulty participating in sporting activities • May result in poor self-esteem when comparing self to peers • Lack of confidence in movement based activities

in routines such as eating and dressing. Common early childhood learning materials, such as pegboards, stacking rings, stringing beads, and puzzles, offer opportunities for infants to practice their fine motor skills. Fine motor movements of the hands are coordinated with perceptual information provided through movements of the eyes, as when seven- to nine-month-old infants use visual information to orient their hands as they reach for an object. Table 7.2 shows the developmental stages of fine motor development.

Movement can be seen and felt and a delay in motor development is usually the first sign of a real problem because it is noticed far sooner than a problem with seeing, hearing or communication. Motor development seems to follow a pattern. Large muscles develop before smaller ones e.g. very young children find it easier to run than cutting with scissors. Children also tend to develop in a head-to-toe pattern. For instance, babies move their eyes, head and hands long before they learn to crawl.

Table 7.2: Stages of Fine Motor Development

Age	*Developmental Milestones*	*Possible Implications If Milestones Not Achieved*
0 - 6 months	• Reflexive grasp (at birth) • Global ineffective reach for • objects (3 months) • Voluntary grasp (3 months) • 2 handed palmar grasp (3 months) • 1 handed palmar grasp (5 months) • Controlled reach (6 months)	• Poor muscle development • Delayed ability to play independently • Delayed sensory development due to delayed interaction with toys and other sensory objects
6 - 12 months	• Reaches, grasps, puts object in mouth • Controlled release of objects • Pincer grasp • Picks things up with pincer grasp (thumb and one finger) • Transfers object from one handto the other • Drops and picks up toy	• Poor development of hand and finger strength • Poor manipulation of objects resulting in delayed play skills • Delayed sensory development due to lack of sensory play experiences
1 -2 years	• Builds tower of three small blocks • Puts four rings on stick • Places five pegs in pegboard • Turns pages two or three at a time • Scribbles • Turns knobs • Paints with whole arm movement, shifts hands, makes strokes • Self-feeds with minimal assistance • Able to use signing to communicate • Brings spoon to mouth • Holds and drinks from cup independently	• Poor development of hand and finger strength • Delayed independent play skills • Delayed development of self care skills such as eating • Delayed manipulation skills
2- 3 years	• Strings four large beads • Turns single pages • Snips with scissors • Holds crayon with thumb and fingers (not fist) • Uses one hand consistently in most activities • Imitates circular, vertical, horizontal strokes • Paints with some wrist action, makes dots, lines, circular strokes • Rolls, pounds, squeezes, and pulls playdough • Eats without assistance	• Delayed self-care skills such as eating • Delayed pre-writing skills development • Delayed manipulation of small • objects such as toys, pencils and scissors • Frustration when manipulating small toys and objects

(Contd.)

Age	*Developmental Milestones*	*Possible Implications If Milestones Not Achieved*
3 - 4 yrs	• Builds tower of nine small blocks • Copies circle • Imitates cross • Manipulates clay material (rolls balls, makes snakes, cookies) • Uses non dominant hand to assist and stabilise the use of objects • Snips paper using scissors	• Delayed pre-writing skills development • Frustration and/or avoidance of pencil based tasks • Poor pencil grasp and pencil control • Poor self-care skills such as eating • Delayed drawing skills
4 -5 yrs	• Cuts on line continuously • Copies cross • Copies square • Writes name • Writes numbers 1-5 • Copies letters • Handedness well established • Dresses and undresses independently	• Difficulties holding and manipulating a pencil • Difficulties learning to write name and other letters of the alphabet Dependence on caregivers for every day activities such as dressing • Frustration and/or avoidance of pencil based tasks
5 - 6 yrs	• Cuts out simple shapes • Copies triangle • Colours within lines • Uses a 3 fingered grasp of pencil and uses fingers to generate movement • Pastes and glues appropriately • Can draw basic pictures	• Difficulties learning to form letters correctly • Poor handwriting • Difficulties demonstrating academic ability on paper • Fatigue during pencil based tasks • Frustration and/or avoidance of pencil based tasks
6 -7 yrs	• Forms most letters and numbers correctly • Writes consistently on the lines • Demonstrates controlled pencil movement • Good endurance for writing • Can build Lego, knex and other blocks independently • Ties shoelaces	• Difficulties getting ideas down on paper • Experiencing fatigue during handwriting tasks • Difficulty keeping up in class due to slow handwriting speed • Poor legibility of handwriting • May impact on self-esteem when comparing work to peers • Possible frustration and/or behaviour difficulties due to avoidance of pencil based tasks
7- 8 yrs	• Maintains legibility of handwriting for entirety of a story	• Difficulty completing handwriting tasks in a timely manner • Experiencing fatigue during handwriting tasks • Poor academic achievement due to difficulty getting ideas down on paper • Difficulties due to avoidance of pencil based tasks

WHY SHOULD WE KNOW ABOUT MOTOR DEVELOPMENT?

- New behaviour is made possible when a child's body develops e.g. a toddler can be toilet trained once the necessary anal sphincter muscles have developed.
- So many new experiences and learning opportunities are opened up when the body is able to do more e.g.
  - being able to hold the head firmly in the midline means the child can focus more easily on an object. It also means the child can now develop hand/eye coordination, a very important skill needed for independent living.
  - being able to reach and grasp means a child can begin to learn about objects in his world o being able to sit means more use of the hands and arms for playing (and therefore learning). It means the child can begin to learn about his position in space. Sitting is an essential skill if the child is to eat easily, dress himself, get the attention of others when speaking, look at computer screens, television etc.
  - being able to crawl increases the child's learning opportunities. It means he can touch things that were only visible before, so much more can be learned about how much space his body takes up by crawling into, under around and over objects.
  - being able to walk means a child is able to carry things. It also means the child can explore and experience more in his environment than before.
  - being able to move independently means a child has more opportunities for social interaction and language learning. Because children can now follow their caregivers from place to place it means they can be talked to and included in more everyday activities. They can run, jump and catch a ball and play with other children, socializing and making friends.

STAGES OF MOTOR DEVELOPMENT

There are three stages of motor development in children.

By the age of 2 years old, this development has begun to level out somewhat. The final stage does not have any marked new developments, rather it is characterized by the mastering and development of the skills achieved in the first two stages.

Stage 1: 0-2 Years or Infanthood (The New Born Child)

The first stage is marked by extremely rapid growth and development. It is argued that many of a newborn's reflexes contribute to motor control as the child learns new motor skills. For example the stepping reflex promotes

Reflex Name	*Method*	*Age Disappears*	*Motor Preparation*
Tonic Neck	Assumes fencing position; 1 arm extended in front of eyes on side to which head is turned. Other arm flexed.	4 Months	May prepare for voluntary reaching
Stepping	Lifts one foot after another in stepping response	2 Months	Prepares for voluntary walking
Palmer Grasp	Spontaneous grasp of adult's finger	3-4 Months	Prepares for voluntary grasping

development areas of the cortex that govern voluntary walking. This and other examples can be seen in the table given above.

Assessing reflexes in newborns will determine the health of the nervous system, as reflexes that are weak or absent, exaggerated or overly rigid may indicate some brain damage. Therefore stages will need to be modified slightly. The average ages at which gross motor skills are achieved during infancy may vary. This range may be seen in the table below:

Motor Skill	*Average Age Achieved*	*Age Range (90% Infants)*
Head erect & steady when held upright	6 weeks	3 weeks-4 months
Lifts self by arms when prone	2 months	3 weeks-4 months
Rolls from side to back	2 months	3 weeks-5 months
Grasps cube	3 months, 3 weeks	2-7 months
Rolls from back to side	4 ½ months	2-7 months
Sits alone	7 months	5-9 months
Crawls	7 months	5-11 months
Pulls to stand	8 months	5-12 months
Plays Pat-a-cake	9 months, 3 weeks	7-15 months
Stands alone	11 months	9-16 months
Walks alone	11 months, 3 weeks	9-17 months
Builds tower of 2 cubes	13 months, 3 weeks	10-19 months
Scribbles vigorously	14 months	10-21 months
Walks up stairs with help	16 months	12-23 months
Jumps in place	23 months, 2 weeks	17-30 months

Although the sequence of motor development is fairly uniform across children, differences may exist individually in the rate at which motor skills develop. A baby who is a late reached may not necessarily be a late crawler/ walker. Concern would arise if the child's development were delayed in many motor skills.

The main points related to the above table are:

- Motor control of the head comes before control of the legs. This head-to-tail sequence is called the *'cephalocaudal'* trend.
- Motor development proceeds from the centre of the body outward; i.e. the head, trunk and arm control is mastered before the coordination of the hands and fingers. This is the *'proximodistical'* trend.
- Physical growth follows these same trends throughout infancy and childhood.

Once the child has grasped these gross motor skills, they are then able to explore their environment further by grasping things, turning them over, and seeing what happens when they are released. Infants are then able to learn a great deal about the sight, sound and feel of objects.

Stage 2: 2-6 Years or Early Childhood

The period of the most rapid development of motor behaviours is the period between 2 and 6 years (also known as the preschool years). Skills that appear are:

- Basic locomotor
- Ball-handling
- Fine eye-hand coordination
- Walking leads to running, jumping, hopping, galloping, and skipping
- Climbing evolves from creeping.

The following points need to be highlighted:

1. By the age of 3 walking is automatic.
2. By 4 years the child has almost achieved an adult style of walking.
3. By 3 years the child has attempted to run, albeit awkward in style and lacking control.
4. By the age of 4-5 years the child has more control over running and can start, stop and turn.
5. By 5-6 skills in running have advanced to the level of an adult manner.
6. Between the ages of 3 and 6 climbing proficiency using ladders, etc., has developed.
7. By 6 years children can hop and gallop skillfully, and jumping distances are longer.
8. At the age of 3 children begin a shuffle which evolves into skipping by the age of 6.
9. At the age of 2 children learn to kick, as their balance mechanism has developed. A full kick with a backswing has developed by the age of 6.
10. Throwing at the age of 2-3 years is not very proficient although is attempted. This has improved by the age of 6 when the child will include a step forward.

At the age of 3 a child can catch a large ball with arms straight; at 4 elbows will be in front when catching; and by the age of 6 years, elbows will be held at the side.

Stage 3: 6-12 Years or Later Childhood

After the age of 6 years old, it becomes increasingly difficult to describe changes and differences in motor skills development. The following characteristics are evident:

- Changes are more subtle, and are often to fine motor skills only
- By 9 years eye-hand coordination has developed to being very good
- Growth is relatively slow
- This stage is terminated by the onset of puberty
- Motor skills are perfected and stabilized
- Links can be made to physical development.

The following are assessed during this stage:

1. Running. This will become faster depending on the length of stride and tempo.
2. Jumping. The ability to jump higher will become greater due to body size, weight, age and strength.
3. Throwing. Boys begin to throw further with a better technique and accuracy.
4. Balancing and coordination. This increases as the child becomes older and control is perfected.

MOTOR DEVELOPMENT AND EDUCATION

Motor development is an important prerequisite for man's motor learning. Along with other development, motor development continues during childhood and adolescence. And in this, much importance is attached to various physical movements and exercises. It is for this reason that in modern school and colleges, academic teaching and training is accompanied by various physical exercises, games and many activities that require motor activity. It helps to develop in child many handicrafts that assist him in his adopting some particular career. Some such handicrafts are stitching and sewing, wood work, typewriting, cooking etc. Motor control is essential in all handicrafts. Motor development is an important part of overall comprehensive development.

Important Factors in Motor Development

Many factors cast a very profound influence upon the child's motor development. The object of motor learning is the acquisition of skill in some particular physical movement or employment. And to gain skill in any work that requires handling, it is essential to start with the fundamental movements, and to progress gradually to the more complex motions. It is only because, the child learns motor control in his childhood that he can, at a later stage, learn the handling and control of motor cars, cycles etc. The motor activity patterns formed in infancy are helpful in the learning of different handicrafts and games. Where these patterns are of help in certain cases, they also hinder the learning of other crafts. The motor patterns that are advantageous to the pursuit of a particular game can prove to be harmful in the playing of another.

Important Factors in the Teaching of Motor Activity

Physical education proves very valuable in the learning of physical skill. In addition to this, in modern school and colleges, the teachers help the students to acquire various kinds of skill and knowledge in handicrafts. The following points should be kept in mind in rendering this assistance:

1. ***Knowledge of effective methods***: Before turning to the teaching of motor skill, it is necessary for the teacher himself to be aware of the most effective ways and means of achieving that skill. It helps him to impart his information more successfully as well as win the admiration and confidence of his students. Once the confidence is developed, it is only natural that they should pay attention to his teaching and to do their best to emulate the movements made and described by him, thereby making his task easier.

2. ***Encouraging the students in the use of effective techniques***: Having gained confidence in the teacher, the student acquires the right mental set for acquiring motor skill. Now, the teacher has to encourage him in the use of methods that have proved successful in the attainment of that motor skill. In the beginning, he is not able to perform these actions perfectly because before the skilled and refined actions can be done, there are the unrefined and unskilled actions to be mastered. The students fails repeatedly in acquiring the skill, he requires by the use of these unskilled and unrefined movements, with the result that he becomes discouraged, and may even become so despondent as to throw up the training. It is for the teacher to foresee this contingency and to prevent it, by tendering encouragement and sympathy. Certain people entertain a groundless fear of water and hence of swimming with the result that when they try to learn it, they are apt to give it up after the first or second decking. In a situation of this kind, it is for instructor to encourage constantly so that enthusiasm many not flag. As in the case of all other learning, the motor learning is also susceptible to the inevitable plateau of learning in its curve. The intelligent instructor can discover the reasons whereby this plateau is arrived at, and contrive to remove it. As a result, the student progresses further, and continue to do so. Hence, in order to develop motor skill, the developed and progressive methods of learning should be employed so that hindrances and obstacles in learning are reduced to a minimum and progress be the most satisfactory and regular. The method of teaching should conform to the needs of education and should change as the subject to be taught changes.

3. *Minimum possible destructive criticism*: Just as the student is susceptible to constant encouragement and good words from the teacher, he is influenced by strong critical comment from the same source. He is so affected that he may become despondent and discouraged. Hence, even if he makes mistakes, the student should be corrected and advised sympathetically, and criticism reduced and kept to the minimum. It should he indulged in only if it becomes inevitable and even then, it should be only as much as is absolutely necessary.

4. *Stress on the right activities:* The main cause of failure in motor skill is the following of wrong activities or actions by student. On the other hand, it is essential to make a habit of the right actions. It is desirable for the teacher to take each action involved in any motor activity separately and demonstrate it to the students, following it up with continuous practice of it in his own presence.

5. *Stress on speed and exactness for skilful working:* Generally some people hold the view that any work done rapidly is not successful. This is quite true of any work at its outset, when one is learning it. In the beginning, it is desirable to make a habit of working slowly but avoiding all mistakes and faults. In learning motor skill, it is particularly important to note that no wrong habits are formed, even if progress is thereby quite slow and retarded. The speed or work should be improved gradually. Sometimes accuracy and skill improves by working rapidly at the outset. In learning cycling, one learns the proper balancing and control only if one immediately takes to riding fast, without any fear of the falls, one is going to suffer. On the other, if he begins by cycling slowly and pays attention to his faults, he is sure to sustain many falls and learn only with great difficulty. But, this fact is not true of many motor skills and activities.

Once a very strong habit of some motor action has been formed, it becomes quite automatic and does not require constant attention to be performed. If a person has learnt his cycling well, he can travel through a crowded market without any apparent attention to his movement. He can in fact allow his thoughts and attention to wander, to some extent, to other things, while he continues forward without endangering his own safety or that of others.

6. ***Proper and adequate practice:*** Constant repetition of some movements is not sufficient in order to generate motor skill in them. It is essential that adequate and proper practice of the activity should be indulged in, in a state of complete mental consciousness of it. The practice must be mentally attended too. Many such factors as the nature of skill, the age and interests of the learner, the conditions of learning, the time taken in learning and practising period of rest, the desired level of skill, etc. influence the result of practice, and changes in these factors are reflected in variations in the final achievement. In practising, it should be remembered that the practice should conform to the method required in actual practice. For example, if a child is required to write with a fountain pen at a later stage, he should be made to practise with a fountain pen and not a quill pen. Similarly, the proper tools of expert use should be employed in training individuals in wood work, carpentry, leather working, etc, and as far as possible, the things made during practice should be the same as are required to be made once the training is completed.

7. ***Practice with an aim:*** While practising for the gaining of motor skill, the learner should be aware of the objective, and should be constantly mindful of it. The teacher should measure his progress by examining him in terms of this objective. If the student is aware of his aim, he progresses faster and more satisfactorily, and his interest also is maintained. Knowing his aim, he is aware of the skill that he must attain. In this, the teacher can also put some example before him. In the absence of such an example, the student may stop working after he has learnt only a very little, in the impression that he has in fact become skilled in his pursuit.

By keeping in mind these factors that influence the teaching of motor skills, the teacher can make very skilled workers of the students. In this, he will have to pay individual attention to each student, because the problems, capabilities and abilities of individual students differ.

Chapter-8
Intellectual or Cognitive Development

It was once believed that infants lacked the ability to think or form complex ideas and remained without cognition until they learned language. It is now known that babies are aware of their surroundings and interested in exploration from the time they are born. From birth, babies begin to actively learn. They gather, sort, and process information from around them, using the data to develop perception and thinking skills.

Cognitive development refers to how a person perceives, thinks, and gains understanding of his or her world through the interaction of genetic and learned factors. Among the areas of cognitive development are information processing, intelligence, reasoning, language development and memory.

Historically, the cognitive development of children has been studied in a variety of ways. The oldest is through intelligence tests, such as the widely used Stanford Binet Intelligence Quotient (IQ) test first adopted for use in the United States by psychologist Lewis Terman (1877–1956) in 1916 from a French model pioneered in 1905. IQ scoring is based on the concept of "mental age," according to which the scores of a child of average intelligence match his or her age, while a gifted child's performance is comparable to that of an older child, and a slow learner's scores are similar to those of a younger child. IQ tests are widely used in the United States, but they have come under increasing criticism for defining intelligence too narrowly and for being biased with regard to race and gender.

In contrast to the emphasis placed on a child's native abilities by intelligence testing, learning theory grew out of work by behaviourist researchers such as John Watson (1878–1958) and B.F. Skinner (1904–1990), who argued that children are completely malleable. Learning theory focuses on the role of environmental factors in shaping the intelligence of children, especially on a child's ability to learn by having certain behaviours rewarded and others discouraged.

MEANING OF COGNITIVE DEVELOPMENT

The term **cognitive development** refers to the process of growth and change in intellectual/mental abilities such as thinking, reasoning and understanding. It includes the acquisition and consolidation of knowledge. Cognitive development is the process by which a child learns to reason, solve problems and to think consciously. Cognitive development allows children to develop their own questions about the world around them and how it works. Children learn by playing, listening, watching, asking questions and doing things for themselves. These activities help a child's brain develop and understand more complex thoughts and processes as they grow.

Children (6 to 12 years old) develop the ability to think in concrete ways (concrete operations), such as how to combine (addition), separate (subtract or divide), order (alphabetize and sort) and transform (change things) objects and actions. They are called concrete because they are performed in the presence of the objects and events being thought about. Adolescence marks the beginning development of more complex thinking processes (also called formal logical operations) including abstract thinking (thinking about possibilities), the ability to reason from known principles (form own new ideas or questions), the ability to consider many points of view according to varying criteria (compare or debate ideas or opinions), and the ability to think about the process of thinking.

DEFINITIONS OF COGNITIVE DEVELOPMENT

1. *"Cognitive development is the construction of thought processes, including remembering, problem solving and decision-making, from childhood through adolescence to adulthood."*
2. *"Cognitive development refers to the development of the ability to think and reason."*

CHARACTERISTICS OF COGNITIVE DEVELOPMENT

A dramatic shift in thinking from concrete to abstract, gives adolescents a whole new set of mental tools. They are now able to analyze situations logically in terms of cause and effect. They can appreciate hypothetical situations. This gives them the ability to think about the future, evaluate alternatives, and set personal goals. They can engage in introspection and mature decision-making. As a result of their growing cognitive abilities, most developing adolescents will:

- Become more independent.
- Take on increased responsibilities, such as babysitting, summer jobs, or household chores.
- Shift their school focus from play-cantered activities to academics.
- Begin to consider future careers and occupations.
- Look to peers and media for information and advice.
- Begin to develop a social conscience: becoming concerned about social issues such as racism, global warming and poverty.
- Develop a sense of values and ethical behaviour: recognizing the value of traits such as honesty, helpfulness, caring for others.

As adolescents begin to exercise their new reasoning skills, some of their behaviours may be confusing for adults. It is normal for them to:

- Argue for the sake of arguing.
- Jump to conclusions.
- Be self-cantered.
- Constantly find fault in the adult's position.
- Be overly dramatic.

COGNITIVE DEVELOPMENTAL OCCUR DURING ADOLESCENCE

During adolescence (between 12 and 18 years of age), the developing teenager acquires the ability to think systematically about all logical relationships within a problem. The transition from concrete thinking to formal logical operations occurs over time. Each adolescent progresses at varying rates in developing his or her ability to think in more complex ways. Each adolescent develops his or her own view of the world. Some adolescents may be able to apply logical operations to school work long before they are able to apply them to personal dilemmas. When emotional issues arise, they often interfere with an adolescent's ability to think in more complex ways. The ability to consider possibilities, as well as facts, may influence decision-making, in either positive or negative ways. Some common indicators indicating a progression from more simple to more complex cognitive development include the following:

Early Adolescence

During early adolescence, the use of more complex thinking is focused on personal decision making in school and home environments, including the following:

- The early adolescent begins to demonstrate use of formal logical operations in schoolwork.
- The early adolescent begins to question authority and society standards.
- The early adolescent begins to form and verbalize his or her own thoughts and views on a variety of topics, usually more related to his or her own life, such as:
- Which sports are better to play
- Which groups are better to be included in
- What personal appearances are desirable or attractive
- What parental rules should be changed

Middle Adolescence

With some experience in using more complex thinking processes, the focus of middle adolescence often expands to include more philosophical and futuristic concerns, including the following:

- The middle adolescent often questions more extensively.
- The middle adolescent often analyzes more extensively.
- The middle adolescent thinks about and begins to form his or her own code of ethics (for example, What do I think is right?).
- The middle adolescent thinks about different possibilities and begins to develop own identity (for example, Who am I?).
- The middle adolescent thinks about and begins to systematically consider possible future goals (for example, What do I want?).
- The middle adolescent thinks about and begins to make his or her own plans.
- The middle adolescent begins to think long-term.
- The middle adolescent's use of systematic thinking begins to influence relationships with others.

Late Adolescence

During late adolescence, complex thinking processes are used to focus on less self-centered concepts as well as personal decision-making, including the following:

- The late adolescent has increased thoughts about more global concepts such as justice, history, politics, and patriotism.
- The late adolescent often develops idealistic views on specific topics or concerns.
- The late adolescent may debate and develop intolerance of opposing views.
- The late adolescent begins to focus thinking on making career decisions.
- The late adolescent begins to focus thinking on emerging role in adult society.

WHAT ENCOURAGES HEALTHY COGNITIVE DEVELOPMENT DURING ADOLESCENCE?

The following suggestions will help to encourage positive and healthy cognitive development in the adolescent:

- Include adolescents in discussions about a variety of topics, issues, and current events.
- Encourage adolescents to share ideas and thoughts with you.
- Encourage adolescents to think independently and develop their own ideas.
- Assist adolescents in setting their own goals.
- Stimulate adolescents to think about possibilities for the future.
- Compliment and praise adolescents for well-thought-out decisions.
- Assist adolescents in re-evaluating poorly made decisions for themselves.

THEORIES OF COGNITIVE DEVELOPMENT

Cognitive theories are concerned with the development of a person's thought processes. It also looks at how these thought processes influence how we understand and interact with the world. Some important theories of cognitive development are as follows:

Piaget's Theory of Intellectual Development

The most systematic and comprehensive theory of cognitive development was given by a Swiss Biologist, Jean Piaget. His approach is known as *genetic epistemology*. Piaget's greatest contribution was his insight that children have a fundamentally different understanding of the world. They were not miniature adults. Piaget demonstrated that children are active learners who learn by observing the consequences of their actions rather than just being passive spectators (Lilienfeld, 2009). Piaget's model of learning is called a constructivist theory. It proposes that children "construct" their understanding of their environment based on observations as a result of their behaviours. There are two major aspects to his theory: the process of coming to know and the stages we move through as we gradually acquire this ability. There are two major aspects to his theory; the process of coming to know and the stages we move through as we gradually acquire this ability. The stages he proposed (see below) mark specific points of a child's development where radical reorganization of thinking takes place. Piaget argued that if human intelligence is to be adaptive, it must have functions to represent both the transformational and the static aspects of reality.

Piaget's Theoretical Concepts

According to Piaget, the development of human intellectual abilities take place as a result of the organization and reorganization of certain pattern of behaviour called '*schema*'. Schemas are the basic structural units of human mind i.e., '*the cognitive structure*'. The process of organization of these schemas take place by three different activities called '*Assimilation, Accommodation and Equilibration*'. These activities constitute the functional aspect of human mind, i.e., '*the cognitive function or cognitive process*'.

Cognitive Structure

According to Piaget- emergence of new cognitive abilities as a result of the modification of human behaviour patterns that are present at the time of birth. These behavioural patterns or the structural units of human mind are called '*schemas*'.

Schemas

Schemas are the basic structural units of human mind. It is the biologically inherited reflexes or abilities to perform a particular task. Sucking, looking, reaching, grasping etc. are the primary schemas of an infant. The infant sucks the breast of his mother, he looks at the objects of his environment, listen different voices in his environment and finally try to reach whatever he sees. As the child grows, it develops different schemas in the form of organized experiences.

Cognitive Functioning

The structure of an organism is said to play an important role in its functioning. The individual has to adapt to his environment for survival as well as proper growth and development. The key to his cognitive development lies in his constant interaction with an adaptation to his physical and social environment. According to Piaget intelligence is a tool by which the individual organizes the schemas and adapt to the world. The process of adaptation or organization of schemas is defined with three different activities – assimilation, accommodation and equilibration.

Assimilation

Assimilation refers to a kind of matching between the already existing cognitive structures and the environmental needs as they arise. It is the process of transforming new experiences into familiar ones by means of organizing past experiences. It takes place when a previous experience is used to comprehend a new experience in its familiar form.

***Example* 1:** When a three month old infant is given a new toy, it is likely to respond by putting the toy in its mouth; because in this period his cognitive structure revolved around the sucking schema, and hence when he get the new toy he put it into his mouth as he suck his mothers breast.

***Example* 2:** A child who has learnt only primary colours such as *red, blue and green* may identify a man wearing a pink-shirt as one wearing a red- shirt.

Accommodation

Accommodation is the modification of existing schemas or behaviour to deal with a new situation. It involves transformation of an old schema or learning a new schema, which is more appropriate for the new situation. In other words accommodation means modifying oneself so as to fit with existing characteristics of the environment. Through accommodation one tries to accommodate or adjust to new ways of thinking and behaving in place of assimilating or behaving in the same old fashion.

***Example* 1:** When the new toy is too big to be picked up and is not able to place in the mouth, the boy will have to change his old ways of thinking and behaving in order to adjust to the new situation. Hence, instead of sucking, now he may respond by pushing or grasping the toy. This is called accommodation.

***Example* 2:** When the child learns to discriminate between red and pink colours, the pre-existing schema of red colour is accommodate with a new experience of identification of the shade of red, that is, pink colour.

Equilibration

According to Piaget, the optimal level of intellectual functioning takes place when there is a balance between assimilation and accommodation. He stressed that the process of assimilation and accommodation helps the organism to adjust or maintain a harmonious relationship between himself and his environment. The process of maintaining this balance is called equilibration. In other words equilibration is the harmonious relationship between the individual and his environment either by assimilation or by accommodation.

Piaget's Stages of Intellectual Development

Cognitive development or intellectual development is the result of continuous interaction between the organism and the environment. It passes through a series of sequential stages. Based upon the nature of this interaction, Piaget divided the cognitive development into four distinctive stages. Each of these stages is marked by the emergence of new patterns of intellectual activities.

They are shown in Figure 8.1 and Table 8.1:

Table 8.1: Stages of Intellectual Development

Intellectual Stage	*Age*
Sensorimotor Stage	(0 – 2 years)
Pre-operational Stage	(2 – 7 years)
Concrete-operational Stage	(7 – 11 years)
Formal-operational Stage	(12– 15 years)

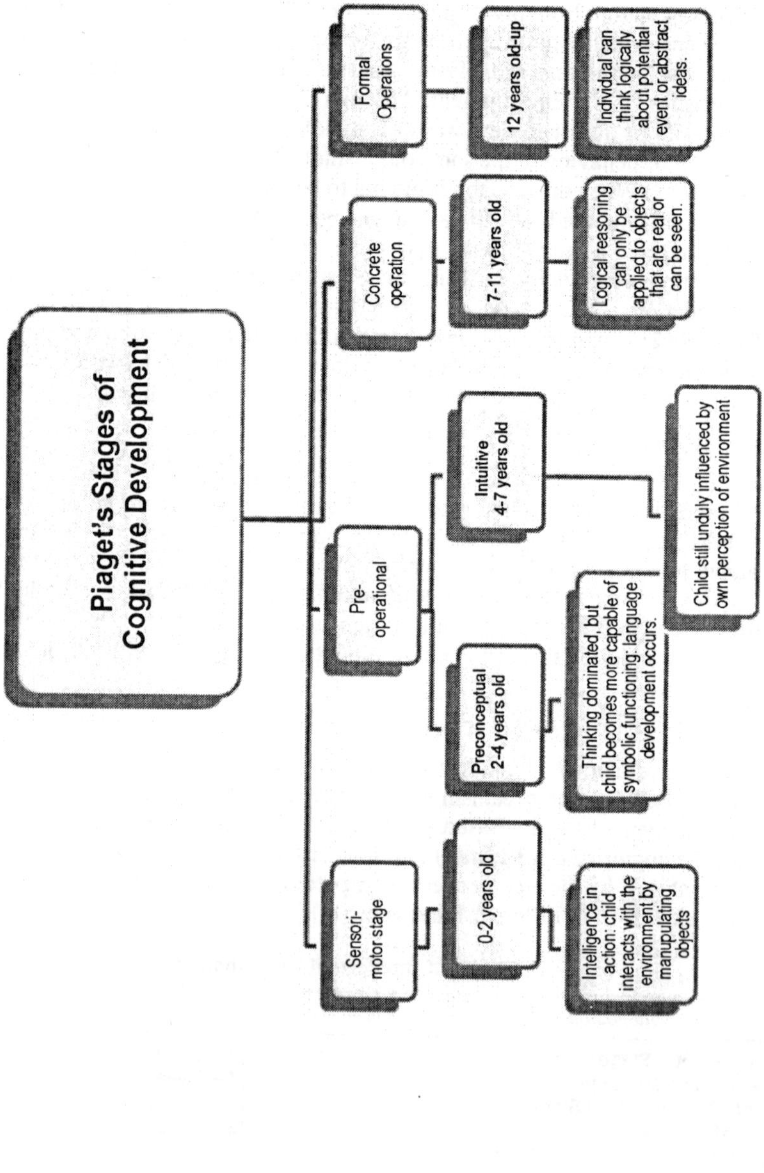

Figure 8.1: Piaget's Stages of Cognitive/Intellectual Development

I. Sensorimotor Stage (0 – 2 years)

In the first two years, infant's mental activities are completely given over to regularizing their sensations and controlling the motor activities. This pre-language period is marked by motor actions and sensations. Hence this period is called as '*sensory-motor period*'. Absence of language is one of the major characteristics of this period. The major characteristics of this period are given in Figure 8.2.

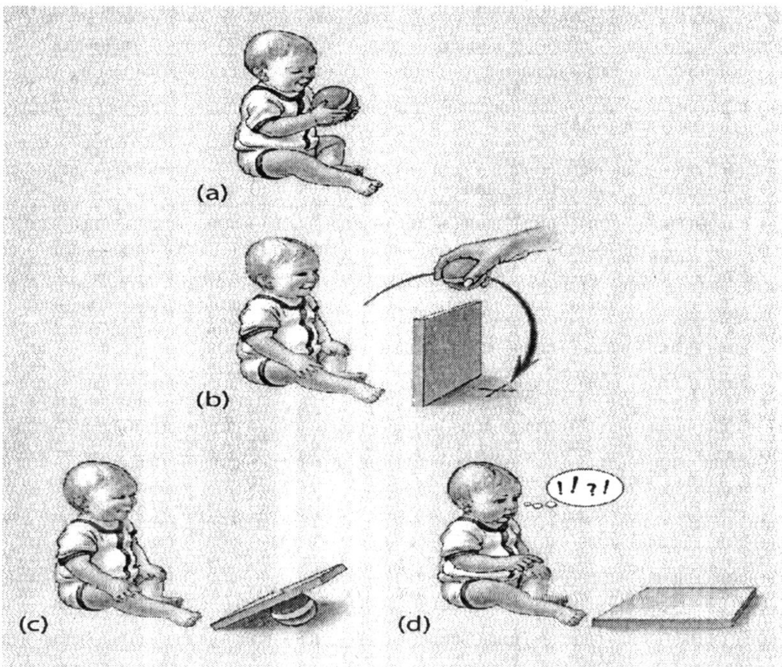

Figure 8.2: Child's Activities during Sensorimotor Stage

- ***Absence of Language:*** Absence of language is one of the major characteristics of this period. The child in this period cannot use any language to communicate with his environment.
- ***Action Schema:*** At birth the infant exhibits a limited number of uncoordinated reflexes such as sucking, looking, reaching and grasping. Gradually these uncoordinated reflexes are coordinated into simple schemas and the infant is able to react to the out objects. Thus they come to know everything around by means of different actions. Piaget called these as action schema.
- ***Absence of Object Permanence:*** As we know a new born baby does not realize that objects are permanent. For him "*what is out of sight is purely out of mind*". For example, if the infant is playing with a toy and you pick it up and hide it somewhere, just after a moment the infant forget about it. For him the hidden toy has disappeared and is no more. Gradually the

concept of object permanence evolves in the cognitive structure of the infant. He begins to realize that the objects continue to exist even though he cannot see or experience them. Thus he begins to search for the hidden objects.

Table 8.2: Sub-stages of Sensorimotor Period

Age	*Sub-stage*	*New Abilities*
Birth - 1 month	Simple Reflexes	Coordination of sensation and action through reflexive behaviours
1 - 4 months	First habits	Coordination of sensation and two schemas: habits and circular reactions
4 - 8 months	Secondary Circular Reactions	Further development of habits
8 - 12 months	Coordination of Secondary Circular Reactions	Coordination of vision and touch
12 - 18 months	Tertiary Circular Reactions, Novelty and Curiosity	Infants become fascinated by objects and the many things they can do
18 - 24 months	Internalism of Schemes	Infants develop the ability to use symbols and form mental pictures

The sub-stages of sensorimotor stage are as follows:

Reflexes (0-1 month): The child uses only innate reflexes. For example, if a nipple or dummy is put into a baby's mouth, they will reflexively suck on it. If an object is placed in their palm, the hand will automatically grab it. These reflexes have the sole function of keeping the child alive.

Primary Circular Actions (1-4 months): The child now has a fixation with it's own body with regards to behaviour (what Piaget refers to as *primary* behaviour); they will perform actions repeatedly on themselves (like sucking their own hand). They also begin to refine reflexes here to form more complex versions of them.

Secondary Circular Reactions (4-8 months): At around 4 months, the child begins to take an interest in their environment (their behaviour is *secondary*). They notice that they can actually influence events in their world, for example they can drop a teddy which bashes a ball on the floor. Although this occurs, the infant will not make conscious connections between what they do and the consequences, they merely observe that their actions have interesting effects.

Co-ordination of Secondary Circular Reactions (8-12 months): At this point, the child begins to engage in *goal-directed* behaviour; they begin to develop cause-effect relationships. So rather than crawl over to a teddy in a cart to pick it up, they might instead pull the cart over with the teddy in to acquire it. The child effectively *knows* that their behaviour will have a certain consequence. At this stage, *object permanence* is acquired – but I will explain this after these sub-stages.

Tertiary Circular Reactions (12-18 months): At this stage, children like to use creativity and flexibility with their previous behaviours, and the result of their experimentation often leads to different outcomes. So rather than grabbing a box, they might instead try to tilt or manipulate it.

Symbolic/Mental Representation (18-24 months): At this stage, the child develops *symbolic thought* and the ability to mentally represent objects in their head. Normally, the child would need to resort to trial-and-error to achieve a desired effect. Now, however, the child can 'plan' to some extent and mentally construct the consequences of an action in their head. Of course, predictions are not always accurate, but it is a step up from trial-and-error.

II. Pre-operational Stage (2–7 years)

During the pre-operational stage the child begins to replace direct action in the form of sensory or motor exploration with symbols. The learning of language helps him in his primary communication. He begins to utter words to ask for something rather than just reaching out to get it. This stage can be further sub-divided into the *Pre-conceptual phase* and *the Intuitive phase.*

Pre-conceptual Phase: (2-4 years)

This is the period of rudimentary concept formation. During this period the child develops the ability to identify and classify objects. The following are the important characteristics of this stage:

- ***Identify Objects by their Names:*** In the early part of this stage, children seem to identify objects by their names but usually make mistakes in identification and concept formation. *For example*, to a child "*all men are daddy and all women are mummy*".
- ***Transductive Reasoning:*** The mode of thinking and reasoning is quite illogical at this stage. It is neither inductive nor deductive but rather transductive in nature, he reasons from the particular to the particular. *For example*, the child at this stage knows that "cows are big animals with four legs and a long tails". After that whenever he saw a bull, a horse or an ass he thinks that 'this animal is also big and has four legs and a tail, therefore it is a cow'.
- ***Representational Thought:*** The child develops the ability to form mental symbols to represent objects or events that are not present. His thinking is sometimes too imaginative and far removed from reality. More over they are unable to distinguish between living and non-living objects. The symbolic function of cognitive development can be seen in two ways:
  - ***Deferred Imitation:*** The child shows the ability to imitate actions performed earlier by adults. An infant might have keenly watched somebody blowing out a candle. The next day he would imitate the same. Since it is delayed one or two day, the infant must have some *memory of actions* and hence Piaget calls this as deferred imitation.
  - ***Symbolic Play:*** This may be seen in their play activities. While playing with a piece of wood, it is turned into a riding horse or a motor cycle, a stick may be used as a gun and a doll into a baby.
- **Ego-centrism***:* One of the major characteristics of this stage is the ego-centric nature of the child. By ego-centrism Piaget means that the child can see the world only from his own views. He thinks that the sun and moon are following him, the stars twinkles to surprise him, the rain falls to delight him and obviously what exists in the external environment is specifically meant for him.

Intuitive Phase: (4–7 years)
Children in this sub-stage become very curious and interested in reasoning. Two abilities that begin to develop, though not fully, during this stage are class inclusion and conservation. Conservation is the understanding that altering the visual appearance of something does not change its physical properties. This was demonstrated in Piaget's conservation tasks. Piaget performed a total of seven tasks that tested conservation of different concepts (number, area, weight, mass etc.).

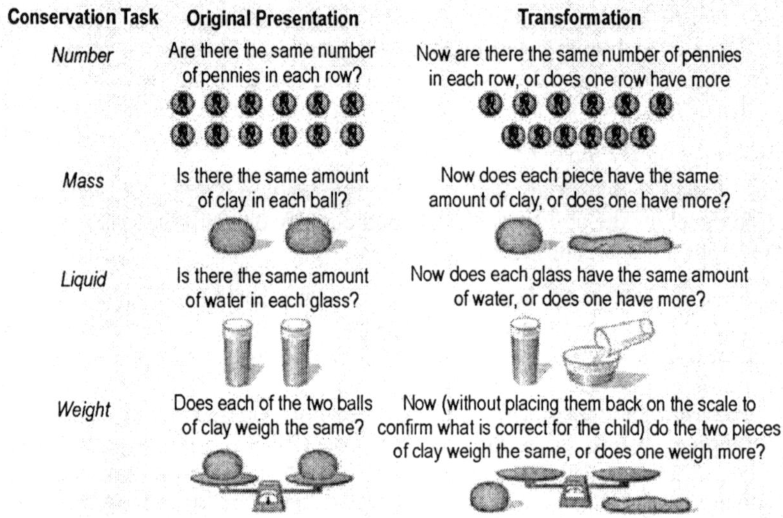

Figure 8.3: Conservation Tasks Related to Pre-operational Stage

During this stage the child progresses towards the formation of various concepts at a more advanced level. For example, now the child will realizes that apples, oranges, bananas etc. are all fruits despite the difference in their shape, colour or taste. But his thinking is based on intuition rather than on systematic logic. The most important characteristic of this stage is as follows:

Thinking is not Logical but Contradictory: During this period the thought process of the child is not logic and systematic but it is full of contradictions. It is due to the absence of *reversibility* and *conservation*. Conservation means the ability to see an object as permanent even though its length, width or shape changes.

Reversibility: It is the ability to reverse or think reversely or vice versa. For example, when a child realizes that not only he has a brother but his brother also has a brother in him, we can say that the child has developed the reversible quality in his cognitive operation. But in the pre-operational stage children are not able to think like this. For them moving from A to B is possible but at the same time movement from B to A is not possible. In another situation, if we teach a child simple mathematics as 2 + 3 = 5, but he cannot comprehend that 5 = 3 + 2 or 5 – 3 = 2. This is due to the absence of reversibility.

Conservation: As mentioned earlier conservation is the ability to see an object as permanent even though its length, width or shape changes. During these stage children lacks the ability to conserve objects in terms of quantity as well as number. For example, a five or six year old child is shown to identical containers filled with the same quantity of water. Now he will agree that both have the same amount.

Figure 8.4: The Child is Seeing the Conservation Task

But after that if we pour the water from one of the containers into a taller but narrower container, the child will reply that the taller container contains more water than the other. The inability to conserve in terms of quantity makes the child think that there is more water in the taller container even though the child has observed that same amount of water has been poured into the taller container; because the level of the water is higher in the taller bur narrower container.

Example 2: A child is shown a set of beads arranged in one-to-one order as shown below.

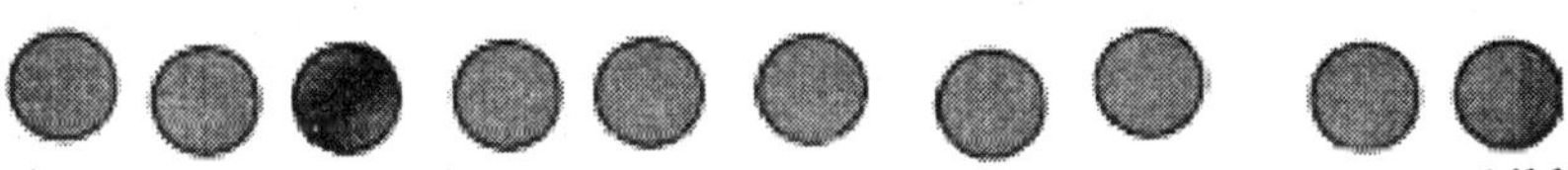

then arrange these beads as adjacent ones as shown below and ask the child which row contains more beads.

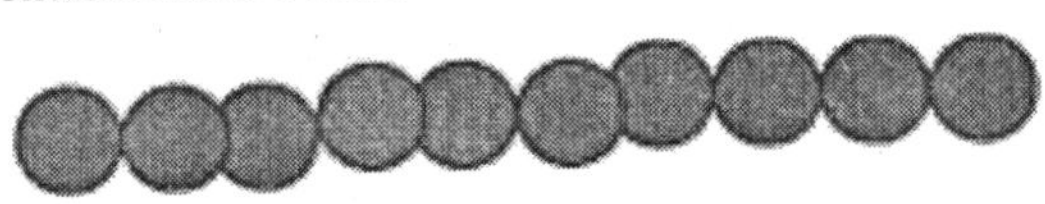

The child is likely to say that the first row has more beads. This is due to the absence of the conservation of number concept. Here the child is unable to realize that a mere change in appearance or arrangement of some objects cannot increase or decrease their number.

Animistic Thinking: Another characteristic of this stage is animism. It is the belief that all things are living. While playing with dolls they feed them milk and food as if they has life.

Table 8.3: Sub-stages of Preoperational Period

Age	*Sub-stage*	*New Abilities*
2 - 4 years	Pre-conceptual	Able to formulate designs of objects that he cannot see Mental abilities of language and pretend play start to occur
4 - 7 years	Intuitive	Children start to grow curious, ask many questions, and reason

III. Concrete Operational Stage (7 – 11 years)

This stage shows marked developments in the cognitive functioning of the child. Here he develops the ability for logical thinking. The major characteristics are described below:

- Here the child learns to ***deals with concepts and ideas*** that exist only *in mental terms*. Now he can think about things and figure out of discrepancies and relationships. For example, now he is able to discriminate between cows and bullocks; as both have four legs and long tails and between a goat and a sheep.
- He begins to ***think in terms of a set of interrelated principles***. For example, as we know Distance, Velocity and Acceleration are inter related terms, i.e., Velocity = Distance divided by Time and Acceleration = Velocity divided by time.
- ***Thinking becomes logic and systematic***: Now the child is able make use of inductive and deductive reasoning. Inductive reasoning means- *'using particular facts and examples to form general rules and principles or from specific to general'*. For example: 'All rocks are solids, so Igneous rocks (Aagneya Shila), Sedimentary rocks (Avasada Shila) Metamorphic rocks (Kayandhariga Shila) etc, are solids. Deductive reasoning means *'from general to specific'*. For example, as mentioned above 'Igneous rocks, Sedimentary rocks, metamorphic rocks, etc. are solids, so we can say 'all rocks are solids'.
- ***Ability of conservation:*** The child develops the ability to conserve both in terms of quantity and number of objects. Now he is able to think that the change in appearance of an object does not alter either its quantity or its number.
- ***Reversibility of thought:*** At this stage the child learns to carry a thought backward and forward in time. For example, as mentioned earlier movement of A à B and B à A or A? B is possible. Or a girl who has a sister now clearly realizes that her sister also has a sister.
- ***Absence of Ego-centrism:*** The child now is no longer ego-centric in his thinking. He is able to think that people may have different opinions and may differ in their modes of thinking and conclusions. Now he is able to appreciate others thoughts and viewpoints.
- ***Classification and Serialization:*** Now the child is able to classify objects on the basis of their merits. For example, by giving a list of objects such as banana, bat, rose, cat, foot ball, elephant, jasmine, dog, apple, lotus, orange,

monkey, etc. the child is able to classify them under the category of Fruits, Animals, Play materials, Flowers etc.

He also develops the ability of serialization like arranging things from largest to smallest and vice versa. The number concept is also developed and is able to recognize the even number, odd number, cardinal number, ordinary number, etc.

Table 8.4: Sub-stages of Concrete Operational Period

Age	*Sub-stage*	*New Abilities*
7 - 11 years	Seriation	Able to sort objects
	Transitivity	Able to recognize logical relationships among elements in a serial order
	Classification	Able to name and identify sets of objects according to characteristics
	Decentering	Takes into account multiple aspects of a problem to solve it
	Reversibility	Understands that numbers and objects can be changed and then returned
	Conservation	Understands quantity, length, or number of items independent of appearance
	Egocentrism Elimination	Able to view things from another person's perspective

IV. Formal Operational Stage (12 – 15 Years)

The intellectual development and cognitive functioning of the child takes a very sophisticated shape. The thought process becomes quite systematic and reasonably well integrated. Following are the major characteristics of this stage:

- ***Ability to deal with abstraction***: Adolescents can think not only in general terms but also in abstract terms. The child learns to utilize the tools of symbolism in the process of thought and learns to deal with abstraction by logical thinking. He begins to construct relationships between concrete operations and between symbols.
- ***Hypothetico-deductive reasoning:*** The child at the formal operational stage starts a form of hypothetico-deductive reasoning. When faced with a problem, he starts with a general theory of all possible factors. Then they test these hypotheses in an orderly fashion to see which one work in the real world. Now the child is able to:
  - Build up multiple hypotheses and a number of alternate solutions
  - Verify all possible solutions in a systematic and logical way
  - Generalize and arrive at abstract rules that cover many specific solutions
- ***Systematic problem solving ability:*** The individual begins to look at problems in many ways and explore various solutions in a systematic and logical way. He develops the ability to build multiple hypotheses and a number of alternate solutions. For example: If a child is shown five colourless, odorless liquids in test tubes and is asked to find out what

combination of the five will produce a red liquid. By adopting a systematic approach he combines the first and second, first and third and so on. By using trial and error method he can simply find out which is the most suitable combination for getting the red colour.

- ***Ability to transfer:*** The development of formal operations enables the adolescent to transfer understanding from one situation another situation.

EDUCATIONAL IMPLICATIONS OF DIFFERENT STAGES OF COGNITIVE DEVELOPMENT

According to Piaget, children of a particular stage tend to reach a particular stage of cognitive development, therefore planning of curriculum and teaching method must be in tune with the cognitive development of that particular stage. This theory guides teachers and parents to provide suitable learning experiences according to the development level and cognitive functioning of their children. Therefore, the educational implications of different stages of cognitive development are as under:

The Sensorimotor Stage

- An experience of sensorimotor stage provides the foundation of cognitive development for later stages. During this stage, children actively use their body and senses. Parents may furnish some soft/hard toys and objects of different shapes. Through the bodily use and manipulation of these objects they may acquire some ideas about their environment.
- As the children try to suck the objects, push, pull, reach and drop them, through sensory and motor activity, they develop cognitively.

The Pre-operational Stage

- As the children at the pre-operational stage can imitate the activity which they have observed previously, the teacher may give instructions through actions.
- They may be encouraged to draw and to describe their drawings, as children's level of thinking is represented through their drawings.
- Parents and teachers should provide them a wide range of opportunities to talk with others to encourage their language development.
- Children may be asked to describe what they are seeing, hearing, tasting to foster their language ability.
- They may be given some cut out letters to build words or some simple tasks on arithmetic, to reveal their level of cognitive development.

The Concrete Operational Stage

- As children at the concrete operational stage are able to seal with concrete objects, teachers should use three dimensional objects and diagrams while teaching them the subjects like Science, History, Geography etc.
- Teach complex ideas through familiar examples.
- Ask them to classify and group objects on the basis of single attribute.
- Present problems that stimulate analytical thinking.

The Formal Operational Stage

- Teachers should continue to provide concrete examples in a more sophisticated form.
- Encourage them to find out general principles.
- The activities should be challenging one but not so difficult.
- Ask them to explain how they arrive at solutions to problems.
- Guide them to reason scientifically and solve problems.
- Provide them some activities those encourage them prepositional thinking.
- Give them the opportunities to gather as much information as possible, combine them and to form new propositions.

EDUCATIONAL IMPLICATIONS OF PIAGET'S STAGES OF COGNITIVE DEVELOPMENT THEORY

An important implication of Piaget's theory is adaptation of instruction to the learner's developmental level. The content of instruction needs to be consistent with the developmental level of the learner. The teacher's role is to facilitate learning by providing a variety of experiences. Opportunities that allow students of differing cognitive levels to work together often encourage less mature students to advance to a more mature understanding. Some suggestions for teachers are:

- hands on experiences
- provide concrete props and visual aids; example- time line
- use familiar examples to facilitate learning more complex ideas; example- story problems in math
- allow opportunities to classify and group information with increasing complexity; example - outlines to assimilate new information with previous knowledge
- present problems that require logical thinking; example- brain teasers
- discuss social, political and cultural issues; example- tie your lesson to some relevant event
- teach broad concepts instead of just facts; example - why you are learning this

BRUNER'S THEORY OF INTELLECTUAL DEVELOPMENT

Bruner was very much a leader in the cognitive revolution, that in the 1950's set out to replace behaviourism. The aim of this revolution was, in Bruner's words *'to discover and to describe formally the meanings that human beings created out of their encounters with the world, and then to propose hypotheses about what meaning-making processes were implicated. It focused on the symbolic activities that human beings employed in constructing and making sense not only of the world, but of themselves'* (Bruner, 1990: p. 2). Bruner felt the emphasis had shifted from the 'construction of meaning' to the 'processing of information' and felt that this metaphor of a computer was too limiting and did not allow for the role of culture in shaping our thoughts and the words we choose to express them.

For Bruner, an understanding of mind must include mental states like believing, desiring, intending, grasping a meaning and must consider the mediating effects of culture and language. Scientists should not continue studying cognition in isolation, because the symbolic systems that individuals used in constructing meaning were systems that were already there, deeply embedded in culture and language. One of Bruner's assumptions is that the outcome of cognitive development is thinking. The intelligent mind creates from experience. 'We are 'information processors' who manipulate mental representations of the world, and this enables us to 'go beyond the information given' to us by our sensory systems.'

Postulates of Intellectual Development

Bruner postulated three stages of intellectual development:

- The first stage he termed *"Enactive"*, when a person learns about the world through actions on physical objects and the outcomes of these actions.
- The second stage was called *"Iconic"* where learning can be obtained through using models and pictures.
- The final stage was *"Symbolic"* in which the learner develops the capacity to think in abstract terms. Based on this three-stage notion, Bruner recommended using a combination of concrete, pictorial then symbolic activities will lead to more effective learning.

Bruner's Stages of Cognitive Development (Representation)

Bruner was concerned with acquisition and use of knowledge. Representation relates to the means by which growing human beings represent their experience of the world; and how they organize for future use what they have encountered. Bruner theorizes that children construct knowledge using three modes of what he called representation that corresponds to developmental stages. According to Bruner, as children develop they master each of these increasingly more complex modes, this involves becoming more skilled in translating between each mode.

According to Bruner, one's intellectual ability evolves as a result of maturation, training and experiences through a series of three stages – the *enactive, iconic and symbolic (see Figure 8.5).*

Enactive (action-based) Stage (Representation)

Sometimes called the concrete stage, this first stage involves a tangible hands-on method of learning. Bruner believed that *"learning begins with an action - touching, feeling and manipulating"*. In mathematics education, *manipulatives* are the concrete objects with which the actions are performed. Common examples of manipulatives used in this stage in math education are algebra tiles, paper, coins, etc. - anything tangible.

In this stage, cognitive experiences are received and represented through motor activities. It is the stage of learning through physical action. At this stage the child knows the world only through the medium of actions – not through words or image, for instance, the infant understands his environment only by touching, biting and grasping. *(Similar to that of Sensori-motor stage of Piaget)*

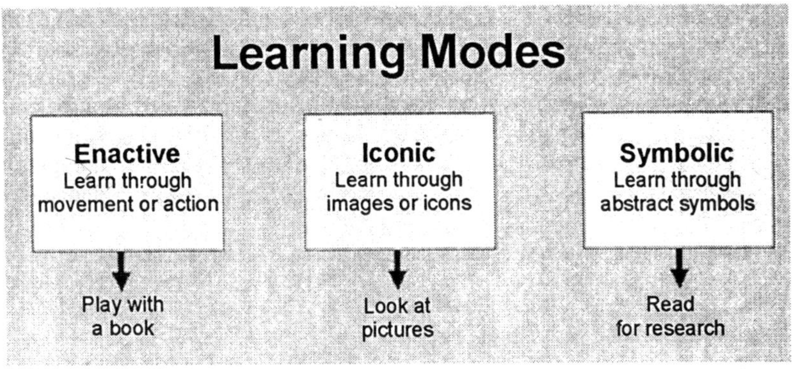

Figure 8.5: Bruner's Stages of Cognitive Development (Representation)

Iconic (image-based) Stage (Representation)

Sometimes called the pictoral stage, this second stage involves images or other visuals to represent the concrete situation enacted in the first stage. One way of doing this is to simply draw images of the objects on paper or to picture them in one's head. Other ways could be through the use of shapes, diagrams, and graphs.

This stage is characterized by the child's representation of things and events in terms of sensory images or mental pictures or icons of perceptual experiences. At this stage, information is gained by imagery and the cognitive process is controlled by perception. Single feature of environment hold attention; visual memory is developed but impressionistic leaps take place.

Symbolic (language-based) Representation

Sometimes called the abstract stage, the last stage takes the images from the second stage and represents those using words and symbols. The use of words and symbols *"allows a student to organize information in the mind by relating concepts together"*. The words and symbols are abstractions; they do not necessarily have a direct connection to the information. For example, a number is a symbol used to describe how many of something there are, but the number in itself has little meaning without the understanding of it means for there to be that number of something. Other examples would be variables such as x or y, or mathematical symbols such as +, -,/, etc. Finally, language and words are another way to abstractly represent the idea. In the context of math, this could be the use of words such as addition, infinite, the number three, etc.

During this stage, cognitive experiences are received and represented through symbols. The child engages in symbolic activities, such as language and mathematics. Here actions and images are translated into words. The symbolic stage allows compactability – that is, condensation of experiences into formulas such as $F = ma$, $E = MC^2$, and into semantically rich statements.

Main Ideas of Jerome Bruner' Theory

Jerome Bruner' theory is very influential and has direct implications on the teaching practices. The main ideas of the theory can be summarized as follows:

- Learning is an active process. Learners select and transform information.
- Learners make appropriate decisions and postulate hypotheses and test their effectiveness.
- Learners use prior experience to fit new information into the pre-existing structures.
- *Scaffolding* is the process through which able peers or adults offer supports for learning. This assistance becomes gradually less frequent as it becomes unnecessary.
- The intellectual development includes three stages. The enactive stage, which refers to learning through actions. The iconic stage which refers to the learner's use of pictures or models. The symbolic stage, which refers to the development of the ability to think in abstract terms.
- The notion of *spiral curriculum* states that a curriculum should revisit basic ideas, building on them until the student grasps the full formal concept.
- Although extrinsic motivation may work in the short run, intrinsic motivation has more value

Features of Bruner's Theory of Instruction

Four features of Bruner's theory of instruction are as follows:

Predisposition to Learn

This feature specifically states the experiences which move the learner toward a love of learning in general, or of learning something in particular. Motivational, cultural, and personal factors contribute to this. Bruner emphasized social factors and early teachers and parents' influence on this. He believed learning and problem solving emerged out of exploration. Part of the task of a teacher is to maintain and direct a child's spontaneous explorations.

Structure of Knowledge

It is possible to structure knowledge in a way that enables the learner to most readily grasp the information. This is a relative feature, as there are many ways to structure a body of knowledge and many preferences among learners. Bruner offered considerable detail about structuring knowledge.

Understanding the fundamental structure of a subject makes it more comprehensible. Bruner viewed categorization as a fundamental process in the structuring of knowledge. Details are better retained when placed within the contest of an ordered and structured pattern. To generate knowledge which is transferable to other contexts, fundamental principles or patterns are best suited. The discrepancy between beginning and advanced knowledge in a subject area is diminished when instruction centers on a structure and principles of orientation. This means that a body of knowledge must be in a simple enough form for the learner to understand it and it must be in a form recognizable to the student's experience.

Modes of Representation: Visual, Words, Symbols

Effective Sequencing: No one sequencing will fit every learner but in general, increasing difficulty. Sequencing, or lack of it, can make learning easier or more difficult.

Implications of Bruner's Intellectual Developmental Theory on the Learning Process

Bruner's learning theory has direct implications on the teaching practices. Here are some of these implications:

- Instruction must be appropriate to the level of the learners. For example, being aware of the learners' learning modes (enactive, iconic, symbolic) will help you plan and prepare appropriate materials for instruction according to the difficulty that matches learners' level.
- The teachers must revisit material to enhance knowledge. Building on pre-taught ideas to grasp the full formal concept is of paramount importance according to Bruner. Feel free to re-introduce vocabulary, grammar points, and other topics now and then in order to push the students to a deeper comprehension and longer retention.
- Material must be presented in a sequence giving the learners the opportunity to:
  - ➢ acquire and construct knowledge
  - ➢ transform and transfer his learning
- Students should be involved in using their prior experiences and structures to learn new knowledge.
- Help students to categorize new information in order to able to see similarities and differences between items.
- Teachers should assist learners in building their knowledge. This assistance should fade away as it becomes unnecessary.
- Teachers should provide feedback that is directed towards intrinsic motivation. Grades and competition are not helpful in the learning process. Bruner states that learners must "experience success and failure not as reward and punishment, but as information"

VYGOTSKY'S VIEW OF KNOWLEDGE CONSTRUCTION

For Vygotsky, cognitive development occurs as a result of **social interactions**. In social interactions, children work with others to make decisions and solve problems. Therefore, their cognitive abilities increase and eventually they gain the ability to function intellectually on their own.

One of the key ideas proposed by Vygotsky is called the **zone of proximal development** (ZPD). ZPD is the range of tasks that are too difficult for a child to master alone, but that can be learned with guidance and assistance of adults or more-skilled children as illustrated in Figure 8.6. Children in the ZPD for a particular task can almost, but not quite, performed the task on their own.

Another important idea to be discussed here is the concept of *scaffolding*. Scaffolding refers to the temporary support that parents, teachers, and more-skilled peers give a child to do a task until the child can do it alone. The concept of scaffolding can be interpreted in the zone of proximal development graph as illustrated in Figure 8.7.

Demonstrating and asking questions are two ways to scaffold students' learning. An art teacher may demonstrate drawing before asking students to try on their own. Another teacher may ask students such question "Can you provide an example of that?"

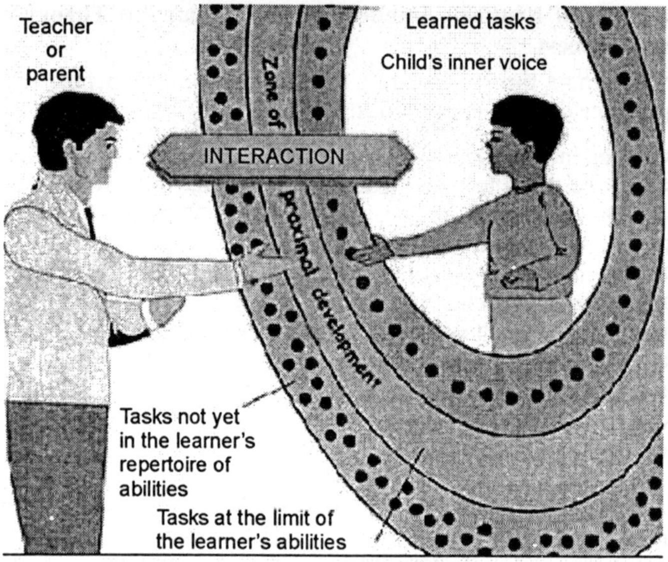

Figure 8.6: Picture that shows Zone of Proximal Development (ZPD) by Vygotsky

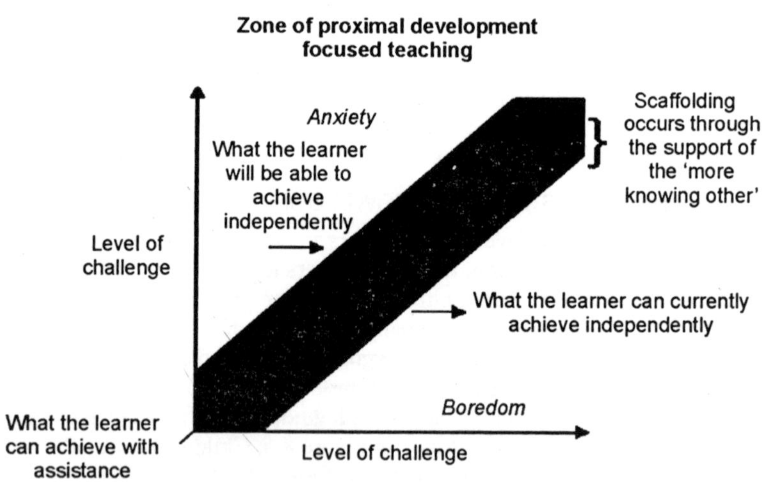

Figure 8.7: Zone of Proximal Development Graph

Applications of Vygotsky's Theory

- Teach within the ZPD such as presenting tasks that students can perform successfully only with assistance.
- Encourage collaborative problem solving such as working in small groups to accomplish complex tasks.

- Use scaffolding to help student's progress through their ZPD such as providing teaching aids that student can use to make difficult tasks easier.
- Use more-skilled peers as teachers.

EDUCATIONAL IMPLICATIONS OF INTELLECTUAL DEVELOPMENT

- Intellectual development during childhood period (Early-childhood and late-childhood) depends on different factors such as heredity, environment (school, home and society.) Role of teachers and guardians are highly important to give a permanent shape to the intellectual curiosity of the growing child.
- Language and communication skill can be promoted through reading, writing, recitation, poetry, essay, composition and story relating creative imagination and rational thinking. Cramming must be replaced by creative practices.
- Involvement of students in practical works, experiments to get first hand knowledge should be encouraged. Picnic, Study tour and fieldtrips are necessary for making learning pleasant and joyful.
- Teachers are required to adopt appropriate methods and techniques of teaching with due consideration to students age and interest which will support intellectual development of the child.

Chapter-9
Language Development

Language refers to a form of communication in which we learn to use complex rules to form and manipulate symbols (words or gestures) that are to generate an endless number meaningful sentences. The growth and development in speech, vocabulary, length of responses are some of the important aspects of language development. The vocabulary of children in the beginning is too limited. There is continuous increase in the size of one's vocabulary during childhood. Later on, as a result of pressure of needs and learning, the vocabulary goes on developing.

MEANING AND SIGNIFICANCE OF LANGUAGE DEVELOPMENT

The major characteristics that distinguish between human beings from animals is their ability to use language. Speech is the most important form of communication. Communication has six forms: 1. Speech, 2. Facial and bodily movements, 3. Touch, 4. Sign language used by the deaf, 5. Arts such as music, dance, painting etc. and 6. Written symbols of words.

DEFINITIONS OF LANGUAGE DEVELOPMENT

Language can be defined in various ways as stated below.

1. Lahey (2004) - *"Language is one of the most significant cognitive developments of the human species."*
2. Feldman (2005)- *"Language is defined as the communication of information through symbols arranged according to systematic rules"*

Language takes several forms of communications that are spoken, written, and signed Language involves two important processes that are, sending and receiving information. To convey information, one must be able to speak or otherwise use words, phrases, and sentences. This ability is referred to as language production. Language comprehension, on the other hand, is the ability to understand message conveyed by words, phrases, and sentences. To understand how language develops, we first need to review some systems of language rules. Let us look at each of these in turn.

SYSTEM OF LANGUAGE RULES OR LEVELS OF LINGUISTIC STRUCTURE

There are 4 rules of language system. The rules are semantics, syntax, phonology and morphology as shown in Figure 9.1.

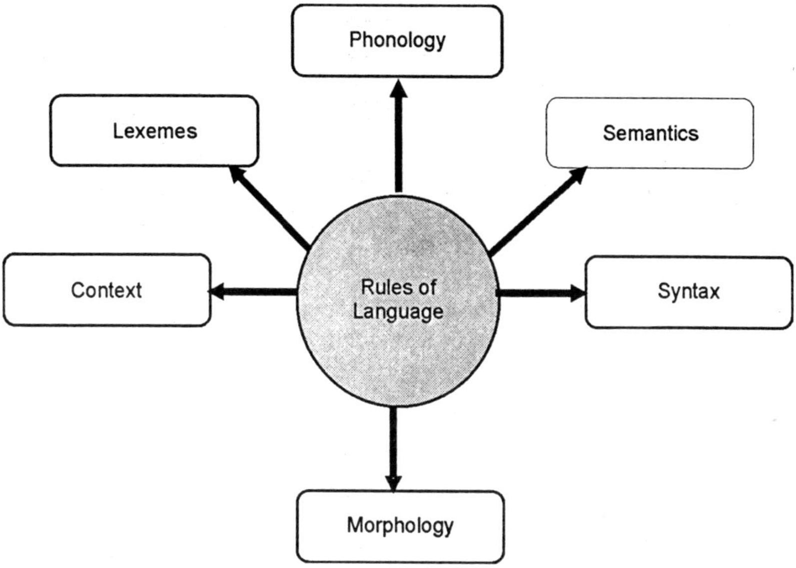

Figure 9.1: Rules for Language System

The rules for language system can be describes as below.

Phonology

A phoneme is the basic unit of phonology. It is the smallest unit of sound that may cause a change of meaning within a language, but that doesn't have meaning by itself. For example, in the words *"bake"* and *"brake"* only one phoneme has been altered but a change in meaning has been triggered. The phoneme/*r*/has no meaning on its own but by appearing in the word it has completely changed the word's meaning.

Morphology

Morphemes, the basic unit of morphology, are the smallest meaningful unit of language. Thus, a morpheme is a series of phonemes that has a special meaning. If a morpheme is altered in any way, the entire meaning of the word can be changed. Some morphemes are individual words (such as "eat" or "water"). These are known as free morphemes because they can exist on their own. Other morphemes are prefixes, suffixes, or other linguistic pieces that aren't full words on their own but do affect meaning (such as the *"-s"* at the end of *"cats"* or the *"re-"* at the beginning of *"redo"*) because these morphemes must be attached to another word to have meaning, they are called bound morphemes.

Syntax

Syntax is a set of rules for constructing full sentences out of words and phrases. Every language has a different set of syntactic rules, but all languages have some form of syntax. In English, the smallest form of a sentence is a noun phrase (which might just be a noun or a pronoun) and a verb phrase (which may be a single verb). Adjectives and adverbs can be added to the sentence to provide further meaning. Word order matters in English, although in some languages, order is of less importance. For example, the English sentences "The baby ate the carrot" and "The carrot ate the baby" do not mean the same thing, even though they contain the exact same words. In languages like Finnish, word order doesn't matter for general meaning—different word orders are used to emphasize different parts of the sentence.

Semantics

Semantics refers to the meaning of words or sentences. Semantics includes knowing the meaning of such words as dragon fruit and love.

Lexemes

Lexemes are the set of inflected forms taken by a single word. For example, members of the lexeme RUN include "run" (the uninflected form), "running" (inflected form), and "ran." This lexeme excludes "runner" (a derived term—it has a derivational morpheme attached). Another way to think about lexemes is that they are the set of words that would be included under one entry in the dictionary—"running" and "ran" would be found under "run," but "runner" would not.

Context

Context is how everything within language works together to convey a particular meaning. Context includes tone of voice, body language, and the words being used. Depending on how a person says something, holds his or her body, or emphasizes certain points of a sentence, a variety of different messages can be conveyed. For example, the word "awesome," when said with a big smile, means the person is excited about a situation. "Awesome," said with crossed arms, rolled eyes, and a sarcastic tone, means the person is not thrilled with the situation.

STAGES OF LANGUAGE ACQUISITION

The stages of language acquisition are given below:

Prelinguistic speech (Crying + cooing + babbling, + imitating language sounds)

Newborn babies signal needs and feelings through cries and facial expressions. Between six weeks and three months, babies start *'cooing'*. Then, they begin making speechlike but meaningless sounds. These sounds are called *'babbling'*. Babies repeat the same sounds such as ba-ba-ba and ma-ma-ma, which are most common across all languages. Language development continues with accidental imitation of language sounds babies hear. They imitate the sounds without understanding the meaning. Crying, cooing, babbling, and imitating language sounds are known as *'prelinguistic speech'*.

Gestures

Shortly before one year of age, babies start using *'gestures'* to communicate.

For example, they learn that nodding the head means yes or blowing means hot.

Linguistic speech

At about one year of age, babies begin to say *'single words'*. The productions of single words mark the beginning of the *'linguistic speech'*. Linguistic speech refers to the verbal expressions that convey meaning. Babies' single words such as go may mean "I want to go out", "I want to sleep" or "Go and get that thing for me". A single words that conveys a complete thought like this is called a *'holophrase'*.

Telegraphic speech

The babies' first brief sentence comes between 18 and 24 months during which they make telegraphic speech to express various actions. In *'telegraphic speech'*, words not critical to the message are left out. Examples of telegraphic speech are "Papa work", "Baby cry" and "No watch TV".

Vocabularies increased

During early childhood, children's vocabularies increase rapidly due to *'fast mapping'* process. Fast mapping allows children aged three to six years old to absorb the meaning of a new word after hearing it once or twice in conversations. In addition, children's grammar and syntax become fairly sophisticated.

Pragmatic

During the school years, children's vocabulary continues to grow. They learn that some words can have more than one meaning. Their understanding of rules of syntax becomes more sophisticated. The major area of linguistic growth during this stage is in *'pragmatics'* or the practical use of language to communicate. For example, when they recognize a breakdown in communication, they do something to repair it and before introducing a topic with which the other person may not be familiar, they first ask simple questions.

Teenage slang

During adolescence, young people know about 80000 words. They can define and discuss such abstractions as love and freedom. They also become more skilled in the ability to understand another person's point of view and level of knowledge and to speak accordingly. Adolescents also like to use *'teenage slang'*. Thus, they speak different language with peers than with adults.

SEQUENCE OF LANGUAGE DEVELOPMENT

- At birth language is particularly absent
- Around 4 weeks - small *throaty sounds* are noticed
- Around 16 weeks – cry, smile, cooing etc.
- Around 28 weeks – babbling stage begins
- Around 40 weeks – try to imitate others sound
- Around 52 weeks – says two or more words
- Around 18 months – baby combines words to from basic sentences

- Around 24 months – baby uses simple phrases and understands simple directions
- Around 36 months – Talks in sentences, answer simple questions
- Around 4 years – use conjunctions and prepositions
- Around 5 years – speaks without infantile articulations

STAGES OF LANGUAGE DEVELOPMENT

The main stages of language development are as follows:

Primitive Stage

This stage is characterized by non-intellectual or thoughtless speech. As babies, we goo and gah, cry and babble. These are examples of the primitive stage of language development. The sounds produced serve no real purpose except to produce the sound. The baby may make sounds without producing speech.

Naïve Stage *(lack of experience in life)*

As the child begins to speak, he learns how to say words far before he learns their meaning and function. An example of this manifestation is "ball". To the child this one word can mean a variety of things such as "where is my ball", "give me the ball", etc. To an adult with an established knowledge of language, this word refers to a child's toy, but to a child's though it can have various meanings.

As the child develops and gains understanding of new words, he begins to produce naïve sentences like "where ball" and "where is the ball." The child uses these structures without any understanding of how to put a sentence together or why the words must go in that order. He only knows that when the words are said in a certain way, others understand his meaning.

Ego-centric Stage or (External Stage)

During the external stage the child begins to use external objects to represent words. For example, the child uses flash cards, objects, or fingers when counting. Another example is the use of his name to remember letters and the sounds they make. The most interesting event is the beginning of egocentric speech. The child will talk to himself when there is no one else around and also during play with others. This is the child's verbalization of thought.

In-growth Stage

As the child's egocentric speech turns inward, he enters the final stage. He uses the skills he has acquired to perform logical tasks internally. Rather than counting aloud, he will count "in his head" using part of his short term memory.

CHOMSKY'S THEORY OF LANGUAGE DEVELOPMENT

Noam Chomsky, the great twentieth century American Linguistic, posited that children are born with a powerful language acquisition device (LAD) which represents knowledge of *universal grammar* or grammar of all human languages. The LAD processes the linguistic input or the language to which a child is exposed and intelligently tests several hypothesis about the nature of the input to quickly and efficiently come up with the knowledge of the rules or grammar of that language.

According to Chomsky, language is being constructed. The primary form of language is stored in human brain. What is to be done is to enable the child to make use of that and acquire knowledge. The main function of language is communication of ideas. We perceive language as the ability to comprehend and speak ideas.

Chomsky's View of Language Acquisition

According to Chomsky, language acquisition is not a process of imitation, but it is a creative process that involves the creation and reliance on a rule system. For example, the English children go through a period in which they produce past tense forms such as 'goed' (past tense of go) and 'comed' (past tense of come) rather than went and came. Such forms are very infrequent in the children's input. Here the child incorrectly applies the regular rules of past tense formation. This indicates that language acquisition involves the development of a rule-based system, a defining feature of generative grammar.

Normal language development involves a number of well defined stages. The basic lexical *(Dictionary word)* and grammatical properties are all acquired within the first three years. At 6-8 months children start to babble, at 10-12 months they speak their first words and at 20-24 months they begin to put words together. When they are between 2 and 3 years they produce simple sentences with infinite verbal forms.

Chomsky's Theoretical Constructs

The important theoretical constructs postulated by Chomsky for explaining his views on linguistic development in children are the following:

Language Acquisition Device (LAD)

It is a neural system of the brain hypothesized to permit understanding of language. According to Chomsky all human beings are born with an innate predisposition (latent tendency) to learn a language fluently, and this predisposition is encased in our biological make-up. This innate, language ability that facilitates the acquisition of language in man is called the Language Acquisition Device. The LAD processes and shapes the primary linguistic data received by the child from the environment and enables him to acquire ideas about the rules of language as applied to one's own language without being aware of.

Noam Chomsky's work discusses the biological basis for language and claims that children have innate abilities to learn language. Chomsky terms this innate ability the *"language acquisition device."* He believes children instinctively learn language without any formal instruction. He also believes children have a natural need to use language, and that in the absence of formal language children will develop a system of communication to meet their needs. He has observed that all children make the same type of language errors, regardless of the language they are taught. Chomsky also believes in the existence of a "universal grammar," which posits that there are certain grammatical rules all human languages share. However, his research does not identify areas of the brain or a genetic basis that enables humans' innate ability for language

Universal Grammar

Chomsky held that all languages of the world have the same basic underlying grammatical structure, and the specific languages have rules that transform these underlying structures into the specific patterns found in given languages. According to Chomsky, all languages have the same basic underlying grammatical structures and principles, which he called Universal Grammar, i.e. all languages of the world share similar characteristics of using nouns, verbs, pronouns, though not necessarily in a similar order.

Generative Grammar

Chomsky defined generative grammar as a finite (limited) set of rules operating on a finite vocabulary to generate an infinite number of acceptable grammatical sentences and no un-acceptable ones. So from a small number of words, using 'some rules', the child can create a vast number of words or sentences.

Semantics

According to Chomsky, the field of linguistics does not include the study of meaning and reference and the use of language. According to linguistic theory, the concepts of the grammar are not based upon semantics, but linguistic theory should provide an explanation to the semantic phenomenon.

Language Acquisition through Universal Grammar

According to Chomsky children are born with a special biological brain mechanism to learn languages, which he called Language Acquisition Device. Chomsky opined that despite many superficial differences found in the surface structure of different languages of the world, they have the same basic underlying grammatical structures and principles, which he called Universal Grammar, i.e. all languages of the world share similar characteristics of using nouns, verbs, pronouns, though not necessarily in a similar order.

All children go through a critical learning period in the first three years of their life during which the child's LAD is active. It accepts the primary linguistic data from the environment as input, processes and transforms it with the help of the Universal Grammar structures, and generate as an output grammar of the language from which the data have been drawn. In this process, the infant acts as a little linguist trying to Figure out the set of abstract rules which generate the sentences that are heard. Chomsky maintains that the extraction of these rules is possible only if the child already knows their basic nature, i.e. he has a LAD which contains knowledge of universal grammar.

During language acquisition, the universal grammar develops into a particular grammar of the language that the child is exposed to, i.e. his native language. The children then extracts and acquires the rules of that language.

THE ROLE OF TEACHER REGARDING LANGUAGE DEVELOPMENT

The teachers need to know the process of language development as language development depends on desire to learn, changes to learn and guidance. Teachers need to act as a model, as with good model to imitate and with guidance in copying it, children will improve their pronunciation.

Students need support from other students and from the teacher to develop their speech. A teacher may encourage cooperative speech by asking children questions and answering their questions. Sometimes students may have speech problem, a teacher may guide by explanations, demonstrations and work with other students-provides opportunities for cooperative learning.

According to Vygotsky, at any given point in development there are certain problems that a child is on the verge of being able to solve. The zone of proximal development is the area where the child cannot solve a problem alone but can be successful under adult guidance or in collaboration with more advanced peer. If the teacher is aware of this aspect, he may provide opportunity to work with someone who is just a bit better. He should encourage using language to organize their thinking and to talk about what they are trying to accomplish. Teacher can do much to help children improve their speech, as language plays a major role in learning, inside and outside the classroom.

Chapter-10
Moral and Psychosocial Development

MEANING OF MORAL DEVELOPMENT

Moral development is the process through which children develop proper attitudes and behaviours toward other people in society, based on social and cultural norms, rules and laws. Moral development is a concern for every teacher and parent. Teaching a child to distinguish right from wrong and to behave accordingly is a goal of parenting. Moral development is a complex issue that—since the beginning of human civilization—has been a topic of discussion among some of the world's most distinguished psychologists, theologians and culture theorists.

Moral development involves children learning how to tell the difference between right and wrong; to use this knowledge to arrive at appropriate decisions when faced with complicated choices; and to have the strength and independence to act in accordance with that right decision (to "do the right thing") despite the fact that it may not be a convenient thing to do. As with other components of development, morality is shaped by multiple factors. Children's interpersonal experiences with family, peers, and other adults, as well as their maturing physical, cognitive, emotional and social skills combine to influence moral development.

DEFINITION OF MORAL DEVELOPMENT

According to Santrock- *"Moral development concerns with rules and conventions about just interactions between people."*

These rules can be studied in three domains such as cognitive, behavioural and emotional. The descriptions of the 3 domains are shown in Figure 10.1.

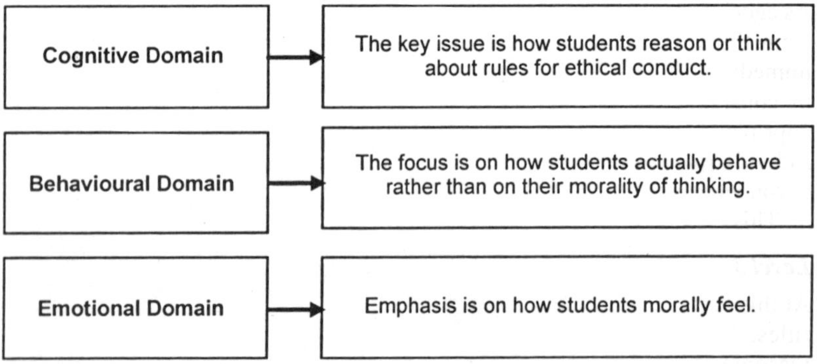

Figure 10.1: Descriptions for Cognitive, Behavioural and Emotional in Rules of Moral Development

KOHLBERG'S THEORY OF MORAL DEVELOPMENT

A second major perspective on moral development was proposed by Lawrence Kohlberg (1958, 1986). Piaget's stage of cognitive stages of development serves as the underpinnings for Kohlberg's theory. Kohlberg arrived at his theory after interviewing children, adolescents and adults (primarily males) about their views on a series of moral dilemmas. Here is an example of the type of dilemma he presented:

> "A woman is near death and is suffering from a special kind of cancer. There is only one drug that doctors think might save her. It was recently discovered by a druggist living in the same town as the woman. The drug was expensive to make, but the druggist is charging 10 times what the drug cost him to make. The sick woman's husband, Heinz tries to borrow the money to buy the drug from every place he can think of but he can't raise enough money. He tells the druggist that his wife is dying and asks him to sell it to him cheaper or let him pay later. But the druggist says, "No, I discovered it and I deserve to make money from it". Later, Heinze get desperate, breaks in to the druggist store, and steals the drug for his wife."

Kohlberg's Level and Stages of Moral Development

Kohlberg constructed a theory of moral development that has 3 main levels with 2 stages at each of the level as shown in Table 10.1.

Level 1: Preconventional Morality

Morality at this stage is determined by the consequences of an action rather than by the inherent goodness or badness of an act. This level consists of 2 stages as shown in Figure 10.2.

That is, they reason that an act is moral if the consequence of obeying a rule results in their obtaining something positive. A child reasoning at this hedonistic stage may argue that Heinz was right in stealing the drug if he left a note promising to do a favour for the druggist.

Level 2: Conventional Morality

As egocentrism continues to decline, the child increasingly views moral issues from the perspective of others. Rather than viewing morality in terms of immediate concrete consequences, the individual now make moral decisions by considering factors of a less concrete and more social nature, such as the approval of others, family loyalty, obedience to the law, and social order. Individuals operating at the conventional level, have internalized the rules or, if you will, the "conventions" of society.

This level of moral reasoning consists of 2 stages as shown in Figure 10.3:

Level 3: Post Conventional Morality

At this level, individuals begin to focus on the principles that underlie these rules. Comparatively few people reach Kohlberg's third level of moral reasoning. This level is made up of 2 stages as shown in Figure 10.4:

Table 11.1: Levels and Stages in Kohlberg's Theory of Development

Level and Stage		*Description*
Level 1 Preconventional Reasoning		♦ The ethics of egocentricity. ♦ Typical of children up to about age 10. ♦ Called preconventional because young children don't really comprehend the rules set down by others. ♦ The consequences of the act determine if it is good or bad.
	Stage 1: Punishment-Obedience	♦ The ethics of "What's in it for me?"
	Stage 2: Market Exchange	♦ Obeying rules and exchanging favours are judged in terms of benefit to the person.
Level 2 Conventional Ethics		♦ The ethics of others. ♦ Typical of ten to twenty years olds. ♦ The names come from conformity to the rules and conventions of society.
	Stage 3: Interpersonal Harmony	♦ Sometimes called "Nice girl/Good boy" ♦ Ethical decisions are based on what pleases, helps, or is approved of others.
	Stage 4: Law and Order	♦ The ethics of order. ♦ Right is doing one's duty, obeying the law, and maintaining an orderly society.
Level 3 Postconventional Ethics		♦ The ethics of principle. ♦ Rarely reached before age twenty and only by a small segment of the population. ♦ Focuses on the principles underlying society's rules.
	Stage 5: Social Contract	♦ Rules are based on principles of justice and common good and are mutually agreed upon by members of society.
	Stage 6: Universal Principles	♦ Rarely encountered in life. ♦ Ethics determine by individual's conscience guided by the abstract principles of justice and equality.

Source: From Lawrence Kohlberg, 1984 in Tan *et al.* (2003) page 83.

Punishment Obedience Stage → Individuals reasoning in the punishment-obedience stage would say that if Ramesh caught stealing the drug, then he was wrong. However, if Ramesh was not caught stealing, then was right.

Market Exchange Stage → In the market-exchange stage, individuals are still driven by the consequences of an action when making decisions about morality, but are also focused on the idea of reciprocity.

Figure 10.2: Two Stages in Preconventional Morality

Interpersonal Harmony Stage → The key feature of the interpersonal harmony stage involves loyalty and gaining the approval of others, who may include family, peers and teachers. An individual at this stage may say that Ramesh was wrong because he did not get approval from the druggist to take his drug, however, another individual at this stage may say that Ramesh was right in stealing because he gained his dying wife's approval.

Law and Order Stage → Individuals in the law and order stage, base moral decision upon whether or not they are congruent with codified law. Individuals in this stage may argue that Ramesh was wrong to steal because stealing is against the law

Figure 10.3: Two Stages in Conventional Morality

Social Contract Stage → In this stage, individual conceptualizes rules as mutually agreed upon and based on principles of justice and the common good. That, is rules are not deemed moral because they are codified law; rather they are moral because they reflect the common good. Individuals in stage 5 may very well contend that Ramesh was right for stealing because his wife's right to life was more important than a law against stealing.

Universal Principles Stage → In the universal principle stage, individuals reason about moral issues by referring to universal abstract principles that transcend society's law. In fact, the specific laws have validity only to the degree that they are in accord with these abstract principles.

Figure 10.4: Two Stages in Post Conventional Morality

ERIKSON'S THEORY OF PSYCHOSOCIAL DEVELOPMENT

Erik Erikson (1902-1994) was a pupil of Sigmund Freud and the first child psychoanalyst in Boston. After extensive study of children from various cultural backgrounds and areas he began to compile this information to form his theories on development, personality and what forms our identity.

Erik Erikson's theory of 'psychosocial development' is one of the best-known theories in psychology. Erikson believed that personality develops in a series of stages and he describes the impact of social experience across the whole lifespan. One of the main elements of Erikson's psychosocial stage theory is the development of 'ego identity' that is the conscious sense of self that we develop through social interaction.

In each stage, the individual experiences a conflict that serves as a turning point in development. These conflicts are centered on either developing a psychological quality or failing to develop that quality. During these times, the potential for personal growth is high, but so is the potential for failure (Erikson, 1994). Erikson's theory breaks down psychosocial development into eight stages. These stages are delineated by age and characterized by a struggle or crisis that must be overcome in order to adapt and continue to develop.

The eight stages of Psychosocial Development are presented in the Figure 10.5.

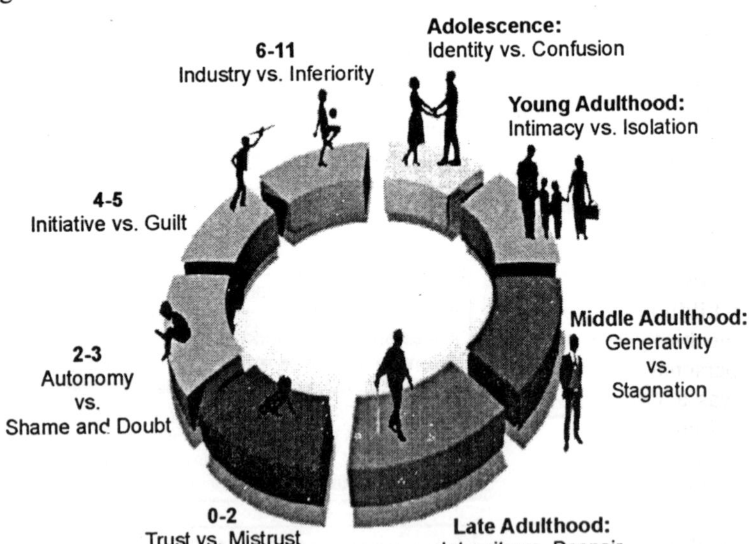

Figure 10.5: Eight Stages of Psychosocial Development

Here is a breakdown of the stages:

Psychosocial Stage 1: Trust vs. Mistrust (Birth-2 Years): The first stage of Erikson's theory of psychosocial development occurs between birth and two years of age. According to Erikson, this stage is the most important period in a person's life. An infant is entirely dependent upon his or her caregivers;

the quality of care plays an important role in the shaping of the infant's personality. The development of trust is based on the dependability and quality of the child's caregivers. During this stage, children learn if they can trust the people around them. Is there anyone to help when the baby cries? When the baby is frightened, is there anyone to comfort him/her? If these needs are consistently met, the child will learn that (s)he can trust the people who are caring for him/her. If these needs are not consistently met, the child will begin to mistrust the people around him. Successful development of trust is important for the individual feeling safe and secure in the world. Failure of developing trust will result in fear and a belief that the world is inconsistent and unpredictable. For healthy development and movement into the next stage, we require our physical and emotional needs to be consistently met.

The main highlights of Stage-1 are as follows:

- The first psychological challenge faced by a child involves developing a sense of trust in others. For the infant, this sense of trust develops if she is predictably cared for when she cries and is warmly treated by her primary caregivers. If an infant, instead, is cared for in unpredictable ways such as not being fed, diapered, or comforted when necessary, Erikson believed this infant would develop basic mistrust of others, which would lead to fear and suspicion.
- One implication for practice is for teachers to develop predictable, consistent classroom routines. It will make the students' feel the classroom is a safe place for them to study and make friends.
- Teachers must always show their genuine concern over student's best interest and make them feel that classroom is safe and loving place. Decorate the classroom with the students.
- Give opportunity for the students to speak in front of the class or write on the whiteboard.
- Give a clap when the student answer questions correctly.
- Classroom teacher must be friendly with the students and communicate with them often.

Psychosocial Stage 2: Autonomy vs. Shame and Doubt [Early Childhood (2 Years-3 Years)]: This stage occurs between the second and the third years of age and is focused on children developing a greater sense of personal control. Just like Freud, Erikson also believed that toilet training was a vital part of this process; however, Erikson's reasoning was quite different. Erikson believed that learning to control one's bodily functions is important for feeling in control and a sense of independence. Other important events are gaining more control over food choices, toy preferences and clothing selection. Children who successfully complete this stage feel secure and confident, while those who do not are left with a sense of inadequacy and self-doubt.

The main highlights of Stage-2 are as follows:

- At ages two and above, children want to do things on their own or act autonomously. Yet this need to become autonomous must be balanced by the reality of safety issues.

- For instance, while Erikson thought it was healthy to allow the two-year-olds to explore the streets alone, this exploration must be done in a constraint way such that the child is not hit by a car. Therefore, Erikson called for a delicate interplay between freedom and restraint.
- As for teachers, their role is to provide safe areas for physical as well as social exploration so that children can practice being autonomous.
- Several educational implications follow.
  - First, when teacher must impose restrictions, never humiliate a child either physically or verbally.
  - Second, provide young children with adequate opportunities to do things for themselves, no matter how messy it would be.
  - Third, set up discipline in which the same consequence is administered consistently each time a rule is broken. This gives the child a sense of a secure and ordered world.

Psychosocial Stage 3: Initiative vs. Guilt [Play Age (4-5 Years)]: This stage occurs during the preschool years, between the ages of four and five when children try their power and control through directing play and other social interactions. Children begin to exercise volition, develop independence and initiate activities. Children can assert control and power over the environment by taking initiative, facing challenges, planning processes and accomplishing tasks. Play and imagination have an important role at this stage. Children have their sense of initiative reinforced by being given the freedom and encouragement to play. During this stage caregivers should encourage exploration and help children make appropriate choices. Children who are successful at this stage feel capable but those who fail to acquire these skills are left with a sense of guilt, self-doubt, and lack of initiative. Success in this stage leads to a sense of purpose, while failure results in a sense of guilt.

The main highlights of Stage-3 are as follows:

- Erikson contends that children when face with new challenges, will want to explore and investigate. He termed this the development of a sense of initiative, whereby children begin to ask many questions about the world.
- The ever-present questions of "why" and "what" seem to engulf a child at this stage as do the inquisitive behaviours that often accompany taking initiative.
- For instance, children may ask question about and want to help with work in the kitchen. In situations in which a child is discouraged from taking the initiative, Erikson believed that the child would develop a sense of guilt regarding her natural tendency to explore and investigate.
- According to tan "A number of implications follow for teachers (Tan 2003: 94)".
  - First, praise children you work with for taking the initiative.
  - A second implication involves the use of developmentally appropriate curriculum in which students have the chance to develop the necessary muscular coordination needed to manipulate the toys and other objects.
  - A third implication is to provide this age group with plenty of opportunities to play.

Psychosocial Stage 4: Industry vs. Inferiority [School Age (6-11 Years)]: This stage occurs between the ages of six and eleven when children need to cope with new social and academic demands. School and social interaction play an important role in a child's life during this period when children become capable of performing increasingly complex tasks. Different kinds of activities at school are fundamental for developing skills and accomplishing results. Reading, writing, drawing, solving problems or social activities are tasks that children need praise and attention for performing successfully. This stage is vital in the development of self-confidence. Successful outcome of this period is the feeling of competence and belief in skills. Children who receive little or no encouragement from parents, teachers, or peers will doubt their abilities to be successful.

The main highlights of Stage-4 are as follows:

- The major psychological task in the fourth stage is the development of competence or industry. The term industry means in this stage children not only continues their interest in trying new things, but they will try to succeed in learning and gain recognition for producing things or good result.
- In this stage of development, which last throughout the elementary school years, children are faced with the challenges of producing good academic work related to reading, writing, and mathematical skills.
- Children also face the challenges to be competence in hobby, playing sports, maintaining a positive relationship with teachers, and developing friendship. Recent research has shown that social skills training as well as attention to social problem solving can be helpful in terms of developing social competence in forming friendships and developing social skills.
- Children, who leave the elementary years without this sense of industry, may feel they are failure at everything. So it is the responsibility of parents and teachers to help them to become academically and socially competence.

Psychosocial Stage 5: Identity vs. Confusion [Adolescence (12-18 Years)]: Identity versus confusion is the fifth stage of Erikson's psychosocial development theory. This stage occurs during adolescence when teens need to develop a sense of self and personal identity. During adolescence, children explore the world and develop their independence and a sense of self. During the transition from childhood to adulthood, teens feel confused or insecure about themselves and how they will be able to fit in to society. As they seek to establish a sense of self, they explore and try out different roles, activities and behaviours. This exploration is very important for forming a strong identity and developing a sense of direction in life. Successful outcome of this period is a strong sense of self and a feeling of independence and control for those who receive proper encouragement and reinforcement through personal exploration. Those who remain unsure of their beliefs and desires will feel insecure and confused about themselves and the future.

The main highlights of Stage-5 are as follows:

- Erikson's fifth stage of psychosocial development is for the secondary and post-secondary school students. The major psychological task is to gain self identity.

- In this stage, adolescents struggle to resolve the questions of "Who am I?" and "Who will I become". That is why they move increasingly from their parents to peers as a point of reference, they need to understand how they are both alike and at the same time uniquely different from everyone else.
- Physical appearance play important role in development of personal identity. For girls personal identity concerns including clothing, make-up, ways of walking and ways of dressing. Along with this search for ideal physical appearance is the advent of the personal fable and imagery audience.
- Personal fable is the self-generated, often romanticized story of one's personal destiny. The adolescent may develop an image of him-or-herself that pretends a destiny, a life story as a great hero, rock star, or the great reformer of the world's evils.
- The potential danger of this notion is that the adolescents think he is invincible and that despite the recognition that bad things happen to others, they will not happen to him. This notion which is not true and the adolescents will suffer the same consequences if they involve in risk taking behaviour.
- Imagery audience is part of adolescent egocentrism, implies that the adolescent assumes that others are focused upon and concerned about the same issues which he personally feels so important such as the ways of dressing.
- The adolescents also strive to find their own personalities. They need a figure or model to identify with. That's why the adolescents often imitate the attitudes and actions of others they admire.
- Adolescents also face the issues of sexual identity that is the adolescent searches for comfortable expressions of sexuality through friendship and dating.
- This in fact is the most difficult time in everyone's life. Teachers and parents have to be patience with the adolescents and guide them to cope effectively with the crises they are facing.
- Parents and teachers should give the adolescent opportunity to explore different jobs such as working temporarily in fast food restaurant, become the chef of a restaurant, work in a bank, work in a factory etc.

Psychosocial Stage 6: Intimacy vs. Isolation [Young Adulthood (18-35 Years)]: This is the sixth stage of Erikson's theory. This stage takes place during young adulthood between the ages of approximately 19 and 40. The major conflict of this stage centers on forming intimate, loving relationships with other people. Previous steps are really important for the success of this stage. A strong sense of personal identity is important for developing intimate relationships. A fully formed sense of self is essential for being able to form intimate relationships. Successful outcome of this stage leads to strong relationships, while failure results in loneliness and isolation. Those who fail to attain this skill will feel unproductive and uninvolved in the world.

At this stage of psychosocial development, a person begins to search for a partner. It becomes the main focus or new struggle once a person has resolved their adolescent identity crisis. The most important event in this stage is a romantic attachment or relationship. This is also the stage in which most start a family, though this has been pushed back somewhat in societal norms today.

The struggle of this stage is *Intimacy vs. Isolation.* If we are successful at this stage we find intimacy on a profound level. If we do not resolve this struggle, we may experience isolation from others. Our most significant relationships are with partners and friends in this stage.

The main highlights of Stage-6 are as follows:

- The major psychosocial crisis in Erikson's six stage is the development of a true and intimate heterosexual relationship. Erikson contends that in this stage individuals should be able to care for others without losing their self-identity.
- Erikson believes individual who never know this intimacy will develop a sense of isolation and tend to avoid relationships with others and make commitments.
- This six stages crises faced mostly by college and university students. One of the ways for the adolescents to face this crisis is to be active in sports, clubs and participate in community social works.

Psychosocial Stage 7: Generativity vs. Stagnation [Middle Adulthood (35-55 Years)]: Generativity versus stagnation is the seventh stage of the model. This stage takes place during middle adulthood between the ages of approximately 40 and 65. During this time, adults are intent on creating or nurturing things and living beings; often by having children or contributing to positive changes that benefits other people. Generativity is related to contribution and 'making your mark' on the world, through caring for others, creating things and accomplishing things that make the world better. During adulthood individuals' focus is on career and family. Those who are successful in this period will feel that they are contributing to the world by being active in their home and community. Those who fail to attain this skill will feel unproductive and uninvolved in the world.

Erikson believed that much of our lives are spent preparing for this stage. Once we have successfully resolved the conflict of young adulthood, we approach a new conflict in middle adulthood. At this stage, work is most crucial to our lives and we tend to be concerned with productivity as well as personal growth. The biggest fear of this stage is feeling meaningless or inactive. Also the stage of the "mid-life crisis," we tend to struggle to find our purpose or greater meaning in life. This struggle is known as *Generativity vs. Self-absorption.* If we become stagnant and fail to grow or resolve our mid-life crisis, it generally leads to self-absorption or self-indulgence.

The main highlights of Stage-7 are as follows:

- The major concern of the people at this age is on the caring and well-being of the next generation rather than being overly self-concerned.
- Most parents focused their energy and time on bringing up their children to be successful academically, socially and emotionally.
- Erikson argued that if a sense of generativity is not present, the individual would experience stagnation and become overly self- preoccupied.

Psychosocial Stage 8: Integrity vs. Despair [Late Adulthood (55-Death)]: This phase occurs during old age and is focused on reflecting back on life. Individuals in this period try to reconsider their accomplishments and qualify themselves. Those who feel proud of their accomplishments will feel a sense of integrity. Successfully completing this phase means looking back with few regrets and a general feeling of satisfaction. These individuals attain wisdom, even when confronting death. Those who are unsuccessful during this stage will feel that their life has been wasted and will experience many regrets. The individual will be left with feelings of bitterness and despair.

The main highlights of Stage-8 are as follows:

- In this last stage, individuals who have managed to adapt to the triumphs and tragedies of life are able to review their lives with a sense of satisfaction and acceptance which Erikson thought to be a prerequisite to achieving a sense of integrity at the end's of one's life. Others who have failed will be absorbed with despairing over missed opportunities, age and failure.
- For those who have achieved a sense of satisfaction in life, it can be well-pictured during celebration such as Hari Raya, Chinese New Year and Deepavali as those who will be surrounded by their children and grandchildren, and have happy moments together year by year until they deceased.

In Erikson's theory of psychosocial development, Erikson highlighted the importance of relationship with others in the formation of one's own identity. Erikson believed that personality develops through eight stages or critical periods of life as shown in Table 10.2.

Table 10.2: Stages in Erikson's Theory of Psychosocial Development

Stages	Ages	Description
Stages 1 Trust versus Mistrust.	Birth to two years	A child have to develop a sense of trust in others.
Stages 2 Autonomy versus Shame and Doubt.	Two to three years	The children want to do things autonomously.
Stages 3 Initiative versus Guilt.	Four to Five years	The children develop a sense of initiative, explore and investigate.
Stages 4 Industry versus Inferiority.	Six to Eleven years	The children go to school, learn reading, writing and counting; eager to produce good work.
Stages 5 Identity versus Role Confusion.	Twelve to Eighteen years	Adolescent have to develop self-identity. Look up for role model.
Stages 6 Intimacy versus Isolation.	Eighteen to Thirty five years	Adolescent try to develop true and intimate relationship with opposite sex friends.
Stages 7 Generativity versus Stagnation.	Thirty Five to Sixty Five years	Married couple taking good care and well-being of next generation.
Stages 8 Integrity versus Despair.	Over Sixty Five Years	Old couple review their life with a sense of satisfaction and acceptance. Their lives have been fruitful, achieve a sense of integrity.

He also contended that at each stage of life, an individual is confronted by a crisis. Erikson assume the personality develops in accordance to one's ability to interact with the environment and to resolve the crises experienced. The manner in which the crises are resolved will have a lasting effect on the person's view of him or herself and the surrounding world.

Chapter-11
Emotional Development

Human beings are endorsed by motives, and as rational beings, to certain extent we go about satisfying them in an intelligent way. But our life does not end with this, we are also emotional beings. Indeed most of our affairs of everyday life are tingled with feelings and emotions. Our finest achievements, miserable failures, our noble characters and ugly behaviours are all directed by emotions.

We feel excited when we pass our examination and jump out of joy. We shout when we get angry, we feel sorry at the death of our loved one. We tremble when we are afraid. Joy, sorrow, fear, sympathy, empathy, love and affection are all emotions which influence our life and behaviour. Life would be dreary without emotions and feelings. They add colour and spice to living. Proper control and expression of our emotions make our living pleasant, lack of control and improper expression leads to misery.

Our emotions play quite a significant role in guiding and directing our behaviour. Many times they seem to dominate us in such a way that we have no solution other than behaving as they want us to. On the other hand, if a person has no emotions in him, then he becomes crippled in term of living his life in a normal way. In this way, emotions play a key role in providing a particular direction to our behaviour and thus shaping our personality according to their development.

DEFINITIONS OF EMOTIONS

Etymologically, the word emotion is derived from the Latin word *'emovere'* which means *'to stir up'* or *'to excite'*. Emotion can thus be understood as an agitated or excited state of our mind and body. Taking clue from its derivation, various psychologists have tried to define the term 'emotion' in their own ways. Let us reproduce a few of such definitions:

1. **Woodworth (1945)** – "*Emotion is a 'moved' or 'stirred-up' state of an organism. It is a stirred-up state of feeling that is the way it appears to the individual himself. It is a disturbed muscular and glandular activity that is the way it appears to an external observer.*"

2. **Crow and Crow (1973)** – "*Emotion is an affective experience that accompanies generalised liner adjustment and mental and physiological stirred-up states in the individual and that shows itself in his overt behaviour.*"

3. **Charles G. Morris (1979)** – "*Emotion is a complex affective experience that involves diffuse physiological changes and can be expressed overtly in characteristic behaviour patterns.*"

4. **McDougall (1949)** – "*Emotion is an affective experience that one undergoes during an instinctive excitement. For example, when a child*

perceives a bull coming towards him (cognition) he experiences an affective experience in the form of the arousal of accompanied emotion of fear and consequently tries to run away (conative aspect of one's behaviour)."

5. According to Kimball Young, *"Emotion is the all around state of the organism marked by increased bodily activity and strong feelings directed to some subject."*

DEFINITION OF INSTINCT

The word instinct is derived from the Latin word "Instinctus" meaning to 'instigate' or 'to motivate'. Instincts are innate, original or inherited tendencies to act or to behave. These are inborn in nature but gain their expression in proper form from with the growth of the child.

According to C.W. Valentine, *"Instincts are innate impulse to act in a certain way fulfilling some biological purpose"*. B. Woodworth defined instincts as unlearned motives. Instincts are prime mover of action.

CLASSIFICATION OF INSTINCT

Freud classified instincts into-(a) Sex Instinct, (b) Eross or Life Instinct or Ego Instinct and (c) Thanatos or Death Instinct.

Thorndike mentioned about two categories of instincts-(a) Individual Instincts and (b) Social Instincts.

McDougall discovered 14 basic instincts and concluded that each and every emotion, whatever it may be, is the product of some instinctive behaviour. These instincts, with their associated emotions can be listed as follows:

Table 11.1: Human Instincts with their Associated Emotions

Sl. No.	*Instinct*	*Emotion accompanying it*
1.	Flight or escape	Fear
2.	Pugnacity or combat	Anger
3.	Repulsion	Disgust
4.	Curiosity	Wonder
5.	Parental	Tender emotion, love
6.	Appeal	Distress
7.	Construction	Feeling of creativeness
8.	Acquisition	Feeling of ownership
9.	Gregariousness	Feeling of loneliness
10.	Sex, mating	Lust
11.	Self-assertion	Positive self-feeling or elation
12.	Submission	Negative self-feeling
13.	Food-seeking	Appetite
14.	Laughter	Amusement

COMPONENTS OF EMOTIONS

There are three components of emotions:

Cognition: This component serves primarily to influence an evaluation of given situation, prompting us to become emotional in one way or another, or not at all.

Feeling: In daily life we think of feelings. The feelings are most readily evident changes in an aroused person. Feelings have immediate motivational significance. They give rise to many physiological processes in the cardiovascular system and produce increased blood pressure, changes in sexual urge. They also stimulate nervous system and prompt widespread electrochemical activities.

Behaviour: The behavioural component involves facial, postural, gestures and vocal responses.

CHARACTERISTICS OF EMOTIONS

The characteristics of emotions are as follows:

- Emotional Experiences are Associated with Some Instincts or Biological Drives: Every emotional experience is associated with one or the other innate instinct. An emotion is aroused under the current or influence of an instinctive excitement. One can experience emotion of anger only after riding on the instinctive waves of pugnacity or combat.
- Emotions are the Product of Perception: Perception of a proper stimulus (object or situation) is needed to start an emotional experience. The organic changes within the body (favourable or unfavourable) then, may intensify the emotional experience.
- The Core of an Emotion is Feeling: Actually every emotional experience, whatever it may be, involves feeling – a sense of response aroused in the heart.
- Emotions are prevalent in every living organism.
- They are present at all stages of development and can be aroused in young as well as in old.
- Emotions are individualistic and they differ from person to person.
- Same emotion can be aroused by a number of different stimuli—objects or situations.
- Emotions rise abruptly but subside slowly. An emotion once aroused, tends to persist and leave behind, an emotional mood.
- Emotions have the quality of displacement. The anger aroused on account of one stimulus gets transferred to another situation. The anger resulting from being rebuked by the boss gets transferred to beating the children at home.
- One emotion can give birth to a number of similar emotions.
- There is a negative correlation between the upsurge of emotions and intelligence. Reasoning and sharp intellect can check sudden upsurge of emotions. Also, under emotional experiences, the reasoning and thinking powers are decreased.

MEANING OF EMOTIONAL DEVELOPMENT

The word emotion has been taken from Latin word *"emovere"* which means to stir up or agitate or to excite. One of the basic aims of education is to develop a sound and stable personality of an individual in order to enable him or her to live healthy social life. In this regard, emotional development plays vital role in the social life of a person. A person with emotional soundness proves to be useful and lead a happy and peaceful life as against a person who is emotionally disturbed. So, education by teachers, educators, parents and guardians of a child, enables students to become emotionally sound and productive individuals for a society.

Adolescents are faced with the large task of establishing a sense of identity. The new cognitive skills of maturing adolescents give them the ability to reflect on who they are and what makes them unique. Identity is made up of two components:

- **Self-concept:** The set of beliefs about oneself, including attributes, roles, goals, interests, values and religious or political beliefs
- **Self-esteem:** How one feels about one's self-concept

The process of developing a sense of identity involves experimenting with different ways of appearing, sounding and behaving. Each adolescent will approach this exploration in his or her own unique way. Adolescents must also develop relationship skills that allow them to get along well with others and to make friends. The specific skills that they need to master as part of their emotional development include:

- Recognizing and managing emotions.
- Developing empathy.
- Learning to resolve conflict constructively.
- Developing a cooperative spirit.

CHARACTERISTICS OF EMOTIONS AT VARIOUS STAGES OF DEVELOPMENT

Characteristics of emotion differ during various stages of development-childhood, adolescence and adulthood.

Childhood Emotion

- Childhood emotions are brief, it lasts for short time.
- There are intense, sudden outbursts are rotted, i.c. a child ways bitterly, in anger he loses control over himself.
- These are transitory i.e. rapid shift from one emotion to another. E.g. from laughter to tears, from anger to smiles, from jealousy to affection.
- Theses appear frequently.
- Symptoms like tension, restlessness, nail biting, thumb sucking, day dreaming and speech difficulties may develop due to childhood conditional disturbance.
- They are very innocent in nature and do not know the art of hiding their feelings and emotions.

Adolescent Emotions

Adolescence is an age of emotional upheavals. There is no mental peace, no serenity of mind for him. It is termed as a period of emotional storm and stress. The emotional characteristics of adolescent emotions are as follows:

- Heightening of emotions due to physical and sexual changes.
- Variations in emotional moods.

- Outbursts of temper, tension and anxiety.
- Capacity to share his/her emotional feelings with others of his peer group.
- Increase in fellow feeling and entering into friendship.
- Emotional patterns like joy, love, jealousy, fear. Worry. Envy etc. common among adolescents.

Adulthood Emotions

In case of adults, emotional development reaches its maturity. At this stage, various emotions like anger, hatred, discrimination, pleasure etc. can be distinctly seen in an individual. Manifestation of emotion is relatively refined and all the emotional reactions are influenced by ideas, values, desires and norms of the society.

FACTORS INFLUENCING EMOTIONAL DEVELOPMENT

Emotional development of an individual is influenced by a number of factors. These factors are as follows:

Health and Physical Development of an Individual: There is a positive correlation between health and physical development and emotional development. Any deficiency in health and physical development- internal or external leads to emotional disturbance. Children who are weak in structure or who suffer occasional illness are more emotionally upset and unstable than children whose health is better. Any abnormal increase or decrease in the normal functioning of the glands creates obstacles in the proper emotional development.

Intelligence and Emotional Development: There is less emotional control, on the average, among those of the lower intellectual level than among children of the same group who are bright. An intelligent person, with his thinking and reasoning powers, is in a better position to exercise control over his emotions.

Family Environment and Emotional Development: A cordial environment i.e. healthy relationship between the parents is very conducive to the emotional development of the child. The treatment meted out to the child by the parents and other members of the family influences his emotional development. The order of birth (whether the first or the younger child), sex (son or daughter), size of the family, socio-economic status of the family, discipline in the family, the parental attitude towards the child (pampered, overprotected or neglected)—all are important factors in the emotional development of the child.

School Environment: The attitude of the teachers, school discipline, academic facilities available, physical facilities, methods of teaching, co-curricular activities, etc. all influence emotional development of children.

Peer Group Relations and Emotional Development: The influence of the classmates and other members of the group affect emotional development.

Neighbourhood, Community and Society's Environment and Emotional Development: A child lives in the society and he picks up so many traits of his emotional behaviour from his surroundings.

THE CHARACTERISTICS OF AN EMOTIONALLY MATURED PERSON

An emotionally matured person demonstrates the following traits and characteristics in his behaviour:

1. Almost all the emotions can be distinctly seen in him and their pattern of expression can be easily recognised.
2. Manifestation of emotions is very much refined. Usually he expresses his emotions in a socially desirable way.
3. He is able to exercise control over his emotions. Sudden inappropriate emotional outbursts are rarely found in him. He is able to hide his feelings and check his emotional tide.
4. The person perceives things in their real perspective. He is not a day dreamer and does not possess the desire to run away from realities.
5. His intellectual powers like thinking and reasoning are properly exercised by him in making any decision. He is guided more by his intellect than his emotions.
6. He does not possess the habit of rationalization i.e. he never argues in defence of his undesirable or improper conduct. Also, he never shifts the responsibility of his mistakes on others. He is always honest in his behaviour.
7. He possesses adequate self-concept and self-respect. He never likes to do things or show such behaviour that can injure his self-respect and is adverse to his ideals.
8. He is not confined to himself. He thinks about others and is keen to maintain social relationships. He never engages himself in such behaviour as is antisocial and can result in social conflicts and strain his social relationships.
9. He can exercise his emotions at a proper time in a proper place. If, there is a danger to his self-prestige or if anyone is in distress, he can rise to the occasion by exercising his emotion of anger. But, if he commits a mistake and is rebuked, he is equally able to check his emotion of anger. Matured emotional behaviour is characterised by greater stability. A person having such maturity does not sudden shift from one emotion to another.

EDUCATIONAL IMPLICATIONS OF INSTINCTS

The educational importance of instincts are as follows:

Instinct	Educational Importance
Curiosity	Towards new knowledge, new ideas etc.
Escape	avoiding punishments or criticism.
Construction	Creative work, learning by doing, art and craft and technical education.
Sex Instincts	Proper sex education may give the scientific knowledge.
Acquisition	Collection of materials, knowledge and social qualities.
Social Instinct	Group feeling and group activities of various kinds.

EDUCATIONAL IMPLICATIONS OF EMOTION

The knowledge of emotion is closely related to the development of educational programme which are discussed as follows:

- Teacher himself should be emotionally mature, should act as a model, and should be a source of inspiration so that the students can copy him.
- Teacher should be sympathetic and patient towards the emotional problems of the students. He should be a very good listener.
- Whenever possible, children should be encouraged to express their emotions. They should find pleasure in day to day activities.
- Counselling can be a great help in matters or cases of acute emotional stress.
- Teachers should not expect much from the students. Aspiration level should be fixed only after consideration of students optimum level.
- Teachers should give the students enough independence. He should have full control over his emotions as well as to can help his students to gain control over their emotional outbursts.
- Teachers should be able to utilize the good effects of emotions because these may act as sources of enjoyment, motivation and strength.
- Teacher should try to get rid of the bad effects of emotions i.e. physiological stress which may damage physical health as well as mental health. It affects the normal personality of an individual and ultimately hampers his normal life.
- Teacher should be aware about various causes of emotional problems like-
  - ➢ Unfavourable relation in home or school.
  - ➢ High social expectations.
  - ➢ School failures or vocational problems.
  - ➢ Conflicts in social or religious beliefs and values.
  - ➢ Difficulty in adjustment to the member of opposite sex.
- Teacher should be aware of various criteria of emotional maturity like-
  - ➢ Self-understanding or adequate self-concept.
  - ➢ Development of one's potentialities to the fullest extent.
  - ➢ Facing the reality without undue stress.
  - ➢ Enjoying perfect social relationship.
  - ➢ Realistic hopes and aspiration.

ROLE OF THE SCHOOL AND THE TEACHER IN EMOTIONAL DEVELOPMENT OF THE CHILD

Following are the role of the schools for healthy emotional development of the children:

Providing Emotional Security: When the child enters the school for the first time, he finds quite a new world from him over there. He was just like a prince in the domain of his home. He likes and dislikes had great significance. He felt himself secure physically as well as emotionally. He had a sense of belongingness and his feeling of self-assertion was also satisfied adequately. But, everything is changed in the school. He has little significance and voice in the matters over there to start with. All the other children appear to him well knit and well adjusted in their own groups while he stands aloof. Sometimes, he is ridiculed by the fellow students. All these things make him very uneasy emotionally. If the teacher is also indifferent to him or he proves to be a bit hard for him, he loses his emotional balance. The teacher should be very careful of this situation. He should try to make the shift from home to school very agreeable for the new-comers. He should see that the new-comer may not feel the change adversely. There may be a welcome committee comprising some pupils under the guidance of a teacher to help the new-comers in desirable adjustment.

Equal Treatment Irrespective of Income: Poverty is not a bad thing in itself but sometimes it happens to be the cause of emotional disturbance, for some pupils in certain situations. At home, the poor child was quite contended and happy in his limited world. But, when poor children come across rich ones in the school, they find colossal differences between themselves and their rich classmates as regards their clothes, their modes of life, their meals and pocket allowances. Some of them may develop jealousy, worry and inferiority complex, if they cannot make proper adjustment with hard realities. Sometimes, the teachers aggravate the situation when they happen to be quite partial and do not treat the poor children at par with the rich ones. Heavy financial demands my also disturb the poor children emotionally, as they are often unable to meet the same easily.

The School is responsible to the poor students as much as to the rich ones. Resources of poor students should be studied individually and effort should be made to meet their monetary needs in connection with their education. Simple living should be a guiding principle in all the educational institutions.

Dynamic Methods of Teaching: Faulty methods of teaching do not develop motivation in the children. Therefore, lessons become drudgery. The children begin to hate the very process of education. There is always tension in their minds. Learning is no more a joyful activity from them. The improvement of the methods of teaching can go a long way in bringing back emotional security for many children. Educational work can easily be turned into play and then it will be interesting, joyful and at the same time more instructive.

Role of Love in Schools: In most of the traditional schools, teaching is based on the emotion of fear. Children know that they will be canned, if they are not successful in studies. They get heavy home task which is often impossible to complete without help and guidance which is not always available at home. They sleep at night with the dreams of canes. They wake up in the morning with fear and constant worry. Under such circumstances, emotional tranquillity is hardly possible. There is a famous saying. *"Love the child and the child will love you. Hate the child and he will hate you."* Love should be the basis of all work.

Balanced Emotional Behaviour of the Teacher: Some teachers themselves need emotional stability. Emotionally unbalanced teachers prove contagious for the innocent children. They themselves become a prey to inferiority complex, persistent worries or over-excited emotions. They are generally irritable and provocative. For the balanced emotional development of children, teachers themselves should be emotionally developed.

Creative and Democratic Concept of Discipline: Traditional methods of discipline are faulty. Sometimes schools are just like jails and some teachers, like jailors. Such discipline is negative. It may serve the purpose superficially but in reality the things are far from being satisfactory. There should be positive devices of discipline. Discipline should be creative. Children should be made responsible from handling their own affairs as far as it is convenient.

Healthy Physical Conditions in the Schools: Poor physical conditions in the school bring fatigue and boredom to the children. They are very soon fed up with the school and its activities. Lack of recreational activities is also responsible for emotional disturbance. The school authorities should be careful in this respect also.

Due Regard to Individual Differences: All children differ mentally, emotionally and physically. But, we provided little individual attention to the children in schools. Some of them are backward in studies, while some of them are very superior. But, they are dragged on the same lines. The backward lag behind still more and result in emotional disturbance. We must do something to help unfortunate ones.

Provision of Co-curricular Activities: All the children and especially adolescents need provision for the expression of their pent-up emotions and for redirection of their emotional behaviour. In the absence of such provision, emotional stability is not possible. Varied co-curricular activities can solve this problem quite satisfactorily.

Provision of Sex Education: During adolescent period, lack of information about sex, causes emotional disturbance. Teacher should provide necessary information about the sex matters and problems. There should be no shyness and should be done seriously.

Continuous Evaluation: The present system of examination is faculty. Chance factor counts much in this system. It does not measure the all-round development of the child and causes disturbance. Evaluation system should be made continuous, comprehensive and objective.

Rich and Varied Curriculum: The curriculum in schools does not relate to the real life of children. Learning in schools is unrelated to the modern needs of children. It is not according to the requirements of the society and hence emotional disturbance is created among students. Curriculum must be activity-based and need-based.

Chapter-12
Social Development

MEANING OF SOCIAL DEVELOPMENT

Social development implies the development of an individual in such a way, as he becomes a useful member of society or the group to which he belongs. He conforms to the norms of the group of the society to which he belongs. An individual becomes a human being only as a member of the society. By nature, he cannot live alone in isolation. He is compelled by biological, psychological and social needs to live in a group or society. Each of us is largely a social product. The Process of the development of such qualities which bring desirable changes in the social behaviour is referred to as social development or socialization of the child.

Social development involves learning the values, knowledge and skills that enable children to relate to others effectively and to contribute in positive ways to family, school and the community. This kind of learning is passed on to children directly by those who care for and teach them, as well as indirectly through social relationships within the family or with friends, and through children's participation in the culture around them. Through their relationships with others and their growing awareness of social values and expectations, children build a sense of who they are and of the social roles available to them. As children develop socially, they both respond to the in?uences around them and play an active part in shaping their relationships.

CONCEPT OF SOCIAL DEVELOPMENT

A child is not born social. He learns to be social. A socially mature child can adjust well with others, make actions which are beneficial both to himself and to the society (Leeladevi, 1975), will trust his classmates, solve interpersonal problems in an adaptive way and earn higher grades (Wentzel, 1991).

Definitions of Social Development

Various thinkers have tried to define social development in the following ways:

1. Freeman and Showel (1940) write, *"Social development is the process of learning to conform to group standards".*
2. L.D. Crow and A. Crow (1944) write, *"Social development means acquisition or the ability to behave in accordance with social expectations."*
3. Herbart Sorenson (1948) thinks, *"By social growth and development, we mean increasing ability to get along well with oneself and others."*
4. James Drever (1952) states, *"Socialization (social development) is a process by which the individual is adapted to his social environment (by*

attaining social conformity) and becomes a recognised, cooperating and efficient member of it."

5. E.B. Hurlock (1956) notes, *"Social development means the attaining of maturity of social setting."*
6. H.E. Garret (1968) is of the view that *"Socialization or social development is the process whereby the biological individual is converted into a human person."*
7. In the views of Shamsuddin (1971) *"the child's reaction and gradual adjustment to changing environments are known as social development."*
8. Leeladevi (1975) defined social development as *"an organized all-round development of a person directed towards his adjustment to social groups."*
9. According to Jupe *et al.* (1985), *"social development is the process of growing up to take one's full place in the society."*
10. Chaube (1996), *"Social development means the ability to behave properly with others and capability of standing on one's own legs."*
11. According to Kuppuswamy (1974), *"Social development is the process by which the child learns to interact with the expectations and obligations of various groups."*
12. To Skinner (1996) social development can be defined as *"the progressive improvement, through directed activity of the individual in the comprehension of the social heritage and the formation of flexible conduct patterns of reasonable conformity with his heritage."*

CHARACTERISTICS OF SOCIAL DEVELOPMENT

The following are the main characteristics of social development:

- Social development beings with the infant's first contact with other people.
- Social development continues throughout life.
- Social development is the net result of the child's constant interaction with his social environment.
- Social development helps in learning and acquiring social qualities of character.
- Social development enables the child to adjust himself to his social environment and to maintain social relationships.

ASPECTS OF SOCIAL DEVELOPMENT

Two aspects of social development are as under:

Socialization: Socialization is a process where an individual becomes a functioning member of the group, acting according to its standards, observing its traditions and adjusting himself to social situation. He learns to control himself in the interest of society and realizes his duties and responsibilities towards them.

Social Horizon: The individual mixes with increasingly large group members of the society. He learns to adjust with other members of the groups. He develops friendships, sense of competition, group loyalties, social perception, belongingness and social acceptance.

STAGES OF SOCIAL DEVELOPMENT

The stages of social development are as follows:

Pre-social Behaviour: The behaviour of human infant from birth to first few months when he/she is self-centered and responds to intense stimuli like loud noises, bright light, strong touch etc.

Beginning of Social Behaviour: From 5th/6th months, child reacts differently to smiling and scolding, differentiate between family members and strangers.

Imitation: By 8th/9th months, child tries to initiate speech and gestures.

Appearance of Fear, Shyness, Uncertainty: By 1 year, the child responds adversely to strangers by crying and cooperates with those familiar to him.

Social Differentiation: At about 1.5 year, the child shows affection for adults and children. Various emotions like fera, anger, jealousy etc. is differentiated.

Period of Solitary Play: Before 2 years, the child plays alone with toys, with increasing age, he desires to play with other children.

Period of Negativism and Fighting: At about 2 years of age, the child rebels against authority, at 5, fighting is less, friendship strong.

Period of Unbound Curiosity: At 5 years, child becomes imaginative and curious to know various things.

Period of Social Adjustment: The school is like a social home to the child. At this stage, his social development is influenced by school environment, teachers and school companions.

Gang Age: By 6-7 years, the child plays in small groups by 11-12 years, the child takes part in team games and his group becomes important during this period.

Period of Sex Cleavages: In early childhood both sexes play together up to 8-10 years. They refuse to play together till puberty.

FACTORS RELATED TO SOCIAL DEVELOPMENT OF ADOLESCENTS

The following factors related to the social development of adolescents must be kept in mind:

Adolescent Identity Exploration: Adolescence is the period of life between the onset of puberty and the full commitment to an adult social role. This period of life is known for the formation of personal and social identity. Like toddlers, adolescents must explore, test limits, become autonomous, and commit to an identity, or sense of self. Different roles, behaviours, and ideologies must be tried out to select an identity. Role confusion and inability to choose vocation can result from a failure to achieve a sense of identity.

Egocentrism in adolescents is a self-conscious desire to feel important in peer groups and receive social acceptance. Since choices made during adolescence can influence later life, high levels of self-awareness and self-control in mid-adolescence will lead to better decisions during the transition to adulthood. Three general approaches to understanding identity development include *self concept, sense of identity,* and *self-esteem.*

Self Concept: Early in adolescence, cognitive developments result in greater self-awareness. This leads to greater awareness of others, and their thoughts and judgments. Adolescents also develop the ability to think about abstract, future possibilities and the ability to consider multiple possibilities at once.

Adolescents can conceptualize multiple 'possible selves' they could become as well as long-term possibilities and consequences of their choices. Differentiation occurs as an adolescent recognizes and distinguishes the contextual influences on his/her own behaviour and the perceptions of others. Adolescents can begin to qualify their traits when asked to describe themselves. Differentiation becomes fully developed by mid-adolescence.

The recognition of inconsistent content in the self-concept is a common source of distress in these years, but this distress may benefit adolescents by encouraging further structural development.

Sense of Identity: Unlike the conflicting aspects of self-concept, identity represents a coherent sense of self that is stable across circumstances and includes past experiences and future goals. Erik Erikson determined that 'identity achievement' resolved the identity crisis in which adolescents must explore different possibilities and integrate different parts of themselves before committing to their chosen identity. Adolescents begin by defining themselves based on their crowd membership, and then hone in on a personal identity. Media eventually extends this by exposing adolescents to the self-image factor.

Self Esteem: Self-esteem is one's thoughts and feelings about one's self-concept and identity. Children who are raised female are often taught that their sense of self is highly linked to their relationships with others; therefore many adolescent girls enjoy high self-esteem when engaged in supportive relationships with friends. The most important function of friendship here is having someone who can provide social and moral support. Children who are raised as male, on the other hand, are often taught to value such things as autonomy and independence; therefore many adolescent boys are more concerned with establishing and asserting their independence and defining their relation to authority. High self-esteem is often derived from their ability to successfully influence their friends.

Social Influences: Sociocultural influences are playing a different role identity formation now than they have in the past. Sociocultural influences on adolescents traditionally appeared in the form of resources available to explore identity choices as well as options for personal commitments. This influence is becoming less significant today due to the growing acceptance of identity options that were once less popular. The changing sociocultural situation is forcing individuals to develop a unique identity based on their own aspirations.

The type of relationship that adolescents have with their parents has a significant role in identity formation. When a solid and positive relationship exists, adolescents are more likely to feel freedom in exploring identity options. However, when the relationship is not as close or supportive, and the adolescent fears rejection from the parent, he/she is more likely to feel less confident in forming a separate, personal identity.

Adolescents that have a post-secondary education tend to make more concrete goals and stable occupational commitments. Academic work has an impact on identity and can be beneficial for an individual. Adolescents receive education on different approaches and paths to take in the process of identity formation.

Psychological Changes: Changes in the levels of the neurotransmitters dopamine and serotonin in the limbic system make adolescents more emotional than younger children and adults, and more sensitive to rewards and stress. Other cognitive development have an impact on identity formation as well. When adolescents are able to think abstractly and reason logically, they have an easier time exploring and contemplating possible identities. When an adolescent has advanced cognitive development and maturity, he/she tends to resolve identity issues more easily than peers who are less cognitively developed. When identity issues are solved more quickly, time and effort is freed up for developing that chosen identity. Having a solid identity earlier is a preferred situation, and is one of the first steps in forming the desired life and goals of an adolescent individual.

FACTORS INFLUENCING SOCIAL DEVELOPMENT OF THE CHILDREN

Below are the main factors that influence the social development of the children:

Health and Physique: Good health helps in social development and can maintain proper social relationship.

Emotional Development: Good emotional development favours social development. Emotionally balanced persons are cheerful and forms healthy social personality.

Intellectual Development: More intelligent the persons, he is more socially adjustable.

Sex: Sex differences influence social attitudes. Girls are more sympathetic than boys.

Culture: Existing customs, traditions, values of home and society influences the child's social development.

Economic Condition: Often children of lower socio-economic groups develop inferiority complex as their legitimate needs are not met with and this hampers their social development.

Language: Language helps to develop social concepts of complex and abstract nature. It is through language that social contracts are established with the outside world.

Family: Character and behaviour of the person is influenced by behaviour and character of his family members.

Neighbours: Habits, interests, attitudes and behaviour patterns of neighbours influence social development of the child.

School: School plays a vital role in social development next to family.

Playmates and Friends: One's beliefs, attitudes, interests and habits are influenced by his playmates and companions. He develops the qualities of leadership, self-confidence in him.

Community: Community influences on the child in parks, play grounds, museums and libraries and it helps children to active personal security, adequacy and progress towards independence.

KEY POINTS FOR SUPPORTING CHILDREN'S SOCIAL DEVELOPMENT

Children's earliest and most extensive learning about social relationships occurs in the family. Parents and teachers can support positive social development when they model respect and consideration and encourage children to be similarly respectful in all their relationships. Following point should be remembered:

- Provide care and support by tuning into children's needs. Show you are willing to listen and take children's feelings into consideration.
- Help children to develop social skills by providing coaching and teaching them to think through and solve the day-to-day social difficulties they encounter. Supervise and support children's social activities without taking over.
- Ask questions that encourage children to put themselves in someone else's shoes. Questions like "How would you feel if ...?" help children learn skills for perspective-taking. Asking questions in a supportive way helps children to think through situations and encourages them to take others' feelings and perspectives into account.
- Discuss moral issues with children and encourage them to state their opinions and reasons.

ROLE OF THE TEACHER IN THE SOCIAL DEVELOPMENT OF THE CHILD

A teacher can play a vital role in the social development of the child under his charge. He exerts a great influence upon the development of the personality of the child. Following are the important suggestions to teachers for the social development of the child:

1. Teachers and parents may encourage the children to mix in inter-caste rather than intra-caste and inter-regional rather than intra-regional groups.
2. The teachers and the parents should respect the personality of children.
3. The mechanism of praise and blame, reward and punishment should be carefully used to socialize the children.
4. Proper social education may be provided to parents, so that they understand the significance of the socialization of the children.
5. The teacher should demonstrate democratic outlook.
6. The teacher should refrain from projecting their class images on students. They should not show any discrimination. They must ensure a safe and healthy social environment in which the children may imbibe desirable values of freedom, equality, integrity, honesty, patriotism etc.
7. Community activities like camps, common meals, social service etc. should be frequently organized.
8. There should be a close cooperation between the teachers and parents on matters relating to the proper socialization of the children.
9. Various aspects of socialization, anxiety of children and juvenile delinquency may be discussed by the heads of schools, inspecting officers, teacher-educators and professional organizations in seminars or small forums.

10. Adequate stress may be laid on group activities.
11. Exhibitions on *"Know Our Country"* may be organized from time to time.
12. Stories depicting self-sacrifices made by great men for the cause of general good may be told to children, so that they are motivated to rise above petty gains and work for the betterment of the humanity.
13. With proper guidance and responsibilities, the student's council can build up a sense of shared responsibility among children.
14. A proper socialization of children very much necessitates that the ideology of the common school system is allowed to function in letter and spirit in India.
15. Children may be taken from time to time to public places like museums, courts, places of historical importance etc.
16. People engaged in different economic activities or vocations may be invited to school for giving a faithful description of what they do and how useful their work is to the nation. This will enable the children to be acquainted with those around them in the society. This will also develop vocational socialization in children.
17. Work experience should be introduced in schools. This will enable the children to have first hand experiences of the activities pursued in farms and factories.
18. Children should be acquainted with the social events like the celebration of the birthdays of leaders.
19. The school or college programme should be full of numerous co-curricular and curricular activities in which children meet, cooperate and learn from each other's personalities.
20. Children should be told about the socially accepted institutions in their society.
21. The introduction of common school dress, common lunch etc. in the schools and the colleges will prevent children of poor and lower middle classes from suffering due to the inflated ego of the children of the well-to-do families.

EDUCATIONAL IMPLICATIONS OF SOCIAL DEVELOPMENT

A famous French Socialist Emile Durkheim writes- *"Education is the influence exercised by adult generations on those that are not yet ready for social life. Its object is to arouse and to develop in the child a certain number of physical, intellectual and moral traits that are demanded of him by both the political society as a whole and the special milieu for which he is specially destined, more briefly, education is a socialization of the young generation. Education is the means by which every society prepares, within their children, the essential conditions of its very existence. It is idle to think that we can rear our children as we wish. There are customs which we are bound to conform: if we flout them too severely, they take their vengeance on our children."*

Chapter-13
Parenting Styles or Child Rearing Practices

MEANING OF PARENTING OR CHILD REARING

Parenting or child rearing is the process of promoting and supporting the physical, emotional, social, financial and intellectual development of a child from infancy to adulthood. Parenting refers to the aspects of raising a child aside from the biological relationship. The most common caretaker in parenting is the biological parent(s) of the child, although others may be an older sibling, a grandparent, a legal guardian, aunt, uncle or other family member or a family friend. Governments and society may have a role in child-rearing as well. In many cases, orphaned or abandoned children receive parental care from non-parent blood relations. Others may be adopted, raised in foster care, or placed in an orphanage. Parenting skills vary, and a parent with good parenting skills may be referred to as a *good parent.*

The practices or style adopted by the parents in rearing their children are quite unique in their nature and are largely determined by the factors like:

- influence of one's own parents and culture i.e. they learn (copy or select) rearing practices from their own parents and culture in which they grow and develop
- temperaments of the children
- their own temperaments
- the circumstances and environment in which they have to rear their Children.

DEFINITIONS OF CHILD REARING

1. *The training or bringing up of child by parents or parent-substitutes. It is used also for child rearing practices in different societies, at different economic levels, in different ethnic groups, etc.*

2. According to Merriam-Webster Learner's Dictionary, child rearing is defined as, *"The process of taking care of and raising children."*

So, all those practices which parents use to raise their children, to develop their personality and to make them familiar with society are called child rearing practices. The UN Convention on the Rights of the Child (CRC) states that the family has the key responsibility to ensure the fundamental rights of children as it is the primary setting within which children are cared for and parented and where first significant relationships develop and the foundations of their development take place.

MEANING OF PARENTING PRACTICE OR CHILD REARING PRACTICES

A parenting practice is a specific behaviour that a parent uses in raising a child. Parenting practices reflect the cultural understanding of children. Child rearing practices are a form of socialization process through which the new members of society are being trained to learn about society, cope up with social issues and to behave in a specific manner with the members of society in order to become a useful member of society.

Parents use different practices to make their children familiar with the world. They treat their children according to their age, gender, beliefs, religion and culture. All those practices which are performed by the family to protect and socialize a person since his/her birth and even before birth are included in child rearing practices.

It is connected to the practices and styles of raising the children. Each parent raises their children differently from other parents – as long as the methods used are appropriate, loving and safe, this is good. Different cultures and countries approach raising children from different philosophies and beliefs. Some may focus on teaching children to be more independent while others tend to focus more on expressing their love for their children.

MEANING OF PARENTING OR CHILD REARING SKILLS

Parenting styles are only a small piece of what it takes to be a "good parent". Parenting takes a lot of skill and patience and is constant work and growth. Research shows that children benefit most when their parents:

- communicate honestly about events or discussions that have happened, and when parents explain clearly to children what happened and how they were involved if they were;
- stay consistent, as children need structure: parents who have regular routines benefits children incredibly;
- utilize resources available to them, reaching out into the community;
- take more interest in their child's educational needs and early development; and
- keep open communication and staying educated on what their child is learning and doing and how it is affecting them.

PARENTING OR CHILD REARING STYLES

Parenting style refers to the way in which parents choose to raise their children. The way that people parent is an important factor in their children's socio-emotional growth and development. In her research, Diana Baumrind (1966) found what she considered to be the two basic elements that help shape successful parenting: parental responsiveness and parental demandingness. Through her studies, Baumrind identified three initial parenting styles: *authoritative parenting, authoritarian parenting,* and *permissive parenting.* Maccoby and Martin (1983) later expanded upon Baumrind's three original parenting styles by adding the *uninvolved or neglectful* style, which has the most pervasive negative consequences across all domains. While not every parent falls neatly into one category, these parenting styles generally correspond with the type of discipline a parent chooses to use with his or her child or children.

A parenting style is a psychological construct representing standard strategies that parents use in their child rearing. The quality of parenting is far more essential than the quantity of time spent with the child. For instance, a parent can spend an entire afternoon with his or her child, yet the parent may be engaging in a different activity and not demonstrating enough interest towards the child. Parenting styles are the representation of how parents respond and demand to their children. Parenting practices are specific behaviours, while parenting styles represent broader patterns of parenting practices.

TYPES OF PARENTING STYLES OR CHILD REARING PRACTICES

In psychology today, there are four major recognized parenting styles: authoritative, neglectful, permissive and authoritarian. Each one carries different characteristics and brings about different reactions in the children which they are used on.

Authoritarian Parenting Style or Child Rearing Practice

In the authoritarian style, parents put a high value on conformity and obedience. The parents are often strict, tightly monitor their children, and express little warmth. These parents exhibit a large amount of control over their child's decisions and behaviour. Authoritarian parents set rigid rules with firm consequences; in contrast to the authoritative style, authoritarian parents probably would not relax bedtime rules during a vacation because they consider the rules to be set, and they expect obedience at all times.

In this style of parenting, children are expected to follow the strict rules established by the parents. Failure to follow such rules usually results in punishment. Authoritarian parents fail to explain the reasoning behind these rules. If asked to explain, the parent might simply reply, *"Because I said so."* These parents have high demands, but are not responsive to their children. According to Baumrind, these parents *"are obedience- and status-oriented, and expect their orders to be obeyed without explanation"* (1991).

Children who grow up in authoritarian homes often become anxious or withdrawn or suffer from self-esteem problems. Due to gender socialization, those raised as male may experience anger problems, while those raised as female may become dependent upon others for approval. Although these children may do poorly in school, they do not tend to engage in antisocial behaviour for fear of their parents' reaction. However, it is important to keep in mind cultural differences: different cultures respond better to different parenting styles than others

Influence of the Authoritarian Parenting Style or Child Rearing Practice on the Development of Children

Authoritarian child rearing practice or style of parenting is said to influence the development of the children in some of the following ways:

- They may become handicapped in taking their own decisions in solving their problems or planning and executing the tasks of their life as they have been reared in the circumstances where their work had been merely to follow and not to take initiative/decision by their own.
- Their intellectual, emotional and social development suffer a great set back

on account of being denied the needed essential opportunities and independent facilities for doing so in their early life by their authoritarian parents.

- Their instinctive and emotional energy does not find the suitable expression and outlet for the desired channelization, sublimation or catharsis in the environment surcharged with authoritarian code of conduct prescribed by their parents. As expected, the repressed wishes, unfulfilled desires and the uneasiness felt by the children in the slave like conditions prevailed in the authoritarian rearing, may force the children to develop serious behavioural and conduct problems. If the demands and descriptions are pushed too forcefully upon the children, it may either make them to seek withdrawal from the positive work and efforts for progress or burst into social deviant, rebellion or delinquents.
- Such type of parenting does not help the children to acquire needed social skills and competencies are for leading their life in a proper way. They can't learn and live with democratic principles and ways of life. The qualities of democratic living and good citizenship can hardly be developed among the children brought up in such authoritarian parenting style.

Authoritative Parenting

Like authoritarian parents, those with an authoritative parenting style establish rules and guidelines that their children are expected to follow. However, this parenting style is much more democratic. Authoritative parents are responsive to their children and willing to listen to questions. When children fail to meet the expectations, these parents are more nurturing and forgiving rather than punishing. Baumrind suggests that these parents "monitor and impart clear standards for their children's conduct. They are assertive, but not intrusive and restrictive. Their disciplinary methods are supportive, rather than punitive. They want their children to be assertive as well as socially responsible, and self-regulated as well as cooperative.

Authoritative parenting is generally regarded as the most successful approach to parenting because of its high level of involvement and balanced levels of control. Authoritative parents set realistic expectations and consistent limits for their children, and provide them with fair or natural consequences. Natural consequences are those that occur as a natural result of the child's behaviour (or lack of a particular behaviour), with no intervention required; for example, if a child touches a hot stove and is burned by the heat, the burn is a natural consequence. Authoritative parents express warmth and affection, listen to their child's point of view, and provide opportunities for independence. Parents set rules and explain the reasons behind them, and they are also flexible and willing to make exceptions to the rules in certain cases—for example, temporarily relaxing bedtime rules to allow for a nighttime swim during a family vacation.

Of the four parenting styles, the authoritative style is the one that is most encouraged in modern society. Children raised by authoritative parents tend to have high self-esteem and social skills and work well with others. However, effective parenting styles vary as a function of culture, and the authoritative style is not necessarily preferred or appropriate in all cultures.

Influence of the Authoritative Parenting Style or Child Rearing Practice on the Development of Children

This type of authoritative rearing practice or parenting style is supposed to carry the following positive and desirable effects on the proper development and progress of the developing children:

- It provides due encouragement for the children to grow and develop their capacities by providing them proper freedom and opportunities but in doing so it does not allow them to go out of track and still places needed limits and controls at their actions. Therefore, there are little chances for the developing children to get lost or de-railed in their developmental path.
- The children rearing so are found to be quite self-satisfied in terms of the fulfillment of their basic needs - physical, social and emotional. They know the ways of channelizing their instincts and emotions and developing their basic potentialities by their own independent efforts.
- They are found to be quite sincere to their duties and remain disciplined in life by observing self-restraint and are law-avoiding by nature. They are observed to feel obliged to their parents in providing them all needed for their proper growth and development with a proper check on their independent activities.

Indulgent/Permissive Parenting

Permissive parenting tends to be warm and loving but lacks follow-through on setting limits or rules. Permissive parents tend to be overindulgent, make few demands, rarely use punishment, and allow their children to make their own decisions, regardless of the consequences. They tend to be very nurturing and loving and may play the role of friend rather than parent. These parents might be caught up in their own lives and therefore inattentive (although not neglectful) and exhibit little control over their children.

Permissive parents, sometimes referred to as indulgent parents, have very few demands to make of their children. These parents rarely discipline their children because they have relatively low expectations of maturity and self-control. According to Baumrind, permissive parents *"are more responsive than they are demanding. They are nontraditional and lenient, do not require mature behaviour, allow considerable self-regulation, and avoid confrontation" (1991)*. Permissive parents are generally nurturing and communicative with their children, often taking on the status of a friend more than that of a parent.

Children raised by permissive parents tend to lack self-discipline, and the permissive parenting style is negatively associated with grades. The permissive style may also contribute to other risky or impulsive behaviours such as alcohol abuse, risky sexual behaviour, especially among female children and increased display of disruptive behaviours by male children. However, there are some positive outcomes associated with children raised by permissive parents: many tend to have higher self-esteem, better social skills, and report lower levels of depression.

Influence of the Indulgent/Permissive Parenting Style or Child Rearing Practice on the Development of Children

Indulgent child rearing practice or parenting style may influence the development of the growing children in the ways outlined below:

- The children brought up in this environment never learn to control their own behaviour and always expect to get their way.
- They grow as more impulsive, unreasonable and immature children and may be observed to demonstrate socially irresponsible deviant and morally deficient behaviour in their teen and adult life in the shape of drug addiction heavy drinking delinquency or other anti-social behaviour.
- Brought up in excessive care and look after, they are hardly to learn independent ways of leading their own life. They depend on others to solve their problems and arrange for the needs of their life.
- The children reared in this set up may have all possibilities of de-figuring of spoiling their future prospectus. Most of them are seen to be turned as "Spoiled brats" or "Spoiled sweet" children proving a red signal for the welfare of their self and the society.

Uninvolved/Neglectful Parenting

An uninvolved parenting style is characterized by few demands, low responsiveness and little communication. While these parents fulfill the child's basic needs, they are generally detached from their child's life. In extreme cases, these parents may even reject or neglect the needs of their children.

With the uninvolved style of parenting, the parents are indifferent and sometimes referred to as neglectful. They don't respond to their child's needs and make relatively few demands. This could be because of severe depression, substance abuse, or other factors such as the parents' extreme focus on work. Neglectful parents may look to their children for support and guidance, and these children often end up "parenting their parents." These parents may provide for the child's basic needs, but little else; in more extreme forms of neglect, basic needs may not be cared for at all or children may be placed in harmful situations.

These children, much like those raised in permissive homes, tend to have myriad problems, but often the problems are often much more serious. Children raised in this parenting style are usually emotionally withdrawn, fearful, and anxious; perform poorly in school; and are at an increased risk of substance abuse.

*Influence of the Neglectful/*Uninvolved *Parenting Style or Child Rearing Practice on the Development of Children*

Neglectful child rearing practice or parenting style may influence the development of growing children in the ways outlined below.

- This type of set up is unable to fulfill the children's social and psychological needs. As a result, they may remain emotionally starved and socially undeveloped throughout their life.
- They may be grasped with the feelings of insecurity or unsafely as an

outcome of the neglectful or indifferent attitude shown by their parents in their upbringing and look after. It may create quite undesirable complexes in their minds many times coupled with the feelings of anxiety, depression or rebellion attitude on the part of the growing children.

- The neglectful rearing environment may provide the children defective model of social relationships and emotional bonds among the members of the family. It may take roots in their behaviour for being practice in the future life.
- The unbridled freedom, coupled with emotional insecurity and lack of support may push the children to adopt withdrawal or rebellion behaviour in their life style. As a result they may be found to suffer from shyness, social and emotional incompetencies delinquent and antisocial behaviour in their adolescence and adult life.

FACTORS THAT AFFECT PARENTING DECISIONS

Social class, wealth, culture and income have a very strong impact on what methods of child rearing are used by parents. Cultural values play a major role in how a parent raises their child. However, parenting is always evolving; as times change, cultural practices and social norms and traditions change.

In psychology, the parental investment theory suggests that basic differences between males and females in parental investment have great adaptive significance and lead to gender differences in mating propensities and preferences. A family's social class plays a large role in the opportunities and resources that will be made available to a child. Working-class children often grow up at a disadvantage with the schooling, communities, and parental attention made available to them compared to middle-class or upper-class upbringings. Also, lower working-class families do not get the kind of networking that the middle and upper classes do through helpful family members, friends, and community individuals and groups as well as various professionals or experts.

ROLE OF TEACHERS, PARENTS AND FAMILY IN CHILD REARING

Fathers are expected to be providers and protectors and take major decisions regarding children; whereas mothers are expected to comply more with the role of nurturing, caring and home maintenance.

Perceptions and Role of Mother in Child Rearing

- Taking care and satisfying regular needs
  - ➢ Takes good care of child
  - ➢ Cooks for and feeds child
  - ➢ Gives food on time and what child wants to eat
  - ➢ Bathes child
  - ➢ Fulfils his necessities
- Showing love and affection
- Showers love and expresses love
- Loves child
- Talks to child affectionately
- Feeds child with love and care

- Tells child nice stories at bedtime
- Providing comfort, sacrifice and place for sharing feelings
    - Mother is willing to do anything, any sacrifice for her children.
    - Wants to make the child happy
    - Comforts him when he cries
    - Does not leave him alone anywhere
    - Lets him accompany her wherever she goes
    - Understands the pain of her child
- Providing opportunities
- Sends child to school and tells them to study
- Treats girls and boys equally
- Lets child mix with friends and go out
- Lets child play
- Lets child participate in special occasions and competitions
- Providing support and appreciation
- Comforts him when someone says anything wrong to child
- Praises child when he does something good
- Providing information and guidance
- Gives child information about household matters and about culture
- Gives advice
- Teaches good things
- Stops child from doing anything bad which can harm him
- Forbids child to say bad things

Perceptions and Role of Father in Child Rearing

- Providing material and financial support:
    - Provides child with all the necessities
    - Buys new clothes (at the time of special occasions, especially during religious festivals such)
- Taking care of the development of the child and providing guidance:
    - Takes child to the doctors when ill
    - Takes care of child's health
    - Protects him from danger
    - Advises for child's good
    - Offers encouragement
    - Does not let child fight or steal something or doing something bad
- Providing opportunities:
- Sends child to school
- Allows child to study as much as he can
- Treats girls and boys equally
- Does not allow early marriage
- Showing affection:
- Loves child very much
- Talks to him affectionately
- Takes him on his lap
- Takes child out on picnics
- Gives child chocolate, sweets, fruits, money according to need

- Active engagement with children to support their development:
- Encourages him to study
- Pays attention to his studies – buys notebooks, school stationery and uniforms
- Helps me with my studies
- Does not make child feel that he is weak in studies or other activities
- Spends time with child
- Feels bad after scolding or hitting child
- Positive discipline, valuing and appreciating children:
- Does not beat child
- Talks to him with care and respect
- Explains what is good and what is bad to child
- Helps child to understand right and wrong
- Forgives child

The main aim of childrearing practices is to develop such qualities in child that may help him to achieve success in life.

Chapter-14
Methods to Understand Children's and Adolescent's Behaviour

It is the responsibility of the teachers to understand and do proper study of the behaviour of their students to understand the need and for guiding the students about their proper growth and development as well as planning and organizing their teaching-learning activities. The task of studying behaviour of the students requires collecting various types of data and information regarding the students. The important methods to understand children's and adolescents' behaviour are given below:

REFLECTIVE JOURNAL

Reflective journals are notebooks or pieces of paper that students use when writing about and reflecting on their own thoughts. The act of reflecting on thoughts, ideas, feelings and their own learning encourages the development of metacognitive skills by helping students self-evaluate and sort what they know from what they don't know. The process of examining one's own thoughts and feelings is particularly helpful for students who are learning new concepts or beginning to grapple with complex issues that go beyond right and wrong answers.

Definition of Reflective Journals: A reflective journal is a personal record of student's learning experiences. It is a space where a learner can record and reflect upon their observations and responses to situations, which can then be used to explore and analyze ways of thinking. Journals, although generally written, can also contain images, drawings and other types of reference materials.

Purpose of Reflective Journals: A reflective journal is a means for learners to reflect on their learning and learning experiences in different ways. They are used to:

- record the development of learners' ideas and insights and/or those of a group in a given context and can include concepts, ideas and main points from experience and theory;
- reflect upon the subject content and personal experiences as a means to increase learners' understanding;
- analyze learning process for self development.

Structure of Reflective Journal: Basically, there are two standard forms of reflective journals:

Structured journals: students are given a specific question, target, or set of guidelines to base their writings on

Unstructured journals/free-form journals: students are required to record thoughts and feeling with minimal direction

Usage of Reflective Journals: Reflective journals are used to explore situations from a personal perspective, but generally within the context of learning from students' own experiences. They are used to reflect on, in and for action. Common questions arising from 'reflection' are:

- What happened? (Reflecting on actions)
- Why did it happen? (Reflecting in actions)
- What can be learnt from this for future actions? (Reflecting for actions)

Advantages of Reflective Journal: Some advantages of reflective journal are:

Active learning: The process of reflection encourages the students to take the initiative to be active, self-driven; allows individual learner to explore concepts and ideas in relation to their thoughts and feelings from different perspectives. Students can become independent thinkers through the practice and to enable themselves to solve various problems on their own.

Understanding the Progress of Students: Reflective journals provide good opportunities for teachers to gain better understanding about how the students think and feel about the course, and the learning progress of the students throughout the course, which will eventually enhance the students' learning process.

Improving Writing Skills: Writing reflective journals can involve students in a new form of writing which they may not have a chance to experience in the past. This exposure can bring out improvement in students' writing skills.

Freely Expressing Personal Views and Criticizing of One-self: Reflective journal assignments provide the platform for students to freely express what they think and feel about the course and their learning process, and also promote their expression of ideas, personal experiences and opinions. This is an ideal place for students who are generally not willing to speak up in the classes and tutorials to express themselves.

Enhance Critical Thinking and Creativity: The process of self-reflection enhances the development of critical thinking skills among students when they relate their knowledge to real world issues. It can help students develop their creativity and a questioning attitude towards different issues and problems.

Disadvantages of Reflective Journal: Some disadvantages of reflective journal are:

Difficult for Objective Marking: Due to the subjective nature of reflective assignments, it is rather difficult for assessors to be objective and have consistent grading. Different assessors when marking may have quite a large discrepancy in their judgment of different types of work.

Time Consuming for Grading: The context of reflective writing can often be very wide, and involves a wide range of concepts, issues, and perspectives. As a result, it often takes considerable amount of time for assessors to read and grade students' works.

Confidentiality: As students have to disclose their personal and private views and information in their reflection, some of them may be unwilling to honestly disclose their real perspectives. They may be concerned that what they wrote will significantly affect the grade they receive.

Clear Guidelines Needed: Many students may not be familiar with the procedure of writing reflective assignments and may feel very lost when working on it for the first time. Teachers have to give clear guidelines to students about what should be included in the reflective journals, what can be learnt from writing it, as well as how they will be graded.

PORTFOLIO

A portfolio is a collection of student's work which gives evidence to show how the student can meet the specified learning outcomes. A typical portfolio consists of work selected by the student, reasons for selecting these works and self-reflection on the learning process. Portfolio is a developmental process, thus it is not only the product that the student or teacher assess upon but also the learning process in which the student develops during the given period. Portfolio is an assessment method that monitors the growth and development of student learning.

Structure of Portfolio Assessment

Unlike most assessments, portfolio assessment can contain many different forms of assessments as it is a collection of student's work. A portfolio assessment is sometimes followed by an oral assessment.

Types of Portfolio

Three Types of Assessment Portfolios are as under:

- *Documentation Portfolio* is to highlight the development and improvement of student learning during a given period of time. It often contains a range of artifacts from brainstormed lists to rough drafts to finished products.
- *Process Portfolio* is similar to documentation portfolio, in which it contains all the evidences required to prove the learning outcomes in the given time, in addition, it integrates reflection and higher-order cognitive activities. It emphasizes metacognitive functioning and encourages students to become active participants in understanding their own learning. Process portfolio often contains documentation of reflection such as learning logs, journals and diaries.
- *Product Portfolio* is a portfolio to demonstrate a student's best work. This type of portfolio is typically used for interview. It is more of a summative assessment and has no reflection on the learning process.

Advantages of Portfolio

Some advantages of portfolio are:

- Portfolio is an assessment method which gives students the opportunity to be responsible for their own learning. Students often develop a proud ownership of their work.

- The self-reflection in each step allows students to improve as they see themselves progressing over time at the different stages.
- Portfolio is an authentic assessment method, it determines meaningful work and often has personal relevance.
- It promotes diversity of assessment methods.
- It encourages motivation due to the visibility of the final portfolio.
- It promotes creativity, individuality and uniqueness in the assessment of learning.
- It assesses all levels of Bloom's taxonomy.
- It shifts teacher's focus from comparative ranking to improving understanding via feedback.
- Learning should not be all about the end result, portfolio is one of those assessment methods which allow students to demonstrate more than the end result – a process orientated method.
- High validity.

Disadvantages of Portfolio

Some disadvantages of portfolio are:

- Portfolio is a very time-consuming assessment method in terms of planning, responding, correcting and providing feedback.
- Clear instructions and guidelines must be given to students, as often students take portfolio as a collection of their work only with no justification on reasoning and reflective statements. A sample or defined portfolio size should also be given.
- Plagiarism can occur.
- It is a subjective assessment method and teachers sometimes find it difficult to assess, as it is difficult to measure reliability.
- Students may overspend their time on the presentation of the portfolio, and not on the actual content. Tutor and peer assessors may also be affected by these effects and overlook the meaningful ideas behind the topic.

INTERVIEW METHOD

Interview method is the most popular method for collecting primary data. It is widely used in every fields or sectors. The interview technique is one of the important and powerful tool for collecting the primary data in social research. The technique involves presentation of oral-verbal stimuli and reply in terms of oral-verbal responses. It is a direct method of data collection. The interview technique can be used through personal interviews and through telephone interviews.

According to Vivien Palmar, *"the interview constitutes a social situation between the two persons, the psychological process involved requiring both the individuals mutually respond through the social research. The purpose of the interview calls for a varied response from the two parties concerned"*.

Merits of Interview Method

The major merits of interview method can be summarized as:

- More accurate information can be obtained.

- Personal information can as well be obtained easily under this method.
- Due to personal presence of the interviewer, there is flexibility in the inquiry.
- Additional supplementary information can also be obtained.
- The interviewer can usually control which person will answer the questions.
- Generally non-response remains very low in this method.
- Observation method can as well as applied to recording verbal answers to various questions.
- Representative and wider distribution of sample is possible by using the method.
- The interviewer contact the informants personally, they can exercise their intelligence, skill, tact etc. to extract correct and relevant information by cross examination of the information, if necessary.
- The language of the interview can be adopted to the ability or educational level of the person interviewed and as such misinterpretations concerning questions can be avoided.
- Very good technique for getting the information about the complex, emotionally laden subjects.
- Can be easily adapted to the ability of the person being interviewed.
- Yields a good percentage of returns.
- Yields perfect sample of the general population.
- Data collected by this method is likely to be more correct compared to the other methods that are used for the data collection.

Demerits of Interview Method

Interview techniques have many merits but it has also many demerits. The main demerits of this method are given below:

- It is a very expensive method, especially when large and widely spread geographical sample is taken.
- There remains the possibility of the bias of interviewer as well as that of the respondent.
- This method is relatively more-time consuming, especially when the sample is large.
- Certain types of respondents may not give true answers to the questions.
- The presence of the interviewer on the spot may over-stimulate the respondent.
- Training and supervising of the interviewers is more complex.
- Systematic errors may arise.
- Time consuming process.
- Involves high cost.
- Requires highly skilled interviewer.
- Requires more energy.
- May sometimes involve systematic errors.
- More confusing and a very complicated method.

Types of Interview Method

Structured Interview: This is also known as a formal interview (like a job interview). The questions are asked in a set/standardized order and the interviewer will not deviate from the interview schedule or probe beyond the answers received (so they are not flexible). These are based on structured, closed-ended questions.

Advantages of Structured Interview

- Structured interviews are easy to replicate as a fixed set of closed questions are used, which are easy to quantify—this means it is easy to test for reliability.
- Structured interviews are fairly quick to conduct which means that many interviews can take place within a short amount of time. This means a large sample can be obtained resulting in the findings being representative and having the ability to be generalized to a large population.

Disadvantages of Structured Interview

- Structure interviews are not flexible. This means new questions cannot be asked impromptu (i.e. during the interview) as an interview schedule must be followed.
- The answers from structured interviews lack detail as only closed questions are asked which generates quantitative data. This means a research will won't know why a person behaves in a certain way.

Unstructured Interview

These are sometimes referred to as 'discovery interviews' & are more like a 'guided conservation' than a strict structured interview. They are sometimes called informal interviews.

An interview schedule might not be used, and even if one is used, they will contain open-ended questions that can be asked in any order. Some questions might be added/missed as the Interview progresses.

Advantages of Unstructured Interview

- Unstructured interviews are more flexible as questions can be adapted and changed depending on the respondents' answers. The interview can deviate from the interview schedule.
- Unstructured interviews generate qualitative data through the use of open questions. This allows the respondent to talk in some depth, choosing their own words. This helps the researcher develop a real sense of a person's understanding of a situation.
- They also have increased validity because it gives the interviewer the opportunity to probe for a deeper understanding, ask for clarification & allow the interviewee to steer the direction of the interview etc.

Disadvantages of Unstructured Interview

- It can be time consuming to conduct an unstructured interview and analyze the qualitative data (using methods such as thematic analysis).
- Employing and training interviewers is expensive, and not as cheap as collecting data via questionnaires. For example, certain skills may be needed by the interviewer. These include the ability to establish rapport & knowing when to probe.

Group Interview

In this interview 5 or 6 applicants are placed together in a situation in which they must interact. The situation may be structured or unstructured. It is usual for the selector to remain silent throughout the discussion and make notes of the applicant's interactions unobtrusively.

The applicant who verbalizes better and who has a better personality is likely to be selected under such circumstances. Sometimes the applicants and the selectors may live together for a few days thus providing a chance to the selectors to know about the personal idiosyncrasies of applicants better. This is known as the "house part" technique.

NATURALISTIC OBSERVATION

Naturalistic observation (i.e. unstructured observation) involves studying the spontaneous behaviour of participants in natural surroundings. The researcher simply records what they see in whatever way they can. Compared with controlled/structured methods it is like the difference between studying wild animals in a zoo and studying them in their natural habitat. Naturalistic observation is a method commonly used by psychologists and other social scientists. This technique involves observing subjects in their natural environment. Naturalistic observation differs from structured observation in that it involves looking at a behaviour as it occurs in its natural setting with no attempts at intervention on the part of the researcher.

Advantages of Naturalistic Observation

- One of the biggest advantages of this type of method is that it allows the teacher to directly observe the subject in a natural setting.
- By being able to observe the flow of behaviour in its own setting studies have greater ecological validity.
- Like case studies naturalistic observation is often used to generate new ideas. Because it gives the researcher the opportunity to study the total situation it often suggests avenues of enquiry not thought of before.

Disadvantages of Naturalistic Observation

- These observations are often conducted on a micro (small) scale and may lack a representative sample (biased in relation to age, gender, social class or ethnicity). This may result in the findings lacking the ability to be generalized to wider society.
- Natural observations are less reliable as other variables cannot be controlled. This makes it difficult for another researcher to repeat the study in exactly the same way.
- A further disadvantage is that the researcher needs to be trained to be able to recognize aspects of a situation that are psychologically significant and worth further attention.
- With observations we do not have manipulations of variables (or control over extraneous variables) which means cause and effect relationships cannot be established.

Types of Observation

Participant Observation

The participant observation means watching the events or situation or activities from inside by taking part in the group to be observed. He freely interacts with the other group members, participates in various activities of the group, acquires the way of life of the observed group or his own, and studies their behaviour or other activities not as an outsider but by becoming a member of that group.

Goode and Hatt define participant observation as *"the procedure used when the investigator can go disguise himself as to be accepted as a member of the group"*. So in this kind of observation the observer has to stay as a member in the group he wants to study. According to P.V. Young, *"the participant observer using non-controlled observation, generally lives or otherwise shares in the life of the group which he is studying"*.

Non-Participant Observation

When the observer observes the group passively from a distance without participating in the group activities, it is known as non-participant observation. Here he does not try to influence them or take part in the group activities. However, purely non-participant observation is extremely difficult. One cannot penetrate into the heart of a matter without proper participation in it. One really cannot imagine a kind of relationship, when the researcher is always present but never participates. This situation is hardly conducive for both the observer and the group. A combination of both participant and non-participant method is sometimes selected.

The observer actively participates in some of the ordinary activities and observes passively from distance in others. Many sociologists therefore treat a non-participant observation in practice as only a quasi-participant observation. It is easier for the observer to perform both the roles than to disguise himself completely.

NARRATIVE

Collecting data on a child involves observing a child and using a method to gather evidence that can help identify and understand the behaviour of a child. A commonly used method of recording data on a student is called narrative recording.

Narrative observation is a useful tool for assessing children's educational, emotional and social development. By keeping a detailed written record of a child's behaviour, including his learning style, the ways in which he interacts with teachers and peers and identifying factors that boost confidence and well-being, teachers and parents can work together to help him achieve his full potential. Narrative observation can be conducted by keeping a diary of a child's activities and by recording activities with digital equipment.

Narrative data should include:

- What the teachers are doing.
- What the students are doing.
- How the students are participating

- (engagement level) in the class discussion/activity.
- How the students are interacting with one another.
- Details of the events in chronological order. Below are advantages and disadvantages for using this particular method of observing children:

Advantages of Narrative

Narrative recording involves providing an ongoing description of the events that take place during an observation as they occur in real time. It is not limited to a particular incident, but rather encompasses all events taking place in a given time frame. It focuses on behaviours of all students, as opposed to a particular behaviour of one child. A narrative observation includes recording details in a sequential manner that helps the observer better understand not only what behaviours took place but also the context in which the behaviour occurred. This can be used as evidence to support claims you make and to provide suggestions when you talk with the teacher after the observation. Accurately written notes in chronological order, along with specific examples about the student's behaviour, can be used to discuss appropriate strategies or techniques that can be used as part a behaviour intervention plan and increase a child's attention, time on-task, and overall learning in the classroom.

Disadvantages of Narrative

Information in narrative recording does not typically contain quantitative data (e.g. the number of times a child raised his hand, the number of tantrums a child has, etc.). It involves a general (or specific) description of events occurring in a particular setting. Recording data in narrative form is time consuming and works well for observing one student. It may be difficult for the observer to track all student behaviour in the classroom, especially in group work. The observer typically sits in isolation away from the students while taking notes. A student may be aware that he/she is being observed which could trigger the student to be on his/her best behaviour. At the same time, this can prove that a child is able to control his/her behaviour in that setting.

Chapter-15
Learning

All complex behaviours are learned. Learning is a theoretical concept. Hence, it is not directly observable. We can infer that learning has taken place if an individual behaves, reacts as a result of experience in a manner different from the way formally behaved.

Learning has no universally agreed definition. The way one defines it emanates from, as well as influences, the way one theorizes learning. Thus there are as many definitions as there are theories of learning. For instance, cognitive theories of learning, which emphasize the thought process and the role of the mind in learning, view it as the mind's ability to acquire, process, and retain new knowledge and information. Thus cognitive psychologists studying learning are interested in unobservable mental activities such as thinking, remembering, creating, and solving problems. On the other hand, behavioural psychologists view that the outcome of learning is change in behaviour and emphasizes the effects of external events on the individual. But experiential theories, which emphasize the role of action and experience in learning, conceptualize it in terms of competencies generated among learners.

MEANING OF LEARNING

Learning is the primary reason for the existence of schools and a means by which socialization is affected. It is difficult to imagine how human beings can be separated from learning, for the two are not separated. Think for a moment, a state that human being would be if there was no learning or he/she did not have capacity to learn. Without learning people would not know their names, their parents and children would not even know where they came from. In this lecture we are going to discuss in details about learning.

By definition *learning* involves a change of behaviour as a result of what one has experienced, and this may be shown in the way a person thinks, acts and feels (Hilgard and Bewer, 1975). This definition claims that there are certain behaviours that may be not the result of learning but due to normal biological development just like walking and seeing.

Learning is a continuous process lasting from a moment when a person is born to the end of his/her life on this surface of the earth (Mwamwenda, 1996). Learning may also be defined as relatively permanent change in behaviour following practice or experience. Many of us think of learning as the process of only acquiring facts and that it is only taking place in schools. But there are many kinds of learning taking place at all times, although our discussion is basically on school learning.

DEFINITIONS OF LEARNING

The important definitions of learning are as follows:

1. Gates and Others (1946)—*"Learning is the modification in behaviour to meet environmental requirements."*

2. F.S. Freeman (1958) —*"Learning is the process of developing the ability to respond adequately to a situation which may or may not have been properly encountered."*

3. H. Faigan (1958)—*"Learning is a sequence of mental events or conditions leading to changes in the learner. As a sequence of events, the learning process is as follows: (1) The individual has needs and is therefore in a state of readiness to respond. There are antecedent conditions within the learner. (2) He meets a learning situation or problem. A new interpretation is required because previously learned responses are not adequate for reaching the goal and satisfying his need. He encounters something new or unexpected and must search for a different response. (3) He interprets the situation with reference to his goals and tries a response or responses which see to satisfy his need. The way he perceives the situation and the response he makes depends both on his 'readiness' and on external conditions of the situation. (4) If his response leads to devised goals or satisfaction, he will tend to interpret and respond to similar future situations in the same way. If not, he keeps on trying and reinterpreting until consequences are attained. The learning process is this whole sequence.*

4. H.J. Klausmeir (1961)—*"Learning is a process whereby a change in behaviour results from some form of experience, activity, training, observation and the like."*

5. E.A. Peel (1962)—*"Learning is a change in the individual following upon changes in the environment."*

6. Blair, Jones and Simpson (1964)—*"Any change of behaviour which is a result of experience and which causes people to face later situations differently may be called learning."*

7. W.C. Morse and G.M. Wingo (1967)—*"Learning can be defined as changing one's potential for seeing, feeling and doing through experiences partly perceptual, partly intellectual, partly emotional and partly motor.*

8. J.F. Travers (1972)—*"Learning is a process that results in the modification of behaviour."*

9. Dictionary of Education by C.V. Good (1973)—*The term 'learning' has been interpreted to mean: "Change in response or behaviour (such as innovation, elimination or modification of responses, involving some degree of performance) caused partly or wholly by experience, such experience being in the main conscious, but sometimes including significant unconscious components, as is common in motor learning or in reaction to unrecognized or subliminal stimuli; includes behaviour changes in the emotional sphere, but more commonly refers to the acquisition of symbolic knowledge or motor skills, does not include psychological changes, such as fatigue or temporary sensory resistance or non-functioning after continued stimulations."*

10. M.L. Bigge (1976)—*"Learning may be considered as a change in insights, behaviour, perception, motivation or a combination of these."*

11. Bernhardt—*"Learning is more or less permanent modification of an individual activity in a given situation, due to the practice in attempts to achieve some goal or solve some problem."*

12. Colvin —*"Learning is the modification of the reactions of an organism through experience."*

13. Cronbach—*"Learning is shown by a change in behaviour as a result of experience."*

14. Eason—*"Learning includes changes in behaviour that are determined primarily by the individual's interaction with his environment."*

15. Gooch—*"Learning as we measure it is a change in performance which occurs under the condition of practice."*

16. Harrimn—*"Learning is the improvement in efficiency of adjustment as a result of practice, insight, observation, imitation and conditioning."*

17. Heidgerken—*"Learning is not an addition of new experience per se, nor is it old experience summed up, rather it is the synthesis of old and the new experiences which result in completely new organisation or pattern of experience."*

18. M.H. Marx—*"Learning is a relatively enduring change in behaviour which is a function of prior behaviour (usually called practice).*

19. Gardner Murphy (1968)—*"The term learning covers every modification in behaviour to meet environmental requirements."*

20. Henry P. Smith (1962)—*"Learning is the acquisition of new behaviour or the strengthening or weakening of old behaviour as the result of experience."*

21. Woodworth (1945)—*"Any activity can be called learning so far as it develops the individual (in any respect, good or bad) and makes him alter behaviour and experiences different from what they would otherwise have been."*

22. Kingsley and R. Garry (1957)—*"Learning is the process by which behaviour (in the broader sense) is originated or changes through practice or training."*

23. Pressey, Robinson and Horrocks (1967)—*"Learning is an episode in which a motivated individual attempts to adapt his behaviour so as to succeed in a situation which he perceives as requiring action to attain a goal."*

24. Crow and Crow (1973)—*"Learning is the acquisition of habits, knowledge and attitudes. It involves new ways of doing things, and it operates in an individual's attempts to overcome obstacles or to adjust to new situations. It represents progressive changes in behaviour...... it enables him to satisfy interests to attain goals."*

25. Hilgard (1958)—*"Learning is the process by which an activity originates or is changed through reaching to an encountered situation, provided that the characteristics of the changes in activity cannot be explained on the basis of native response, tendencies, maturation, or temporary states of the organism (e.g. fatigue or drugs, etc.)."*

26. Kimble (1961)—*"Learning is a relatively permanent change in behavioural potentiality that occurs as a result of reinforced practice."*

27. Skinner (1960)—*"Learning is a process of progressive behaviour adaptation."*

28. Leagans (1961)—*"Learning is a process by which a person becomes changed in his behaviour through self-activity."*

29. Kolb (1984)—*"Learning is the process whereby knowledge is created through the transformation of experience."*

30. Van den Ban & Hawkins (1988) defined learning as—*"the acquiring or improving the ability to perform a behavioural pattern through experience and practice."*

31. Weiss (1990)—*"Learning is any relatively permanent change in behaviour that occurs as a result of experience or practice."*

32. Atkinson *et al.* (1993)—*"Learning is a relatively permanent change in behaviour that results from practice."*

33. According to Woolfolk (1995), *"learning occurs when experience causes a relatively permanent change in an individual's knowledge or behaviour."*

The above definitions reveals the following facts about learning:

- Learning is a process and a product (outcome).
- It involves all those experiences and training of an individual (right from birth) which help him to produce changes in his behaviour.
- Learning leads to changes in behaviour but this does not necessarily mean that these changes always bring about improvement or positive development. One has an equal chance to drift to the negative side of human personality.
- Instead of change in existing behaviour or acquisition of new behaviour, learning may also result in discontinuance or abandonment of existing behaviour. Through it is referred to as unlearning, actually unlearning is also a learning process.
- Learning prepares an individual for any adjustment and adaptation that may be necessary.
- Learning is purposeful and goal-oriented. In case there is no propose, there would definitely be hardly any learning.
- The scope of learning is too wide to be explained in words. It is a very comprehensive process which covers nearly all fields—conative, cognitive and affective - of human behaviour.
- Learning is universal and continuous. Every creature that lives learns. In human beings, it is not restricted to any particular age, sex, race o culture. It is a continuous, never-ending process that extends from the womb to the tomb.
- As maintained by Crow and Crow, learning involves new ways of doing things but there is no limit to adopting these ways and means. All learning does not take place in the same manner. Therefore, learning as a process is of different types and involves different methods.
- As mentioned by Hilgard, the concept of learning excludes changes in behaviour on the basis of native response tendencies like instincts and reflexes, etc. Instinctive or species specific programmes cannot be termed as learned behaviour. Similarly, reflexes, the innate involuntary responses to stimulation e.g., blinking at bright lights and the infant's sucking behaviour, cannot be attributed to learning.
- Learning does not include changes in behaviour on account of maturation, fatigue, illness or drugs etc.

NATURE OF LEARNING

The nature of learning is as follows:

Learning is Universal: Every creature that lives learns. Man learns most. The human nervous system is very complex, so are human reactions and so are human acquisition. Positive learning vital for children's growth and development.

Learning is through Experience: Learning always involves some kind of experience, direct or indirect (vicarious).

Learning is from all Sides: Today learning is from all sides. Children learn from parents, teachers, environment, nature, media etc.

Learning is Continuous: It denotes the lifelong nature of learning. Every day new situations are faced and the individual has to bring essential changes in his style of behaviour adopted to tackle them. Learning is birth to death.

It Results in Change in Behaviour: It is a change of behaviour influenced by previous behaviour. It is any activity that leaves a more or less permanent effect on later activity.

Learning is an Adjustment: Learning helps the individual to adjust himself adequately to the new situations. Most learning in children consists in modifying, adapting, and developing their original nature. In later life the individuals acquire new forms of behaviour.

It Comes About as a Result of Practice: It is the basis of drill and practice. It has been proven that students learn best and retain information longer when they have meaningful practice and repetition. Every time practice occurs, learning continues.

Learning is a Relatively Permanent Change: After a rat wake up from his nap he still remembers the path to the food. Even if you have been on a bicycle for years, in just a few minutes practice you can be quite proficient again.

Learning as Growth and Development: It is never ending growth and development. At reach stage the learner acquires new visions of his future growth and news ideals of achievement in the direction of his effort. According to Woodworth, "All activity can be called learning so far as it develops the individual."

Learning is Not Directly Observable: The only way to study learning is through some observable behaviour. Actually, we cannot observe learning; we see only what precedes performance, the performance itself and the consequences of performance.

PRINCIPLES OF LEARNING

There are some principles of learning which are very much applicable in extension. The principles are generalized guidelines, which form the basis for taking action. Following are some of the principles of learning along with their implications for teaching:

Principle of Association

Learning is growth-like and continuous. The kind of learning that takes place is the result of the kind of experience we have. Previous learning always sets the stage for subsequent learning. New learning may be associated with previous successful and satisfying responses. For example, if the farmers have obtained profitable return by the application of nitrogenous fertilizer, they may be motivated to use balanced fertilizers containing phosphate and potash, for still higher return.

Implications for Teaching: Implications of this principle are:

- Begin at the level of the learner.
- New must be related to the old.
- Adjust the pace to the learner's capacity, one idea at a time.
- Bring the idea to the attention of the learner repeatedly (in a variety of ways) and over a period of time.

Principle of Clarity of Objectives

Learning is more effective when it is purposeful. The learning must be useful to the learners. Objectives must be clear and meaningful to the learners. What is to be learnt must be important to a relatively large number of participants in the group and must be attainable.

Implications for Teaching

- Learning must make sense to the learning.
- Progress must be constantly appraised and redirected.
- Purpose must be kept in sharp focus (objectives must be clear to the learner and teacher).

Principle of Self Activity

Learning is an active process on the part of the learners. The instructor can create a situation and stimulate a person to learn. The door to learning is "locked on the inside" and unless the learner opens the door herself/himself, learning cannot take place. Activities appropriate to the specific learning must be used. For example, conducting demonstration by the farmers in their own fields provides opportunity of self-activity, that is, *learning by doing*. This makes learning effective and permanent.

Implications for Teaching

- Activities appropriate to specific learning situation must be used.
- Learning activities should engage a maximum number of senses.

Principle of Motivation

To learn, people need to feel the need for learning. When this desire exists, the learner will exert a high level of effort. The learning experience, therefore, should be designed so learners can see how it will help them achieve those goals they have set for themselves.

Implications for Teaching

- Teacher motivation of the student is essential in making learning more challenging.
- Standards demanded of the learner should be suitable to their ability or capacity.
- Appropriate and timely recognition should be given to student achievement.

Principle of Practice

When learner actually practice what they have read, heard, or seen, they gain confidence and are less likely to make errors or to forget what they have learned. Active involvement through practice, therefore, should be made part of the learning process.

Implications for Teaching

- Course content should be organized into meaningful units.
- Theory should be related to practice.
- Provide activities that stimulate actual use situation.

Principle of Disassociation

Learning is affected by emotions. The most effective way of eliminating an undesirable response is to set up a desirable substitute that must be more satisfying than the original reaction. For example, when planting a crop in lines gives better yield, the farmer may be advised not to practice broadcasting.

Implications for Teaching

- Strive to increase pleasant emotions and decrease unpleasant emotions of students in connection with the learning process.
- Train the expression of emotions in the right direction.

Principle of Readiness: Learning takes place more effectively when one is ready to learn.

Principle of Set or Attitude: An unfavourable attitude or set retards learning and a favourable attitude accelerates it.

Principle of Reinforcement: Behaviours that are positively reinforced (rewarded) are encouraged and sustained. When the behaviour is punished, it is temporarily suppressed but is unlikely to be extinguished.

Principle of Transfer of Learning: It does not make much sense to perfect a skill in the classroom and then find that you cannot successfully transfer it to the job. Therefore, learning should be designed to foster transferability.

Principle of Feedback: Learning is facilitated when the learners are provided with knowledge of progress of learning.

Principle of Abilities: Learning abilities varies widely among individuals. The level of communication and the level of understandability of the subject matter taught must be in line with the learner's ability.

CHARACTERISTICS OF LEARNING

The main characteristics of learning are discussed below:

Learning is Growth: The word growth is generally associated with the body which is growing, but through the mental growth of the learner. Although it is latent yet we can perceive its growth. Through his daily activities the child grows both mentally and physically. Therefore, we say that learning is growth through experience.

Learning is Experience: The individual learns through experiences. Human life is fall of experiences. All these experiences provide new knowledge, understanding, skills and attitudes. Learning is not mere acquisition of the knowledge, skills and attitudes. It is also the reorganization of experiences or the synthesis of the old experiences with the new.

Motivation is a Key Component in Learning: Not only is it the case that motivation helps learning, it is essential for learning. This ideas of motivation as described here is broadly conceived to include an understanding of ways in which the knowledge can be used. Unless we know "the reasons why", we may not be very involved in using the knowledge that may be instilled in us. even by the most severe and direct teaching.

Learning is Adjustment: Learning helps the individual to adjust himself adequately to the new situations. Children meet with new situations which demand solution. Repeated efforts are required to react to them effectively. Life is full of experiences and each experience leaves behind some effects in the mental structure. These effects modify our behaviour.

Learning is Organizing Experience: Learning is not mere addition to knowledge. It is not mere acquisition of facts and skills through drill and repetition. It is the reorganization of experience.

Learning is Purposeful: All true learning is based on purpose. Purpose plays a big role in learning. According to Ryburn, "This purpose is always connected with the use of some instinctive power, with the use of the energy with which we are endowed with birth". We do not learn anything and everything that comes in our way, in a haphazard manner. All school activities should be purposeful so that the child should feel real urge for learning.

Learning Involves Language: The language we use influences learning. On the empirical level, researchers have noted that people talk to themselves as they learn. On a more general level, there is a collection of arguments, presented most forcefully by Vigotsky, that language and learning are inextricably intertwined.

Learning is Intelligent: Meaningless efforts do not produce permanent result. Any work done mechanically is without any soul. When a child learns something unintelligently, he is likely to forget it very soon. He does not assimilate but simply commits to memory. Only efforts made intelligently have lasting effects.

Learning is an Active Process: Learning is an active process in which the learner uses sensory input and constructs meaning out of it. The more traditional formulation of this idea involves the terminology of the active learner (Dewey's term) stressing that the learner needs to do something; that learning is not the passive acceptance of knowledge which exists "out there" but that learning involves the learner s engaging with the world.

Learning does not take place without a purpose and self-activity. In the teaching-learning process, the activity of the learner counts more than the activity of the teacher. The principle of learning by doing is the main principle and it has been recommended by all modern educationists. It is the basis of all progressive methods of education such as the Dalton, the Project, the Montessori and the Basic.

Learning is Both Individual and Social: Learning is more than an individual activity. It is a social activity also. Individual mind is affected by the group mind consciously as well as unconsciously as individual is influenced by his friends, relatives, classmates, parents, etc. and learns their ideas, feelings and notions. Social agencies like the family, church, film and gangs of playmates have a tremendous influence on the child and are always moulding and re-moulding him.

Although learning is an individual activity, it is social also. Individual mind is consciously or unconsciously affected by the group activities. Individual is influenced by his peers, friends, relatives' parents and classmates and learns their ideas, feelings and attitudes in some way or others. The social agencies like family, church, markets, and clubs exert immense, influence on the individual minds. As such, learning becomes both individual as well as social.

Our learning is intimately associated with our connection with other human beings, our teachers, our peers, our family as well as casual acquaintances, including the people before us or next to us at the exhibit. We are more likely to be successful in our efforts to educate if we recognize this principle rather than try to avoid it. Much of traditional education, as Dewey pointed out, is directed towards isolating the learner from all social interaction, and towards seeing education as a one-on-one relationship between the learner and the objective material to be learned. In contrast, progressive education (to continue to use Dewey's formulation) recognizes the social aspect of learning and uses conversation, interaction with others, and the application of knowledge as an integral aspect of learning.

Learning is the Product of the Environment: Environment plays an important role in the growth and development of the individual. Environment should be healthy and rich in educative possibilities. The individual lives in interaction of the society. Particularly, environment plays an important part in the growth and development of the individual. The physical, social, intellectual and emotional development of the child is molded and remolded by the objects and individuals in his environment. Therefore, emphasized that child's environment should be made free from unhealthy and vicious matters to make it more effective for learning.

People Learn to Learn as they Learn: Learning consists both of constructing meaning and constructing systems of meaning. For example, if we learn the chronology of dates of a series of historical events, we are simultaneously learning the meaning of a chronology. Each meaning we construct makes us better able to give meaning to other sensations which can fit a similar pattern.

The Crucial Action of Constructing Meaning is Mental: It happens in the mind. Physical actions, hands-on experience may be necessary for learning, especially for children, but it is not sufficient; we need to provide activities which engage the mind as well as the hands.

True Learning Affects the Conduct of the Learner: There is a change in the mental structure of the learner after every experience. Learning is called the modification of behaviour. It affects the learner's behaviour and conduct. Every learning experience brings about changes in the mental structure of the learner. Therefore attempts are made to provide such learning experiences which can mould the desired conduct and habits in the learners.

Learning is Contextual: We do not learn isolated facts and theories in some abstract ethereal land of the mind separate from the rest of our lives: we learn in relationship to what else we know, what we believe, our prejudices and our fears. On reflection, it becomes clear that this point is actually a corollary of the idea that learning is active and social. We cannot divorce our learning from our lives.

One Needs Knowledge to Learn: It is not possible to assimilate new knowledge without having some structure developed from previous knowledge to build on. The more we know, the more we can learn. Therefore any effort to teach must be connected to the state of the learner, must provide a path into the subject for the learner based on that learner's previous knowledge.

It Takes Time to Learn: Learning is not instantaneous. For significant learning we need to revisit ideas, ponder them try them out, play with them and use them. This cannot happen in the 5-10 minutes usually spent in a gallery (and certainly not in the few seconds usually spent contemplating a single museum object.) If you reflect on anything you have learned, you soon realize that it is the product of repeated exposure and thought. Even, or especially, moments of profound insight, can be traced back to longer periods of preparation.

LAWS OF LEARNING

On the basis of research findings, Thorndike (1932) formulated Three Laws that govern learning:

The Law of Effect: This law states that a satisfying state of affairs leads to repetition of a given behaviour, whereas an annoying state of weakness delays a response. If putting up his hand in class gains a pupil the teacher's attention and recognition, his behaviour has resulted in a satisfying state of affairs, thus this is likely to repeat. On the other hand, if a pupil raises hand to attract teacher's attention and the teacher does not recognize it, the pupil is less likely to repeat such behaviour. This, too, shows how learning occurs.

The Law of Readiness: Given a situation where a person is ready or prepared to engage in certain behaviour and is provided with an opportunity, the whole experience will be pleasing or satisfying one. Therefore it is important to note that learner's readiness is important in learning. Secondly, if a person is denied the chance to engage in behaviour for which he/she is prepared, this will result in frustration and annoyance. Third, if a person is forced to engage in certain behaviour for which is not ready, the end result will be annoying.

The Law of Exercise: A strong connection or bond is established between a stimulus and a response as a result of practice. Indeed as it is often said "*practice makes perfect*". The more the skill or body of information is practiced the more it will be mastered, applied and retained in memory. In Tanzanian primary schools for example, it a common practice for pupils to memorise multiplication tables. This practice applies the law of exercise.

LEARNING CURVE

A learning curve is a graphic representation which is drawn to represent the progress of learning of an individual or a group in a given period. Usually the abscissa (x-axis) of a learning curve is described in terms of number of trails or some measure of time. The ordinate (y-axis) is usually represented by scores (latency, frequency, etc). The slope of the curve indicates the rate of progress (increase or decrease).

Two telegraphists, namely Bryan and Harter were the originators of a learning curve. While transmitting telegrams, they came across this phenomenon.

If we take trails on X-axis and progress on y-axis and join the points, we have with us a learning curve (Figure 15.1).

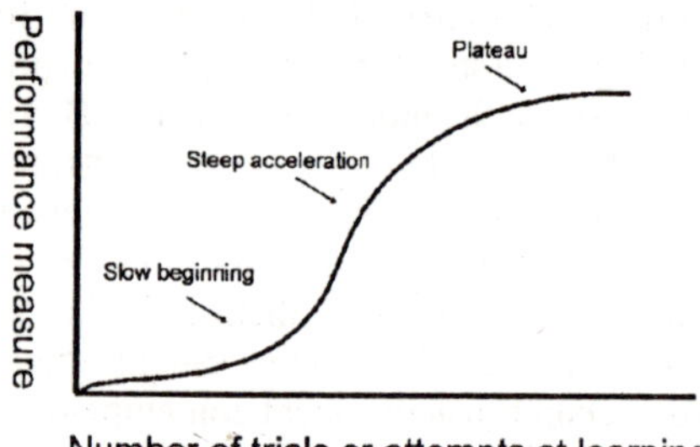

Figure 15.1: Learning Curve

The learning curves connected with child learning are almost confined entirely to the sensory-motor types of learning. They represent acquisition of skills such as telegraphy, typewriting, learning (memorization) and retention or forgetting of practice material like nonsense syllables. Since, such material is divisible into units and it capable of quantitative expression, the drawing of learning curves representing these skills is possible.

Types of Learning Curves

The progress made in the acquisition of skills when graphically plotted takes the form of several types of curves. The different types of learning curves are as follows:

Straight Line Curve: Such a curve shows a constant or uniform rate of progress (Figure 15.2). This type of curve is seldom found. Here the increment of gain is the same for each successive trail.

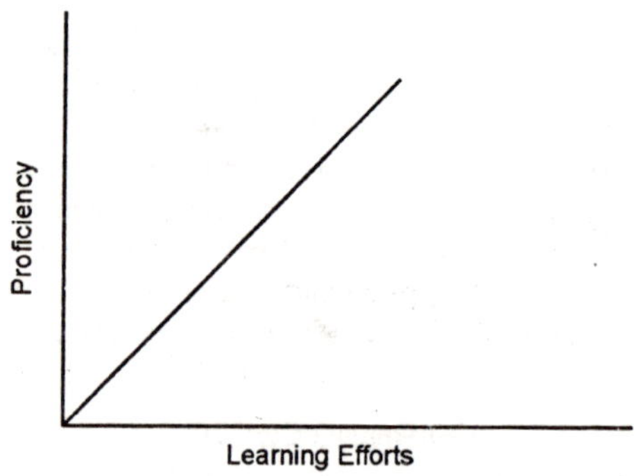

Figure 15.2: Straight Line Learning Curve

Convex Learning Curve or Negatively Accelerated Learning Curve: In convex curve, there is the fastest rate of gain in the beginning but decreases as practice continues. Such a rate is called *negative acceleration.* Improvement is still being made but the increment of gain decreases in successive trails. (Figure 1.3). Such learning curve is frequently found.

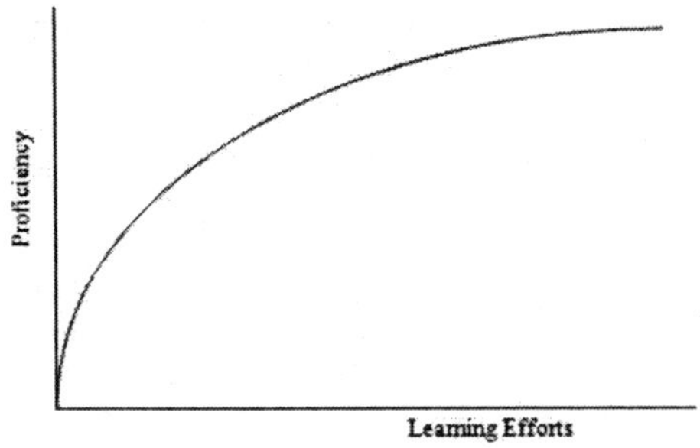

Figure 15.3: Convex Learning Curve

Concave Learning Curve or Positively Accelerated Curve: This curve shows that the initial rate of gain gradually increases (Figure 15.4). This increase in the rate of improvement is called *positive acceleration.* An example of positive acceleration is found in the increase of children's vocabulary. It must be remembered that positive acceleration cannot continue indefinitely. Sooner or later one reaches the highest stage of mastery.

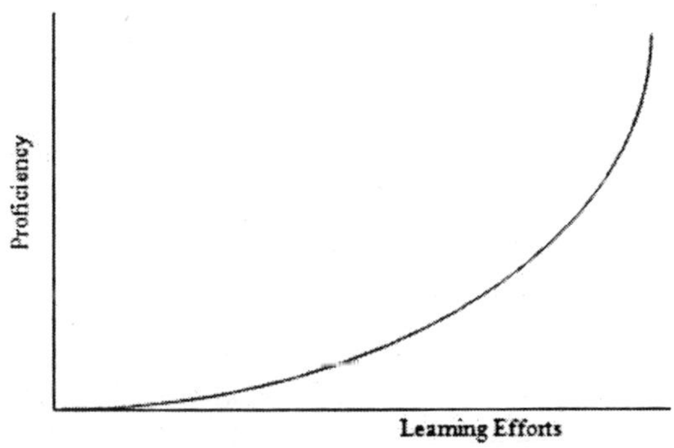

Figure 15.4: Concave Learning Curve

Combination of Convex and Concave Curve: Such a curve represents negative and positive accelerations as well.

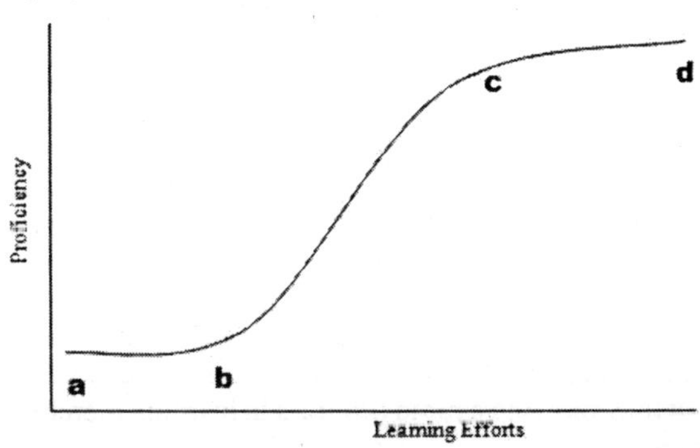

Figure 15.5: Convex and Concave Learning Curve

On account of individual differences, these curves vary from person to person and from subject to subject. The form of the curve depends partly on the nature of the work and partly on the learner's ability to perform a task, his method of work, previous training and the circumstances under which he works.

Factors Affecting Shape/Type of Learning Curve

The following factors Affects thy shape/type of learning curve:

Nature of the Learner: The learners' interests, attitudes, potentials capabilities etc affects the shape of the curve., e.g- more interests, more learning, more upward moves the curve.

Nature of Learning Material: The more interesting the learning materials, the more the child are motivated to learn and vice versa.

Length of Practice Period: If the task is very difficult but is also given lot of time then it leads to progress. But if the task is difficult and not given enough time than the progress is affected, it may lead to less or even no learning.

Previous Learning: It adopts the principle of moving from the Known to unknown. This leads to progress in learning.

Environmental Factors: Factors like proper ventilation, lighting, seating arrangements etc. leads to better learning as these factors help child to pay more attention. It leads to progress in learning. On the other hand poor environmental condition affects learning and leads to downward moving curve.

To Known the Extent to Which Objective have been Achieved: Objective achieved leads to progress—curve moves upward. Objectives not achieved—leads to no or less learning, decline in the progress.

Drawbacks/Limitation of Learning Curve

The main drawbacks of learning curve are as follows:

- The data for learning curve is very limited—e.g. acquisition of skills, memory, forgetting (how much you forget after each interval)
- Disregard to individual learning in its environment i.e. it ignores the learning environment.
- It does not show progress in terms of learning that has taken place as per unit time i.e. how much learning has taken place in each interval.
- Learning curve does not show latent learning i.e. hidden learning. e.g..– a small child learning to speak in the initial phases of life. The learning of language cannot be measured.

Phases of Typical Learning Curve

The phases of a typical learning curve are:

A Period of Slow Progress: Here since the learning material is new or because the child has just started learning, the rate of progress in this initial stage is very slow. e.g. child learning types of noun for the first time—slow learning.

A Period of Rapid Progress: Now slowly-slowly the child gets turned into the process of learning or in case of new material with the more practice gains mastery over it thus showing a rapid progress in learning thereby accelerating the curve upward.

Period of No Progress: Now since the child has gained mastery over the learning material, he may revise the some material or may take some rest because of which no new learning takes place and therefore the curve stays stable.

Period of Sudden Rise: Now again the child takes place up something new and learns it because of which learning has taken place which leads to o rise in learning curve.

Leveling Off: The phase of leveling off is reached when your physiological limits are reached. When your brains are saturated and you are not physically and mentally ready to do any more learning. At such time you need to take a break from learning and take some rest.

FACTORS THAT MAY AFFECT THE LEARNING PROCESS

Some of the important factors which may affect the learning process are as follows:

Intellectual Factor

The term refers to the individual mental level. Success in school is generally closely related to level of the intellect. Pupils with low intelligence often encounter serious difficulty in mastering schoolwork. Sometimes pupils do not learn because of special intellectual disabilities. A low score in one subject and his scores in other subjects indicate the possible presence of a special deficiency. Psychology reveals to use that an individual possess different kinds to intelligence. Knowledge of the nature of the pupil's intellect is of considerable value in the guidance and the diagnosis of disability. The native capacity of the individual is of prime importance in determining the effectiveness of the, learning process.

Learning Factors

Factors owing to lack of mastery of what has been taught, faulty methods of work or study, and narrowness of experimental background may affect the learning process of any pupil. If the school proceeds too rapidly and does not constantly check up on the extent to which the pupil is mastering what is being taught, the pupil accumulates a number of deficiencies that interfere with successful progress.

In arithmetic, for instance, knowledge of basic addition is essential to successful work in multiplication. Weakness in addition will contribute directly to the deficiency in multiplication. Likewise, failure in history may be due to low reading ability or weakness in English. Similarly, because of faulty instruction, the pupil may have learned inefficient methods of study. Many other kinds of difficulty which are directly related to learning factors may interfere with progress.

Physical Factors

Under this group are included such factors as health, physical development, nutrition, visual and physical defects, and glandular abnormality. It is generally recognized that ill health retards physical and motor development, and malnutrition interferes with learning and physical growth.

Children suffering from visual, auditory, and other physical defects are seriously handicapped in developing skills such as reading and spelling. It has been demonstrated that various glands of internal secretion, such as the thyroid and pituitary glands, affect behaviour. The health of the learner will likely affect his ability to learn and his power to concentrate.

Mental Factors

Attitude falls under mental factors attitudes are made up of organic and kinesthetic elements. They are not to be confused with emotions that are characterized by internal visceral disturbances. Attitudes are more or less of definite sort. They play a large part in the mental organization and general behaviour of the individual.

Attitudes are also important in the development of personality. Among these attitudes aw interest, cheerfulness, affection, prejudice, -open mindedness, and loyalty. Attitudes exercise a stimulating effect upon the rate of learning and teaching and upon the progress in school. The efficiency of the work from day to day and the rapidity with which it is achieved are influenced by the attitude of the learner. A favourable mental attitude facilitates learning. The factor of interest is very closely related in nature to that of symbolic drive and reward.

Emotional and Social Factors

Personal factors, such as instincts and emotions, and social factors, such as cooperation and rivalry, are directly related to a complex psychology of motivation. It is a recognized fact that the various responses of the individual to various kinds of stimuli are determined by a wide variety of tendencies.

Some of these innate tendencies are constructive and others are harmful. For some reason a pupil may have developed a dislike for some subject because he may fail to see its value, or may lack foundation. This dislike results in a bad emotional state. Some pupils are in a continuing state of unhappiness because of their fear of being victims of the disapproval of their teachers and classmates. This is an unwholesome attitude and affects the learning process to a considerable degree. This is oftentimes the result of bad training.

Environmental Factor

Physical conditions needed for learning is under environmental factor. One of the factors that affect the efficiency of learning is the condition in which learning takes place. This includes the classrooms, textbooks, equipment, school supplies, and other instructional materials.

In the school and at the home, the conditions for learning must be favourable and adequate if teaching is to produce the desired results. It cannot be denied that the type and quality of instructional materials and equipment play an important part in the instructional efficiency of the school.

It is difficult to do a good job of teaching in a poor type of building and without adequate equipment and instructional materials. A school building or a classroom has no merit when built without due regard to its educational objectives and functions.

Teacher's Personality

The teacher as an individual personality is an important element in the learning environment or in the failures and success of the learner. The way in which his personality interacts with the personalities of the pupils being taught helps to determine the kind of behaviour which emerges from the learning situation.

The supreme value of a teacher is not in the regular performance of routine duties, but in his power to lead and to inspire his pupils through the influence of his moral personality and example. Strictly speaking, personality is made up of all the factors that make the individual what he is, the complex pattern of characteristics that distinguishes him from the others of his kind. Personality is the product of many integrating forces.

In other words, an individual's personality is a composite of his physical appearance, his mental capacity, his emotional behaviour, and his attitudes towards others. Effective teaching and learning are the results of an integrated personality of the teacher.

Generally speaking, pupils do- not like a grouchy teacher who cannot control his temper before the class. It is impossible for a teacher with a temper to create enthusiasm and to radiate light and sunshine to those about him.

Pupils love a happy, sympathetic, enthusiastic, and cheerful teacher. Effective teaching and learning are the results of love for the pupils, sympathy for their interests, tolerance, and a definite capacity for understanding.

The teacher must therefore recognize that in all his activities in the classroom he is directly affecting the behaviour of the growing and learning organism.

FACTORS ASSOCIATED WITH LEARNER THAT AFFECTS LEARNING

Learner is the key figure in any learning task. He has to learn or bring desired modification in his behaviour. How he will learn or what he will achieve, through a particular learning act depends heavily upon his own characteristics and ways or learning. Such things or factors associated with this can be described as follows:

Learner's Physical and Mental Health

Learning is greatly affected by the learner's physical and mental health maintained by him particularly, at the time of learning. A simple headache or a stomachache can play havoc with the process and products of learning. A child who does not maintain satisfactory physical health, have to suffer adversely in term of gains in learning. Similarly, the mental state and the health of a learner at the time of learning become potent factors in deciding the outcome of his learning. A tense, emotionally and mentally disturbed learner cannot show satisfactory results in learning.

The Basic Potential of the Learner

The results achieved by the learner through a process of learning depend heavily upon his basic potential to undergo such learning. Such potential may consist of the things given below.

- Learner's innate abilities and capacities for learning a thing.
- Learner's basic potential in terms of general intelligence and specific knowledge, understanding and skills related to a particular learning area.
- Learner's basic interests, aptitudes and attitudes related to the learning of a particular thing or area.

The Level of Aspiration and Achievement Motivation

Learning is greatly influenced by the level of aspiration and nature of achievement motivation possessed by a learner. How can we expect learner to achieve a thing for which he has no aspiration? Also, too much of aspirations make it impossible for an individual to achieve this. A person has to maintain the level of his aspiration and achievement motivation at a reasonable level. That is to say, his aspirations should be neither too high which will result in non-achievement of any of his goals, nor too low as not to try to achieve goals which he is quite capable.

Goals of Life

The philosophy of immediate as well as ultimate goals of one's life affects the process and product of learning. His mode and ways of looking towards things, his inclination towards learning a particular subject and patience and persistence in pursuing his learning despite the heavy odds—all depend up on his goals and philosophy of life.

Readiness and Will Power

A learner's readiness and power to learn is a great deciding factor of his results in learning. No power on earth can help a learner if he is not ready to learn. Certainly, if he has a will to learn a thing, then automatically, he will himself find ways for effective learning.

FACTORS ASSOCIATED WITH THE TYPES OF LEARNING EXPERIENCES THAT AFFECTS LEARNING

The type of changes or modifications found in learner's behaviour depends much on the type of learning experience and training received by him for this purpose. This task involves a variety of factors like those given below.

Nature of Learning Experience

Learning is influenced by the nature of the subject matter and the learning experiences presented to a learner such as the following:

- Whether the nature of learning experience is formal or informal, incidental or well-planned, direct or indirect and the like.
- Whether learning experiences are suitably selected on the basis of the principle of child-centeredness, principle of activity, criterion of activity, age, grade and experiences of a learner.
- Whether learning experiences are suitably organised for the attainment of desired educational objections or not.

Methodology of Learning

Learning depends upon the methods, techniques and approaches employed for the teaching and learning of the selected contents. Let us think about the truth of this statement fresh from various angles:

Linking the Recent Learning with those of the Past: The quality of result in learning depends much on the abilities of a teacher and a learner to link the present new learning with the past experiences of the learner. Past experiences help the learner to assimilate and understand the new learning.

Correlating Learning in one Area with that of Another: Correlation facilitates the task of learning as it allows maximum transfer of training or learning from one area to another. Accordingly, one can expect good results in learning, if learning experiences are given in view of seeking correlation (a) among the different subjects of areas, (b) within the branches or experiences of the same area and (c) with real life happenings and situations.

Utilization of Maximum Number of Sense: Senses are said to be the gateway of knowledge and consequently the results in learning are very much influenced by the nature and type of utilization of one's senses in the acquisition of learning experiences. A learner, who learns through utilization of his maximum senses like sense of sight, hearing, touch, smell, taste and also tries to learn by doing things for him, always has an advantageous edge over others.

Revision and Practice: Review and practice always brings good results in the achievements of learning. A learner who makes use of sufficient drill work, practice work, revision and review of his learning can be expected to harvest a good yield in terms of his good retention, reproduction and utilization at the proper time.

Provision of Proper Feedback and Reinforcement: Learning yields are dependent upon the nature and quality of the reinforcement provided to the learner in his learning task. One must be acquainted with the progress of his learning in term of his strength and weakness and remedial action if needed may be taken at the proper time. Knowledge of the results and the progress may work for providing immediate reinforcement to the learner. In addition to it, learning process can be suitably designed if we take due care to make planning of proper reinforcement schedules.

The Selection of the Suitable Learning Methods of Techniques: There are sufficient methods and a number of good techniques available for the teaching and learning of different subjects and areas of experiences. The results of learning are always influenced by the nature and quality of the methods and techniques employed for the teaching and learning of a particular content, subject matter or learning experiences.

FACTORS ASSOCIATED WITH THE MEN AND MATERIAL RESOURCES THAT AFFECTS LEARNING

A learner is helped by the available resources (men and material) for bringing desirable changes in his behaviour. How effectively such changes will take place in his behaviour depend much on the quality and management of these resources. Certain factors which affect learning may be listed in the following manner:

- Quality of teacher in term of his mastery over the subject matter, teaching skills, rich experiences, teacher qualities and behaviour.

- Socio-emotional climate available in the institution in the form of teacher-pupil relationships, pupil-pupil relationships and school-staff relationships and the like.
- Availability of appropriate learning material and facilities like teaching-learning aids, text books, library and laboratory facilities, project works etc.
- Availability of proper conducive environment and learning situations like:
  - ➢ Proper seating arrangement.
  - ➢ Calm and peaceful environment.
  - ➢ Management and control of the factors leading to distraction.
  - ➢ Cooperative and competitive group situations.
  - ➢ Congenial learning environment at home.
  - ➢ Provision of proper change, rest and recreation.
  - ➢ Provision of opportunity for creativity and self expression.

Classroom Implications of Learning

Classroom implications of learning may be summarized as under:

Who is Learn?

The child is to learn and therefore, his age, abilities, aptitudes and interests may be taken note of by all those who are charged with the learning of the child.

From Whom to Learn? :

Learning is from the teacher. Therefore, a teacher must present good models of teaching-learning.

Why to Learn?

Learning is not merely in terms of the traditional 3 R's, i.e. reading, writing and arithmetic but in terms of 7R's, i.e. reading, writing, arithmetic, rights, responsibilities and their relationships and recreation. Learning is for individual good as well as for the good of the society.

How to Learn?

It involves various methods of learning, for instance learning through rote memory, learning through imitation, learning through insight etc.

When to Learn

This is concerned with motivational situations for the learner.

Where to Learn?

Learning takes place in the classroom, on the playfield, in the workshop, in the neighbourhood, etc. School is not the only place of learning.

Chapter-16
Behaviourism Perspective of Learning

According to behaviourism, learning is a mechanical process of associating the stimulus with response, which produces a new behaviour. Such behaviour is strengthened by the reinforcement. Behaviourists view the learner as a passive person, who responds to the stimuli. According to them, the learner starts as '*tabula rasa*' (which means clean slate) and the behaviour is shaped by reinforcement. Positive as well as negative reinforcement increase the probability of the repetition of behaviour. However, the punishment decreases the chance of repetition of the behaviour. Learning is therefore defined as a change in the behaviour of the learner.

The behaviourist school sees the mind as a "black box," in the sense that a response to a stimulus can be observed quantitatively, totally ignoring the effect of thought processes occurring in the mind. The school, therefore, looks at overt behaviours that can be observed and measured as indicators of learning.

KEY IDEAS OF BEHAVIOURISM

The key ideas of behaviourism are as follows:

- Behaviourism focuses on observable learning events as demonstrated by stimulus and response relationships.
- Learning always involves a change in behaviour.
- Mental processes should be excluded from the scientific study of learning.
- The laws governing learning apply equally to all organisms, including human organisms.
- Organisms begin life as blank slates: there are no innate laws of behaviour.
- Learning results from external events in the environment.
- Behaviourism is a deterministic theory: the subject has no choice but to respond to appropriate stimuli.

BEHAVIOURIST ASSUMPTIONS ABOUT LEARNING

The main assumptions of behaviourist learning are as follows:

- Observable behaviour is more important than understanding internal activities;
- Behaviour should be focused on simple elements: specific stimuli and responses;
- Learning is about behaviour change.

KEY PRINCIPLES OF BEHAVIOURISM

The key principles of behaviourism are as follows:

Reinforcement: Positive or negative feedback which will lead the learner to form a strong association between the stimulus and the desired behaviour.

Contiguity: The more immediate the feedback, the stronger the association is.

Repetition: The more frequent the stimulus-response the more likely is the desired outcome.

Variation: Varying the pattern of the stimulus generalizes the response.

Intermittent Reinforcement: Not rewarding the response every time is found to be more effective than constant reward; it helps keep the learner guessing.

Extinction: If the stimulus-response bond is not reinforced the association will die.

BEHAVIOURAL APPROACHES TO LEARNING

Common behavioural approaches to learning are as follows:

- The learner takes on a predominantly passive and reactive role.
- Instruction is structured and systematic.
- Concrete and defined instructional goals, objectives and strategies aimed at learners in general and not on thc individual learner.
- Learning can be measured.
- It assumes that a well-planned instructional intervention can result in a desired learning outcome.
- Focus on simplification (start with easy and progress to more difficult) and repetition (rote learning/drill and practice).
- Instruction is instructor-controlled.

STRENGTHS OF BEHAVIOURISM

The main strengths of Behaviourism are as follows:

- It can be used to formulate behavioural contracts in the school as well as at home.
- It is helpful in bringing about behaviour modification (desired outcome) with the help of reinforcement, punishment and extinction.
- Cueing responses to behaviour allow the learner to react in a predictable way under certain conditions.
- Success of outcomes is easily measurable.
- Guarantees specific learning.
- Ease of application.

WEAKNESSES OF BEHAVIOURISM

The main weaknesses of Behaviourism are as follows:

- It is an extrapolation of animal behaviour to humans.
- Behaviourism fails to explain the development of human languages.
- Effect of environment in shaping the behaviour of a human, is not taken into account by the behaviourists.

IMPLICATIONS OF BEHAVIOURISM

- Learners should be told the explicit outcomes of the learning, so that they can set expectations and can judge for themselves, whether or not they have achieved the outcome of the day's lesson.

- Learners must be tested to determine whether or not they have achieved the learning outcome. Testing and assessment should be integrated into the learning sequence to check the learner's achievement level and to provide appropriate feedback.
- Learning materials must be sequenced appropriately to promote learning. The sequencing could take the form of simple to complex, known to unknown, and knowledge to application.
- Learners must be provided with feedback so that they can monitor how they are doing and take corrective action if required.
- The techniques of reinforcement and punishment have been employed by the teachers in the classrooms to promote desirable behaviour and discourage unwanted behaviour of the learners.

PRACTICAL IMPLICATIONS OF BEHAVIOURISM

Current educational practice is influenced by behaviourist features like:

Curriculum Planning

The following list outlines curriculum-planning steps commonly undertaken by teachers at different educational levels:

- identify the need for the programme;
- determine the aims and instructional objectives of the programme;
- define the characteristics of the target group;
- list the precise learning outcomes;
- categorize learning outcomes according to Bloom's taxonomies;
- break the material down into small units;
- carefully sequence these units;
- provide frequent practice to strengthen the stimulus–response bond;
- ensure that the learner responds (does things);
- observe and assess any behavioural changes;
- provide opportunities for frequent learner feedback;
- reinforce 'correct' behaviour with immediate rewards;
- evaluate the effectiveness of the programme;
- modify and improve the programme.

Learning Outcomes

Learning outcomes, which have developed from the behavioural educational objectives described above, are increasingly used at all levels of education, although their application is more straightforward when the behaviours are easily observed. Their use is more difficult when applied to complex and internal thought processes. A learning outcome is an explicit statement of what a learner will be able to do as a result of completing a course of study. A learning outcome statement includes:

- action, expressed using precise behavioural verbs;
- context, which requires reference to the conditions of performance;
- threshold, which is an indication of acceptable performance – that is, a statement about the performance threshold required.

Learning outcomes help learners at all levels to understand exactly what is expected of them and to tailor their learning activities accordingly. One of the major contributions of behaviourism to contemporary educational practice has been to remove the mystique and vagueness that has frequently characterized the discourse of educational aims and objectives.

Assessment

It is commonly held that effective assessment tasks should test the performance of behaviours stated in learning outcomes under the same conditions as those under which they were learnt. For example, if the learning outcome states that apprentice carpenters will be able to hang a door, the assessment should require them to hang a door rather than describe the technique in a written examination, which is what often happens.

Behaviourist principles are useful as part of formative assessment, which is a kind of assessment designed to provide feedback for the learner and teacher, rather than to record or certify achievement. Formative assessment may be seen as a form of reinforcement, designed to motivate and encourage learners. To be effective, the reinforcement of desired behaviour must be provided consistently and in a timely manner so that the correct response is reinforced. When it comes to assessment, therefore, learners should receive feedback as quickly as possible after the assessment task.

Behaviour Management

Changing or strengthening learners' behaviours is the aim of most elementary learning programmes, with this strengthening of specific behaviours acting as a precursor to the development of cognitive skills. As part of the process of behaviour management, teachers can use operant conditioning techniques, which Skinner claims work best in providing motivation for learning. Indeed, positive reinforcement or the use of praise as a motivator lies behind practices that seek to reward learners when they demonstrate the behaviour the teacher has set out to inculcate. Reinforcers may be:

- material, such as prizes and awards;
- social, such as teacher attention, approval or praise;
- activity-related, such as an opportunity to engage in a favourite activity;
- intrinsic, such as feelings of self-actualization or pride.

Chapter-17
Cognitivism Perspective of Learning

How is it that if someone speaks your name, you immediately hear it even though you are not consciously attending to it? Certain automatic brain processes have taken place for this to occur, and these processes are studied by cognitive psychologists.

Cognitivism involves the study of mental processes such as sensation, perception, attention, encoding and memory that behaviourists were reluctant to study, because cognition occurs inside the 'black box' of the brain. Cognitivists believe that learning results from organizing and processing information effectively. If educators understand how learners process information, they can design learning experiences that optimize this activity. For example, an awareness of how learners transfer short-term memories into meaningful knowledge is likely to be useful in the classroom.

Cognitivism refers to the study of the mind and how it obtains, processes and stores information. This theory was a response to behaviourism. It was argued that not all learning occurs through shaping and changing of behaviours. In this theory, learners are active participants in their learning and the mind functions like a computer processor. Information comes in as input, the mind processes the information for the time being and the information is stored away to be retrieved later. Learning is shaped by acquired learning strategies and prior knowledge and attitudes, called schemas. The cognitive view of learning is teacher-centered and information must be presented in an organized manner in order to achieve the most efficient learning.

KEY IDEAS OF COGNITIVISM

The key ideas of cognitivism are as follows:

- Learning does not always involve a change in behaviour.
- Cognitivism focuses on internal mental learning processes.
- The key metaphor in cognitivism is the computer model.
- This model assumes discrete stages through which information is processed.
- Learners actively process, store and retrieve information for use.
- Learners organize and interpret information to create knowledge.

The Development of Cognitivism: Four factors influenced the development of cognitivism as a separate discipline in psychology:

- the development of experimental psychology;
- the move from an interest in external behaviours to internal brain processes;
- the inadequacy of behaviourism to explain language acquisition;
- the development of computers and an interest in artificial intelligence.

Experimental Psychology: There is a long tradition of experimental memory research by psychologists beginning in the 1880s with Hermann Ebbinghaus, who used nonsense syllables and words to investigate how memory is laid down. The British psychologist Frederic Bartlett, who wrote a book called *Remembering* in 1932, is best known for his development of the concept of 'schema'. G.A. Miller wrote a classic article, 'The magical number seven, plus or minus two', which investigated short-term memory as a separate cognitive entity. This early work on memory paved the way for more sustained research

The Shift from Behaviourism to Cognitivism: Behaviourists came to realize that not all learning could be explained by Pavlov's and Watson's theories of simple stimulus–response and reinforcement. In 1927 Köhler demonstrated that apes solved problems through a form of thinking he termed 'insightful behaviourism'.

Neo-behaviourists such as Tolman expanded this mental focus to a consideration of purposive behaviour in animals and people. He demonstrated that rats build up a mental representation or cognitive map of their environment and develop expectations rather than a set of inflexible links between stimuli and response.

Language Acquisition: Evidence of human cognition came from contested theories of language acquisition. Skinner's book *Verbal Behaviour* (1957) claimed that language was an activity shaped by the stimulus–response mechanism. The structural linguist Naom Chomsky challenged this by arguing that stimulus–response does not explain how children can generate sentences they have not heard before.

Computers and Artificial Intelligence: Computer scientists in the 1950s were interested in mental processes that could be reproduced by machines. The computer came to be used as a metaphor for cognitive function, and the brain came to be seen as a computing device. For example, cognitive theory employs an information-processing, input-process-output model, similar to that used in the computer industry (see Figure 17.1).

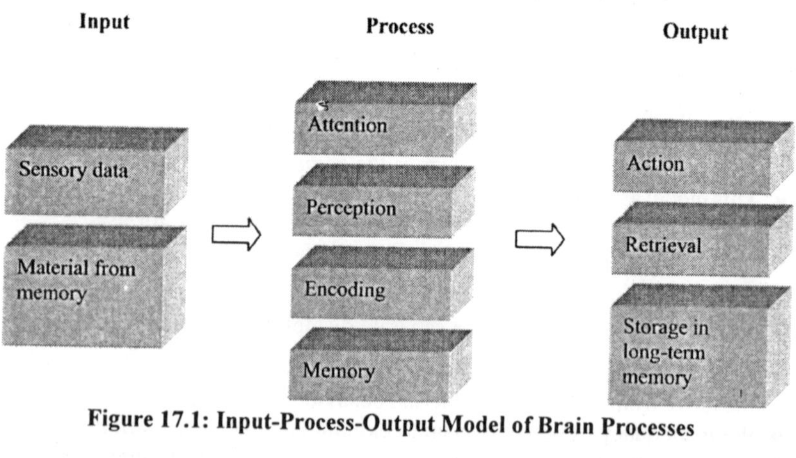

Figure 17.1: Input-Process-Output Model of Brain Processes

KEY PRINCIPLES OF COGNITIVISM

According to Hartley (1998), the key principles of learning associated with cognitive psychology are:

- ***Instruction should be well-organized:*** Well-organized materials are easier to learn and to remember.
- ***Instruction should be clearly structured*:** Subject matters are said to have inherent structures—logical relationships between key ideas and concepts—which link the parts together.
- ***The perceptual features of the task are important:*** Learners attend selectively to different aspects of the environment. Thus, the way a problem is displayed is important if learners are to comprehend it.
- ***Prior knowledge is important*:** Things must fit with what is already known if it is to be learnt.
- ***Differences between individuals are important as they will affect learning:*** Differences in 'cognitive style' or methods of approach influence learning.
- ***Cognitive feedback gives information to learners about their success or failure concerning the task at hand:*** Reinforcement can come through giving information—'knowledge of results'—rather than simply a reward.

PRACTICAL IMPLICATIONS OF COGNITIVISM FOR EDUCATORS

Cognitivists maintain that learning involves developing effective ways of building schemata and processing information. Knowing how learners process information should be helpful in designing appropriate learning experiences. For cognitivists, the teacher is in control of the learning, although they also hold that people learn best when encouraged to discover information pertinent to their own needs. Thus, teachers should design material that stimulates learners' cognitive processes and encourages learners to make mental connections for themselves.

In this section, we outline some of the practical educational implications of cognitivism as

Sensation

Teachers and instructional designers need to consider carefully the amount and type of information they present and the speed at which it is presented. Paivio (1986) argues that the mind processes visual and auditory material along different channels and in different ways for encoding, storage and later retrieval. In order to take account of processes of sensation teachers should:

- limit competing and distracting sensory impressions;
- use materials and draw on experiences that involve all the senses;
- present information in more than one sensory mode to facilitate dual encoding;
- direct the processing of sensory information.

Perception

Information-processing is both 'bottom up' and 'top down'. Top-down processing is perhaps the more important. In order to take account of processes of perception teachers should:

- arouse perceptual interest with strongly defined material;
- emphasize the distinctiveness of material in processing;
- point out patterns in materials;
- present material in a structured form – e.g. diagrams or stories;
- place learning in context and take contextual factors into account;
- review knowledge and assist learners to see relationships between old and new;
- explore attitudes and emotional responses to a topic and deal with any negativity.

Attention

A key concern for teachers is how to direct learners' attention when there are competing sensory impressions and memory. One way that teachers can address the issue of engaging learners' attention is by means of Howard Gardner's work on multiple intelligences (MI) theory. He suggested that 'any rich, nourishing topic—any concept worth teaching—can be approached in at least five different ways that will map onto the multiple intelligences' (Gardner 1991: 245). Gardner thinks of a topic as a room with several entry points that will engage the attention of different types of learners. These entry points and the means that teachers can use to access them include the:

- *Narrational* by means of a story;
- *Logical-quantitative* by deductive reasoning;
- *Foundational* by discussing underlying concepts;
- *Aesthetic* by appeal to artistic sensitivity;
- *Experiential* by some direct experience.

Attention is linked to learner motivation. Keller's ARCS motivational model proposes that motivation includes four categories—attention, relevance, confidence and satisfaction (Keller 1983; Keller and Kopp 1987). In order to gain and maintain attention teachers should:

- arouse initial interest by novelty and departure from the expected;
- present the subject in an interesting way—e.g. presenting a problem;
- vary teaching methods with exercises and activities that maintain interest;
- promote active listening in lectures or presentations.

Short-term Memory

Short-term memory (STM) is limited both in capacity and duration. In order to take account of these limitations on STM teachers should:

- limit the number of lists or items to be committed to memory at one time;
- be aware that learners remember first and last items on a list better than central ones;
- group items into 'chunks' with less than ten items to be memorized at one time;
- be conscious of interference between different types of information to be learnt;
- use repetition or maintenance rehearsal to retain information for a short period.

Working Memory

The concept of working memory has replaced STM as a model for more active and non-serial processing of information. Encoding is the process of organizing material and making it meaningful so that it can eventually be placed in long-term memory. In order to activate working memory teachers should:

- tell learners which information is most important;
- begin with an overview or outline of the material to be learnt;
- state the objectives or learning outcomes of a learning session;
- develop automaticity and speed of response in learners through regular practice;
- encourage learners to use the knowledge they already possess;
- encourage reflection and meta-cognition;
- link difficult-to-remember items to more meaningful ones;
- encourage visualization–use image representations; use verbal memory aids such as mnemonics;
- use mind-mapping techniques;
- use guided questioning to activate existing schemata and concepts;
- match encoding strategies with material to be learned;
- understand that learners may need to make schemata explicit and challenge their own assumptions;
- present content in increasing order of complexity;
- revisit topics to strengthen retention.

Long-term Memory

Long-term memory (LTM) is the permanent repository of accumulated information. Retrieval requires cues that may be sensory, cognitive or emotional. Cues create associations that activate (LTM). For example, particular songs often arouse powerful memories. In order to promote recall teachers should:

- link materials to cues that can be used to recall them;
- remind learners that cues are sufficient to recall the material;
- encourage learners to create their own cues;
- teach revision techniques;
- encourage learners to discover and use their strengths and styles.

STRENGTHS OF COGNITIVISM

The main strengths of cognitivism are as follows:

- Organized structure to learning: information comes in and is processed into short term memory before being stored away in long term memory.
- When problems are broken down into smaller parts, learners are not overwhelmed with incoming information and have time to process smaller bits.

WEAKNESSES OF COGNITIVISM

Because learning is very structured, it may become difficult to adapt to changes in what has already been processed and learned.

APPLICATION OF COGNITIVISM

Cognitivism is suited well for problem solving, where the concepts are complex and must be broken down into smaller parts. Ideas and concepts from these problems are linked to prior knowledge, which in turn helps the learner develop a stronger comprehension. (Stavredes, 2011)

EDUCATIONAL IMPLICATIONS OF COGNITIVISM

- Learners should be told why they should take the lesson, so that they can attend to the information throughout the lesson.
- Information critical for learning should be highlighted to focus learners' attention.
- The difficulty level of the material must match the cognitive level of the learner, so that the learner can both attend to and relate to the material. Links to both simpler and more complicated materials can be used to accommodate learners at different knowledge levels.
- Strategies should be used to allow learners to retrieve existing information from longterm memory to help make sense of the new information. Learners must construct a memory link between the new information and some related information already stored in long-term memory.
- Information should be chunked to prevent overload during processing in working memory (*Miller, 1956*).To facilitate deep processing, learners should be asked to generate the information maps during the learning process or as a summary activity after the lesson (*Bonk & Reynolds, 1997*).
- Other strategies that promote deep processing should be used to help transfer information to long-term storage. Strategies that require learners to apply, analyze, and evaluate promote higher-level learning, which makes the transfer to long-term memory more effective.
- Promote active listening;
- Don't overload short term memory by presenting too much material at once;
- Don't lecture for more than about twenty minutes without a break;
- Chunk material into groups or categories to facilitate retention;
- Make the structure and patterning of the material explicit for learners;
- Present material in more than one form to facilitate transfer to long term memory;
- Give learners the opportunity to revisit topics to strengthen retention;
- Use key words and terms as memory cues;
- Outline the metacognitive strategies needed for a given subject.

Chapter-18
Constructivism Perspective of Learning

Some teachers take a great interest when their pupils offer an incorrect answer to a question. In such a situation, these teachers proceed by asking pupils to explain how they arrived at that answer. It is likely that these teachers are operating from a constructivist perspective, which sees learners as constructors of meaning. By investigating the origins of a wrong answer, the teacher can uncover the learner's thinking processes, subsequently challenging and refining faulty mental constructs.

It is difficult to draw a clear distinction between constructivism and cognitivism because constructivism is a natural progression from cognitivism and both are interested in cognitive processes. But whereas cognitivism focuses on how information is processed, constructivism focuses on what people do with information to develop knowledge. In particular, constructivism holds that people actively build knowledge and understanding by synthesizing the knowledge they already possess with new information. For constructivists, learning is an active process through which learners 'construct' new meaning.

Constructivism is the study of a learner's own construction of knowledge. This knowledge is constructed through one's own personal experiences and interactions with the outside world. The learner takes in new information and gives meaning to it using his or her own prior attitudes, beliefs, and experiences as references. Learners are active participants in the construction of knowledge while the instructor serves as a facilitator.

Constructivists see learners as being active rather than passive. Knowledge is not received from the outside or from someone else; rather, it is the individual learner's interpretation and processing of what is received through the senses that creates knowledge. The learner is the center of the learning, with the instructor playing an advising and facilitating role. Learners should be allowed to construct knowledge rather than being given knowledge through instruction.

A major emphasis of constructivists is situated learning, which sees learning as contextual. Learning activities that allow learners to contextualize the information should be used in online instruction. If the information has to be applied in many contexts, then learning strategies that promote multi-contextual learning should be used to make sure that learners can indeed apply the information broadly. Learning is moving away from one-way instruction to construction and discovery of knowledge.

WHAT IS CONSTRUCTIVISM?

Constructivism is basically a theory, based on observation and scientific study about how people learn. It says that people construct their own understanding and knowledge of the world, through experiencing things and reflecting on those experiences. When we encounter something new, we have to reconcile it with our previous ideas and experience, may be changing what we believe, or may be discarding the new information as irrelevant. In any case, we are active creators of our own knowledge. To do this, we must ask questions, explore and assess what we know.

In the classroom, the constructivist view of learning can point towards a number of different teaching practices. In the most general sense, it usually means encouraging students to use active techniques (experiments, real-world problem solving) to create more knowledge and then to reflect on and talk about what they are doing and how their understanding is changing. The teacher makes sure that he understands the students' preexisting conceptions, and guides the activity to address them and then build on them.

According to constructivism theory:

- learners construct knowledge (rather than acquiring it) individually through their interactions with the environment (including other learners) based on their current as well as prior knowledge, authentic experience, mental structures, and beliefs that are used to interpret objects and events in relation to the context and environment in which learning takes place.
- the learner is an active processor of information and creator of personal knowledge;
- instruction is a process of supporting that construction;
- knowledge is not purely objective; and
- the instructor's major role is that of a facilitator of learning.

DEFINING CONSTRUCTIVISM

Constructivism is *theory of learning* based on the idea that knowledge is constructed by the knower based on mental activity. Learners are considered to be active organisms seeking meaning. Constructivism is founded on the premise that, by reflecting on our experiences, we construct our own understanding of the world consciously we live in. Each of us generates our own "rules" and "mental models," which we use to make sense of our experiences. Learning, therefore, is simply the process of adjusting our mental models to accommodate new experiences. Constructions of meaning may initially bear little relationship to reality (as in the naive theories of children), but will become increasing more complex, differentiated and realistic as time goes on.

KEY IDEAS OF CONSTRUCTIVISM

The key ideas of constructivism are as follows:

- Knowledge is situated and constructed in social contexts.
- The learner is an active agent in the interpretation of the world.
- Constructivism focuses on meaning-making and the understanding of knowledge.
- Learning involves the interpretation of experience to construct meaning.
- Mental constructs may be modified as a result of confirmation or challenge.
- Other people are important in the formation and modification of mental constructs.

ASSUMPTIONS OF CONSTRUCTIVISM

According to Merrill's (1991), the assumptions of constructivism are:

- knowledge is constructed from experience;
- learning is a personal interpretation of the world;
- learning is an active process in which meaning is developed on the basis of experience;
- conceptual growth comes from the negotiation of meaning, the sharing of multiple perspectives and the changing of our internal representations through collaborative learning;
- learning should be situated in realistic settings; testing should be integrated with the task and not a separate activity.

GUIDING PRINCIPLES OF CONSTRUCTIVISM

The guiding principles of constructivism are as follows:

- Knowledge is constructed, not transmitted.
- Prior knowledge impacts the learning process.
- Initial understanding is local, not global.
- Building useful knowledge structures requires effortful and purposeful activity.

HOW CONSTRUCTIVISM IMPACTS LEARNING

Constructivist learning theory does not necessarily imply that one must follow a "constructivist" pedagogical strategy. In other words, most researches firmly believe that knowledge is constructed, but some (e.g. main stream instructional designers) do not adopt an instructional design that is labeled "constructivist".

Typically, a constructivist teaching strategy is based on the belief that students learn best when they gain knowledge through exploration and active learning. Hands-on materials are used instead of textbooks, and students are encouraged to think and explain their reasoning instead of memorizing and reciting facts. Education is centered on themes and concepts and the connections between them, rather than isolated information.

Instruction: Under the theory of constructivism, educators focus on making connections between facts and fostering new understanding in students. Instructors tailor their teaching strategies to student responses and encourage students to analyze, interpret, and predict information. Teachers also rely heavily on open-ended questions and promote extensive dialogue among students.

Assessment: Constructivism calls for the elimination of grades and standardized testing. Instead, assessment becomes part of the learning process so that students play a larger role in judging their own progress.

COMPONENTS OF CONSTRUCTIVISM

The following components comprise the theoretical framework of Constructivism (Wilson, Teslow, and Osman-Jouchoux, 1995):

- mind is real: mental events are worthy of study;
- knowledge resides in the mind;

- knowledge is dynamic;
- meaning is constructed;
- reflection/abstraction is critical to becoming an expert;
- learning includes constructing representations;
- teaching is negotiating construction of meaning;
- thinking and perception are inseparable;
- problem solving is central to cognition;

FACES OR SCHOOLS OF CONSTRUCTIVISM

The faces or schools of constructivism are given below:

Trivial (Cognitive) Constructivism

It is the concept that knowledge is actively constructed by the learner, not passively received by the environment. It is derived from the assimilation - accommodation and schema models of Piaget.

Radical Constructivism

Derived from Von Glaserfeld (1990). Von Glaserfeld put forth the notion that the learner's constructions do not necessarily reflect knowledge of a "real world." Coming to know is a process of dynamic adaptation toward viable interpretations of experiences. We have no way of knowing what "real" reality might be, since input is filtered. Previous constructs also influence our perceptions of current experience. We construct "viable" models of what reality is based on social and physical constraints.

Social Constructivism or Socio-Constructivism

The social world of a learner includes the *people that directly affect that person, including teachers, friends, students, administrators, and participants in all forms of activity*. This takes into account the *social nature of both the local processes in collaborative learning and in the discussion of wider social collaboration* in a given subject, such as science.

This was the theory of Vygotsky in the late 1970's. Vygotsky's point of view was that acquisition and participation were synergistic strategies in learning situations. Aspects of participation involved teaching in contexts that could be meaningful to students based on their personal and social history, negotiating, class discussions, small group collaborative learning with projects and tasks, and valuing meaningful activity over correct answers. Social Constructivism emphasizes that learning takes place through interactions with other students, teachers, and the world-at-large.

Cultural Constructivism

Brings in a wider context to learning, including customs, religion, language, physiology, tools available (Computers, books, etc.). Tools are used to redistribute the cognitive load between the learner and the tool, and can affect the mind beyond actual use by changing one's skills, perspectives, and responses.

Beyond the immediate social environment of a learning situation are the *wider context of cultural influences, including custom, religion, biology, tools and language*. For example, the format of books can affect learning, by promoting views about the organization, accessibility and status of the information they contain.

According to Vosniadou (1996)—"*[What we need] is a new conception of the mind, not as an individual information processor, but as a biological, developing system that exists equally well within an individual brain and in the tools, artefacts, and symbolic systems used to facilitate social and cultural interaction.*"

Higher mental functions are, by definition, culturally mediated. They involve not a direct action on the world but an indirect one, one that takes a bit of material matter used previously and incorporates it as an aspect of action. Insofar as that matter itself has been shaped by prior human practice (e.g. it is an artifact), current action incorporates the mental work that produced the particular form of that matter.

Cobern (1993) writes of the world of subject matter and the internal mental world of the student as competing conceptual "ecologies", an image which invokes pictures of competing constructs, adaptation and survival-of-the-fittest. This is a somewhat more complex picture than radical constructivism. It highlights the need to consider both contexts fully, that of the student and that of the knowledge to be learned.

Critical Constructivism

Critical Constructivism adds a dimension of critical evaluation and cultural reform to the educational process. This approach incorporates the use of Communicative Ethics which defines the conditions for establishing dialog oriented toward mutual understanding among learners and teachers. Communicative Ethics promotes (1) primary concern for maintaining empathetic, caring, and trusting relationships, (2) commitment to achieve reciprocal understanding of goals, interests and standards, and (3) concern for and critical awareness of the often-invisible rules of the classroom, including social and cultural myths.

Critical constructivism looks at constructivism within a social and cultural environment, but adds a critical dimension aimed at *reforming these environments in order to improve the success of constructivism applied as a referent*. Taylor (1996) describes critical constructivism as a social epistemology that addresses the socio-cultural context of knowledge construction and serves as a referent for cultural reform. It confirms the relativism of radical constructivism, and also identifies the learner as being suspended in semiotic systems similar to those earlier identified in social and cultural constructivism. To these, critical constructivism adds a greater emphasis on the actions for change of a learning teacher.

Cultural myths that are prevalent in today's education systems include (Taylor, 1996):

- The rationalist myth of cold reason - where knowledge is seen as discovery of an external truth. This can lead to the picture of the teacher in a central role as transmitter of objective truths to students. This philosophy does not promote clarifying relevance to the lives of students, but instead promotes a curriculum to be delivered.

- The myth of hard control - which renders the teacher's classroom role as controller, and "locks teachers and students into grossly asymmetrical power relationships designed to reproduce, rather than challenge, the established culture".

Characteristics of Critical Constructivism

The main characteristics of critical constructivism are as under:

- Knowledge is socially constructed: World and information co-construct one another
- Consciousness is a social construction
- Political struggles: Power plays an exaggerated role in the production of knowledge and consciousness
- The necessity of understanding consciousness—even though it does not lend itself to traditional reductionistic modes of measurability
- The importance of uniting logic and emotion in the process of knowledge and producing knowledge
- The inseparability of the knower and the known
- The centrality of the perspectives of oppressed peoples—the value of the insights of those who have suffered as the result of existing social arrangements
- The existence of multiple realities: Making sense of a world far more complex that we originally imagined
- Becoming humble knowledge workers: Understanding our location in the tangled web of reality
- Standpoint epistemology: Locating ourselves in the web of reality, we are better equipped to produce our own knowledge
- Constructing practical knowledge for critical social action
- Complexity: Overcoming reductionism
- Knowledge is always entrenched in a larger process
- The centrality of interpretation: Critical hermeneutics
- The new frontier of classroom knowledge: Personal experiences intersecting with pluriversal information
- Constructing new ways of being human: Critical ontology

Trivial Constructivism

Knowledge is actively constructed by the learner, not passively received from the environment.

Constructionism

Constructionism is a constructivist learning theory and theory of instruction. It states that building knowledge occurs best through building things that are tangible an sharable "Constructionism (in the context of learning) is the idea that people learn effectively through making things. Constructionism is connected with experiential learning and builds on some of the ideas of Jean Piaget." Constructionism asserts that constructivism occurs especially well when the learner is engaged in constructing something for others to see:

According to Papert (1990) - *"Constructionism shares constructivism's* *connotation of learning as `building knowledge structures' irrespective of the circumstances of the learning. It then adds that this happens especially felicitously in a context where the learner is consciously engaged in constructing a public entity, whether it's a sandcastle or a theory of the universe... If one eschews pipeline models of transmitting knowledge in talking among ourselves as well as in theorizing about classrooms, then one must expect that I will not be able to tell you about my idea of constructionism. Doing so is bound to trivialize it. Instead, I must confine myself to engage you in experiences (including verbal ones) liable to encourage your own personal construction of something in some sense like it. Only in this way will there be something rich enough in your mind to be worth talking about."*

Important concepts are *consciously engaged* and *public entity*. Constructionism is not just learning-by-doing, but engaging reflexively and socially in the task. Both the creation process and the produced artifacts ought to be socially shared. Artifacts popular with constructionists include digital artifacts (e.g. things one can build with microworlds. "As adults, we all have times when we need to teach or explain something we know to someone else. To do this, we may have to bone up on the subject, talk with others, prepare notes and draw diagrams. In the process, we learn our subject well because we have to think hard about it and think of the best ways to convey it to others.

EDUCATIONAL IMPLICATIONS OF CONSTRUCTIVISM

Because constructivism is principally a theory about how people learn, we can draw many educational implications from the work of the key constructivist theorists, and those who have used constructivist principles. Some constructivist practices in education include:

- the diagnosis of learners' individual learning styles;
- the identification of learners' strengths or intelligences;
- curricular practices such as Individual Learning Plans (ILPs);
- attention to cultural inclusivity;
- innovative learning and teaching strategies such as problem-based learning;
- links between community-based learning and formal education;
- authentic assessment practices, which incorporate learners' views.

STRENGTHS OF CONSTRUCTIVISM

- Constructivist activities are generally relevant to the learner and real-world based.
- Learners construct knowledge and meaning as they can relate the information to their own experiences, beliefs, and attitudes.

WEAKNESSES OF CONSTRUCTIVISM

- Individual experiences and attitudes can vary.
- A specific, desired outcome may not always be achieved when different people approach the problem or task.

APPLICATION OF CONSTRUCTIVISM

Constructivism is best utilized when learners take control of the learning situation, such as in Problem-Based Learning. As learners engage themselves in an activity like this, they develop an understanding of the importance of the problem, comprehend the relevance of the topic, and construct knowledge through their experiences. It is more important to focus on the whole rather than the individual parts in constructivist learning. Constructivism is sometimes misconstrued as a theory that compels students to reinvent the wheel, but instead, it implores students to attempt to learn how it functions and apply this to real world learning.

IMPLICATIONS OF CONSTRUCTIVISM

- Learning should be an active process. Keeping learners active doing meaningful activities results in high-level processing, which facilitates the creation of personalized meaning. Asking learners to apply the information in a practical situation is an active process, and facilitates personal interpretation and relevance.
- Learners should construct their own knowledge rather than accepting that given by the instructor. Knowledge construction is facilitated by good interactive online instruction, since the students have to take the initiative to learn and to interact with other students and the instructor, and because the learning agenda is controlled by the student.
- Collaborative learning should be encouraged to facilitate constructivist learning. Working with other learners gives learners real-life experience of working in a group, and allows them to use their metacognitive skills. Learners will also be able to use the strengths of other learners, and to learn from others. When assigning learners for group work, membership should be based on the expertise level and learning style of individual group members, so that individual team members can benefit from one another's strengths.
- Learners should be given control of the learning process. There should be a form of guided discovery where learners are allowed to make decision on learning goals, but with some guidance from the instructor.
- Learning should be made meaningful for learners. The learning materials should include examples that relate to students, so that they can make sense of the information. Assignments and projects should allow learners to choose meaningful activities to help them apply and personalize the information.
- Learning should be interactive to promote higher-level learning and social presence, and to help develop personal meaning. Learning is the development of new knowledge, skills, and attitudes as the learner interacts with information and the environment.

Chapter-19
Humanism Perspective of Learning

Some psychologists disliked psychodynamic and behaviourist explanations of personality. They felt that these theories ignored the qualities that make humans unique among animals, such as striving for self-determination and self-realization. In the 1950s, some of these psychologists began a school of psychology called *humanism.*

Humanistic psychologists try to see people's lives as those people would see them. They tend to have an optimistic perspective on human nature. They focus on the ability of human beings to think consciously and rationally, to control their biological urges, and to achieve their full potential. In the humanistic view, people are responsible for their lives and actions and have the freedom and will to change their attitudes and behaviour.

ASSUMPTIONS OF HUMANISTIC PSYCHOLOGISTS

Humanistic psychologists start from the assumption that every person has his/her own unique way of *perceiving* and understanding the world and that the things they do only make sense in this light. Consequently, the kinds of questions they ask about people differ from those asked by psychologists from other approaches. Whereas other approaches take an *objective* view of people, in essence asking about them, *'what is this person like?'* humanistic psychologists' priority is understanding people's *subjectivity*, asking *'what is it like to be this person?'* As a result, they reject the objective *scientific method* as a way of studying people. Humanistic psychologists explicitly endorse the idea that people have *free will* and are capable of choosing their own actions (although they may not always realize this). They also take the view that all people have a tendency towards *growth* and the fulfillment of their potential. Much of their research has focused on how people can be helped to fulfill their potential and lead more contented lives.

PRINCIPLES OF HUMANISTIC EDUCATION

There are five basic principles of humanistic education:

- Students should be able to choose what they want to learn. Humanistic teachers believe that students will be motivated to learn a subject if it's something they need and want to know.
- The goal of education should be to foster students' desire to learn and teach them how to learn. Students should be self-motivated in their studies and desire to learn on their own.
- Humanistic educators believe that grades are irrelevant and that only self-evaluation is meaningful. Grading encourages students to work for a grade and not for personal satisfaction. In addition, humanistic educators are

opposed to objective tests because they test a student's ability to memorize and do not provide sufficient educational feedback to the teacher and student.

- Humanistic teachers believe that both feelings and knowledge are important to the learning process. Unlike traditional educators, humanistic teachers do not separate the cognitive and affective domains.
- Humanistic teachers insist that schools need to provide students with a non-threatening environment so that they will feel secure to learn. Once students feel secure, learning becomes easier and more meaningful.

HUMANISTIC APPROACH TO LEARNING

The more recent *humanist theories* take into account the way that, in our society, previously polarized views of right and wrong have dissolved into a variety of potentially equally valuable truths, i.e., a pluralistic approach. The stress on valuing diversity in many organizations and in society generally is a reflection of this ideology.

An emphasis on active learning is at the core of these humanistic approaches to learning. The terms '*andragogy*' and '*pedagogy*' highlight the difference between earlier models of training and the more usual approach nowadays.

Pedagogy and Andragogy: Pedagogy and andragogy are terms derived from the Greek words meaning *'child'* and *'man'* respectively.

Pedagogy: Pedagogy is essentially based on instruction; knowledge is transmitted formally from one who knows to one who does not know. This type of model has often been used in institutional settings, where it can be administratively easier to assume control of the learning experience, while ignoring the ability or needs of the person to engage in self-directed learning – for example in schools and other educational establishments. Unfortunately, this model can engender resistance or rebellion, particularly in older children, adolescents and adults.

It could be claimed that pedagogy actually misses the point: providing training or education does not necessarily mean that the learner will enjoy or remember the experience, even less transfer it to useful settings.

Andragogy: Andragogy, however, provides us with a process model in which the learner discovers knowledge at a pace to suit him/herself, supported by a facilitator, perhaps a coach or mentor. Andragogical theory is based on four assumptions that define its unique position, as against pedagogy or traditional learning methods:

- The learner needs freedom to develop his/her own learning.
- The existing experiences of the learner are fundamental for understanding and new learning to take place effectively.
- The person needs to be ready to learn, as opposed to being motivated by fear or coercion.
- The orientation to learning is paramount: in other words, it is not subject-orientated but learner centred.

Informal individual support is important in andragogy theory, as is the development of a group environment that is both positive and accepting.

Sharing experiences can deepen individual learning, not only for cognitive (intellectual) processes, but also affective (emotional) processes. Participative methods build on both individual and group experiences, aiding reflection, lengthening the span of attention and increasing self-awareness. Learning in this way is often referred to as *'experiential learning'*.

Two psychologists, Abraham Maslow and Carl Rogers became well known for their humanistic theories.

Carl Rogers (1902-1987) was a humanistic psychologist who agreed with the main assumptions of Abraham Maslow, but added that for a person to "grow", they need an environment that provides them with genuineness (openness and self-disclosure), acceptance (being seen with unconditional positive regard), and empathy (being listened to and understood). Without these, relationships and healthy personalities will not develop as they should, much like a tree will not grow without sunlight and water. Rogers believed that every person can achieve their goals, wishes and desires in life. When, or rather if they did so, *self actualization* took place. This was one of Carl Rogers most important contributions to psychology and for a person to reach their potential a number of factors must be satisfied.

CARL ROGERS, FREEDOM TO LEARN (1994)

According to Rogers, learning is facilitated when:

- the student participates completely in the learning process and has control over its nature and direction
- it is primarily based upon direct confrontation with practical, social, personal or research problems, and
- self-evaluation is the principal method of assessing progress or success. Rogers also emphasizes the importance of learning to learn and an openness to change.

ROGER'S PRINCIPLES OF LEARNING

- Significant learning takes place when the subject matter is relevant to the personal interests of the student
- Learning which is threatening to the self (e.g., new attitudes or perspectives) is more easily assimilated when external threats are at a minimum
- Learning proceeds faster when the threat to the self is low
- Self-initiated learning is the most lasting and pervasive.

SELF ACTUALIZATION

According to Rogers (1951), "*The organism has one basic tendency and striving - to actualize, maintain, and enhance the experiencing organism*" Rogers rejected the deterministic nature of both psychoanalysis and behaviourism and maintained that we behave as we do because of the way we perceive our situation. "As no one else can know how we perceive, we are the best experts on ourselves."

Carl Rogers (1959) believed that humans have one basic motive, that is the tendency to self-actualize - i.e. to fulfill one's potential and achieve the highest level of 'human-beingness' we can. Like a flower that will grow to its full potential if the conditions are right, but which is constrained by its environment, so people will flourish and reach their potential if their environment is good enough.

However, unlike a flower, the potential of the individual human is unique, and we are meant to develop in different ways according to our personality. Rogers believed that people are inherently good and creative. They become destructive only when a poor self-concept or external constraints override the valuing process. Carl Rogers believed that for a person to achieve self-actualization they must be in a state of congruence.

This means that self-actualization occurs when a person's "ideal self" (i.e. who they would like to be) is congruent with their actual behaviour (self-image). Rogers describes an individual who is actualizing as a fully functioning person. The main determinant of whether we will become self-actualized is childhood experience.

Characteristics of Self-Actualized People: Following are the main characteristics of self-actualized people:

- They are realistically oriented.
- They accept themselves, other people, and the natural world for what they are.
- They have a great deal of spontaneity.
- They are problem-centred rather than self-centered.
- They have an air of detachment and a need for privacy.
- They are autonomous and independent.
- Their appreciation of people and things is fresh rather than stereotyped.
- Most of them have had profound mystical or spiritual experiences, although not necessarily religious in character.
- They identify with humanity.
- Their intimate relationships with a few specially loved people tend to be profound and deeply emotional rather than superficial.
- Their values and attitudes are democratic.
- They do not confuse means with ends
- Their sense of humor is philosophical rather than hostile.
- They have a great fund of creativeness.
- They resist conformity to the culture.
- They transcend the environment rather than just coping with it.

CARL ROGERS'S THEORY OF PERSONALITY

As we interact with others, starting from home, our friends, neighbors and then eventually at school, we start creating an image of ourselves. According to Carl Rogers, *"we have an organized, consistent set of perceptions and beliefs about our self which is also known as our self-concept."* In accordance to this, our self-concept is developed as a result of our positive or negative responses from the influence of people around us.

Carl Rogers was a humanist and psychotherapist. He believed if an individual attained self-actualization they would be a fully functioning person living *"the good life"*. By this, he means that the individual would have a positive healthy psychological outlook, trust their own feelings and have congruence in their lives between self and experience (Rogers 2004).

Carl Roger's theory is phenomenological and idiographic. He believed that human nature is *"exquisitely rational"* (Rogers, 2004 p. 194). His theory came from his work as a psychotherapist. The aim of the therapy is to facilitate a reintegration of the *self-concept*. Rogers believed that people know what is causing the psychological imbalance in their lives and that deep down they know what they need to do to regain their balance or *self-actualization* to become "Fully Functioning" persons (Rogers 2004). Psychotherapy is the change agent that assists individuals in making personal changes to regain balance and achieve their potential or self-actualization.

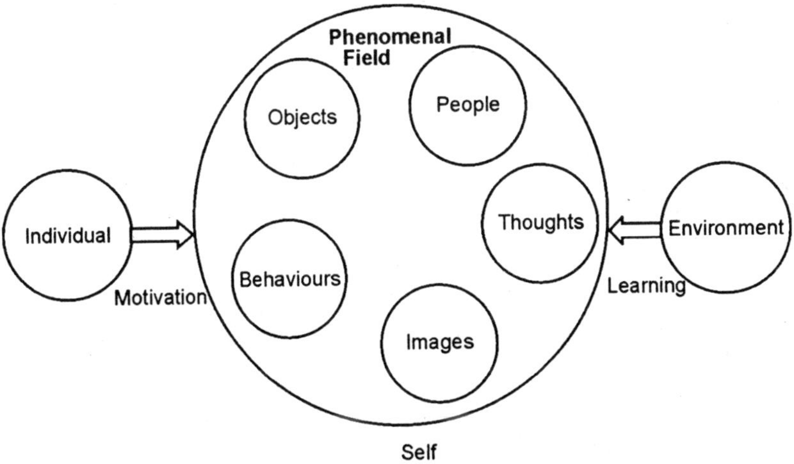

Figure 19.1: Carl Rogers's Theory of Personality

Central to Rogers' personality theory is the notion of self or self-concept. This is defined as *"the organized, consistent set of perceptions and beliefs about oneself"*. The self is the humanistic term for who we really are as a person. The self is our inner personality, and can be likened to the soul, or Freud's psyche. The self is influenced by the experiences a person has in their life, and out interpretations of those experiences. Two primary sources that influence our self-concept are childhood experiences and evaluation by others.

According to Rogers (1959), we want to feel, experience and behave in ways which are consistent with our self-image and which reflect what we would like to be like, our ideal-self. The closer our self-image and ideal-self are to each other, the more consistent or congruent we are and the higher our sense of self-worth. A person is said to be in a state of incongruence if some of the totality of their experience is unacceptable to them and is denied or distorted in the self-image.

Components of Personality

Carl Rogers believed that there are three important components of human personality:

Self-Actualization: Rogers believed humans are born with a desire to be the best they can. Self-actualization is the motivating force to achieving their full potential. As infants the main goal towards self-actualization is to have needs met e.g. to be fed.

Real Self: What a person is capable of becoming if they lived in an ideal world. An individual would have lived in an environment of unconditional positive regard. Their parents would have accepted and loved them just as they are. Such individuals would be psychologically healthy with a positive unconditional self-regard and the potential to attain self-actualization.

Self-Concept: A person's perception of themselves is shaped by how others see them. The self is the central construct in this theory. It is based largely on life experiences, social evaluation and the attitude of the individual's significant other. If the individual experiences conditional positive regard from their parents, the individual develops their parent's values and conditions of worth. If self-concept is based on the values of the significant other this can give rise to incongruence between self and experience.

Components of Self-Concept: Carl Rogers believed that there are three different parts of self-concept:

Self-Image or How You See Yourself: Self-image includes the influence of our body image on inner personality. Basically, we might see ourselves as a good or bad person, beautiful or ugly because our self-image influence how we think, feel and behave in this world. However, we have to know that self-image does not necessary coincide with reality. For example, a teenage boy thinks he is timid, when he is really quite demure. A girl believes that she is not appealing, when she is really quite pretty. Each person's self-image is perhaps a combination of different aspects such as your physical characteristics, personality traits, and social roles.

Self-Worth or Self-Esteem or What We Think About Ourselves: Rogers believed feelings of self-worth developed in early childhood and were formed from the interaction of the child with the mother and father. As a child grows older, interactions with significant others will affect feelings of self-worth. The way we compare ourselves to others and how others respond to us affects our self-worth. For instance, when a boy behaves well and the teacher recognizes his good behaviour, the boy may develop a positive self-esteem. When a person cannot afford to buy a car but he sees his friend has a new car, it can have a negative impact on his self-esteem.

Ideal-Self or How You Wish You Could Be: This is the person who we would like to be. It consists of our purpose, goals and what we aspire in life. It changes continually as we grow old; for this reason, the ideal self in childhood is not the ideal self in teens or late twenties and so on. Most of the time, the way we see ourselves is different how we would like to see ourselves.

Carl Rogers (1951) viewed the child as having two basic needs: positive regard from other people and self-worth. Our feelings of self-worth and how we think about ourselves are very important to be psychologically healthy and in achieving our goals and ambitions in life, eventually our self-actualization.

CARL ROGERS'S PERSON-CENTERED THEORY OR PERSON CENTERED THERAPY (PCT) OR PERSON CENTERED APPROACH

Person-centered therapy (PCT) is also known as person-centered psychotherapy, person-centered counseling, client-centered therapy and Rogerian psychotherapy. PCT is a form of talk-psychotherapy developed by psychologist Carl Rogers in the 1940s and 1950s. The goal of PCT is to provide clients with an opportunity to develop a sense of self where they can realize how their attitudes, feelings and behaviour are being negatively affected.

Carl Rogers proposed a theory called the person-centered theory. Like Freud, Rogers drew on clinical case studies to come up with his theory. He also drew from the ideas of Maslow and others. In Rogers's view, the *self-concept* is the most important feature of personality, and it includes all the thoughts, feelings, and beliefs people have about themselves. Rogers believed that people are aware of their self-concepts.

Propositions of Carl Roger's Person-Centered Theory: Carl Roger's theory (as of 1951) was based on 19 propositions:

1. All individuals (organisms) exist in a continually changing world of experience (phenomenal field) of which they are the center.
2. The organism reacts to the field as it is experienced and perceived. This perceptual field is "reality" for the individual.
3. The organism reacts as an organized whole to this phenomenal field.
4. A portion of the total perceptual field gradually becomes differentiated as the self.
5. As a result of interaction with the environment, and particularly as a result of evaluational interaction with others, the structure of the self is formed – an organized, fluid but consistent conceptual pattern of perceptions of characteristics and relationships of the "I" or the "me", together with values attached to these concepts.
6. The organism has one basic tendency and striving - to actualize, maintain and enhance the experiencing organism.
7. The best vantage point for understanding behaviour is from the internal frame of reference of the individual.
8. Behaviour is basically the goal-directed attempt of the organism to satisfy its needs as experienced, in the field as perceived.
9. Emotion accompanies, and in general facilitates, such goal directed behaviour, the kind of emotion being related to the perceived significance of the behaviour for the maintenance and enhancement of the organism.
10. The values attached to experiences, and the values that are a part of the self-structure, in some instances, are values experienced directly by the organism, and in some instances are values introjected or taken over from others, but perceived in distorted fashion, as if they had been experienced directly.
11. As experiences occur in the life of the individual, they are either, (a) symbolized, perceived and organized into some relation to the self, (b) ignored because there is no perceived relationship to the self structure, (c) denied symbolization or given distorted symbolization because the experience is inconsistent with the structure of the self.

12. Most of the ways of behaving that are adopted by the organism are those that are consistent with the concept of self.
13. In some instances, behaviour may be brought about by organic experiences and needs which have not been symbolized. Such behaviour may be inconsistent with the structure of the self but in such instances the behaviour is not "owned" by the individual.
14. Psychological adjustment exists when the concept of the self is such that all the sensory and visceral experiences of the organism are, or may be, assimilated on a symbolic level into a consistent relationship with the concept of self.
15. Psychological maladjustment exists when the organism denies awareness of significant sensory and visceral experiences, which consequently are not symbolized and organized into the gestalt of the self structure. When this situation exists, there is a basic or potential psychological tension.
16. Any experience which is inconsistent with the organization of the structure of the self may be perceived as a threat, and the more of these perceptions there are, the more rigidly the self structure is organized to maintain itself.
17. Under certain conditions, involving primarily complete absence of threat to the self structure, experiences which are inconsistent with it may be perceived and examined, and the structure of self revised to assimilate and include such experiences.
18. When the individual perceives and accepts into one consistent and integrated system all his sensory and visceral experiences, then he is necessarily more understanding of others and is more accepting of others as separate individuals.
19. As the individual perceives and accepts into his self structure more of his organic experiences, he finds that he is replacing his present value system- based extensively on introjections which have been distortedly symbolized- with a continuing organismic valuing process.

Core Conditions

Client-centered therapy operates according to three basic principles that reflect the attitude of the therapist to the client:

- The therapist is *congruent* with the client.
- The therapist provides the client with *unconditional positive regard.*
- The therapist shows *empathetic* understanding to the client.

Congruence in Counseling: Congruence is also called genuineness. Congruence is the most important attribute in counseling, according to Rogers. This means that, unlike the psychodynamic therapist who generally maintains a 'blank screen' and reveals little of their own personality in therapy, the Rogerian is keen to allow the client to experience them as they really are. The therapist does not have a façade (like psychoanalysis), that is, the therapist's internal and external experiences are one in the same. In short, the therapist is authentic.

Unconditional Positive Regard: The next Rogerian core condition is *unconditional positive regard.* Rogers believed that for people to grow and fulfill their potential it is important that they are valued as themselves.

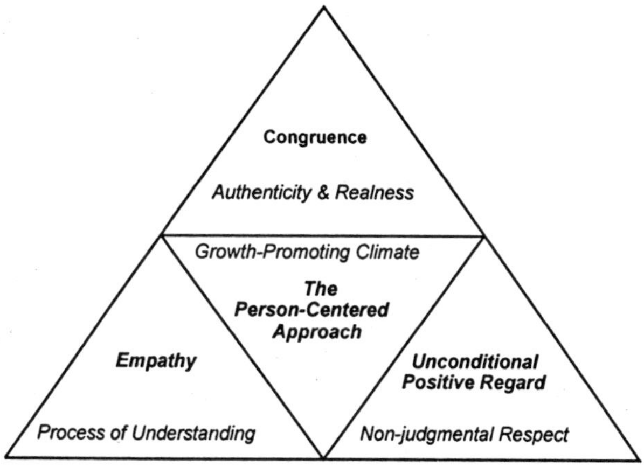

Figure 19.2: The Person-Centered Approach

This refers to the therapist's deep and genuine caring for the client. The therapist may not approve of some of the client's actions but the therapist does approve of the client. In short, the therapist needs an attitude of "I'll accept you as you are." The person-centered counselor is thus careful to always maintain a positive attitude to the client, even when disgusted by the client's actions.

Empathy: Empathy is the ability to understand what the client is feeling. This refers to the therapist's ability to understand sensitively and accurately [but not sympathetically] the client's experience and feelings in the here-and-now.

Chapter-20
Theories of Learning

Learning theories play explicitly or implicitly a major role in instructional design models upon which the approaches to teaching by instructors are based; they form the foundation for effective instructional models and provide frameworks for providing the conditions for, and interpreting observations of teaching and learning. Effective instructional models are based on learning theories emphasizes the fact that instructional designers must understand the strengths and weaknesses of each learning theory to optimize their use in appropriate instructional design strategies. Mayes (2004) states that for good pedagogical design, there is simply no escaping the need to adopt a theory of learning. The present chapter describe the four different views of learning

THORNDIKE'S TRIAL-AND-ERROR LEARNING THEORY

The experimental study of animal learning by E.L. Thorndike (1874-1949) in the United States and his theory on trial-and-error learning provided the impetus for Skinner's experiments on instrumental or operant conditioning. Thorndike's doctoral research on *'Animal Intelligence'* in 1898 provided the psychological world the first miniature system of learning known as trial-and-error learning.

Trial and Error is based on random activities to reach the goal. Thorndike's research on animals showed that learning is a matter of connecting responses to stimuli in a very mechanical way. There is no involvement of consciousness, thinking, reasoning or understanding. The animal performs responses mechanically. The responses that bring reward are learned; the responses that do not bring reward are not learned. The animal does not show ability to understand, think, and reason. The animal learns mechanically through trial-and-error.

Indeed many forms of human learning, particularly the learning of sensory-motor skills, are achieved through trial-and-error. Learning to walk, to swim, or to ride a bicycle is based on trial-and-error. At the beginning, we make wrong movements and commit errors. As we go through a series of practice trials, errors are reduced and responses are mastered. The gradual reduction of errors over trials gives the name, trial-and-error form of learning.

Thorndike's Puzzle Box Experiment on Cat

His classic experiment used a hungry cat as the subject, a piece of fish as the reward, and a puzzle box as the instrument for studying trial-and-error learning.

In this typical experiment, a hungry cat was placed inside the puzzle box, and a piece of fish was kept outside the box. The cat could not reach the fish unless it opened the door. In order to escape from the box, the cat had to perform a simple action as required by the experimenter. The cat had to pull a loop or press a lever in order to open the door. Once the door was opened, the cat could escape and get the fish as a reward.

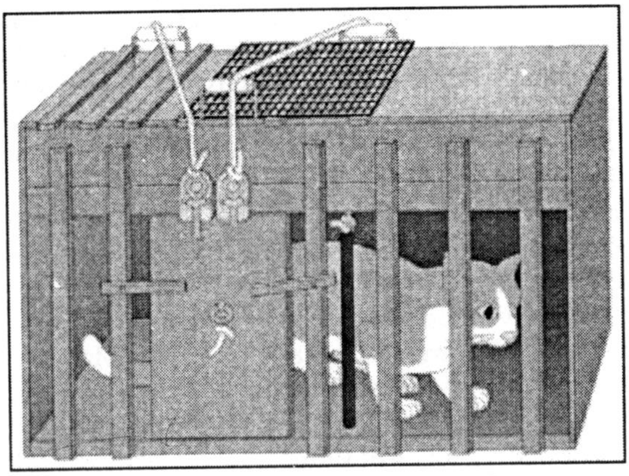

Figure 20.1: Thorndike's Puzzle Box

Result of the Experiment

Trial & Error is based on random activities to reach the goal. Random activities are block or hindrances, drive, goal, random movements, multiple response, chance, success, selection and fixation. Experiment sums up the following stages in the process of learning:

Drive: Hungry cat intensified by the sight of the food.

Goal: To get food by getting out of the box.

Block: The cat was confined in the box with a closed door.

Random movements: The cat persistently tried to come out of the box without knowing how.

Chance success: Striving and random movements the cat by chance succeeded in opening the door.

Selection: Gradually cat recognized the correct way to manipulate the latch.

Fixation: At last cat learned the proper way to open the door by eliminating all the incorrect responses and fixing only the right response.

Features of Trial and Error Learning

- Learning by trial and error is gradual process.
- For learning to occur, the learner must be definitely motivated.
- The learner makes random and variable response.
- Some responses do lead to the goal (annoying response)
- Some responses lead to the goal. (satisfying responses)
- With the increase in number of trials the annoying responses will tend to be eliminated and the satisfying responses will be strengthened and repeated.
- The time taken to perform the task (to repeat the satisfying response) decreases with successive trials.

Thorndike's Laws of Learning

1. *Law of Readiness:* First primary law of learning, according to him, is

the *'Law of Readiness'* or the *'Law of Action Tendency'*, which means that learning takes place when an action tendency is aroused through preparatory adjustment, set or attitude. Readiness means a preparation of action. If one is not prepared to learn, learning cannot be automatically instilled in him, for example, unless the typist, in order to learn typing prepares himself to start, he would not make much progress in a lethargic and unprepared manner.

2. *Law of Exercise:* The second law of learning is the *'Law of Exercise'*, which means that drill or practice helps in increasing efficiency and durability of learning and according to Throndike's S-R Bond Theory, the connections are strengthened with trail or practice and the connections are weakened when trial or practice is discontinued. The 'law of exercise', therefore, is also understood as the 'law of use and disuse' in which case connections or bonds made in the brain cortex are weakened or loosened. Many examples of this case are found in case of human learning. Learning to drive a motor-car, typewriting, singing or memorizing a poem or a mathematical table, and music etc. need exercise and repetition of various movements and actions many times.

Law of Effect: The third law is the *'Law of Effect'*, according to which the trial or steps leading to satisfaction stamps in the bond or connection. Satisfying states lead to consolidation and strengthening of the connection, whereas dissatisfaction, annoyance or pain leads to the weakening or stamping out of the connection. In fact, the 'law of effect' signifies that if the response satisfies the subject, they are learnt and selected, while those which are not satisfying are eliminated. Teaching, therefore, must be pleasing. The educator must obey the tastes and interests of his pupils. In other words, greater the satisfaction stronger will be the motive to learn. Thus, intensity is an important condition of 'law of effect'.

Besides these three basic laws, Throndike also refer to five subordinate laws which further help to explain the learning process. These are:

i. Law of Multiple Response: According to it, the organism varies or changes its response till an appropriate behaviour is hit upon. Without varying the responses, the correspondence for the solution might never be elicited. If the individual wants to solve a puzzle, he is to try in different ways rather than mechanically persisting in the same way. Throndike's cat in the puzzle box moved about and tried many ways to come out till finally it hit the latch with her paw which opened the door and it jumped out.

ii. The Law of Set or Attitude: Learning is guided by a total set or attitude of the organism, which determines not only what the person will do but what will satisfy or annoy him. For instance, unless the cricketer sets himself to make a century, he will not be able to score more runs. A student, similarly, unless he sets to get first position and has the attitude of being at the top, would while away the time and would not learn much. Hence, learning is affected more in the individual if he is set to learn more or to excel.

iii. Pre-potency of Elements: According to this law, the learner reacts selectively to the important or essential in the situation and neglects the other features or elements which may be irrelevant or non- essential. The ability to deal with the essential or the relevant part of the situation makes analytical and insightful learning possible. In this law of pre-potency of elements,

Thorndike is really anticipating insight in learning which was more emphasized by the Gestaltions.

iv. Law of Response by Analogy: According to this law, the individual makes use of old experiences or acquisitions while learning a new situation. There is a tendency to utilize common elements in the new situation as existed in a similar past situation. The learning of driving a car, for instance, is facilitated by the earlier acquired skill of driving a motor cycle or even riding a bicycle because the perspective or maintaining a balance and controlling the handle helps in steering the car.

v. The Law of Associative Shifting: According to this law we may get an response, of which a learner is capable, associated with any other situation to which he is sensitive. Thorndike illustrated this by the act of teaching a cat to stand up at a command. A fish was dangled before the cat while he said 'stand up'. After a number trails by presenting the fish after uttering the command 'stand up', he later ousted the fish and the overall command of 'stand up' was found sufficient to evoke the response in the cat by standing up or her hind legs.

Educational Implications of Thorndike's Laws of Learning: In brief, the educational implications of the Thorndike's Theory are:

1. According to this theory the task can be started from the easier aspect towards its difficult side. This approach will benefit the weaker and backward children.
2. A small child learns some skills through trial and error method only such as sitting, standing, walking, running etc. In teaching also the child rectifies the writing after committing mistakes.
3. In this theory more emphasis has been laid on motivation. Thus, before starting teaching in the classroom the students should be properly motivated.
4. Practice leads a man towards maturity. Practice is the main feature of trial and error method. Practice helps in reducing the errors committed by the child in learning any concept.
5. Habits are formed as a result of repetition. With the help of this theory the wrong habits of the children can be modified and the good habits strengthened.
6. The effects of rewards and punishment also affect the learning of the child. Thus, the theory lays emphasis on the use of reward and punishment in the class by the teacher.
7. The theory may be found quite helpful in changing the behaviour of the delinquent children. The teacher should cure such children making use of this theory.
8. With the help of this theory the teacher can control the negative emotions of the children such as anger, jealousy etc.
9. The teacher can improve his teaching methods making use of this theory. He must observe the effects of his teaching methods on the students and should not hesitate to make necessary changes in them, if required.
10. The theory pays more emphasis on oral drill work. Thus, a teacher should conduct oral drill of the taught contents. This help in strengthening the learning more.

SKINNER'S OPERANT CONDITIONING LEARNING THEORY

Burhaus Frederic Skinner (1938) is the best-known psychologist in the US behaviourist tradition. In the 1930s, he adopted a carefully structured approach called *'operant conditioning'* in which the behaviour of the subject determines the response to the subject's own actions.

WHAT IS OPERANT CONDITIONING?

B.F. Skinner (1938) coined the term operant conditioning; it means roughly changing of behaviour by the use of reinforcement which is given after the desired response. Skinner identified three types of responses or operant that can follow behaviour:

1. **Neutral Operants**: responses from the environment that neither increase nor decrease the probability of a behaviour being repeated.
2. **Reinforcers**: Responses from the environment that increase the probability of a behaviour being repeated. Reinforcers can be either positive or negative.
3. **Punishers**: Responses from the environment that decrease the likelihood of a behaviour being repeated. Punishment weakens behaviour.

Operant conditioning proposes that we learn through consequence. It works on the assumption of learning through reward and punishment. Behaviour which is positively reinforced tends to be repeated, whereas behaviour which is negatively reinforced tends to be avoided. This learning theory was first investigated by Skinner, who developed the "Skinner box" in which rats were placed in a box and required to press a lever for food to be dispensed (the reward). The consequence of receiving food if they pressed the lever caused the rats to repeat this behaviour again and again.

Skinner (1948) studied operant conditioning by conducting experiments using animals which he placed in a *'Skinner Box'* which was similar to Thorndike's puzzle box.

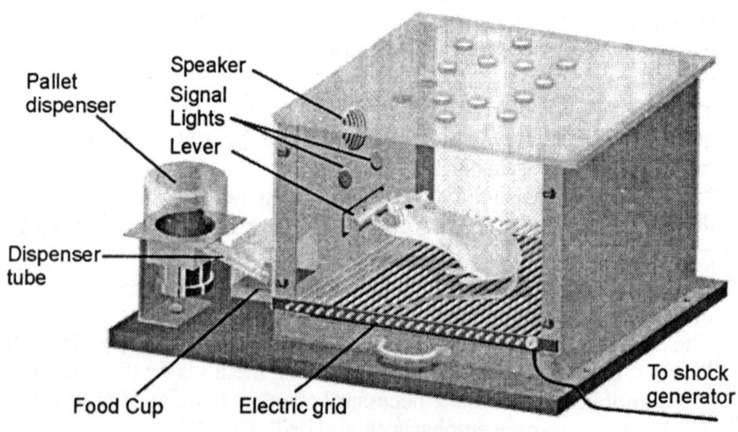

Figure 20.2: Skinner's Box

In his *'Skinner Box'*, Skinner used positive reinforcement to train rats to press a lever to obtain food pellets. The positive reinforcement provided by the food increases the probability that the rats will press the lever again. Negative reinforcement removes an aversive stimulus after the correct response – for example, rats press a lever to remove an electric shock. The relief from painful experience also increases the probability that the lever will be pressed again. Skinner uses the term 'reinforcer' rather than 'reward' because 'reinforcer' has an association with behaviour whereas 'reward' does not. A response followed by a reinforcing stimulus is strengthened and is therefore more likely to occur again. The larger and more appealing the reinforcer, the faster a response will be learned. A response that is not followed by a reinforcing stimulus is weakened, and is therefore less likely to occur again. The link between stimulus and response gradually becomes weaker and subsequently dies – for example, rats repeatedly pressing a lever without receiving food pellets will eventually abandon that behaviour. This results in extinction.

Therefore:

- desired behaviours are rewarded causing their frequency to increase;
- undesired behaviours are punished causing their frequency to decrease.

Although Skinner did not consider punishment as effective as reinforcement in modifying behaviour it is still commonly used as a deterrent. Types of reward and punishment are shown in Figure 20.3.

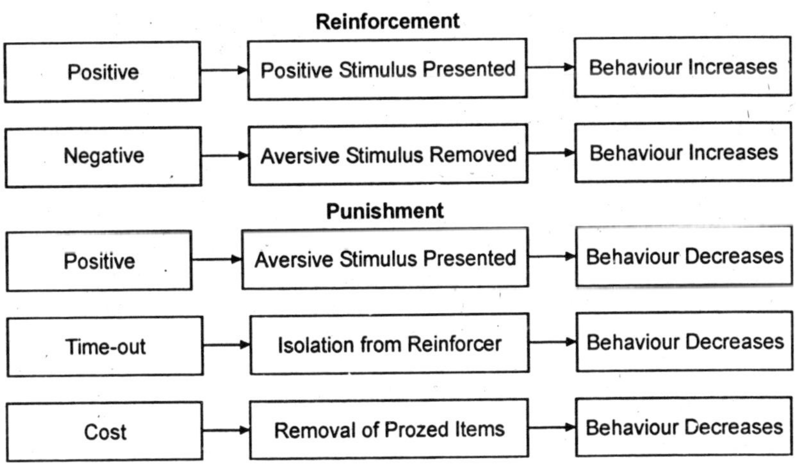

Source: based on Oates *et al.* (2005: 55).

Figure 20.3: Reinforcement and Punishment

Skinner experimented with what he called continuous and variable reinforcement schedules. In continuous reinforcement, every correct response is reinforced; in variable reinforcement, only some are. Skinner found that variable reinforcement schedules lead to steadier response rates because of the possibility that the next response will pay off.

In other experiments, Skinner (1958a) trained pigeons to play a type of table tennis by a process called 'shaping'. At first pigeons were rewarded when they performed an action that vaguely approximated to the target behaviour. Then the reward was restricted to actions that more closely matched the target behaviour. Gradually their behaviour was 'shaped' until it was satisfactory. A summary of the key terms used in operant conditioning is given in Table 20.1.

Table 20.1: Key Terms in Operant Conditioning

Operant Conditioning	The process of shaping behaviour by following it with reinforcement that increases in frequency
Reinforcement	An event that increases the probability that the event preceding it will be repeated
Continuous Reinforcement	A pattern in which every desirable response is followed by reinforcement
Variable Reinforcement	A pattern in which only some desirable responses are followed by reinforcement
Magnitude	A term that describes the scale of a large and appealing reinforce that is likely to produce faster learning of responses
Repetition	The frequency of reinforced operant behaviour that strengthens association between stimulus and response
Extinction	The elimination of behaviour by removing reinforcement
Shaping	The process of reinforcing behaviour as it becomes more like the target behaviour

Educational Implications of Operant Conditioning Theory

Conditioning Study Behaviour: Teaching is the arrangement of contingencies of reinforcement which expedite learning. For effective teaching teacher should arranged effective contingencies of reinforcement. Example: For Self learning of a student, teacher should reinforce student behaviour through variety of incentives such as prize, medal, smile, praise, affectionate patting on the back or by giving higher marks.

Conditioning and Classroom Behaviour: During learning process child acquire unpleasant experiences also. This unpleasantness becomes conditioned to the teacher subject and the classroom and learner dislike the subject and a teacher. Suitable behavioural contingencies, atmosphere of recognition, acceptance, affection and esteem helps child in approaching teacher and the subject. If student is not serious in study, teacher make use of negative reinforcement like showing negligence, criticising student etc. but if student is serious in study, teacher make use of positive reinforcement like prize, medal, praise and smile. Example: student having transistor in classroom neglected by the teacher indulged in talking with others for longer time. After long time student asked teacher till now you are receiving assignments, I will also submit you. Thus behaviour is conditioned.

Managing Problem Behaviour: Two types of behaviour is seen in the classroom—undesired behaviour and problematic behaviour. Operant conditioning is a behaviour therapy technique that shape students behaviour. For this teacher should admit positive contingencies like praise, encouragement etc. for learning. One should not admit negative contingencies. Example punishment (student will run away from the dull and dreary classes – escape stimulation.

Dealing with Anxieties through Conditioning

Through conditioning fear, anxieties, prejudices, attitudes, perceptual meaning develops. Example of anxiety:

- Signals on the road
- Siren blown during war time
- Child receiving painful injection from a doctor

Anxiety is a generalized fear response. To break the habits of fear, desensitization techniques should be used by a teacher. Initially teacher should provide very weak form of conditioned stimulus. Gradually the strength of stimulus should be increased.

Conditioning Group Behaviour: Conditioning makes entire group learn and complete change in behaviour is seen due to reinforcement. It breaks undesired and unsocial behaviour too. Example: Putting questions or telling lie to teachers will make teachers annoyed in such circumstances students learn to keep mum in the class. Asking questions, active participation in class discussion will make the teacher feel happy – interaction will increase and teaching learning process becomes more effective.

Conditioning and Cognitive Processes: Reinforcement is given in different form, for the progress of knowledge and in the feedback form. When response is correct positive reinforcement is given. Example: A student who stands first in the class in the month of January is rewarded in the month of December. To overcome this Programme instruction is used. In this subject matter is broken down into steps. Organizing in logical sequence helps in learning. Each step is build upon the preceding step. Progress is seen in the process of learning. Immediate reinforcement is given at each step.

Shaping Complex Behaviour: Complex behaviour exists in form of a chain of small behaviour. Control is required for such kind of behaviour. This extended form of learning is shaping technique. Smallest Behaviour is controlled at initial stage. On behalf of different contingencies next order of chain of behaviours is controlled. Example: Vocabulary in English. Teaching spelling is mainly a process of shaping complex form of behaviour.

PAVLOV'S CLASSICAL CONDITIONING THEORY OF LEARNING

Behaviourism had its origins in the last years of the nineteenth century, when physiologists such as Ivan Pavlov investigated animals' automatic and involuntary responses to stimuli. Classical behaviourists believe that all learning conforms to observable scientific laws governing behavioural associations and patterns; the learner simply responds to external stimuli in a deterministic manner.

Classical Conditioning is one important type of learning. It was actually discovered accidentally by Ivan Pavlov (1849-1936). Pavlov was a Russian physiologist who discovered this phenomenon while doing research on digestion. His research was aimed at better understanding the digestive patterns in dogs.

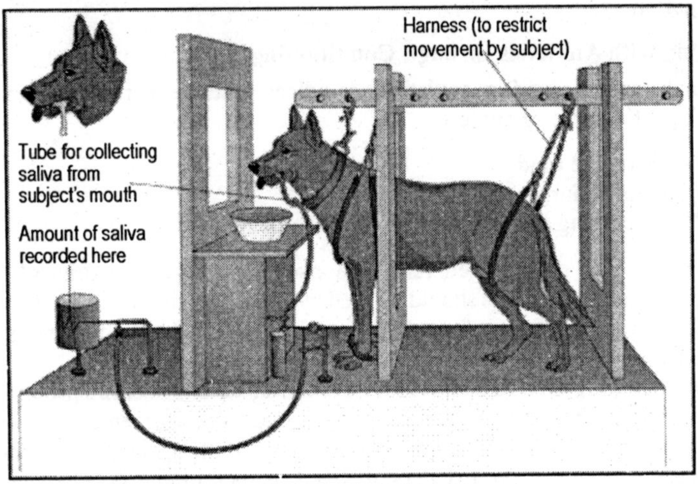

Figure 20.4: Pavlov's Experiment

During his experiments, he would put meat powder in the mouths of dogs that had tubes inserted into various organs to measure bodily responses. What he discovered was that the dogs began to salivate before the meat powder was presented to them. Then, the dogs began to salivate as soon as the person feeding them would enter the room. He soon began to gain interest in this phenomenon and abandoned his digestion research in favour of his now famous Classical Conditioning study.

Basically, the findings support the idea that we develop responses to certain stimuli that are not naturally occurring. When we touch a hot stove, our reflex pulls our hand back. It does this instinctually, no learning involved. It is merely a survival instinct. But why now do some people, after getting burned, pull their hands back even when the stove is not turned on? Pavlov discovered that we make associations which cause us to generalize our response to one stimulus onto neutral stimuli it is paired with. In other words, hot burner = ouch, stove = burner, therefore, stove = ouch.

Basic Principles of Classical Conditioning

Classical conditioning is a form of learning whereby a *conditioned stimulus (CS)* becomes associated with an unrelated *unconditioned stimulus (US)* in order to produce a behavioural response known as a *conditioned response (CR)*. The conditioned response is the learned response to the previously neutral stimulus. The unconditioned stimulus is usually a biologically significant stimulus such as food or pain that elicits an *unconditioned response (UR)* from the start. The conditioned stimulus is usually neutral and produces no particular response at first but after conditioning it elicits the conditioned response.

Extinction is the decrease in the conditioned response when the unconditioned stimulus is no longer presented with the conditioned stimulus. When presented with the conditioned stimulus alone, the individual would show a weaker and weaker response, and finally no response. In classical-conditioning terms, there is a gradual weakening and disappearance of the conditioned response. Related to this, *spontaneous recovery* refers to the return of a previously extinguished conditioned response following a rest period. Research has found that with repeated extinction/recovery cycles, the conditioned response tends to be less intense with each period of recovery.

Key Terms in Classical Conditioning

The key terms used in classical conditioning are:

Table 20.2: Key Terms in Classical Conditioning

Term	Meaning
Classical Conditioning	Learning in which a subject comes to respond to a conditional stimulus repeatedly presented along with an unconditional stimulus
Unconditional Stimulus	Any stimulus that elicits an automatic reaction in an organism
Neutral Stimulus	A stimulus that does not cause the organism to respond
Conditional Stimulus	A neutral stimulus that elicits a particular reaction by association with an unconditional stimulus
Unconditional Response	An automatic reaction elicited by a stimulus
Conditional Response	The behaviour that occurs when the conditional stimulus is presented
Contiguity	The close association in time of conditional and unconditional stimuli
Extinction	The elimination of behaviour by removing the unconditional stimulus
Variation	The process of varying the stimuli in order to produce a more generalized response
Generalization	The behaviour that occurs when organisms respond in the same way to stimuli that are similar to an original conditional stimulus
Drive Stimuli	Needs such as hunger, thirst and sleep
Repetition	The pattern in which frequent and contiguous presentation of the stimulus and response is designed to produce an association between them
Habit Strength	The frequency of association between a particular stimulus and response, which usually leads an organism to choose the response connected to the strongest habit

Educational Implications of Classical Conditioning Learning Theory

The educational implications of Classical Conditioning Learning Theory are as under:

- The formulation of positive attitudes, fears, love, prejudices or hatred towards an object, phenomenon or event can be developed through conditioning. Thus, classical conditioning can be used to develop favourable or unfavourable attitude towards learning, teacher and the school.

- We should associates faults with punishment so that whenever a child feels like committing faults, he/she anticipates the punishments. Thus, reward and punishments may be given right at the time of the act and not to be delayed.
- Repetition and habit formation is to be strengthed in the process of learning.
- Most of our learning is associated with the process of conditioning from the beginning. Thus, the teacher is to develop the good reading habits through conditioning.
- This learning theory is helpful for developing good habits such as cleanliness, respect, for elders, honesty, punctuality etc. in the learners.
- It can be used to eliminate the bad habits and conditioned fear from the behaviour of the students.
- The principle of classical conditioning can be used in removing complexes from the minds of abnormal children.

Comparison between Classical Conditioning and Operant Conditioning

The comparison between Classical Conditioning and Operant Conditioning is given in Table 20.3

ROBERT GAGNE'S THEORY OF LEARNING

Robert Gagne (1916–2002) was an American educational psychologist who pioneered the science of instruction in the 1940s. His book *"The Conditions of Learning,"* first published in 1965, identified the mental conditions that are necessary for effective learning.

Robert Gagné's seminal work is his conditions of learning theory. It includes five categories of learning outcomes and the nine events of instruction. Together, these two themes of Gagné's learning theory provide a framework for learning conditions.

Gagné's work (1985) focuses on intentional or purposeful learning, which is the type of learning that occurs in school or specific training programmes. He believed that events in the environment influence the learning process. His theory identifies the general types of human capabilities that are learned. These capabilities are the behavioural changes (learning outcomes) in a learner that a learning theory must explain. Once the learning outcomes are identified, an analysis of the conditions that govern learning and remembering can occur.

For example, a learner who is participating in a situation where the right conditions for learning are invoked, then he or she will experience the five categories of learning outcomes that include the human capabilities of intellectual skills, verbal information, cognitive strategies, motor skills, and attitudes.

Description of Gagné's Conditions of Learning Theory

Gagné's conditions of learning theory draws upon general concepts from various learning theories in order to define what learning is. The theory looks at the observable changes in human behaviour that confirm that learning has occurred. Gagné's theory provides an answer to the question, *"what is learning?"* In answering that question, Gagné provides a description of the conditions under which learning takes place by referring to situations in

Table 20.3: Comparison between Classical Conditioning and Operant Conditioning

Classical Conditioning	*Operant Conditioning*
It was developed by Russian Physiologist Ivan P. Pavlov.	It was developed by B.F. Skinner.
It is called Pavlovian or Type-1 learning (respondent).	It is called Skinnerian or type-2 learning (operant).
It is signal conditioning.	It is instrumental conditioning.
The occurrence of conditioned response (CR) is relaxively forced by unconditioned stimulus (UCS).	The response is more voluntary and spontaneous.
The unconditioned stimulus (UCS) occurs without regard to the subject's behaviour.	The reward is contingent upon the occu-rrence of response.
It is described as preparatory or anticipa-tory response and is also called signal learning.	It serves primarily to emphasize or guide an organism which already has certain responses available in its repertoire.
The association between stimulus and response (S-R) is on the basis of Law of Contiguity.	The association between stimulus and response (S-R) is on the basis of Law of Effect.
It is controlled by autonomic nervous sys-tem in the organism.	It is controlled by central nervous system in the organism.
Bondage between specific unconditioned stimulus (UCS)/conditioned stimulus (CS) is established	Tendency to respond in a specific manner is developed.
Reinforcement comes first as in Pavlov's experiment. Food is presented first to elicit the response.	Reinforcement is provided after the response is made by the organism.
Conditioned stimulus (CS) and unconditio-ned stimulus (UCS) can be placed in different temporal sequences, close contiguity is followed.	Close contiguity is followed and R-S chain is formed.
It focuses on the single (S-R) stimulus-response bondage.	It is concerned with sequences of response. A chain of responses is formed which leads to the desired goal.
We present the unconditioned response (UCS) irrespective of the behaviour.	We present the stimulus only if the organism makes the desired response.
It presents different pictures of behaviour and learning in which an arbitrary stimulus is associated with a high specific, elicitable response.	The situation describes the differentia-tion and discrimination of a response out of a mass behaviour emitted in response to complex stimulus field.
The essence of learning is stimulus substitution.	The essence of learning is response modification.
The classical conditioned reflexes may have zero strength initially.	The operant cannot have zero strength because it has to occur at least once before it can be reinforced.
The classical conditioned response is corre-lated with and controlled by an antecedent event, an eliciting stimulus which is initially the UCS and subsequently the CS.	In operant conditioning, there is no ante-cedent and the behaviour is controlled by its consequences.
Respondent behaviour is internal.	Operant is external behaviour.

ordinary life and in school where learning occurs and by referring to experimental studies in learning.

Gagné (1985) postulates that proof of learning shows by a difference in a learner's performance before and after participating in a learning situation. He claims that the presence of the performance does not make it possible to conclude that learning has occurred; but instead, it is necessary to show that there has been a change in performance. In other words, the capability for exhibiting the performance before learning requires consideration as well as the capability that exists after learning.

The following four elements provide the framework for Gagné's Conditions of learning theory.

i. Conditions of Learning
ii. Association Learning
iii. The Five Categories of Learning Outcomes
iv. The Nine Events of Instruction

Conditions of Learning

Gagné (1985) describes two different types of conditions that exist in learning: *internal and external.*

Internal Conditions: Capabilities that already exist in a learner before any new learning begins make up the internal conditions necessary for learning. These internal conditions are transformed during the learning process.

External Conditions: It include different stimulus's that exist outside the learner such as the environment, the teacher, and the learning situation. This means that each new learning situation begins from a different point of prior learning and will consist of a different external situation, depending on the learner and on the learning environment.

Therefore, the useful prototypes of learning by association (described next) are delineated by internal and external learning conditions.

Gagné's Hierarchy or Conditions of Learning

Robert M. Gagné proposed a system of classifying different types of learning in terms of the degree of complexity of the mental processes involved. He identified eight basic types and arranged these in the hierarchy shown in Figure 20.5. According to Gagné, the higher orders of learning in this hierarchy build upon the lower levels, requiring progressively greater amounts of previous learning for their success. The lowest four orders tend to focus on the more behavioural aspects of learning, while the highest four focus on the more cognitive aspects.

The brief descriptions of Gagné's eight categories of learning are as under:

Signal Learning: This is the simplest form of learning, and consists essentially of the classical conditioning first described by the behavioural psychologist Pavlov. In this, the subject is 'conditioned' to emit a desired response as a result of a stimulus that would not normally produce that response. This is done by first exposing the subject to the chosen stimulus (known as the conditioned stimulus) along with another stimulus (known as the unconditioned stimulus) which produces the desired response naturally; after

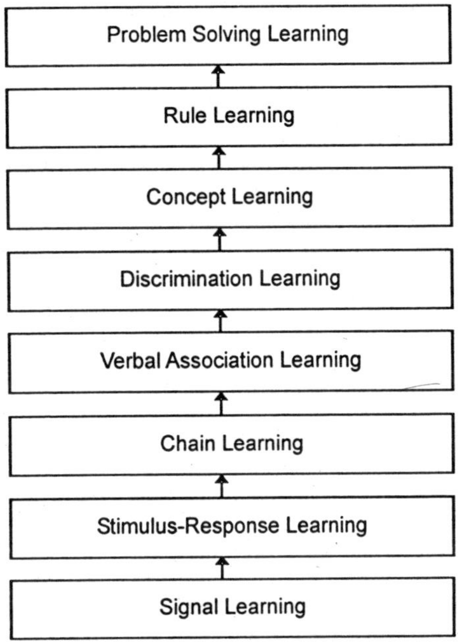

Figure 20.5: Gagné's Hierarchy of Learning

a certain number of repetitions of the double stimulus, it is found that the subject emits the desired response when exposed to the conditioned stimulus on its own. The applications of classical conditioning in facilitating human learning are, however, very limited.

Stimulus-Response Learning: This somewhat more sophisticated form of learning, which is also known as operant conditioning, was originally developed by Skinner. It involves developing desired stimulus-response bonds in the subject through a carefully-planned reinforcement schedule based on the use of 'rewards' and 'punishments'. Operant conditioning differs from classical conditioning in that the reinforcing agent (the 'reward' or 'punishment') is presented after the response. It is this type of conditioning that forms the basis of programmed learning in all its various manifestations.

Chaining: This is a more advanced form of learning in which the subject develops the ability to connect two or more previously-learned stimulus-response bonds into a linked sequence. It is the process whereby most complex psychomotor skills (e.g. riding a bicycle or playing the piano) are learned.

Verbal Association: This is a form of chaining in which the links between the items being connected are verbal in nature. Verbal association is one of the key processes in the development of language skills.

Discrimination Learning: This involves developing the ability to make appropriate (different) responses to a series of similar stimuli that differ in a systematic way. The process is made more complex (and hence more difficult) by the phenomenon of interference, whereby one piece of learning inhibits another. Interference is thought to be one of the main causes of forgetting.

Concept Learning: This involves developing the ability to make a consistent response to different stimuli that form a common class or category of some sort. It forms the basis of the ability to generalize, classify etc.

Rule Learning: This is a very-high-level cognitive process that involves being able to learn relationships between concepts and apply these relationships in different situations, including situations not previously encountered. It forms the basis of the learning of general rules, procedures, etc.

Problem Solving: This is the highest level of cognitive process according to Gagné. It involves developing the ability to invent a complex rule, algorithm or procedure for the purpose of solving one particular problem, and then using the method to solve other problems of a similar nature.

HULL'S SYSTEMATIC BEHAVIOUR LEARNING THEORY OR DRIVE REDUCTION LEARNING THEORY

C.L. Hull (1884-1952) who was professor of psychology at Yale University synthesized into a unified system many of the achievements of his predecessors and built a new system on their strength and avoided some of their pitfalls. His system of behaviour studied under S-R reinforcement theorists is deductive, mathematical and testable. Its important features are:

- It is based on the association theory of stimulus –response.
- It is based in survival model of life.
- It is based on biological needs and their fulfillment.

Hull's Drive Reduction Theory is the notion that behaviour occurs in response to *"drives"* such as hunger, thirst, sexual interest, feeling cold, etc. When the goal of the drive is attained (food, water, mating, warmth) the drive is reduced and this constitutes reinforcement of the behaviours that lead to the drive reduction and ultimately learning.

Hull viewed the drive as a stimulus, arising from a tissue need, which in turn stimulates behaviour. The strength of the drive is determined upon the length of the deprivation, or the intensity/strength of the resulting behaviour. He believed the drive to be non-specific, which means that the drive does not direct behaviour rather it functions to energize it. In addition this drive reduction is the reinforcement.

Clark Hull's learning theory focuses mainly on the principle of reinforcement; when an S-R relationship is followed by a reduction of the need, the probability increases that in future similar situations the same stimulus will create the same prior response. Reinforcement can be defined in terms of reduction of a primary need. Just as Hull believed that there were secondary drives, he also felt that there were secondary reinforcements - *"If the intensity of the stimulus is reduced as the result of a secondary or learned drive, it will act as a secondary reinforcement"*.

Important Concepts related to Hull's Learning Theory

With a view to understand Hull's theory of learning, following concepts may be explained:

Need: Need is a state of the organism in which a deviation of the organism, from the optimum of biological conditions necessary for survival, takes place. When a need arises, the organism acts in order to reduce the need. Therefore, Hull's theory of learning is called need- reduction theory. Need would produce the behaviour and the particular behaviour that reduces the need would be gradually learned.

Drive: It is a common denominator for all primary motivations whether due to food, water, sex or any other cause.

Reinforcement: Hull explained reinforcement as "Whenever a reaction (R) takes place in temporal contiguity within afferent receptor impulse (s) resulting from the impact upon a receptor of stimulus energy (S) and this conjunction is followed closely by the diminution in a need, in the tendency if that stimulus on subsequent occasions to evoke that reactions."

Unlearned Behaviour: Hull recognized the importance of unlearned stimulus-response associations. Unlearned associations are found more frequently on the lower phylogenetic levels than on the higher. Learning's super-structure is built upon these inherited associations. The nature of inherited response patterns was formulated on the basis of association- doctrine. Hull developed an elaborate symbolism for his theory. The symbol SUR stands for the unlearned stimulus-response association. U is an abbreviation of unlearned. The S and R represent the stimulus and response components of learning respectively.

The Stimulus: The theories of the behaviourists measure the objective physical stimulus, usually relate to the internal neural activities to a response. For Hull, responses are conditioned to the neural after effects of stimuli rather than to the stimuli themselves. The effective stimulus, in learning, is the trace in the nervous system caused by the environmental objects. According to Hull, the stimuli in the object would give rise to stimulus traces in the organism. The first may be designated S and the seconds s. Learning involves S and not the s.

The Response: A distinction may be made between tendency within the person to make a response and the actual response itself. If we designate the overt response R, we can refer to the pre-existing neural activities which initiate the response as r. These internal response tendencies are not observable but inferred fiom behaviour. Symbolically the learned association, of S and R is represented as SHR. H represents habit. Changes in SHR constitute learning in Hull's system.

Learning and Biological Needs: There is a difference between learning and performance. Several factors can influence performance but learning itself as influenced only by one factor, the number of times, the particular response occurring together (contiguity) has been followed by reinforcement.

Reinforcement: According to Hull all behaviour has its origin in the biological needs which are most demanding early in human life. The complex human behaviour is based on these biological needs. Reinforcement according to Hull is like Thorndike's rewarded in one way. It is stimulus which has the ability to alter the probabilities of certain R following certain S. When a response is reinforced; this implies that it has been followed by one of a certain class of stimuli. Hull envisaged that reinforcing stimuli were those which reduced stimuli uniquely associated with the biological drives.

Educational Implications of Hull's Systematic Behaviour Learning Theory

Hulls system of learning is acclaimed and remembered for putting forward a most systematic, scientific and mathematical theory of learning.

- Hull's theory rejected the trigger-like mechanism of stimuli-response advocated by Thorndike and introduced the concept of intervening variables between S and R. The things within the individual definitely act and react with what is received in terms of stimuli from the external environment before emitting of an overt response. He termed the environmental influences upon the individual as 'inputs' and his responses as 'outputs' and what goes from the individual as 'processes'.
- Hull's theory attached sufficient importance to the needs, drives, incentives, reinforcement and adequate motivation for achieving satisfactory results in the process of teaching and learning.
- Hull's theory tried to extend the concept of reinforcement was considered only in terms of rewards and satisfaction but Hull stated that to escape pain or punishment or to reduce need is also a kind of reward helps in reinforcement.
- Hull's theory laid great emphasis on the formation of good habits as a means of the learning of desirable behaviour. In practice, Hull reduced the art of the learning to mere habit formation and its proper reinforcement.
- Hull's theory emphasized the need for proper rest and other measure to reduce the ill-effects of fatigue in any act of learning the principle of work and appropriate rest, may thus be said to have evolved as a result of the experimental findings of this theory.
- Hull's system of learning advocated the following chain sequence for improved results in the teaching-learning process:
  - Drive:-this is something which is needed by the learner in order to behave or respond.
  - Cue:-There must be something to which the learner must respond. Response:-The learner must be made to respond or do something in order to learn some act.
  - Reward:-The learners' response must be reinforced or rewarded, thus enabling him to learn what he wants to learn.

KURT LEWIN'S FIELD THEORY OF LEARNING

Kurt Lewin was considered by some as the father of modern social psychology due to his act of breaking new ground in employing scientific methods and experimentation in the study of social behaviour. His focus on fusing psychology with the philosophy of science resulted in an extensive number of empirical studies performed in the realms of child development, motivation and social behaviour, particularly having to do with observational studies and experiments on children's behaviour.

Lewin not only adapted Gestalt principles but further applied them to a theory of personality and development into what is now known as the Psychological Field Theory. He translated Gestalt philosophy into social experience involving people who should be considered as wholes instead of being composed of discrete parts. A person is presented as a whole system consisting of subsystems that are somewhat separate yet are still capable of interacting and combining with each other.

He was one of the first psychologists to propose that the development of an individual was the product of the interaction between inborn predispositions (nature) and life experiences (nurture). This conception was presented by Lewin in the form of a mathematical equation known as Lewin's Equation for behaviour, stating that behaviour is the function of the person interacting within his environment or B = f (P,E).

According to Levin, behaviour exists in a totality of interacting facts which comprise a dynamic field. The circumstances or conditions in any part of the field are influenced by and depend on every other part of the field. This psychological field is otherwise known as the life space which comprises the individual and his psychological or behavioural environment also known as facts that affect the behaviour or thoughts of the individual at a certain point in time.

Main Concepts Used in Lewin's Learning Theory

The main concepts used in Lewin's theory are as follows:

Field: For a psychologist, a field means a psychological world that covers an individual himself, his concepts and expectations. It does not correspond with a Geographical or a Physical world. A field situation is perceived in such a way that any change in the field depends upon the nature of the field at that time. An astronomer used 'field' to describe the universe and predict the orbits of stars. A biologist relates the function of cells to their location in a growth 'field'.

Person: The person is often represented as a point moving about in his life space, affected by pulls and pushes upon him, circumventing barriers in his locomotion in his own life space. A person is a psychological self. A person is not limited to a mind or body, nor mind and body. It refer to what is 'I', 'my', 'mine', 'me'. Life space contains the person himself, the goals he is seeking (positive valences), the goals he is avoiding (negative valences), the 'barriers' that restrict his movements, and the 'paths' he must follow to get what he wants. In an ideal situation, the person being kept in the present state of isolation wants to reach his goal 'G'. But, in between person himself (P) and goal (G) stands barriers (B), the apologizing barrier. Thus, the person is nothing but a teaching itself.

Life Space: It is also called the psychological field. The psychological field is the space in which the person moves psychologically. It contains the whole of one' psychological reality - one's self and what one gains from one's physical and social environment.

Regions: The life space also consists of numerous relationships between person and his environment, numerous inter-dependent variables and total patterns of factors and influences together with the individual with all his needs, percepts, concepts, ideas, knowledge, beliefs and images of concrete objects. The life space can be divided into numerous regions depending upon one's similar experiences or reference material. Each region may consist of numerous positive-negative vectors and valences.

In cognitive field term, a generalization arises through a person's categorization of sub-regions into a unified region of his life space. When a child learns that vegetables, flowers, bushes and trees are plants or a student learns that hopes, dreams, beliefs and anticipations are all sub-regions of a 'future' region in his contemporaneous life space, he is generalizing. A student of professional education, through differentiation of various instances of learning, may develop a generalized concept, learning to cover any learning in any situation.

Valence: When a person is attracted by an object that object is said to have a positive valence. When person is repelled by an object, that is said to have a negative valence. The person tends to move away towards a region in life space that has positive valence and he tends to move away from a region in life space that has negative valence. Because life space may contain regions with several valences active at ones, these give rise to conflict, especially when the opposing forces are approximately in balance.

The concept of valence is related with conflict, which means that a person is confronted with a complicated situation to the different aspects of which he has learned to make in compitable responses. Every person, incident or object tends to attract or repel you in some degree.

Vectors: The term vectors represent a force which is influence movement towards a goal or away form it. If there is only one vector, she is movement in the direction of the vector; however, if there are two or more vectors acting simultaneously in different directions, the movement is in the direction of the resultant force.

Foreign Hull: The two principal aspects of a lift space and a person and his psychological environment. The two are not mutually exclusive. Both are surrounded by a non-psychological Foreign Hull. The Foreign Hull of a life space is composed of those aspects of a person's physical-social environment that are observable not by the person himself but by the one who is studying the particular person but which, at the juncture under consideration have no significance for the person being studied.

Topology: It is also called topological. Two basic concepts which topological space denotes are: (i) connectedness, and (ii) part whole relationships. Topological concepts are used to represent the structure of life space in such a way as to define the range of possible perceptions and actions. This is accomplished by showing the arrangements of the functional parts of life space. The parts are shown as various regions and their boundaries. When an individual structures his life space, he divides it into regions.

Topology is a kind of Geometry, which is concerned with inside, outside, boundary etc. and not with length, breadth, height, thickness. Here, we do not pay importance to the distance. Topology explains the position of man in reference to his functions, goals and barriers.

Educational Implications of Lewin's Field Theory of Learning

The educational implications of Lewin's Field Theory of Learning are as under:

- Lewin's field theory emphasizes on motivation and perception. Therefore, for effective learning the teacher should provide suitable psychological environment and have an insight and understanding into the relationship between individual, environment and his behaviour.
- The teacher should keep in setting the goals for different individuals to attain according to their capacities and abilities and try to guide the learners effectively to overcome difficulties, threats and barriers of learning.
- Total situation of the problem should be made very clear and understandable to the learner so that they will be motivated to learn.
- Teacher should use reward and punishment according to the needs of the situation as Lewin's accepted the value of reward and punishment for learning.

TOLMAN'S SIGN THEORY OF LEARNING

Edward Chace Tolman (1886 - 1959) was born in Newton, Massachusetts on April, 14th, 1886.

He was a Cognitive Behaviourist who believed that animals had the ability to learn things that they could use later in a variety of ways. This point of view was in opposition to the idea that learning occurs as an automatic response to environmental stimuli.

Tolman is well-known for his theory on Latent Learning, which states that learning occurs even if there is no reward. He demonstrated this in an experiment where rats were trained to run a maze without a reward.

Edward C. Tolman's theory of learning is known by several names such as "Sign significance theory", "Expectancy theory", "Purposive behaviourism" or simple "Sign Theory". The main features of this theory are as follows:

- It accepts behaviourism as basis. Main characteristics of behaviour are:
  - Behaviour goal directed i.e. it is purposive.
  - Behaviour makes use of environmental factors as means for getting at the goal.
  - Behaviour consists of the formation of cognitive maps.
  - The organism has a selective preference for the "Principle of least effort", for arriving at the goal.
  - Molar behaviour is docile.
- According to Tolman the behaviour depends upon:
  - The need system, (b) the belief value matrix, and (c) The behaviour space.
- This theory takes into consideration that learning is based upon some signs or clues leading to the goal. The organism learns not the movement patterns, but the sign-significant relations.

Tolman's Laws of Learning

- Learning of an organism depends upon its capacity to learn (Capacity law).
- Learning depends upon the nature of the material to be learnt.

- Learning depends upon the manner of presentation of learning material.

Types of Learning

Tolman distinguished six types of learning. They are:

Cathexis: In this type of learning an association appears to be formed between certain objectives and certain drives states. Persons belonging to cold countries where liquors are usually consumed for satisfying the thirst drive will certainly tend to seek such drinks in preferences to a simple glass of water mainly because for them water has not been associated with the satisfaction of thirst drive.

Equivalence Beliefs: Sometimes a sub goal like scoring of high grades provides the same motivation as might be provided by the main goal like winning love and appreciation, etc. The learning performed in such a condition is said to the equivalence beliefs learning.

Field Expectancy: In this type of learning the learning, the learning takes place on account of the expectancy of something occurring in one's environment. Upon seeing a certain sign for instance one expects that a certain other sign will follow. The only reward in such learning is the fulfillment the expectation.

Field Cognition Models: This type of learning involves the learning of a strategy or a way of approaching a problem solving situation by arranging the perceptual field in a specific way for application to each new field with which one is presented.

Drive Discrimination: This type of learning requires the learner to identify and determine his own drive states and responds accordingly. The individual therefore has to learn the behaviour needed for satisfying his thirst drive quite differently from the learning of the behaviour needed to satisfy his drive for love and affection.

Motor Patterns: In such learning the motor patterns are associated with or conditioned by behaviour.

Educational Implications of Tolman's Sign Theory of Learning

- This theory highlighted what is to be taught to the child therefore should purposeful and should lead him towards some clear cut goals and objectives.
- No learning is wasteful attempts attempt at learning are never in vain although no immediate purpose may appear to be served through such efforts.
- Children while learning should not be forced to follow a routine or obvious path but should be encouraged to explore as many as possibilities for solving the problems and performing the tasks.
- A reward or reinforcement is not essential for every step taken towards reaching a goal or learning. We learn so many things throughout our life for which we are reinforced by no other reward than the satisfaction of the learning itself.
- Intervening variables like environmental surroundings drives, previous learning, age, etc play a major role in influencing the learning processes every effort should be made to take proper note of these variables in any teaching – learning situation.

In conclusion, we can say that through Tolman theory, changed track from Engnearing to Psychology. He has left an imprint in learning theories. His theory is unique in the sense that he totally transformed the earlier views of Thorndike, Skinner, Pavlov and Kohler by introducing a number of new terms and concepts. He has raised behaviourism from its lifeless and mechanistic approach to the higher meaningful and goal directed behaviour.

KOHLER'S INSIGHT LEARNING THEORY

The theory of learning by insight is the contribution of *Gestalt Psychologists*. Gestalt is a term derived from the German word *'gestalten'*, has no English equivalent. The nearest English translation of Gestalt is *'configuration'* or an *'organized whole'* or the *'totality of a situation'*. *Wolfgang Kohler, Max Wertheimer, Kurt Koffka* etc. were the prominent Gestalt Psychologists. They believe that *"The whole is more imp rtant than its parts"*.

Dissatisfied with the behaviourist approach of learning, the cognitivists tried to see learning as a more deliberate and conscious effort of the individual rather than a mere product of *habit formation* or a machine-like *'stimulus-response connection'*. According to them the learner does not merely respond to a stimulus, but definitely process what he receives or perceives. Thus learning is a purposive, explorative and creative activity instead of trial and error.

It is a theory regarding *'perception'*. Gestaltists consider learning as the development of insight, which is primarily concerned with the nature of perception. *Perception is a process by which an organism interprets and organizes sensation to produce a meaningful experience of the world.* It is the ultimate experience of the world and typically involves further processing of sensory input.

While learning, the learner always perceives the situation as a whole and after seeing and evaluating the different relationships takes the proper decision intelligently. Gestalt psychology used the term 'insight' to describe the perception of the whole situation by the learner and his intelligence in responding to the proper relationships. Insight refers the sudden flash in the mind about the solution of the problem.

Kohler conducted many experiments with his chimpanzee *"Sulthan"* to describe the term *"insight"*. Some of the Kohler's experiments for 'Learning by Insight' are:

1. In one experiment, Kohler put the chimpanzee, "Sulthan" inside a cage and a banana was hung from the roof of a cage. A box was placed inside the cage. The chimpanzee tried to reach the banana by jumping but could not succeed. Suddenly he got an idea and used the box as a jumping platform by placing it just below the hanging banana.
2. In another experiment Kohler made this problem complicated that two or three boxes were required to reach the banana.
3. In a more complicated experiment, a banana was kept far outside the cage and two sticks – one larger than the other- were kept inside the box. When failed to reach the banana by one stick, with a sudden bright idea the chimpanzee tried to reach the banana by joining the two sticks.

These experiments demonstrated the role of intelligence and cognitive abilities in higher learning and problem solving situations.

Steps in the Insight Learning

Identifying the Problem: The learner recognizes the presence of intervening obstacles on his way to the goal.

Understanding the Problem: The learner observes the problematic situation, analyze it and perceive the relation between the goal and the obstacles.

Incubation of Ideas: After analyzing the total situation he reaches in conclusions by means of hesitation, pause, concentrated attention etc.

Trail of Mode of Response: The learner makes initial efforts in the form of a simple trial and error mechanism.

Sustained Attention: The learner maintains frequently recurrent attention to the goal and motivation.

Insight Development: In a certain moment there is a sudden perception of the relationship in the total situation and the organism directly performs the required acts.

Steady Repetition of Adaptive Behaviour: After getting an insightful solution, the individual tries to implement it in another situation.

Comprehension of Ability: The learner reaches the ability to understand the relevant parts of the situation and overlooking the irrelevant ones.

GESTALT LAWS OF LEARNING

There are four important laws regarding insight learning. They are as follows:

Law of Similarity: Grasp things which are similar. Similar ideas and experiences get associated together. An object revives another object which resembles it. Example: seeing a man and remembering an intimate friend by some resemblance in his personal appearance though never saw them together in past. A photo reminds us of the person when it represents.

Law of Proximity: Perceptual groups are favoured according to the nearness of their respective parts. Items form groups if they are spaced together. Example Triangle and circle. The law of *proximity* states that *"objects which are close together are likely to be seen as a group"*. For example, look at the following line:

III II IIII I

You are likely to perceive this as four separate groups, comprising three, two, four and one members respectively, rather than to view it as a line of ten I s. This doesn't only apply to visual perception, think for example of music, perceived as a melody rather than a procession of single notes.

Law of Closure: According to the law of *closure,* we prefer complete forms to incomplete forms. When the outline of an object is left unfinished, as long as the gap is less than half the total circumference then the object is identified and perceived as whole rather than as a different shape. Thus, in the drawing below, we mentally close the gaps and perceive it as IBM. This tendency allows us to perceive whole objects from incomplete and imperfect forms.

Law of Continuity: Experiences occurred together. Simultaneously and close succession which tends towards reviving one another. The law states that *"we link individual elements of a configuration so that they form continuous pattern that makes sense to us"*. That is, we tend to perceive the components of a perceptual filed as smoothly flowing rather than discontinuous forms. Example: Perception of ripe mango suggests idea of its sweet taste and flavor. Because this idea is perceive together in the past. Idea of inkpot suggest idea of pen. Idea of bat suggest idea of ball.

Laws of Contrasts: On the basis of above principles, children should be taught tune or melody rather than separate notes. Whole dance pattern rather than steps. Simple meaningful sentences rather than discrete words.

Educational Implications of Gestalt Learning Theory

Proceeding From Whole to Parts: The teacher should present the subject matter as a whole to facilitate insight learning. It means the teacher should teach the whole concept, i.e. begin from the globe an then come to country, state, district and block etc.

Integrated Approach: While planning curriculum, gestalt principles should be given due consideration. A particular subject should not be treated as the mere collection of isolated facts. It should be closely integrated into a whole.

Importance of Motivation: The teacher should arouse the child's curiosity, interest and motivation. He should gain full attention of the whole class before teaching.

Emphasis on Understanding: It has made learning an intelligent task requiring mental abilities than a stimulus – response association. So the learner must be given opportunities for using his mental abilities.

Problem Solving Approach: This theory emphasis that as the learner is able to solve problems by his insight, meaningful learning, learning by understanding, reasoning, etc. must be encouraged in the school.

Checking of Previous Experiences: As insight depends upon the previous experiences of the learner, the teacher must check the previous experiences of the child and relate them with the new learning situation.

Goal Orientation: As learning is a purposeful and goal oriented task, the learner has to be well acquainted with these objectives. He should be fully familiar with the goals and purposes of every task.

GUTHRIE'S CONTIGUITY THEORY OR ONE TRIAL LEARNING

Contiguity theory or *law of contiguity* and *one trial learning* are ideas introduced in 1920s by American philosopher, mathematician and psychologist Edwin Guthrie in collaboration with Stevenson Smith. Law of contiguity states that a '*close temporal relationship*' between a stimulus and a response is the only necessary condition for an association between the two to be established.

Guthrie attempted to explain learning through '*association*' of stimuli with responses. Learning, in terms of behaviour is a function of the environment. According to Guthrie, learning is associating a particular stimulus with a particular response. This association, however, will only occur if '*stimuli and responses occur soon enough*' one after another (*the contiguity law*). The association is established on the '*first experienced instance of the stimulus*' (*one trial learning*). Repetitions or '*reinforcements*' in terms of reward or punishment do not influence the strength of this connection. Still, every stimulus is a bit different, which results in many trials in order to form a general response. This was according to Guthrie the only type of learning identifying him not as *reinforcement theorist*, but *contiguity theorist*.

More complex behaviours are composed of a '*series of movements*' (*habits*), where each movement is a small stimulus-response combination. This movements or are actually what is being learned in each one trial learning rather than behaviours. Learning a number of moves forms an act (incremental learning). Unsuccessful acts remain not learned because they are replaced by later successfully learned acts. Other researchers like John Watson studied whole acts just because it was easier, but movements are, according to Guthrie what should actually be studied.

Forgetting occurs not due to time passage, but due to interference. As time passes, stimulus can become associated with new responses.

Educational Implications of Guthrie's Theory of Learning

- Guthrie's analysis of extinction, punishment, habit breaking and other phenomenon had considerable impact on theory of education.
- His theory provided theoretical model for later workers.
- Behaviour therapists apply his method of breaking habits in correcting deviant behaviour in children.
- The principle of Association by Contiguity is important to analyze emotional responses of human beings in daily life.

HEBB'S NEUROPHYSIOLOGICAL THEORY OF LEARNING

Donald Olding Hebb has been called the *"Father of Cognitive Psychobiology"*. The writings of James, Freud and Watson stimulated his interest in psychology and as a part time graduate student at McGill University, Hebb was exposed to Pavlov's programme. Hebb went to work with Lashley and in 1936 completed his Ph.D. at Harvard on the effects of early visual deprivation upon size and brightness perception in the rat. He joined the faculty at McGill University.

Hebb described his system as *"psuedo-behaviouristic"*. He was preoccupied with explaining higher mental processes such as thinking and perception. These are not usually within the scope of rigid behaviourism. Hebb was inspired by the work of B.F. Skinner and always stated with complete conviction that he regarded Skinner as the greatest psychologist of the century. Over the course of his career, Hebb moved away from behaviourism and argued that thoughts are processes represented in the head and that behaviourism, in an over-reaction against introspectionism, was begging the important questions in psychology.

Hebb's theory describes a basic device for synaptic plasticity where an increase in synaptic effectiveness arises from the presynaptic cell's repeated and continual stimulation of the postsynaptic cell (Cooper, 2005). His neurological postulate as presented in 'The Organization of Behaviour' is as follows:

> "Let us assume that the persistence or repetition of a reverberatory activity (or 'trace') tends to induce lasting cellular changes that add to its stability.... When an axon of cell A is near enough to excite a cell B and repeatedly or persistently takes part in firing it, some growth process or metabolic change takes place in one or both cells such that A's efficiency, as one of the cells firing B, is increased."(p. 62) (Hebb, 1949).
>
> In his book, Hebb talks of the "intrinsic organization of cortical activity" (Hebb, 1949). In establishing his theory, Hebb rejected the Gestalt psychologist's views on perception, where small figures are perceived as a whole, without the need of any learning process. Hebb believed that perception of even small simple figures requires assembly from simpler elements and at first requires associative learning to take place. Hebb deduced that visual perception is compiled from smaller attributes and that associative learning binds these attributes into a perceived whole. Hebb conversely asserted that a similar process takes place in infant development in acquiring perceptual abilities.

According to Hebb's theory, Hebbian synapses produce cell-assemblies, which can be connected together associatively to generate phase sequences, and these phase sequences represent the neural basis of higher-order thought (Cooper, 2005). However, a major issue emerges here; while it is possible in theory to examine structural changes occurring at synapses (synaptic plasticity), experimentally, it cannot be accomplished for cell assemblies and phase sequences (Cooper, 2005).

Major Theoretical Concepts of Hebb's Neurophysiological Theory of Learning

Hebb had made three observations about his theory:

- The brain does not act as a simple switchboard, as the behaviourists and associationists had assumed.
- Intelligence comes from experience and, therefore, is not genetically determined.
- Childhood experiences are more important in determining intelligence than adult experiences.

Contribution of Hebb's Theory for Education

Hebb's most important contribution was his conceptual demonstration that we could study higher cognitive processes by using single neurons and synapses as our fundamental tools. In this respect, Hebb differentiated his position from theories relying on abstract S-R bonds. Although contemporary students of psychological or neuroscience may take for granted the fundamental relationship between synaptic activity and all higher-order brain phenomena, Hebb was the first researcher to make that connection and to build simple models of how higher processes are constructed from synaptic events. More than fifty years after Hebb developed his theory, it continues to exert a heuristic influence in the neurosciences, as well as in computer research with neural networks.

Hebb's fundamental learning principle required only repetition and contiguity, and it was guided by a reasonable understanding of what neurons actually could do. Although he was willing to modify his basic neuropsychological postulate to include learning via reinforcement, Hebb's theory clearly does not need such a process. The postulate can account for everything from perceptual learning to conditioning via reinforces to higher emotional and cognitive processes. In this and is scientifically appealing for its simplicity—not because it relies on biological or physiological mechanism.

For Hebb, there were two kinds of learning. The first involves the gradual build-up of cell assemblies and phase sequences during infancy and early childhood. This early learning results in the objects and events in the environment having neurological representation. When this neural development has taken place, the child can think of an object or event, or a series of objects and events, when it is not physically present. In a sense, copies of those environmental objects now exist in the child's nervous system. During this early learning, an enriched environment would be important for the child, including wide variety of sights, sounds, textures, shapes, objects, and so on. The more complex the environment, the more there is to be represented on the neurological level. The more that is represented on the neural level, the more the child can think about. Thus, the Hebbian teacher dealing with young children would create an educational environment with great variety. According to Hebb, during early learning certain associationistic principles may be operating. Those that seem most important for the development of cell assemblies and phase sequences are the principles of contiguity and frequency. For example, if a series of environment events occurs often enough, it becomes represented neurologically as a phase sequence. Reinforcement appears to have nothing to do with it.

The second kind of learning, according to Hebb, is explained more by Gestalt principles than by associationistic ones. Once cell assemblies and phase sequences have been developed early in life, subsequent learning typically involves their rearrangement. In other words, once the building blocks have been established, they can be rearranged in almost an infinite number of configurations. Later learning then is perceptual, rapid, and insightful. The job of the teacher dealing with older children is to help them see what they have already learned in new, creative ways.

Hebb also said that the physical characteristics of the learning environment are very important for any given task and for any given student; there is an optimal level of arousal that will allow most efficient learning. Because arousal level is controlled primarily by external stimulation, the level of stimulation in the learning environment will determine, to a large extent, how much leaning takes place. If there is too much stimulation (e.g. commotion in the classroom), learning will be difficult Likewise, if there is not enough stimulation (e.g. a deadly quit classroom), learning will also be difficult. What is needed in an optimal level of stimulation for both the task and the student at hand.

ALBERT BANDURA'S SOCIAL LEARNING THEORY OR OBSERVATIONAL LEARNING THEORY OR LEARNING BY IMITATION

Albert Bandura was born in Alberta, Canada in 1925. Bandura's early work in the 1960's represents one of the bridges from behaviourism to cognitive models for learning. He developed most of the principles of contemporary social learning theory/social-cognitive theory which is one of the more prominent and influential theories of development today.

Social learning theory argues that learning occurs within social situations and contexts. Social learning theory also considers how people learn from each other and includes related concepts such as observational learning, imitation and behavioural modeling.

In social learning, three variables: modeled behaviours, the person and the learning environment influence each other

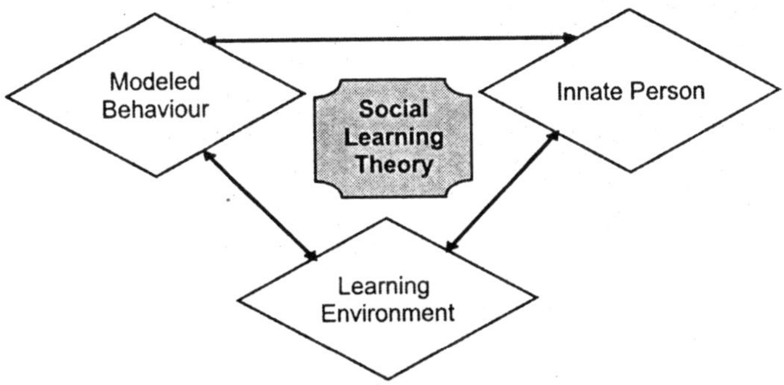

Figure 20.6: Variables of Social Learning Theory

Alfred Bandura's view of social learning emphasizes the value of observing and modeling behaviours, attitudes and emotional reactions of others. In 1977, he said that *"...learning would be exceedingly labourious, not to mention hazardous, if [we] had to rely solely on the effects of [our] own actions to inform [our own understanding of something] ... fortunately, most human behaviour is learned observationally through modeling: from observing others one forms an idea of how new behaviours are performed, and on later occasions this coded information serves as a guide for action..."*. Bandura's work is related to the theories of Vygotsky and Lave which emphasize the central role of social learning in the developing the intellectual and the social capacity of learners.

What is Observational Learning Theory?

Observational learning also called social learning theory, occurs when an observer's behaviour changes after viewing the behaviour of a model. An observer's behaviour can be affected by the positive or negative consequences–called vicarious reinforcement or vicarious punishment of a model's behaviour.

Observational learning is the process of learning by observing a model and then duplicating a skill, process, strategy, or task that is demonstrated by the model. This occurs without overt instructional activity and the model may not even know he/she is serving as an instrument of learning for the observer. According to Bandura, this type of learning is an information processing activity.

According to Bandura's Social Learning Theory, the child is regarded as an active learner, capable of acting upon and influencing his environment, and being influenced by it as well. This participation in an interactive relationship was termed as "reciprocal determinism" by Bandura. To a certain extent, the child "creates" his environment, which he is at the same time a product of. Majority of a child's learning stems from his act of actively imitating or modeling behaviour that he has witnessed or heard from other people/ models that comprise his environment.

Bandura's Social learning theory serves as a link that connects the behaviourist perspective and the cognitive perspective, supporting the behaviourist's belief in the importance of reinforcement on maintaining behaviour on one hand, while acknowledging the influence of cognitions on learning on the other.

Principles of Observational or Social Learning Theory

There are several guiding principles behind observational learning or social learning theory:

- People learn by observing the behaviours of others and by observing the outcome of those behaviours
- People are able to learn through observation alone
- Cognition plays a certain role in learning. Awareness and expectations of future reinforcements or punishments have an impact on the behaviours people exhibit
- Social learning theory is a type of bridge or transition between behaviourist learning theories and cognitive theories
- The observer will imitate the model's behaviour, if the model possesses characteristics– things such as talent, intelligence, power, good looks, or popularity–that the observer finds attractive or desirable.
- The observer will react to the way the model is treated and mimic the model's behaviour. When the model's behaviour is rewarded, the observer is more likely to reproduce the rewarded behaviour. When the model is punished, an example of vicarious punishment, the observer is less likely to reproduce the same behaviour.
- A distinction exists between an observer's "acquiring" a behaviour and "performing" a behaviour. Through observation, the observer can acquire the behaviour without performing it. The observer may then later, in situations where there is an incentive to do so, display the behaviour

Role of Reinforcement and Punishment in Social Learning

The role of reinforcement and punishment in Social Learning are:

- Reinforcement and punishment have indirect effects on learning; they are not the sole or main cause.
- Reinforcement and punishment influence the extent to which individuals exhibit behaviours that have been learned.

- Expectation of reinforcement influences cognitive processes that promote learning; attention plays a critical role in learning. Attention is influenced by the expectation of reinforcement; where a teacher tells students what they will study next is not be on the test; students will not pay attention because they are not expected to know the information for a test

Cognitive Factors in Social Learning

Social learning theory has cognitive factors as well as behaviourist or operant factors as below:

- *Learning without performance:* Bandura makes a distinction between learning through observation and imitation of what has been learned.
- *Cognitive processing during learning:* social learning theorists argue that attention is a critical factor in learning.
- *Expectations:* as a result of being reinforced, people form expectations about the consequences that their behaviours are likely to bring. They expect certain behaviours to bring reinforcements and others to bring punishments. The learner needs to be aware of response reinforcements and response punishments. Reinforcement increases the response when the learner is aware of that connection.
- *Reciprocal causation:* Bandura proposed that behaviour can influence both the environment and the person. In fact each of these variables, person, behaviour and environment influence each other.
- *Modeling:* there are different models; a live model, and an actual person demonstrating the behaviour. There is a symbolic model which puts a person or action in some other medium such as television, videotape, computer programmes.

Learning Behaviours through Modeling

Many behaviours can be learned through modeling. For Examples, students watch their parents reading, students watch demonstrations of mathematics problems or someone acting bravely. Aggression can also be learned through modelling. Research shows that children are more aggressive when observing aggressive or violent modeling. Moral thinking and behaviours are also influenced by modeling and observing. This includes moral judgments regarding right and wrong.

Role of Conditions for Effective Modeling

Bandura mentions four conditions necessary for individuals to model:

- ***Attention:*** the person must first pay attention to the model
- ***Retention:*** the observer must be able to remember what is observed; one way of increasing this is using the technique of rehearsal
- ***Motor reproduction:*** the third condition is the ability to replicate behaviours the model demonstrates; this means that observers must be able to replicate the action, which may pose a problem for learners who are not developmentally ready
- ***Motivation:*** the final ingredient for modeling is motivation; learners must

want to demonstrate what they have learned; because the four conditions vary, different people will reproduce the same behaviour differently

Effects of Modeling on Behaviours

The effects of modeling in behaviours are as follows:

- Modeling teaches new behaviours
- Modeling influences the frequency of previously learned behaviours
- Modeling may encourage previously forbidden behaviours
- Modeling increases the frequency of similar behaviours; a student might see a friend excel in basketball and might try to excel in football because he is not tall enough for basketball

Bandura's Bobo Doll Experiment

In his famous Bobo doll experiment, Bandura demonstrated that children learn and imitate behaviours they have observed in other people. The children in Bandura's studies observed an adult acting violently toward a Bobo doll. When the children were later allowed to play in a room with the Bobo doll, they began to imitate the aggressive actions they had previously observed.

Models of Observational Learning

Bandura identified three basic models of observational learning:

- A live model, which involves an actual individual demonstrating or acting out a behaviour.
- A verbal instructional model, which involves descriptions and explanations of a behaviour.
- A symbolic model, which involves real or fictional characters displaying behaviours in books, films, television programmes, or online media.

Elements of Observational Learning: Four elements of observational learning are:

Attention: In order for an individual to learn something, they must pay attention to the features of the modeled behaviour.

Memory: Humans need to be able to remember details of the behaviour in order to learn and later reproduce the behaviour.

Imitation: In reproducing or imitating a behaviour, an individual must organize his or her responses in accordance with the model behaviour. This ability can improve with practice.

Motivation: There must be an incentive or motivation driving the individual's reproduction of the behaviour. Even if all of the above factors are present, the person will not engage in the behaviour without motivation.

Educational Implications of Social Learning Theory

Social learning theory has numerous implications for classrooms:

- Students learn a great deal simply by observing others
- Describing the consequences of behaviour increases appropriate behaviours, decreasing inappropriate ones; this includes discussing the rewards of various behaviours

- Modeling provides an alternative to teaching new behaviours. Instead of using shaping, an operant conditioning, modeling is a faster, more efficient means of teaching. To promote effective modeling, teachers must ensure the four essential conditions exist; attention, retention, motor reproduction and motivation
- Teachers must model appropriate behavioursand take care they do not model inappropriate behaviours
- Teachers should expose students to a variety of models; this is important to break down stereotypes
- Students must believe that they are capable of accomplishing a task; it is important to develop a sense of self-efficacy for students. Teachers can promote such self-efficacy by having students receive confidence-building messages, watch others be successful, and experience success on their own
- Teachers should help students set realistic expectations; ensuring that expectations are realistically challenging. Sometimes a task is beyond a student's ability
- Self-regulation techniques provide an effective method for improving student behaviours

SITUATED LEARNING THEORY

Situated learning theory is a theory developed by Jean Lave and Etienne Wenger and owes much to the work of John Dewey and Lev Vygotsky who believed students were more likely to learn by actively participating in their learning as opposed to listening to lecturers. Situated learning is a matter of creating meaning from the real activities of daily living where learning occurs in a pro-social but informal setting. This notion suggests that learning takes place through social relationships, within a cultural milieu, and by connecting prior knowledge to new contexts. Situated learning emphasizes the idea that what is learned is specific to the situation (context) in which it is learned. Wilson and Myers (2000) describe it as cognition that "emphasizes the web of social and activity systems within which authentic practice takes placc."

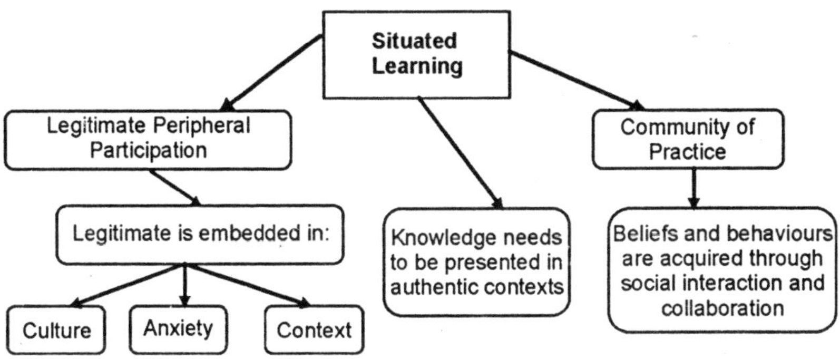

Figure 20.7: Situated Learning Theory

The situated model of learning is part of Lave and Wenger's theory of communities of practice which states that learning should not be viewed as mere transmission of knowledge but as a distinctly embedded and active process. They argue that this type of learning is stimulated by specific contexts (where learning is socially-situated) and within authentic social and physical environments.

Key Concepts of Situated Learning

The key concepts of Situated Learning are:

- Knowledge is not an object and memory is not a location; knowledge is socially-constructed
- Knowledge is thus located in the actions of people and groups of people; it evolves naturally as a result of individuals participating in and negotiating their way through new situations
- Knowing, learning and cognition are socially-constructed, expressed and reified in the actions of people and people interacting
- Construction of meaning is tied to specific contexts and purposes
- Mediation artifacts: cultural models are not held by individuals but live in the practices of a community and how people engage with each other, as well as any tools they use, and the specific cultural context
- As situations shape individual cognition, individual thinking and action shape the situation; the reciprocal influence constitutes an alternative conception of systemic causality to the more commonly assumed linear object causality (Wilson and Myers, 2000).

Chapter-21
Transfer of Learning

INTRODUCTION

The ability of the individual to apply the previous experience on the new related experience is what we call transfer of learning. Unless students are able to transfer prior skills and knowledge on new ones, the continuity of learning will be difficult.

MEANING OF TRANSFER OF LEARNING

The essence of learning is that a previously learnt fact should be linked with a present experience. This is because human being must be dynamic and that the prior experience will make them to develop the new skills and knowledge. The influence that past experience has on the succeeding experience is called transfer of learning.

DEFINITIONS OF TRANSFER OF LEARNING

1. M.J. Peterson (1957), *"Transfer is generalization, for it is the extension of idea to a new field."*
2. L.D. Crow and A.C. Crow (1963), *"The carry-over habits of thinking, feeling or working of knowledge or skills from one learning area to another usually is referred to as the transfer of training."*
3. B.L. Bigge (1964), *"Transfer of learning occurs when a person's learning in one situation influences his learning and performance in other situations."*
4. H.C. Ellis (1965), *"Transfer of learning means that experience or performance on one task influences performance on some subsequent task."*
5. K. Lovell (1970), *"Transfer of learning is the effect which some particular course of training has on learning or execution of a second performance. Such an effect may be a helpful nature or it may hinder."*
6. Guthrie and Powers, *"Transfer may be defined as a process of extending and applying behaviour."*
7. Cormier and Hagman, (1987) define transfer of learning as *"the application of skills and knowledge learned in one context being applied in another context."*
8. Oladele (1998) defines transfer of learning as the *"effect of prior learning on the present."*

Learning is meaningful when the past learning smoothens the progress of something else. For example, if a learnt experience refuses to aid the new learning, the goal of training has seized to be accomplished. In the school, the teacher teaches some subjects in order that the experience gained in those subjects could be transferred into another.

Charham (1987) affirms that human and animal learning is normally affected by the past experience, and that the various subjects are included in the school curriculum because of their utility and wide application to real life situations For instance, the teacher who has taught his/her students some skills in Mathematics would believe that such skills be transferred to related subjects like Physics or Accounting. If the students fail to apply these skills in their subsequent learning, it means that the students have not been successful in transferring the learning.

TYPES OF TRANSFER OF LEARNING

The above example gives us clues into the different types of transfer of learning that we have. These are explained below:

Positive Transfer: When learning of one activity helps in the learning of another activity is called positive transfer e.g. Knowledge of typing is help full to learn computer typing. This is a situation whereby a previously learnt fact or information aids in the understanding of a new task. Aside from aiding the learners in their subsequent learning, it also helps the learners to learn the new task effectively.

Negative Transfer: When previously learnt activity become obstacle in learning another activity then it is known as negative transfer pronunciation of mother tongue become obstacle while pronunciation of English language. This is a type of learning in which prior experience impacts negatively on the new one. In this case, the understanding of past skills inhibits the mastering of new ones. For example, if a student wrongly connects information, it can lead to negative transfer.

Zero Transfer: When learning of one activity neither facilitates nor interferes with the learning of a new work. It is said to be zero transfer. There may be zero transfer in language and mathematics. This type of learning reveals no link between the previously learnt task and the recent one. The evidence of zero transfer is hardly seen, it reveals no clear positive or negative effect.

THEORIES OF TRANSFER OF LEARNING

The important theories of transfer of learning are as follows:

Theory of Mental Faculties or Formal Discipline Theory

This theory was propounded by the Greek Philosophers, notable among them was Aristotle. The basic tenet of the theory is that human mind is sub-divided into different powers of faculties like memory, judgment, reasoning or thinking. It is therefore believed that each of these faculties is reinforced and developed by continuous memorization of poetry/poem and similar works. This theory believes that exercises and regular practice will strengthen the mental faculties. The theory therefore dismisses the concept of transfer of learning. To it, a well trained and disciplined mind is the ingredient needed for understanding of new information.

Theory of Identical Elements

This theory was developed by Thorndike and Woodworth (American Psychologists). It indicates that it is possible for an individual to transfer the prior skills and knowledge to recent ones because both experiences are identical (share things in common). This theory suggests that a successful or effective learning will happen if there are connections or interrelatedness between the old and the new experiences. For example, it is expected that a student who has learnt about anatomical parts of human being in a Biology lesson, should be able to do well when he/she is asked to name anatomical parts of a goat during Agriculture lesson.

Theory of Generalization

This theory was advocated by the Psychologist, Charles Judd. The assumption of the theory is that general principles aid transfer of learning better than segregated facts. This theory believes in Gestalt, an assertion which views learning from a whole or complete form rather than in isolated form. For example, the theory of generalization indicates that a learnt experience should be useful in other day-to -day related activities.

EDUCATIONAL IMPLICATIONS OF TRANSFER OF LEARNING

The knowledge and understanding of transfer of learning can be useful for the teachers for the following purpose:

- The teacher should know that transfer of learning will not take place when both the old and new are unrelated. Hence, the teacher should endeavor to teach his/her subject-matter in a more meaningful and detailed way rather than by rote.
- The teacher should provide the opportunity for his/her students to practice a subject-matter being discussed along with him/her. When the learners are allowed to take active part in teaching learning activities, they will be able to repeat the task at another time.
- For a transfer of learning to take place, the teacher should always emphasize the relationship that exists between one subject-matter and another.
- The teacher should endeavor to develop positive attitudes towards a learning task so that the students can be motivated to like the task rather avoiding it.
- It is believed that what students see, touch, feel or manipulate will be better remembered than the one they are not familiar with. Hence, for a meaningful transfer of learning to take place, the teacher should incorporate exercises that task the various senses of learners in the learning process.
- Transfer of learning takes place because of similarity of content and techniques and because of generalization hence teacher should show similarity in different content and teach how to use it.
- Teacher should provide varied experience to the student.
- Greater transfer from subject matter can be achieved by changing the methods of teaching. Teacher should use appropriate method as per demand of the subject matter.
- Emphasis should be given on correlation is important. previous knowledge may be used in the new task.

- Coordination between theoretical knowledge and practical experience should be done in the classroom.
- The teacher should keep in mind that for maximum transfer, the generalization should be thoroughly mastered and completely understood.
- Teacher should make the use of law of association for providing different type of knowledge.
- Teacher should remember that transfer is not accomplished with equal facility or in equal amounts by all individuals. It depends upon one's ability to generalize his experience and the ability to perceive relationship between two situations.

Chapter-22
Motivation

Significance of Motives, individual and collective behaviour is guided by some or other motives. These motives play the most effective role in bringing change in the behaviour of an individual and groups. In the education field, behaviour of students is channelized through behaviour. Motives cannot be directly seen. A motive is a construct or mediating variable referring to the drive for particular goal. Objects, goals and targets can be specified in a motive. The child can be hostile towards his elder brother but not toward every other people. Some children are highly motivated to achieve in school and academic subjects but may not in sports. Motive is inferred from behaviour. Individual differences in strength of motive are inferred from the directionality of the individual's behaviour and his perseverance in trying to obtain the much desired goal. A motive may be highly salient and, yet it may not lead directly to behaviour that gratifies that motive. Fear or anxiety may inhabit goal directed behaviour inspite of a motive to achieve the goals.

The knowledge of how to stimulate the students to participate meaningfully in classroom will go a long way in assisting the teachers. This unit therefore provides the learners the opportunity to understand different theories of motivation and how to apply these theories to their day-to-day classroom teaching/learning activities.

MEANING OF MOTIVATION

Motivation is defined as an inspiration that propels someone into an action. It is an internal state or condition that activates and gives direction to our thoughts, feelings, and actions (Lahey, 1995). In the opinion of Oladele (1998), motivation is a process by which the learner's internal energies are directed toward various goal objects in his/her environment. These energies or arousals push an individual in achieving his goals. An individual may be highly motivated to perform well in a task and completely unmotivated in another. This means that when people are motivated, they will work tirelessly to achieve their aspirations.

Maslow (1970) believed that motivation leads to growth and development, and that need, satisfaction is the most important sole factor underlying motivation. Maslow further explained that man is perpetually in need and that the resources to satisfy those needs are limited. In view of this, man places his/her wants on the scale of preference, that he/she selects the most pressing need. After this need has been satisfied, it becomes less important, paving way for the next on the rank.

The needs of man may either be primary or secondary. Primary needs are the physiological wants of man. It may be the need for water, rest, sexual intercourse, hunger and thirst. Secondary needs are the desire for autonomy, affection, or the need for safety and security. For example, the desire of a labourer to take a glass of water after thirst is a primary need. At the same time, craving of the students to stay in a serene classroom environment is a secondary need.

DEFINING MOTIVATION

Motivation is to inspire people to work, individually or in groups in the ways such as to produce best results. It is the will to act. It is the willingness to exert high levels of effort towards organizational goals, conditioned by the efforts and ability to satisfy some individual need.

Motivation is getting somebody to do something because they want to do it. It was once assumed that motivation had to be injected from outside, but it is now understood that everyone is motivated by several differing forces.

Motivation is a general term applied to the entire class of drives, desires, needs, wishes and similar forces. To say that managers motivate their subordinates is to say that they do those things which they hope will satisfy these drives and desires and induce the subordinates to act in a desired manner.

To motivate others is the most important of management tasks. It comprises the abilities to communicate, to set an example, to challenge, to encourage, to obtain feedback, to involve, to delegate, to develop and train, to inform, to brief and to provide a just reward.

DEFINITIONS OF MOTIVATION

1. Skinner (1947), *"Motivation in school learning involves arousing, persisting, sustaining and directing desirable behaviour."*
2. G.M. Blair and Others (1947), *"Motivation is a process in which the learner's internal energies or need are directed towards various goal objects in his environment."*
3. J.P. Guilford (1950), *"A motive is any particular internal factor of condition that tends to initiate and sustain activity."*
4. A.H. Maslow (1954), *"The self-actualisation tendency is growth motivation. Self-actualisation is the development of personality which frees the person from the deficiency problems of growth. Motivation is constant, never ending, fluctuating and complex and that it is an almost universal characteristics of particularly every organismic state of affairs."*
5. W.A. Kelly (1955). *"Motivation is the central factor in the effective management of the process of learning. Some type of motivation must be present in all learning."*
6. L.D. Crow and A. Crow (1962), *"Motivation is considered with the arousal of the interest in learning and to that extent is basic to learning."*
7. K. Lovell (1964), *"Motivation in school learning involves arousing, persisting, sustaining and directing desirable behaviour."*
8. H.W. Bernard (1965), *"Motivation is the stimulation of actions towards a particular objective where previously there was little or no attraction to that goal."*
9. T.W. Atkinson (1966), *"The term motivation refers to the arousal of tendency to act to produce one or more effects."*

10. F.G. McDonald (1972), *"Motivation is an energy change within the person characterised by affective arousal and anticipatory goal relations."*
11. C.W. Good (1973), *"Motivation is the process of arousing, sustaining and regulating activity."*
12. D.O. Hebb (1975), *"The term motivation refers (i) to existence of an organised phase sequence (ii) to its direction and content (iii) to its persistence in given direction or stability of content."*
13. Bernard (1980), *"Motivation is the stimulation of actions towards a particular objective where previously there was little or no attraction to that goal."*
14. According to Goods, *"motivation is the process of arousing sustaining and regulating activity."*
15. According to Maslow, *"Motivation is constant, never ending, fluctuating and complex and is an almost universal characteristic of particularly every organic state of affairs."*
16. Coleman, *"Motives refer to any inner condition of the individual that initiates or directs behaviour towards a specific goal."*
17. According to Morgan, *"Motivation refers to behaviour that is instigated by needs within the individual and is directed toward goals that satisfy these needs."*
18. Bernad, *"Motivation refers to all those phenomena which are involved in the stimulation of action towards particular objectives where previously there was little or no movement towards those goals."*

The child expects to achieve his goals as a result of the behaviour. In another case, a child becomes anxious to express a motive on the one hand and does not try to grafity his motives as he will be rejected in the process. Many of the motives involve an approach avoidance conflict. This means there will be on the one hand a desire to approach a goal and on the other, anxiety associated with the attainment of the goal

TYPES OF MOTIVES

Psychologists have divided motives into three types -biological motives, social motives and personal motives:

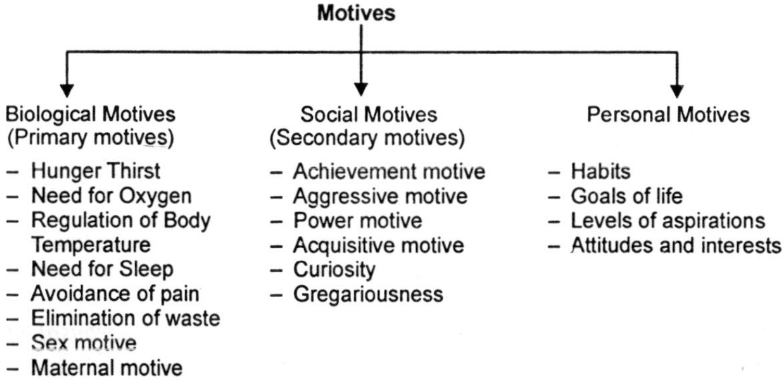

Figure 22.1: Types of Motivation

(A) Biological Motives and Homeostasis

Biological motives are called as physiological motives. These motives are essential for the survival of the organism. Such motives are triggered when there is imbalancement in the body. The body always tends to maintain a state of equilibrium called *"Homeostasis"*- in many of its internal physiological processes.

This balance is very essential for the normal life. Homeostasis helps to maintain internal physiological processes at optimal levels. The nutritional level, fluid level, temperature level, etc., are maintained at certain optimal level or homeostasis levels. When there is some variation in these levels the individual is motivated for restoring the state of equilibrium.

Types of Biological or Physiological Motives: Below are the types of biological motives or physiological motives:

Hunger Motive: We eat to live. The food we take is digested and nutritional substances are absorbed. The biochemical processes get their energy from the food in order to sustain life. When these substances are exhausted, some imbalancement exists.

We develop hunger motive in order to maintain homeostasis. This is indicated by contraction of stomach muscles causing some pain or discomfort called hunger pangs. Psychologists have demonstrated this phenomenon by experiments.

Thirst Motive: In our daily life regularly we take fluids in the form of water and other beverages. These fluids are essential for our body tissues for normal functioning. When the water level in the body decreases we develop motive to drink water. Usually thirst motive is indicated by dryness of mouth. Experiments by psychologists have shown that just dried mouth getting wetted is not enough. We need to drink sufficient quantity of water to satiate our thirst.

Need for Oxygen: Our body needs oxygen continuously. We get it through continuous respiration. Oxygen is necessary for the purification of blood. We cannot survive without regular supply of oxygen. Lack of oxygen supply may lead to serious consequences like damage to brain or death.

Motive for Regulation of Body Temperature: Maintenance of normal body temperature (98.6°F or 37.0°C) is necessary. Rise or fall in the body temperature causes many problems. There are some automatic mechanisms to regulate body temperature, like sweating when the temperature rises above normal or, shivering when it falls below normal.

These changes motivate us to take necessary steps. For example, opening of windows, put on fans, take cool drinks, remove clothes, etc., when the temperature increases to above normal level; and closing doors and windows, wear sweaters, take hot beverages when temperature falls down. In this way we try to regulate the body temperature.

Need for Sleep: Sleep is an essential process for normal functioning of body and mind. When our body and mind are tired they need rest for rejuvenation of energy. It is observed that there is excess accumulation of a toxin called 'Lactic acid' when tired.

After sleep it disappears and the person becomes active. Sleep deprivation also leads to psychological problems like confusion, inability to concentrate, droopy eyelids, muscle tremors, etc.

Need for Avoidance of Pain: No organism can continue to bear pain. Whenever we experience pain we try to avoid it. We are motivated to escape from painful stimulus. For example, when we are under hot sun we go to shade. When something is pinching we avoid it.

Drive for Elimination of Waste: Our body cannot bear anything excess or anything waste. Excess water is sent out in the form of urine or sweat. So also digested food particles after absorption of nutritional substances are sent out in the form of stools. We experience discomfort until these wastes are eliminated.

Sex Motive: This is a biological motive, arises in the organism as a result of secretion of sex hormones-like androgens and estrogens. Sex need is not essential for the survival of the individual, but it is essential for the survival of the species. However, fulfillment of the sex need is not like satisfying hunger or thirst. The society and the law exercise certain codes of conduct. Human being has to adhere to these rules. Usually this need is fulfilled through marriage.

Maternal Drive: This is an instinct or an inborn tendency. Every normal woman aspires to become a mother. Psychologists have learnt from related studies that, this is a most powerful drive. That is why in many cases the women who cannot bear children of their own, will sublimate that motive and satisfy it through socially acceptable ways, like working in orphan schools, baby sittings or adopting other's children.

(B) Social Motives

Physiological motives discussed above pertain to both animals as well as human beings, but the social motives are specific only to human beings. These are called social motives, because they are learnt in social groups as a result of interaction with the family and society. That is why their strength differs from one individual to another.

Types of Social Motives: Many social motives are recognized by psychologists. Some of the common social motives are:

Achievement Motive: Achievement motivation refers to a desire to achieve some goal. This motive is developed in the individual who has seen some people in the society attaining high success, reaching high positions and standards.

It is the drive to pursue and attain goals. An individual with achievement motivation wishes to achieve objectives and advance up on the ladder of success. Here, accomplishment is important for its own shake and not for the rewards that accompany it.

He/she develops a concern to do better, to improve performance. David C Mc Clelland who conducted a longitudinal study on characteristics of high and low achievers found that the high achievers choose and perform better at challenging tasks, prefers personal responsibility, seeks and utilizes feedback about the performance standard, having innovative ideas to improve performance.

On the other hand, low achievers do not accept challenges, puts on average standards and accepts failures easily. Parents must try to inculcate leadership qualities in children for better achievement in their future life. They must allow children to take decisions independently, and guide them for higher achievement from the childhood, so that the children develop high achievement motivation.

Affiliation Motive: It is a drive to relate to people on a social basis. Persons with affiliation motivation perform work better when they are complimented for their favourable attitudes and co-operation.

Aggressive Motive: It is a motive to react aggressively when faced frustrations. Frustration may occur when a person is obstructed from reaching a goal or when he is insulted by others. Even in a fearful and dangerous do or die situation the individual may resort to aggressive behaviour. Individual expresses such behaviour to overcome opposition forcefully, which may be physical or verbal aggression.

Power Motive: People with power motive will be concerned with having an impact on others. They try to influence people by their reputation. They expect people to bow their heads and obey their instructions.

Usually people with high power motive choose jobs, where they can exert their powers. They want people as followers. They expect high prestige and recognition from others. For example, a person may aspire to go for jobs like Police Officer, Politician, Deputy Commissioner, etc.

Acquisitive Motive: This motive directs the individual for the acquisition of material property. It may be money or other property. This motive arises as we come across different people who have earned a lot of money and leading a good life. It is a human tendency to acquire all those things which appear attractive to him.

Curiosity Motive: This is otherwise called stimulus and exploration motive. Curiosity is a tendency to explore and know new things. We see people indulge in a travelling to look at new places, new things and new developments taking place outside their environment.

People want to extend their knowledge and experiences by exploring new things. Curiosity motive will be very powerful during childhood. That is why they do not accept any toy or other articles unless they examine them from different angles, even at the cost of spoiling or breaking the objects.

Gregariousness: This is also known as affiliation need. Gregariousness is a tendency to associate oneself with other members of the group or same species. The individual will be interested in establishing, maintaining and repairing friendly relationships and will be interested in participating in group activities.

Individual will conform to social norms, mores and other ethical codes of the groups in which he/she is interested. To the greater extent gregariousness is developed because many of the needs like basic needs, safety and security needs are fulfilled.

In addition to the above there are some other social motives like need for self-esteem, social approval, self-actualization, autonomy, master motive, combat, defense, abasement, etc.

(C) Personal Motives

In addition to the above said physiological and social motives, there are some other motives which are allied with both of the above said motives. These are highly personalized and very much individualized motives.

Types of Personal Motives: Below are the types of biological motives or physiological motives:

Force of Habits: We see different people having formed different habits like chewing tobacco, smoking, alcohol consumption, etc. There may be good habits also like regular exercising, reading newspapers, prayers, meditations, etc. Once these habits are formed, they act as drivers and compel the person to perform the act. The specialty of habits is that, they motivate the individual to indulge in that action automatically.

Incentive Motivation: It is where a person or a team reaps a reward from an activity. It is *"You do this and you get that"*, attitude. It is the types of awards and prizes that drive people to work a little harder.

Fear Motivation: Fear motivation coercions a person to act against will. It is instantaneous and gets the job done quickly. It is helpful in the short run.

Goals of Life: Every normal individual will have some goals in the life. They may be related to education, occupation, income, sports, acquisition of property, public service, social service, etc. Once a goal is set, he will be motivated to fulfill that goal. The goals people set, depend upon various factors like knowledge, information, guidance, support, personality, facilities available, aspirations, family and social background, etc.

Attitude Motivation: Attitude motivation is how people think and feel. It is their self confidence, their belief in them, their attitude to life. It is how they feel about the future and how they react to the past.

Competence Motivation: It is the drive to be good at something, allowing the individual to perform high quality work. Competence motivated people seek job mastery, take pride in developing and using their problem-solving skills and strive to be creative when confronted with obstacles. They learn from their experience.

Power Motivation: It is the drive to influence people and change situations. Power motivated people wish to create an impact on their organization and are willing to take risks to do so.

Levels of Aspirations: Aspiration is aspiring to achieve or to get something or a goal. But such achievement depends upon the level of motivation the individual has. Every individual will have a goal in his life and strive to reach that goal. But the effort to attain that goal varies from one individual to another. The amount of satisfaction he gains depends upon his level of aspiration.

For example, if a student is expecting 80 per cent of marks in examination, gets only 75 per cent, he may be unhappy. On the other hand, a student expecting failure may feel very happy if he gets just 35 per cent passing marks, because, the student with high level of aspiration works hard, whereas the student with low level may not.

Hence, always higher level of aspiration is advisable. However, it should be on par with his abilities also. Because, if an individual aspires for higher level of achievement without possessing required ability, he will have to face frustration and disappointment.

Attitudes and Interests: Our attitudes and interests determine our motivation. These are specific to individual. For example, a person within the family, may have positive attitude towards family planning and all others having negative attitudes.

So also, interests differ from one individual to another. Example, interest in sports, T.V., etc. Whenever we have a positive attitude, we will have motivation to attain. In negative attitude, we will be motivated to avoid. If a person is interested in music, he will be motivated to learn it. In this way, our personal motives determine our behaviour.

CATEGORIES OF MOTIVATION

There are two categories of motivation or arousals. They can either be internally or externally driven. The desire for food or sex arises from within us (intrinsic), while the yearning to obtain recognition or approval is influenced by the conditions in our environment (extrinsic). In view of the above explanation, motivation is divided into intrinsic and extrinsic.

Intrinsic Motivation: Is an internal force or motive within the individual which propels him/her into emitting certain behaviour. It is an innate or genetically predetermined disposition to behave in a particular way when he/she faces a particular situation. This type of motivation can make an individual to have the feelings of self-confidence and competence (Deci and Ryan, 1985). A student who is intrinsically motivated may carry out a task because of the enjoyment he/she derives from such a task. In another way, a dog that sees a bone and runs for it, did that because of the satisfaction it derives from eating bone. This type of behaviour does not require any prior learning. Sighting the bone changes the behaviour of the dog and propels it to act.

Extrinsic Motivation: Is the external or environmental factor, which sets the individual's behaviour into motion. The incentive/reinforcer drives an individual's behaviour towards a goal. A student, who is extrinsically motivated, will execute an action in order to obtain some reward or avoid some sanctions. For example, a student who studied hard for the examination did so because of the desire to obtain better grade. The case also goes for a runner who wants to win a prize; he/she will need constant practice than a person who wants to run for the fun of it. Extrinsic rewards should be used with caution because they have the potential for decreasing intrinsic motivation.

For example extrinsic incentive may spur a student to actively participate in the task for which the student has no interest, but may undermine intrinsic and continuing motivation in him/her (Deci *et al*, 1985). Therefore, students' motivation automatically has to do with the students' desire to participate in the learning process. It also concerns the reasons or goals that underlie their involvement or non-involvement in academic activities.

STRATEGIES TO MOTIVATE STUDENTS

By way of concluding above discussion, we mention below some ways of arousing motivation of students in order to enable them to put in their best in the process of learning:

- Teacher should make the teaching child-centred. He should teach according to capacities, abilities, aptitudes and interests of students.
- Teacher should help the students to be clear about their goals. Various motives should be directed towards the fulfilment of a major goal.
- Knowledge of progress should be given to the pupils at suitable time.
- Teacher should make judicious use of reward and punishment.
- Various suitable opportunities should be provided for participation in the activities.
- Ample opportunities for self- expression should be provided to the student.
- Teacher should try to develop spirit of group competition and co- operation (i.e. working and living together) in the students.
- Teachers should try his best to improve the system of evaluation. Occasional and frequent test should be arranged.

CLASSROOM IMPLICATIONS OF THEORY OF MOTIVATION

The classroom implications of theory of motivation are as follows:

- It is important for the teacher to know the basic needs of his/her students and cater for these according to level of their important. For example, the teacher needs to think first of students' food, rest or health before thinking of teaching them.
- When the teacher praises his/her students for doing well in their study or assignment, they will be spurred to sustain that effort.
- A classroom, which is well decorated or adorned with beautiful charts, and learning materials will be students' friendly. The students' minds will always be attracted to the activities in a beautifully adorned classroom.
- In the classroom, students like being recognized or respected. When their views are recognized or respected, they will have their confidence boosted and developed.
- From the beginning of the lesson, the teacher should endeavor to make his/her students know possible outcome of the lesson. It is when the students know what they are likely to achieve from the lesson that their attention will be arrested and sustained.
- Feedback is necessary if the interest of the students must be sustained in the classroom. So the teacher should always strive to let them know how they are performing in the teaching-learning activities.
- The teacher should also provide/plan for extra-curricular activities for his/her students. When the teacher does this, the students will have opportunity of establishing a genuine interaction among them. Besides, they will be able to display their hidden talents.
- When dealing with the students in the classroom, the teacher should take into consideration, the developmental changes and differences in the students before deciding on the particular motivation pattern to be employed.

THEORIES OF MOTIVATION

Motivation is the answer to the question *"Why we do what we do?"* The motivation theories try to figure out what the *"M"* is in the equation: *"M motivates P"* (Motivator motivates the Person). There are different views on motivation. These views are explained as theories of motivation. The theories of motivation, try to provide general sets of principles to guide our understanding of the urges, wants, needs, desires, strivings and goals that come under the heading motivation.

Motivation theories can be classified broadly into two different perspectives: Content and Process theories.

Content Theories of Motivation

Content theories deal with *"what"* motivates people and it is concerned with individual needs and goals. Maslow, Alderfer, Herzberg and McCelland studied motivation from a *"content"* perspective.

Abraham Maslow's Theory of Motivation: When motivation theory is being considered, the first theory that is being recalled is Maslow's hierarchy of needs, which he has introduced in his 1943 article named as *"A Theory of Human Motivation"*. According to this theory, individual strives to seek a higher need when lower needs are fulfilled. Once a lower-level need is satisfied, it no longer serves as a source of motivation. Needs are motivators only when they are unsatisfied.

These needs according to the Maslow are:

Physiological Needs: These are the biological or survival needs of man. They are the most basic needs that control the other needs. Until these needs are fulfilled or satisfied, man will not be able to go to the next level. Examples of these needs are the desire to eat food when hungry, drink water when thirsty or the need for rest, sex, air or to excrete unwanted materials from the body systems. After these survivals needs have been adequately taken care, they become less important and one moves to the next which is the desire for security and safety.

Safety and Security Needs: Human beings require safety and protection from danger or external aggressors. After one has successfully dealt with physiological needs, it is desirable to cater for psychological needs. At this point, Man will be thinking of where to live and efforts will be made to keep him/herself from impending dangers, threats or hazards. The hallmark of these needs is the quest by an individual to seek for conducive or peaceful abode. For example, the desire of war victims to migrate from their original country to become refugees in another country is the need for safety and security. Also, a chicken that quickly hibernates under its mother on sighting an eagle did so because of its desire for safety.

Love and Belongingness Needs: This involves the aspiration of man to establish a cordial relationship with others. It is the need of man to love and be loved. At this level of need, people will like to extend their hands of fellowship or comradeship to their friends, mates, co-workers or neighbours. They equally will expect that such gestures be reciprocated by others. Onyehalu (1988) believes that this need is manifested in our affiliations and friendships.

Achievement Needs: Achievement needs are divided into two. These are the need to achieve success and the need to avoid failure or setback. The need to attain success or freedom drives man to go extra miles. This need motivates an individual to emit a behaviour that will make him/her command respect from others.

Self-Esteem Needs: These are the things we desire in order that our ego will be boosted. After the individual has been accorded respect or recognition by others, the next thing for him/her is to start seeking for the things that will make him/her enjoy considerable influence from others. The ability of someone to fulfil this condition makes him/her feel superior and self-confident. Inability to fulfil this need, makes a person feel dejected or inferior.

Aesthetic Needs: These needs include the desire of people to pursue or admire beautiful things; their desire for beautiful and expensive cars, houses, materials, gorgeous and expensive dresses and beautiful surroundings with well trimmed and maintained flowers.

Self-Actualization Needs: When a person has successfully achieved or gained the most basic needs or wants, then such an individual will want to get a rare opportunity. It is the time when a person will like to distinguish him/herself, by seeking for power or extra-ordinary achievement. At this point, the person is said to have reached the peak of his potentials.

Incentive Theory of Motivation

Incentive theory suggests that employee will increase her/his effort to obtain a desired reward. This is based on the general principle of reinforcement. The desired outcome is usually "money". This theory is coherent with the early economic theories where man is supposed to be rational and forecasts are based on the principle of "economic man".

Process Theories of Motivation

Process theories deal with the *"process"* of motivation and are concerned with *"how"* motivation occurs. Vroom, Porter and Lawler, Adams and Locke studied motivation from a *"process"* perspective.

Expectancy Theory of Motivation

Expectancy Theory argues that humans act according to their conscious expectations that a particular behaviour will lead to specific desirable goals. Victor H. Vroom developed the expectancy theory in 1964, producing a systematic explanatory theory of workplace motivation. Theory asserts that the motivation to behave in a particular way is determined by an individual's expectation that behaviour will lead to a particular outcome, multiplied by the preference or valence that person has for that outcome.

Components of Expectancy Theory

Three components of Expectancy theory are:

*1. **Expectancy:*** Expectancy is a variable that represents the belief that the effort (E) of an individual is an outcome of a need to attain the performance (P) goals that he desires. The theory states that there are three factors that influence the expectancy perception of a person, which include:

Self efficacy: the individual's belief regarding his own ability to perform a specific behaviour successfully.

Goal difficulty: occurs when the desired performance goals are too high that might result to low expectancy perceptions.

Control: the degree of a person's perceived control over his performance.

2. Instrumentality: Instrumentality refers to the notion that a person will get a reward upon the satisfaction of the expected performance. The reward may present in various forms—it can be intrinsic or extrinsic, monetary or non-monetary. If this reward is similar for all the activities that a person must perform, instrumentality is said to be low. There are three factors influencing instrumentality: policies, control and trust. It is the belief of the person that she/he will receive a reward (R) if the performance (P) expectation is met.

3. Valence: Valence refers to the value that a person sets on the reinforcements or rewards. Setting values are usually based on an individual's values, needs, goals and intrinsic or extrinsic sources of motivation. Valence include -1, which means the person is trying to avoid the outcome, 0, which means the person feels indifferent towards the results, and +1, which means that he welcomes the results. It is the value of the reward according to the person. (e.g. Is the reward attractive to the person?)

Motivational Force

The product of the three aforementioned variables i.e. expectancy, valence and instrumentality is called the motivational force. This is the proper formula for motivational force:

Motivational Force (MF) = Expectancy x Instrumentality x Valence

If these three variables are "high" or strong in an individual, then his motivation is also greater.

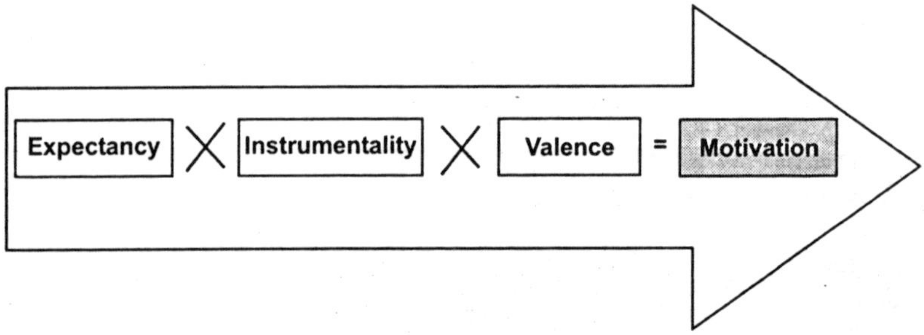

Figure 22.2: Expectancy Theory of Motivation

The equation suggests that human behaviour is directed by subjective probability.

Weiner's Attribution Theory of Motivation

In the 1970's, Bernard Weiner proposed a theory that looked at how people interpret success and failure. According to Weiner, humans feel the need to explain both success and failure, although this need is more prevalent in situations in which the outcome was not unexpected.

Attribution theory (Weiner, 1980, 1992) is probably the most influential contemporary theory with implications for academic motivation. It incorporates behaviour modification in the sense that it emphasizes the idea that learners are strongly motivated by the pleasant outcome of being able to feel good about themselves. It emphasizes that learners' current self-perceptions will strongly influence the ways in which they will interpret the success or failure of their current efforts and hence their future tendency to perform these same behaviours.

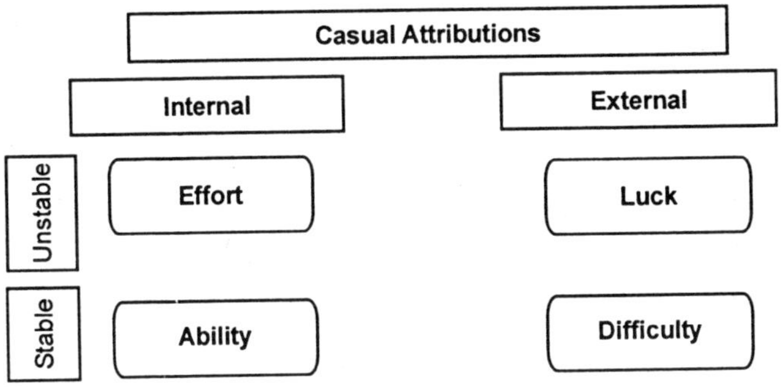

Figure 22.3: Weiner's Attribution Theory of Motivation

Wiener's Attribution Theory is defined as, *"describing our attempts to determine causes for events happening in our lives and subsequently impacts our level of motivation"*. Weiner's theory describes how we make attributions along three dimensions:

1. ***Locus:*** The locus is the perception that an outcome results from either an internal or external factor. If one were to say, "I did well because I studied", that student would be described as having an internal locus. Conversely, if he were to say, "I failed because the test was written poorly", he would be described as having an external locus.
2. ***Stability:*** The second attributable dimension is the perceived *stability* of an outcome to reoccur. For example, a student who claims to always get good grades because he is smart would have a stable perception.
3. ***Controllability:*** The third attribution dimension is controllability. This perception reflects whether an outcome was under someone's control. One who admits to doing poorly on a test because he did not study would be described as having a controllable perception, while another student who blames the teacher for doing poorly would be described as perceiving the outcome as uncontrollable.

There are four factors related to attribution theory that influence motivation in education:

1. ***Ability*** is a relatively *internal* and *stable* factor over which the learner *does not exercise much direct control* i.e., *'I have always been a good dancer.'*
2. ***Task difficulty*** is an *external* and *stable* factor that is *largely beyond the learner's control* i.e., *'Those dance moves were really easy.'*
3. ***Effort*** is an *internal* and *unstable* factor over which the learner *can exercise a great deal of control* i.e., *'I worked hard and studied those dance moves for hours.'*
4. ***Luck*** is an *external* and *unstable* factor over which the learner exercises

very little control 'I was lucky that I was already familiar with those dance moves.'

Weiner's *attribution theory* states that an individual's causal attributions of achievement affect subsequent behaviours and motivation. One of the primary assumptions of attribution theory is that people will interpret their environment in such a way as to maintain a positive self-image.

No one wants to be the bad guy, and assigning attribution is one of the ways that people seek to see themselves in a more positive light. By blaming other people and avoiding personal recrimination, individuals strive to keep a positive self-image. If people believe they are responsible for bad outcomes, they are less motivated to repeat their behaviours. By shifting blame, people avoid accountability and therefore feel able to repeat the same behaviours.

As an example, imagine a thief who breaks into a home and commits a burglary. If the thief sees himself as a 'bad person,' he will feel remorse and be less likely to repeat the behaviour. However, if the thief can blame his actions on society and believe he is entitled to steal, then he is more motivated to perform additional burglaries.

Application of Attribution Theory

When applying attribution theory in a learning environment, it is essential for the instructor to assist learners to accept their effort as the main predictor of achievement. To do so, instructors must utilize the three causal dimensions together to influence the outcome of a behaviour or task. The outcome of each behaviour or task will be different and require different learner attributes.

When examining the instructor's influence on a learner's locus of control, instructors can assist learners in developing an internal locus of control by utilizing learner-centered instructional strategies when presenting new content. By utilizing learner-centered instructional strategies, learners are able to acquire new knowledge in a manner where they are required to apply and utilize their knowledge in a practical setting. When utilizing learner-centered instructional strategies, the instructor becomes a facilitator of knowledge. Therefore, learners develop knowledge based on their experiences and interaction with the content, rather than through verbal instruction. When learners are taught through learner-centered instructional strategies, their individual internal locus of control is strengthened. Examples of learner-centered instructional strategies are:

- individualized application,
- demonstration,
- inquiry-based instruction, and
- problem-based learning.

Chapter-23
Bruner's Discovery Learning

MEANING OF DISCOVERY LEARNING

Discovery learning is an inquiry-based, constructivist learning theory and belief that learners are best educated when they discover facts about their world for themselves. It involves Inquiry-based learning as well as constructivism. Real life scenarios are given to the learner where they face the challenge of solving these problems on their own. The learner uses what they know as well as previous experiences to draw upon conclusions for solving and learning. The learner interacts with the world around them all the while exploring and questioning during experimentation and the use of trial and error. Children love being in charge of their own learning it gives them the sense of self worth. It makes the learning more desirable and attainable. Teachers give a problem to their students and set their students free to solve it on their own, discovering as they go.

Learning for Bruner is an active process. The learning process include according to Bruner:

- selection and transformation of information,
- decision-making,
- generating hypotheses,
- and making meaning from information and experiences.

Learners are able to construct new knowledge based on their current or past knowledge.

Bruner's definition of "discovery" was not restricted to *"the act of finding out something that before was unknown to mankind, but rather (included) all forms of obtaining knowledge for oneself by the use of one's own mind."* He went on to state that there are *"powerful effects that come from permitting the student to put things together for himself, to be his own discoverer."*

Discovery learning is:

- a learning method that encourages students to ask questions and formulate their own tentative answers, and to deduce general principles from practical examples or experiences.
- a learning situation in which the principal content of what is to be learned is not given, but must be independently discovered by the learner, making the student an active participant in the learning process.

In discovery learning, the learner is encouraged to actively use their intuition, imagination, and creativity. In this approach, students are presented with a problem and some evidence: they must seek to reconcile that information and "discover" the solution to the problem. For example, the teacher presents examples and the students work with the examples until they discover the interrelationships. Bruner believed that classroom learning should take place through inductive reasoning by using specific examples to formulate general principle. He suggested that teachers can nurture inductive thinking by encouraging students to make guesses based on incomplete evidence and then to confirm or disprove the guesses systematically.

MAIN IDEA OF THE DISCOVERY LEARNING THEORY

Jerome Bruner' theory is very influential and has direct implications on the teaching practices. The main ideas of the theory can be summarized as follows:

- Learning is an active process. Learners select and transform information.
- Learners make appropriate decisions and postulate hypotheses and test their effectiveness.
- Learners use prior experience to fit new information into the pre-existing structures.
- *Scaffolding* is the process through which able peers or adults offer supports for learning. This assistance becomes gradually less frequent as it becomes unnecessary.
- The intellectual development includes three stages. The **enactive** stage which refers to learning through actions. The **iconic** stage which refers to the learners use of pictures or models. The **symbolic** stage which refers to the development of the ability to think in abstract terms.
- The notion of *spiral curriculum* states that a curriculum should revisit basic ideas, building on them until the student grasps the full formal concept.
- Although extrinsic motivation may work in the short run, intrinsic motivation has more value

METHODS OF DISCOVERY LEARNING

Methods for offering discovery learning can include:

- *Case-based learning:* Students learn vicariously through stories or vignettes
- *Incidental learning:* Students learn through fun, game-like activities, such as a game show or a crossword puzzle
- *Exploring:* Students learn through an organized question-and-answer session with the instructor and other students
- *Reflection:* By modeling the instructor or online system, students learn how to ask better questions
- *Simulation:* Students learn by practicing skills or witnessing their application in a realistic but artificial environment

ADVANTAGES OF DISCOVERY LEARNING

The following are the advantages of discovery learning:

- Supports active engagement of the learner in the learning process
- Fosters curiosity
- Enables the development of life-long learning skills

- Personalizes the learning experience
- Highly motivating as it allows individuals the opportunity to experiment and discover something for themselves
- Builds on learner's prior knowledge and understanding
- Develops a sense of independence and autonomy
- Make them responsible for their own mistakes and results
- Learning as most adults learn on the job and in real life situations
- A reason to record their procedure and discoveries - such as not repeating mistakes, a way to analyze what happened, and a way to record a victorious discovery
- Develops problem solving and creative skills
- Finds new and interesting avenues of information and learning - such as gravy made with too much cornstarch can become a molding medium

DISADVANTAGES OF DISCOVERY LEARNING

Most researchers would argue that pure discovery learning as a general and global teaching strategy for beginning and intermediary learners doesn't work. The debate on how much guiding is needed is somewhat open. Typical criticisms are:

- (Sometimes huge) cognitive overload, potential to confuse the learner if no initial framework is available, etc.
- Measurable performance (compared to hard-core instructional designs) is worse for most learning situations.
- Creations of misconceptions ("knowing less after instruction")
- Weak students have a tendency to "fly under the radar" (Aleven *et al.* 2003) and teacher's fail to detect situations needing strong remediation or scaffolding.
- Some studies admit that strong students can benefit from weak treatments and others conclude that there is no difference, but more importantly they also conclude that weak students benefit strongly from strong treatments.

PLANNING A DISCOVERY LEARNING EXPERIENCE

The following points must be considered at the time of planning a discovery learning experience:

Select an Activity: To begin pick an activity that is relatively short so that follow-up attempts are easier to predict and plan for. Select a subject with which you are personally familiar and comfortable. Also in the beginning it is often best to choose an activity that does not have just one correct answer. Role-playing, creating sculptures, observing characteristics of objects, or searching for or classifying similar items all work well.

Gather Materials: Remember to have enough materials for each learner to repeat the activity at least once.

Stay Focused: Avoid learning tangents that may be interesting but will keep the learner from finishing the project, unless they are truly of great curiosity and value. Instead take notes concerning the new interest to follow-up on once the initial activity is completed.

Use Caution: While the idea of discovery learning is for the instructor to step back and observe allowing the child to work independently, be sure that safety is observed. Activities such as cooking and cutting should always be supervised by an adult and experimenting with magnets is nice unless an important video or cassette tape is ruined.

Plan Extra Time: Understand that children working on their own will most likely take longer than they would with an adult moving them from step to step. Also be sure to plan time for repeated activities in case there is a failure or other reason to repeat the activity.

Record Process and Results: Include in the activity a requirement for older children to record their procedure and results. For young children guide, assist, or model record keeping.

Discuss and Review: After and activity is completed and before it is repeated a second time (if needed), discuss the activity and its outcome with the child. Use the records which were kept to assist during this step. Once the activity has been analyzed, record any observations or mistakes.

Try Again: Have the child repeat the activity if necessary. Encourage her to take into account what was done and the discussion that occurred. Allow her to use any records that were kept to assist her in successfully completing the activity. Give assistance and guidance as necessary.

Plan for More Discovery Learning Activities: Think over how this activity worked for the child. As you plan more discovery activities take the answers to these questions into consideration. What went well? What could have gone better? How can any problem areas be corrected or alleviated?

TEACHER'S ROLE IN DISCOVERY LEARNING

In a Bruner classroom, the teacher is transformed from the "sage on the stage" to the "guide by the side." Specific teacher behaviours include:

- Identifying the key elements of an academic discipline
- Designing activities and tools matched to students' cognitive abilities
- Translating information into the learner's mode of representation
- Constructing interesting, challenging exercises that incite curiosity and create a motivation to learn
- Activating problem solving by modeling trial and error, curiosity, and enthusiasm
- Facilitating the student's reflection and recoding processes by providing aids and dialogues
- Helping the students see relationships and patterns
- Leading students to develop concepts and make sense of operations
- Coaching students to discover principles for themselves
- Interacting one-on-one with students
- Providing timely feedback and reinforcement

STUDENT'S ROLE IN DISCOVERY LEARNING

According to Bruner, "The student is not a bench-bound listener, but is taking a part in the formulation and at times may play the principal role in it". Student behaviours in a discovery-learning classroom include:

- Participating in the knowledge-getting process

- Testing hypotheses
- Interacting with the environment
- Solving problems
- Developing generalizations
- Engaging in dialogue and collaborating with the teacher and other students
- Creating products such as new ideas, solutions, processes, presentations, blogs, or research papers.

EDUCATIONAL IMPLICATIONS OF BRUNER'S DISCOVERY LEARNING

Bruner's learning theory has direct implications on the teaching practices. Here are some of these educational implications:

- Instruction must be appropriate to the level of the learners. For example, being aware of the learners' learning modes (enactive, iconic, symbolic) will help you plan and prepare appropriate materials for instruction according to the difficulty that matches learners' level.
- The teachers must revisit material to enhance knowledge. Building on pre-taught ideas to grasp the full formal concept is of paramount importance according to Bruner. Feel free to re-introduce vocabulary, grammar points, and other topics now and then in order to push the students to a deeper comprehension and longer retention.
- Material must be presented in a sequence giving the learners the opportunity to: (a) acquire and construct knowledge, (b) transform and transfer his learning.
- Students should be involved in using their prior experiences and structures to learn new knowledge.
- Help students to categorize new information in order to able to see similarities and differences between items.
- Teachers should assist learners in building their knowledge. This assistance should fade away as it becomes unnecessary.
- Teachers should provide feedback that is directed towards intrinsic motivation. Grades and competition are not helpful in the learning process. Bruner states that learners must "experience success and failure not as reward and punishment, but as information".

Chapter-24
Children in Marginalized Environment

MEANING OF MARGINALIZATION

Marginalization in its simple meaning stands for the process or act of marginalizing, In the available dictionaries (Meriam Webster, Oxford etc.) the action verb "marginalize" has been defined as: *to put or keep (someone) in a powerless or unimportant position within a society or group.* Accordingly, the term marginalization may stand for the process or act of a majority community or group to put or keep an individual or a minority group in a deprived state, *i.e.,* making them deprived of the power or privilege enjoyed by the members of the community in general. Agreeing with such meaning and concept of the term marginalization, The Encyclopedia of Public Health (2002) has tried to define the term marginalization as; *"to be marginalized means to be placed in the margins and thus get excluded from the privilege and power found "at the center."* All over the world, the societies and the nations suffer from this widespread problem known as marginalization reflecting through the social exclusion of a particular minority group, locality, community and society from the main stream of the society on one or the other accounts. In its practical application thus the term marginalization and social exclusion are used interchangeably and thus both of them may stand for the process in which individuals or entire communities of people are systematically blocked from (or denied full access to) various rights, opportunities and resources that are normally availabie to members of the majority or ruling group.

TYPES OF MARGINALIZATION

According to Mangal (2015) marginalization suffered on the part of individuals in our societies may be visible in two of the main forms: (i) Individual marginalization and (ii) Community marginalization.

Individual Marginalization: It is concerned with the social exclusion of the individuals at their personal or individual level. It results in an individual's exclusive marginalization. As a result he or she may be (i) debarred from meaningful participation in society (ii) denied access to a number of rights and privileges otherwise available to the members of the society. As examples of such as marginalization or social exclusion we may name: marginalization of widows, single mothers, poor, disabled persons, children, senior citizens and persons suffering from Aids, cancers and leprosy etc. The state or conditions of the marginalization suffered by these individuals may be well judged through the instances like below:

- A girl child belonging to the same family may fall victim of the marginalization on account of her gender. She may get less attention, love and affection, incentives and encouragement, opportunity of education, development and progress in comparison to her male siblings or cousins.

- A senior citizen (male or female) may be subjected to seclusion and marginalization at the hands of his own kith and kin. He may be given no attention and most often is denied the essentials of his proper living to the extent of facing social and emotion deprivation.
- A disabled child may not be allowed to make use of the educational facilities available in his or her neighborhood. He is debarred from taking parts in the social functions of the family and community.
- A youth fails to get employment despite his ability and performance shown in the interview of the State Staff selection Board on account of being marginalized and discriminated at the hands of the members of the board dominated by a particular community/caste

Community Marginalization: In such marginalization an entire community or a group having minority status may be found to face marginalization at the hands of the majority group The marginalization of the blacks in European countries, women, untouchables, and scheduled caste people in India may be cited examples of such marginalization. The state or conditions of the marginalization suffered by the groups or community as a whole may be visualized well through the instances like below (Mangal, 2015):

- The people belonging to a socially untouchable, scheduled caste or tribe may be denied or deprived of taking water from a well, the only source of drinking water in the village. They may also be denied the right of worship by not gelling entry in the temples, and casting their franchise in a democratic way. Their children may also be deprived of educational opportunities by not getting admission in the village schools since they are considered untouchable by the higher caste people, If admitted on a legal basis, they suffer from acute humiliation and discrimination on one or the other fronts.
- The rural community may feel deprived of many such facilities that are easily available to the urban people. Similarly a minority community may get victimized at the hands of majority and consequently may feel quite uncomfortable and unsafe even in their living and enjoying civic rights.
- Many of the district or regions of a particular state or nation may also suffer from seclusion and denied opportunities and facilities available to other citizens on account of political reasons or exploiting tendencies of the ruling part or government. The people of Bangladesh remained victims of acute discrimination and exploitation in the hands of the mighty Pakistan, then rulers who showered undue favour to the progress of the western Pakistan at the cost of the present Bangladesh.
- An acute impact of marginalization was faced by us as a whole at the hands of the British rulers who deprived us of our rights and privileges in the same way as faced by oppressed and down trodden classes like women, scheduled castes and tribes (especially in the rural India), poor and have notes etc. in today's democratic and free India.

THE FACTORS OR CONTRIBUTORS TO MARGINALIZATION

Marginalization (visible on the individual or group/community basis) is resulted on account of the apathy shown and discriminatory attitude adopted for the individuals and minority groups by the majority, powerful and status enjoying section of the society. This apathy and discriminatory attitude germinated in the mind and behaviour of the majority group is based on the stereotypes prevailed in the society and negative attitude developed in their mind on one or the account. The major contributors in this connection thus may include the factors like below:

- Gender linked factors like negative attitude towards girls and women, bisexuals, prostitutes, transsexuals, third genders etc.
- Economy linked factors like poverty, low socio-economic status and unemployment.
- Socio-culturally linked factors, like belongingness to different caste, race, colour, creed, religion, language, political affiliation, possessing radical views quite contrary to society and government, and migrants from other regions, states or countries.
- Exceptionality linked factors (being too much diverse from the norms) like being gifted or genius, backward or slow learner, suffering from one or the other disabilities or incapacities etc.

THE CONSEQUENCES OR IMPACTS OF MARGINALIZATION

The outcome or impact of marginalization or social exclusion is that affected individuals or communities are prevented from participating fully in the economic, social, and political life of the society in which they live. Apart from being excluded, they often become victims of acute apathy, hate and discrimination on the part of majority and powerful segment of the society. They are deprived from taking parts in the usual activities of the society and denied access to many essential amenities and privileges enjoyed by the majority group

Marginalized individuals or groups thus may have to suffer from a number or deprivations- socio-cultural, economical, psychological, and educational so much so as to make them suffer badly in terms of their well- being and progress children and Indents are no exceptions. They also have to suffer badly on account of the ill consequences and damaging impact of the phenomenon of marginalization.

We should also be quite clear in visualizing that the developing children feel the heat of marginalization on two fronts. One on account of the marginalization feed by their parents and family and the other on account of the marginalization suffered by themselves in their home, school and society.

The Impact of Marginalization Suffered by their Parents and Family: The developing children depend on their parents and family for the support and facilities needed for their education, adjustment and development. In case where their parents and family get marginalized at the hands of the majority group or society, the ill consequences suffered by them on account of such marginalization get automatically transferred to the developing children. In general, the marginalization of the parent and family members by the majority and powerful section of the society may lead to the family to the following disadvantages:

- Affecting the economy of the family in a quite adverse way to the extent of making it suffer from poverty and lack of essentials for living.
- Compelling the family to live in unhygienic conditions
- Non-availability or denial of the essential medical and health facilities
- Non availability or denial of the proper educational facilities to the self and children
- Getting psychological shocks on account of the ill treatment faced at the hands of the majority group

A marginalized family deprived in the manner given above then fails to contribute appropriately for the growth and development of its developing children. The children here suffers from mal-nourishment right from their very conception in the womb of the mother; are forced to drink contaminated water; do not get health and medical assistance in time, suffer from ailments and diseases; do not get due attention and caring from their parents on account of their struggling to earn livelihood; do not get help from the parents and family members for the development of language and communication power on account of the helplessness and illiteracy of their parents and family members; do not get appropriate opportunity to imbibe healthy proper habits from the peers and neighbors on account of the poor neighborhood and incapable playing mates and peers; fail to get appropriate educational opportunities in terms of admission in the good schools and discrimination or marginalization suffered in the school on account of the seclusion and socio-economic status of their families; remain deprived from the company, contacts and interactions with the members of the community and other social institutions and agencies helpful in their proper social, emotional and mental development. In this way, the physical and socio-cultural environment available in the marginalized and deprived families fails to provide the children what is needed for the satisfaction of their physical and socio-psychological needs and age related wholesome development (Mangal, 2015). On the contrary it leads them to poor physical and mental health and ailments, social and emotional maladjustment, socially and morally undesirable habits, delinquent or socially deviant behaviour, drug addiction and alcoholism, communication and language problems, backwardness and learning difficulties, failures and drop outs, shutting up the doors of higher education, employment and proper settlement in life.

The Impact of Marginalization Suffered by the Children Themselves: In addition to the ill consequence suffered by the children on account of the side effects and contributions of the marginalization of their families, the children are bound to suffer badly on account of their own marginalization and victimization in their families, schools and society. Let us try to think in this direction.

Marginalization in Family: It is quite possible for the children to suffer from acute marginalization and discrimination at the hands of their own parents, step mother and father, care taker and family members in a number of ways.

The apathy and antagonistic attitude of the family members towards, the girl child, widow child, or children losing their mother/father or both, disabled etc. in our society is well known. In such discriminatory and deprived physical and socio-psychological environment of the family the children fails to get needed love and affection, attention and care, rearing and nourishing supplements, healthy interactions and timely guidance, incentives and reinforcement for their good behaviour and progress. As a result there arises a big gap in the physical and socio-psychological needs and their satisfaction.

Marginalization in School: The students may suffer from acute discrimination and marginalization in the school on one or the other accounts like belonging to a particular gender, caste, colour, creed, religion, social status, region, language group and nationality, suffering from one or the other types of disabilities and incapacities, or may face the wrath and blunt of the personal disliking, negative attitude, jealousy and envy of the teachers and authorities developed towards them. Inconsequence, they may exclude and prevent a child from taking part in the regular activities of the school, ridicule or treat him badly in front of others, do injustice in evaluating their performance and achievements and thus harm him psychologically and educationally in a way as to put a lot of barriers in his adequate adjustment, development and progress. Such marginalized students then with no fault of them may be seen to be drifting towards backwardness, failure, truancy, delinquency, drug addiction, arid other types of antisocial and morally deviant behaviour.

Marginalization in the Society: Members of the majority community and the environment also try to display a lot of marginalization and discrimination towards the developing children by not allowing them to take parts in the activities, festivals, rituals, worships and functions organized in the community venues from time to time. The discrimination and prohibition may be on any ground (such as being a women/girl, widow, disabled, lower caste or untouchable, poor, villager, following other sects, faiths or religion, black colour or disliked nationality) but in all its way it casts a quite negative and damaging influence on the adjustment, and development of the children by snatching the valuable opportunities of social interaction, community and social learning and outward self-expression.

ROLE OF TEACHER IN A MARGINALIZED LEARNING ENVIRONMENT SETTING

A marginalized learning environment setting refers to a learning setting or the classroom situation where some students in a given learning set up are seen to get marginalized, secluded, discriminated or deprived of a number of rights, learning opportunities and resources while others may be seen to have full access to all of these. Such scenes may be witnessed in the learning environment of the schools where a great deal of marginalization is applied to the students on the basis of gender, caste, colour, religion, rural or urban background, or socio economic status of the their family.

In a society where an acute sense of marginalization and discrimination is adopted to the people on one or the other grounds, the same may naturally reflect in the school set up and attitudes of the school people, including teachers and students. Accordingly, there is no surprise to witness a vindictive and antagonistic environment against the girl child, widow girl child, the disabled children, the scheduled caste and scheduled tribes children, children belonging (o poor and weaker sections, speaking other language, and belonging to other states or nations.

A teacher by the dignity of his profession has to be quite fair and Impartial to all of his disciples despite their belongingness to any social group or characterized with any distinction or differences with respect to gender, colour, performance or abilities. He has to take necessary precautions in dealing with his students In the prevailing environment of marginalization in the class and school. The things to be done on his part for this purpose may be broadly summarized as below:

- First of all he must try to imbibe him with a required level of sensitivity towards marginalization, seclusion and discrimination prevalent in the society and field of teaching-learning in respect of its concept and ill consequences.
- He should then try to get acquainted with the type and nature of the marginalization practices prevalent in the school against one or the other types of students.
- He should then take into confidence his higher ones and colleagues to say halt to the practices and policies of marginalization, seclusion and discrimination prevalent in the school. It should lead the teachers to remain cautious and vigilant in relation to:
  - knowing the reasons of some students getting marginalized in the school along with the reasons of the marginalization of their families in the society.
  - sorting out the ways and means of putting checks and control over the practice of marginalization in the school.
  - getting assured that no student should get discriminated and victimized on the basis of marginalization in the classrooms and school.
  - persuading the peers and classmates to have no apathy and antagonism with the student who differ from them in terms of gender, race, religion, cast colour or creed socio-economic status, language, abilities and capacities, region or nationality.
- He should build up necessary confidence in the students belonging to marginalized group of society (such as girl students, widow students, scheduled castes and scheduled students, minority status students, migrant students and foreigners) and provide them necessary help and guidance for helping them in their adequate adjustment, education and development.
- He should work for the setting and successful working of an inclusive learning up in the school so that the disadvantaged or deprived ones including the disabled may get equal and conducive learning environment for their adjustment and holistic development well in tune with their abilities and capacities.

Chapter-25
Deprivation and Deprived Children

MEANING AND NATURE OF DEPRIVATION

The term *'deprivation'* has been derived from the word *'deprive'*. The meanings of the word deprive is *'to take from'*, *'to bar'*, *'to dispose'* and *'to strip'* etc. When we say that he has been deprived of something, we may mean either of the following:

- That very thing has been taken from him.
- He has been debarred from enjoying the privilege of that thing.
- The possession of a thing has been snatched from him and given to somebody else.
- He has been stripped of some rights or privileges.

The term deprive indicates a sort of deficiency or loss of a thing, an object or opportunity of doing and progressing or being debarred or denied by some rights or privileges. In case one does not get his due share, right or privilege, then he is named as being deprived of that share, right or privilege. Many of the youngsters have to suffer severe deprivation, on account of the sudden demise of their parents. It makes them deprived of the needed parental love and affection, sense of security, encouragement and incentives etc. for their proper development. In many cases, poverty becomes the sole reason for depriving the individuals of the basic necessities of life and this deprivation may prove a hurdle or major deficiency for their normal progress and development. We may come across a number of instances and examples of such economic, social cultural, physical and psychological deprivation in our surroundings.

A deprived child is one who is:

- Without proper parental care or control, subsistence, education as required by law, or other care or control necessary for his physical, mental, or emotional health or morals.
- Has been placed for care or adoption in violation of law.
- Has been abandoned by parents or other legal custodian.
- Is without a parent, guardian, or custodian

In this way the term 'deprivation' stands for all those deficiencies, defects and ailments prevailing in one environment that may cause to face disfavour, loss of deficit in respect of the desired facilities, opportunities, help and guidance for his proper development and adjustment in comparison to other people living in the same or some other environment.

TYPES OF DEPRIVATION

The following types of deprivation usually prevalent in the Indian society (Mangal, 2015):

- Economic Deprivation
- Social and Cultural Deprivation
- Educational Deprivation
- Emotional Deprivation

Economic Deprivation: Proper economic conditions and well being have greater value in today's materialized world. Every facility of life and opportunities for one's welfare and development is closely linked with one's prosperity in terms of wealth, money and sound means of earning livelihood. The term economic deprivation stands for all those deficiencies, deficits and obstacles suffered by an individual, on account of the paucity of economic resources, *i.e.,* poverty, for the satisfaction of his basic needs, his proper growth and development and adjustment to his self and the environment.

In the circumstances of such economic deprivation, *i.e.,* poverty, the children and other members of the family can't get adequate means even for the satisfaction of their most essential basic needs like food, water, rest and sleep etc. They don't get shelter for living and clothes for wearing. When they venture for schooling, they have no money for the school fees, books, dress or other educationally essential materials. In such a deprived condition how can we think about their all round development and adequate adjustment?

In this way their whole behaviour and personality are ultimately shaped in the struggle for their economic existence and survival, In contrast to these poverty ridden children and individuals there is an affluent layer of the who has everything for the satisfaction of its basic needs and progress. The children bclonging to these strata arc born with a silver spoon in their mouth and as a result do not have to bear the wrath of economic deprivation. Therefore, it is hut natural, that such inequalities and wide variation in the economic level of the different layers of the society will ultimately lead to widespread dissatisfaction, conflicts and tensions in the mind of those who suffer on account of such inequalities, deficiencies and deprivation.

Social and Cultural Deprivation: Social deprivation is the reduction or prevention of culturally normal interaction between an individual and the rest of society. This social deprivation is included in a broad network of correlated factors that contribute to social exclusion; these factors include mental illness, poverty, poor education, and low socioeconomic status.

The term "social deprivation" is slightly ambiguous and lacks a concrete definition. There are several important aspects that are consistently found within research on the subject. With social deprivation one may have limited access to the social world due to factors such as low socioeconomic status or poor education. The socially deprived may experience "a deprivation of basic capabilities due to a lack of freedom, rather than merely low income."[1] This lack of freedoms may include reduced opportunity, political voice, or dignity.[1]

This sort of deprivation is directly linked with the deficiencies, deficits and obstacles faced by the individual family or the whole community in relation to the satisfaction of their socio-cultural needs. When a child is deprived of the company of other children for playing or utilizing his leisure time, he is said to be a victim of social deprivation. A family may fall victim of the socio-cultural deprivation in a colony, sector or village when all the other families residing there either belong to a separate religion, faith, region or linguistic groups or have a quite high or low socio-economic status.

Educational Deprivation: The term educational deprivation stands for all those deficiencies, deficits and obstacles, which are responsible for depriving the individuals, families or communities from the opportunities of getting education or having a feeling that some injustice or disfavour is being done to them in comparison to other individuals, families or communities residing in the same or other regions.

Some children get deprived of education on account of poverty, illiteracy, ignorance and socio-cultural backwardness of their parents, families and communities. Some become victims of such deprivation on account of lack of proper educational facilities and opportunities like absence of school, lack of the provision for girls' education, non availability of the provision for higher, technical, vocational and professional education within the reach of their means.

Emotional Deprivation: The term emotional deprivation stands for all those deficiencies, deficits and obstacles lying in one's environment that interferes with the normal process of the satisfaction of one's socio-psychological needs, more particularly his emotional needs to the extent of being drifted towards severe emotional maladjustment. The following situations and factors present in one's family and school environment are generally responsible for such emotional deprivation:

- The conflicts and clashes between the parents, to the extent of separation or divorce, the death of one or both the parents.
- The insulting, indifferent, partial, prejudiced and unjust behaviour of the parents to the child.
- The behaviour of the other members of the family, relatives, guardians or other members of the society in case of the non-existence of the parents either due to their death or of their in competencies and indifference to the child.
- The conflicts, clashes, fighting and cold war among the members of the family leading to an uncongenial environment at the home.
- Non attention or careless attitudes of the parents or members of the family towards proper rearing and bringing up of the child on account of ignorance, illiteracy, socio-cultural backwardness, selfish interests or some other reasons.
- The unjust, insulting, partial or prejudiced behaviour of the teachers or elder students of the class or school to the child.
- The nonessential restrictions, lack of reasonable freedom and autocratic, unreasonable disciplinary systems both at the school and home.
- Lack of self-expression and opportunities for the self actualization at home and the school.

MEANING OF DEPRIVED CHILDREN

The term deprived children may be referred to those children who suffer from one or the offer types of disadvantages or deprivation to the extent of proving a big obstacle in the path of their proper upbringing, development, adjustment, education and progress in life. These children may be further classified as economically deprived, socially and culturally deprived, educationally and emotionally deprived depending upon the type of deprivation or disadvantages coming in the way of their development and progress.

CHILDHOOD IN THE CONTEXT OF POVERTY

Poverty is a great sin and poverty ridden children are the worst sufferers in terms of various types of deprivations and disadvantages suffered by them on one or the other accounts. The story of their sufferings and deprivations in this connection starts well from the time of their conception in the womb of their mothers and then gets continued throughout their developmental period affecting their growth and development, education and progress as well as interests and welfare in a variety of ways (Mangal, 2015).

- The poverty ridden children may inherit many of the hereditary diseases and ailments, inabilities and incapacities, weaknesses and limitations through the defective genes and chromosomes transmitted to them by their immediate parents who are unfortunate enough to get inflicted by them on account of their poverty ridden defective environment and humiliating conditions of living and working. This defective inheritance may prove them quite costly in terms of the poor base and weak structure for starting their journey of development and progress in their life.
- In the womb of the mother these poverty ridden children do not get needed nourishment and care for their proper growth and development.
- At the time of birth also there may arise a number of problems and adversity to these new born children. There may be no proper facilities available for the delivery of these poverty ridden children.
- After birth on wards these children are deprived with what is needed to them in terms of their proper nourishment, care and satisfaction of their basic needs, availability of essential material facilities, education and progress in their developmental period. The poverty and poor socio economic status of their parents and family may be found to stand firmly well against their progress in their development in many ways and consequently they may have to face the blunt of so many disadvantages, discriminations, prejudices, stereotypes, marginalization and deprivations of one or the other kind resulting in various negative outcomes, to them as summarized below.

SUGGESTION TO MINIMIZE THE EFFECTS OF POVERTY ON CHILDHOOD

The suggestion below may prove fruitful in this direction:

- There should be well planned scheme on the part of government and non government organizations for providing financial assistance and incentives' to the poverty ridden children for their schooling.

- The schooling should be free to the poverty ridden children. The community and government should take care of their dress and other reading material needed by them for their education.
- There should be a fixed proportion of seats reserved for the poverty ridden children in all types of schools (Government, Aided and Private or Public schools.).
- There should be proper arrangement of midday meal programme especially suited In the poverty ridden children.
- Care should be taken for paying attention up on the living conditions of the poverty ridden families. They should be helped in improving their sanitary conditions, and feeding them in a proper way. They should also be helped in having their pakka houses, electricity supply, kitchen gas and clean water to drink with a sufficient subsidy and concessional rates.
- There should be free and concessional provision of essential medical facilities to the poverty ridden families and children.
- The community services, games and entertainment facilities should be suitably available to the poverty ridden children with no cost.
- They should be given all incentives to take part in co-curricular activities and programmes helpful in the wholesome development of their personality.
- They should be helped in knowing and learning that poverty does not come in the progress and development of a person if he tries to proceed on his path with a firm determination. There should be arrangement of such motivational lectures, dialogues and workshops in the schools as well as in community centers.
- Whenever, a poverty ridden child is found to excel in one or the other field, he should be duly encouraged for his or her efforts and attempts should be made to produce him or her as a living example to others.

CHILDREN IN THE CONTEXT OF GLOBALIZATION

These problems and difficulties of the poverty ridden children are very much enhanced and multiplied in their nature and ill effects when the poverty of the children gets associated with the ill impacts and evil influences of the phenomenon of globalization. As a matter of getting acquainted with the concept of globalization we may consider it as a global socio cultural, political, economic and educational phenomenon responsible for narrowing the distances and bringing the world community closer to each other irrespective of the various disparity and inequality lying among them. In its impacts and outcomes, globalization is well associated with a rapid emergence of:

- the institutions of rapid industrialization, urbanization and modernization,
- establishment of multicultural society believing in the philosophy of pragmatism and capitalist economic order and
- employment of the ICT and other scientific means and methods for carrying out the world order and processes

Some of the striking ill impacts and evil influences brought through the courtesy of globalization to the childhood of developing children especially in the developing country like India are:

Exploitation of the Children in the Form of Child Labour: With the emergence of heavy industrialization and competitive market of import and export on the scene through the courtesy of globalization, children in a quite large number are getting exploited in the shape of child labour. They may be seen working in various small and big industrial or business organizations all over the country in the quite pathetic and inhuman conditions. This exploitation takes it worst shape when the children are kept as bonded labour and treated inhumanly like slaves.

Exploitation of Children in the Form of Child Prostitutes: Globalization has made possible visit and tour of the places a quite pleasing matter. There has been a great increase in the number of tourists and visitors to the places of their choice. With a number of attractions for visiting a place on the part of visiting tourists nowadays one thing is strikingly appearing on the scene in a big way is child prostitution. In a report of UNESCO it has been pointed out a quite alarming factor for the wellbeing of the children all over the globe especially for the developing and economy crisis countries (especially East Asian, and East European countries) where poverty ridden children can be easily forced into prostitution. Here the girls and boys of tender age are both involved in pleasing and serving the sex desire of the visitors and tourists belonging to the region and far and near corners of the globe.

Exploitation of the Children in the Form of Child Pornography: The other major field for the exploitation of the younger children (both boys and girls) is concerned with child pornography. Globalization has brought an era of rapid computerization and revolution in the field of ICT and electronic appliances. The internet, web services, audio video' recording devices, multimedia cameras and smart phone technology have made possible the use of child pornography in a quite amazing and damaging way.

Exploitation of Children in the Form of Sale Commodity and Adoption: Another form of exploitation made possible through globalization nowadays exists in the form of buying the younger children as a commodity for their exploitation in one or the other ways. Poverty ridden younger boys and girls are also being purchased for getting exploited as domestic servants. The game of such buying of the younger children is also in practice in the name of adoption. The people of western countries are buying children from the poverty ridden countries in the mode of fake adoption.

CHILDREN LIVING IN SLUM AREAS

The rapid increase in the size and intensity of heavy industrialization and urbanization resulted through the process of globalization in the modern era has given birth to a number of slum areas and localities as habitats for the labours and other people coming to the big towns and cities to earn their livelihood. These slum areas or localities may be seen to portrait the real hail or worst places for the living of human beings in the manner depicted below:

- They are often located in the unused and unauthorized or waste lands and places prohibited for living such as the land available on railway stations, area adjacent to dirty drainage or foul water collected in the low lying lands or nearby the pollution spreading factories.

- They do not possess the essentials of living such as proper pathways and roads, sewerage system and sanitation arrangement, water for drinking and other uses, electricity, gas supply etc.
- The houses are most often built through temporary stuff such as tent house old clothing, plastic sheets, muds and thatches, and bamboo sticks etc. unable to bear the blunt of summer, winter or rains.
- There is no provision of toilets and bathrooms, People have to bath in open and toilet in the areas adjacent to their localities causing hygienic problems to themselves and others.
- Since these are located in the unauthorized land and are not falling within the jurisdiction of the municipal committee or city boards, there exists nothing like parks, open places for the recreation and playing of their children, elementary schools and community centers.
- These are characterized with the heavy doses of air, water and noise pollutions.
- The inhabitants of these localities generally are the poverty ridden masses, labourers serving in the nearby factories, rickshaw pullers, porters, domestic servants and low earning people. Most of them are illiterate or semi- literates with no social exposure of the globalized world.
- They are not much conscious about the sanitation, cleanliness and essential health measures being taken for the health and wellbeing of the pregnant mothers and developing children (Mangal, 2015).

Impact on the Development, Adjustment and Education of the Developing Children: The children belong to urban slums may be found to suffer from a host of deficiencies, deprivations, and adversities affecting their adjustment, education and development in a quite detrimental way much in the ways as suffered by the poverty ridden children. We have discussed all such ill impacts and negative influences on them already in this chapter. However, one thing more here needs to be mentioned in addition to what has already said. It is concerned with the special damaging impact carried out on the developing children on account of the type of environment available to them for their adjustment and education and development. We can summarize it in the manner below:

- They may be found to get inflicted with a number of diseases and ailments on account of poor sanitation and unhealthy living conditions and the adverse impacts of such unhealthy environment may cost them dearly in the impairment of their health and physical development.
- They have nothing solid in their environment that can prove friendly, inspirational and helpful for their proper growth and development. In the form of peers and elderly models available for the observation, imitation and imbibing the habits and learning of the desirable behaviour their environment provides them quite a negative and undesirable models before them at their home, neighborhood unit locality. These may be school failures, drop cuts, truants, problem children, alcoholics, drug addicts, gamblers, thieves, smugglers, delinquents and criminal.
- They may face a lot of discrimination, marginalization and deprivation on

this account. As a part of reactionary measure, it may drift them towards aggression, problematic, and delinquent behaviour. on the other hand there are more possibilities on their part for getting drifted into the state of failure, frustration, and depressions on account of lowering of their morale, self-confidence, self- esteem and self-efficacy in a considerable way.

MEASURES FOR IMPROVEMENT IN DEPRIVED STUDENTS

- Earnest attempts must be made for bringing improvement in the living condition of slum dwellers. These colonies should be regularized and arrangement should be made for equipping them with the needed living amenities like toilets, pure drinking water, electric and kitchen gas supply, pakka houses, proper food, stuff on the subsidized rates, drainage system and sewerage, community centres community parks, neighborhood school and transport facilities.
- The slum dwellers must be helped in making them literates and helping, them advance further in their learning pursuits.
- They must be properly educated for being conscious about bringing improvement in their living and behaving. They should feel their responsibility of providing opportunities to their children for their education and development and reality that they should not do anything that may influence the behaviour and habits of the children in a negative and damaging way.
- Attempts should be made to save the slum children from the company of the bad elements. In case they somehow entrapped in the net of the vested interests, they should be helped in coming out and lead their life in a new way.

SOCIALLY DEPRIVED GIRLS

There has been prevailing a continuous trend and practice of hatred, indifference, prejudices, discrimination and marginalization towards the girl child in the Indian indifference from the time immemorial on one or the other account. As a result, the girl child has been a clear cut object of social deprivation being witnessed in the ways and manners outlined below:

- In most of the Indian families even at this age of so much technological progress and awareness, the birth of a girl child is not the subject of celebration, it is considered quite unfortunate to give birth to a girl child by the mothers and they are cursed and held responsible for bringing misfortune to the family.
- There prevails a clear cut differentiation and discrimination in the upbringing of the girl and boy children on the part of parents and elders such as (Mangal, 2015):
  - Boys enjoy all privileges, care and attention in the satisfaction of their bustle needs at the cost of their sisters.
  - Girls are denied the opportunity of schooling on the plea that they are made for house hold duties.
  - They are denied balanced and nutritious diets on the plea that boys require more energy and stamina for performing man like responsibilities

and duty should be healthier and stronger than their female counter parts.

- ➢ The behaviour of the boy child is not condemned and decried even if it U undesirable and problem generating. On the other hand a simple natural slip in the behaviour of a girl child is punished and decried in every sort.
- ➢ Girls are denied opportunity to participate in outside activities, games and sports, driving and swimming, and any adventurism events on the plea that these task and activities are not feminine and fall predominantly in the task area of the boys.
- ➢ There is a lot of discrimination and differentiation observed by the society in dealing with girls. They are always neglected in comparison to the boys in one or the other matters related to common welfare. In our society, women and girls are always treated just like commodities, the things of utilizing in the service of manhood.

- In schools also girls have to suffer from the menace of gender discrimination, differentiation and deprivation. They are not supposed to study mathematics, computer and engineering, the study areas of boys. Similarly, they are deprived with the opportunities and activities promoting inventiveness, constructivism and discovery on their part. They are discouraged to have competition with boys in martial arts, sports and act of adventurism and take part in outdoor social and community activities thus snatching many valuable opportunities for their wholesome development and progress.

The picture portrayed regarding the discrimination and deprivation of the girls in our society is quite alarming. However, in this connection there is good news that things are changing fast on account of globalization, urbanization, modernization, mass media, spread of literacy and development in ICT and computer applications. The girl child is no more considered as a curse and burden on the family.

CHILDREN SEPARATED FROM PARENTS

It is a hard fact that there is no substitute of parents in the matter of rearing, nourishing and developing the children to their maximum. However, all children are not so fortunate as to enjoy protection, care, love and affection of their parents from their birth onwards. Many of them are found to get separated from their parents on a number of grounds such as:

- Stealing and kidnapping by some vested interests.
- Accidental separation from the parents and family in a fair crowd, visit to places and rail, motor or air accidents.
- Incidental or untimely death of mother, father, or both.
- The parental marital discord, separation or divorce.
- Time bound separation from the parents for full day or few hours on account of their business or professional compulsion.
- Intentionally leaving the children in boarding houses or institutions on account of their abnormal emotional, physical or mental state.

Now the question may arise what happens to these children who get separated from their parents on one or the other ground and are reared or guarded by somebody else.

Children Rearing in the Hands of Bad Peoples and Criminals

You may well imagine the pathetic conditions and consequences suffered by the separated children at the hands of the vested interests. You may have witnessed on the TV and movie screen the scenes how the body parts of the children (kidnapped or falling into the hands of the bad guys) are damaged for forcing them into begging; how these are left to die by extracting one or the other life organs of their body; how these innocent one's are pushed into the world of sex trade and crimes and how these are exploited in terms of bonded labour.

Children Rearing in the Boarding Houses and Institutions

For the children with special needs who are sent to boarding houses or day core special institutions by their parents, there is nothing bad. Such separation, rearing and educational practice may in fact may prove quite beneficial to them for their needed adjustment, education and progress well within their capacities and limitations.

Children Rearing by Single Parent

In the case of marital discord, the custody of the child is given to either of the parent, mother or father. The same responsibility of rearing child all alone also full on the shoulders of a mother or father when one of them is died. In such a situation we may see that every person has his or her own style of rearing. Depending up on one's capacity and resources in terms of time and facilities every single parent tries to provide appropriate caring to the child.

Children Rearing by the Near Relatives

In the situation where the children are so separated from their parents (on account of their marital discord or death) that neither of the parents is available for their rearing, the task may be left to their close relatives. Here the children may feel a lot of problems and difficulties in the way of their adequate adjustment, development and education. Depending up on the nature and behaviour of their keepers they may be fortunate Of unfortunate for passing through their developmental years in a satisfactory or unsatisfactory way.

Children Rearing in Crutches

With an increasing pressure on the parents to earn money for their living and also for the sake of career building and self-satisfaction, both mother and father nowadays. may be found to remain away from their infants. They have the compulsion for leaving the child under the care of (lie other members of the family such as grant parents m some near relatives staying in the home. However, such facility is rarely available on account of the upsurge of the concept of nuclear family and the parents are forced in leave their infants for their rearing in crutches. The numbers of these crutches is increasing day by day in the urban localities of big towns and cities where we may find heavy concentration of the educated working mothers attending offices, schools and business establishments for a considerable length of the day.

Children Rearing in Orphanages

A number of children separated from their parents are forced to get shelter in orphanages when:

- help from relatives are not available
- when they are saved from The clutches of the kidnappers and bad guys
- when they are deliberately abandoned by relatives and single parents in the orphanages (many children are left in temples, lonely places and the premises of orphanages by the unmarried mothers, widows, illegitimate relationship couples etc.)

In such an uncongenial environment it is quite natural for the children rearing in orphanages to suffer from one or the other deprivation or disadvantages such as:

- Deprivation suffered in terms of the satisfaction of their physical needs like availability of enough food for satisfying their hunger, lack of nutritious elements in their food stuff, clean water, cloths and other material for living.
- Deprivation suffered in terms of satisfying their socio- cultural needs such as little or no opportunities for having company and interaction with the social and cultural life of the outside world.
- Deprivation suffered in terms of satisfying their educational needs as no serious attempts are made for their proper education and schooling.
- Deprivation suffered in terms of the satisfaction of their psychological needs such as need to get love and affection, empathy and cooperation etc.

Chapter-26
Thinking

CONCEPT OF THINKING

Thinking is a complex process which involves manipulation of information as we form concepts. It also engages in problem solving, reasoning and making decisions. Thinking is a higher cognitive function and the analysis of thinking processes is part of cognitive psychology. Thinking is a pattern of behaviour in which we make use of internal representations (symbols, signs etc.) of things and events for the solution of some specific, purposeful problem.

DEFINITIONS OF THINKING

Some definitions of thinking are:

1. Kolesnik, *"Thinking is the reorganization of concepts."*
2. Woodworth, *"Thinking is mental exploration to find out solution to a problem."*
3. Bartlett (1958) defined thinking as *"interpolation (i.e. filling in gaps of information), extrapolation (i.e. going beyond the information given) and re-interpretation (i.e. rearranging information)."*
4. Warren (1934) defined thinking as *"a predetermined course of ideas, symbolic in character initiated by a problem or task and leading to a conclusion."*
5. Dewey (1933) defined thinking as *"an attempt to examine and evaluate information based on certain criteria."*
6. Fraenkel (1980) defined thinking as "the formation of ideas, reorganization of one's experience and the organization of information in a particular form."
7. Chaffee (1988) characterises thinking as *"an unusual process used in making decisions and solving problems."*
8. Bourne, Ekstrand and Dominowski (1985) define thinking as *"a complex, multifaceted process that is essentially internal involving symbolic representation of events and objects initiated by some external events."*
9. According to Ross, *"Thinking is mental activity in its cognitive aspect or mental activity with regard to psychological objects"*
10. *"Thinking is an implicit problem solving behaviour."*
11. According to Garett, *"Thinking is behaviour which is often implicit and hidden and in which symbol are ordinarily employed."*
12. Nickerson, Perkins and Smith (1985) looked upon thinking as *"a collection of skills or mental operations used by individuals."*
13. Mayer (1983) viewed thinking from three perspectives:

- Cognitive (i.e. involving knowing, preceiving and conceiving) which occurs internally in the mind or cognitive system and is inferred indrectly from behaviour
- Manipulation of a set of operations of knowledge in the cognitive system
- Results in behaviour directed towards the solution of a problem.

A synthesis of the various definitions of thinkings reveals the following 5 characteristics of thinking (see Figure 26.1):

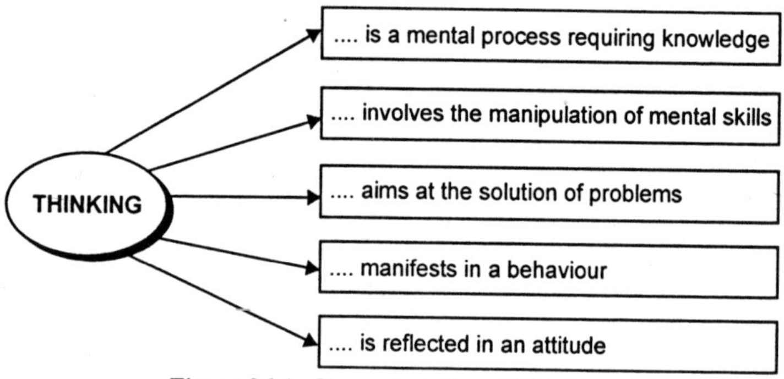

Figure 26.1: Characteristics of Thinking

- First, it is evident that thinking is a process that requires knowledge because it is quite impossible to think in a vacuum. For example, a boy who is dreaming about owning a 16-speed bike and thinking about ways to get the bike. Knowledge about ways to get the bike might include the following: doing odd jobs to save money, borrowing the money from a friend or buyingg a used bike.
- Second, thinking involves the manipulation of mental or cognitive skills such as comparing, classifying, analysis, synthesis and so forth. These skills can be performed well or poorly. When performed poorly, it can be improved or enhanced.
- Third, thinking is targeted at the solution of a problem. For example, thinking how to write an essay, solving a mathematical problem or raising money for the poor.
- Fourth, thinking is manifested in a behaviour or ability such as being able to compare, classify, differentiate and so forth.
- Fifth, thinking is reflected in certain attitudes that are indicative of good and poor thinking.

CHARACTERISTICS OF THINKING

The main characteristics of thinking are:

- It is one of the most important aspects of one's cognitive behaviour.
- It depends on both – perception and memory.
- Thinking is a mental process which starts with a problem and concludes with its solution.
- It involves trial and error; analysis and synthesis; foresight and hindsight.

- It is a symbolic behaviour.
- It is a cognitive activity.
- It is always directed to achieve some purpose.
- It is different from day-dreaming and imagination.
- It is a problem-solving behaviour.
- It is mental exploration instead of motor exploration.(e.g.: if a person gets locked in a room and loses his keys and he starts searching for them in different places. This becomes motor exploration. But if he tries to think of different ways of how he can get out of the room then this becomes mental exploration- Thinking.)
- Thinking is a symbolic activity. (e.g.: engineers use mental images and symbols to design the plan for buildings)

ATTRIBUTES OF GOOD THINKERS

If there is no agreed upon definition of thinking, how does one go about determining good and poor thinkers? Glatthorn and Baron (1985) and Nickerson (1987) developed a list of attributes of good and poor thinkers (see Table 26.1).

Table 26.1: Attributes of Good and Poor Thinkers

Good Thinker	*Poor Thinker*
Welcomes problematic situations	Prefers situations which are more definite
Open to multiple possibilities	Prefers limited possibilities
Uses evidence skillfully	Ignore evidence
Make judgement only after considering all angles	Quick to make judgement
Listens to other people's views	Ignore other people's views
Reflective	Impulsive
Perseveres in searching for information	Gives up easily and is lazy to think further

According to them, a good thinker unlike a poor thinker welcomes problematic situations and is tolerant of ambiguity. A good thinker is self-critical and looks for alternative possibilities and goals, and seeks evidence on both sides, while the poor thinker is satisfied with first attempts. The good thinker is reflective and deliberative while the poor thinker is impulsive and gives up prematurely. While the good thinker believes in the value of rationality, the poor thinker overvalues intuition and believes that thinking would not help. The good thinker is open to multiple suggestions and considers alternatives while the poor thinker prefers to deal with limited possibilities and is reluctant to seek alternatives. The good thinker uses evidence that challenges favoured possibilities while the poor thinker tends to ignore evidence that challenges favoured possibilities.

TYPES OF THINKING

The thinking can be divided into the following types:

Perceptual Thinking: It is a form of thinking in which we make use of sensation and perceptions. For example -the teacher punishes the student for not doing his homework. Now, whenever the student sees that teacher, he recollects that very incident. It is thinking of a lower order such king of thinking is present even in animals and children.

Imaginative Thinking: In such type of thinking mental images are used and employed by using mental images and memory the individual thinks about his future

Conceptual Thinking: In this type of thinking we depend upon the concepts. Concepts are formed with the help of observation, analysis, comparison and mental unification. On the bases of past experiences, we reach at some definite decision whole keeping in view the future

Logical Thinking: It is the highest type of thinking in this type of thinking we makes use of various concepts with a definite aim in view and likes them together in a logical order

Convergent Thinking: Convergent thinking is a term coined by Joy Paul Guilford as the opposite of divergent thinking. It generally means the ability to give the "correct" answer to standard questions that do not require significant creativity.

It is the basic of intelligence. In convergent thinking the person has the tendency to find out one most appropriate idea or responses. Convergent thinking is rigid, stereotyped and mechanically operated. In convergent thinking, we include remembering, recognition and manipulation of some concrete material. Convergent thinking is stimulus bound.

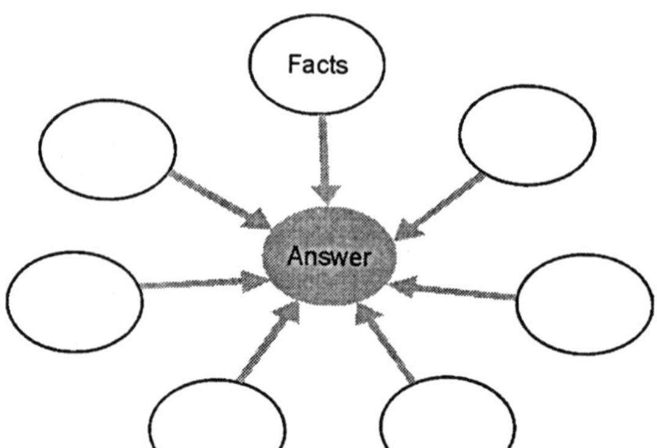

Figure 26.2: Convergent Thinking

Convergent thinking proceeds on the assumption that there is one single best solution to any problem and also that the solution can be arrived at on the basis of the existing knowledge. Thus, convergent thinking involves the direction of all thought process in one single direction. "Convergent" thinking is that in which the person is good at bringing material from a variety of sources to bear on a problem, in such a way as to produce the 'correct answer'.

Divergent Thinking: "Divergent" thinking may start from existing knowledge, but it proceeds in different directions and is not limited or bound by existing knowledge. At times, the divergent thinker may question and doubt the adequacy of the existing knowledge. This type of thinking may start from a common point and move outward into a variety of perspectives. When fostering divergent thinking, teachers use the content as a vehicle to prompt diverse or unique thinking among students rather than a common view. Divergent thinking is also creative thinking. It generates something new or different. It involves having a different idea that works as well or better than previous ideas. Thus, divergent thinkers have an open mind. He is not controlled by the belief that there is 'one best solution' to any problem or 'the correct answer' to any question.

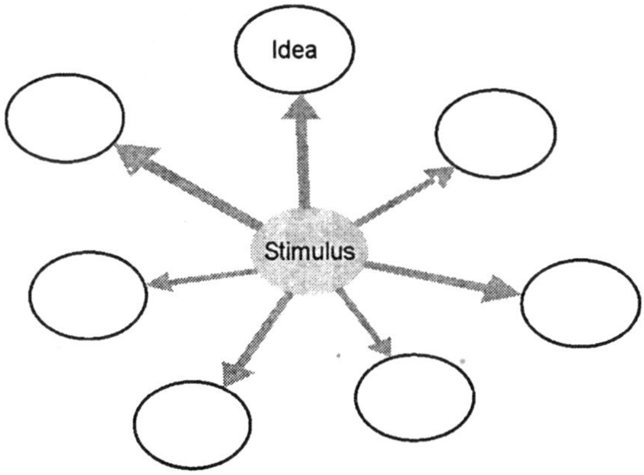

Figure 26.3: Divergent Thinking

Basically divergent thinking is a mode in which a person or group makes themselves open to new ideas. Generally speaking, they are working with, what we might call, an open ended problem, a problem for which there is, there may be, many creative possible solutions. So the divergent thinking process is one in which we are open to all those ideas and we generate lots of new ideas. The difference between the two can be seen in the table 26.2.

It forms the bases of creativity. Divergent Thinking has been regarded as the distinctive aspect of creative thinking. Divergent thinking allows as many responses as possible. This type of thinking is characterized by flexibility, originality and fluency.

Flexibility: It refers to the case with which one changes or stuffs from one set of assumption or approach to another.

Originality: It refers to the novel approach

Fluency: Fluency refers to the number of ideas provided in a given unit

Thus in divergent thinking, we think in different directions, reaching and seeking some variety and novelty.

Difference between Convergent Thinking and Divergent Thinking

The difference between Convergent Thinking and Divergent Thinking is given in Table 26.2:

Table 26.2: Difference between Convergent Thinking and Divergent Thinking

Convergent Thinking	*Divergent Thinking*
Non creative people have convergent thinking.	Creative people have divergent thinking.
Produces single correct answer.	Produces variety of responses.
It is stimulus bound.	It is stimulus free.
The problem is solved by known or common method.	The problem is solved by different innovative methods.
It is rigid, stereotyped & mechanically operated.	It is novel, exploratory & venturesome.
It is measured by intelligence test which includes remembering, recognition & manipulation of some concrete material.	It is measured by creativity tests in which novelty, flexibility & originality are given more weightage.
It is known as Reasoning or Rational Thinking.	It is known as Creative Thinking, Imaginative or Original Thinking.

Critical Thinking

The term of critical thinking is sometimes misunderstood to mean an activity aimed at criticizing or pointing out the weaknesses and finding fault with others. However, this interpretation of the definition is not accurate. The term "critical" is derived from the Greek word *kritikos* which means to question, to make sense of, to be able to analyze. There has been a tendency for some educators to interpret critical thinking more broadly and to include all good thinking as critical thinking. However, other educators prefer the narrower concept of critical thinking.

Critical thinking assesses the worth and validity of something existent. It involves precise, persistent, objective analysis. When teachers try to get several learners to think convergently, they try to help them develop common understanding.

In general, critical thinking includes:

- taking the initiative to question what you read, hear, and observe
- challenging the underlying assumptions of what you are questioning
- analyzing what you question in a reasoned and unbiased way
- remaining open to new ideas and perspectives
- changing your position on an issue when convinced by the logic of another position
- reflecting constantly on your learning in order to find patterns, linkages, or related elements that could be applied to other problems or issues.

Reflective Thinking

Reflective thinking is normally a slow process. It takes considerable time to work on inferring and combining by reflecting upon what we have learnt. This is a higher form of thinking. According to Dewey, *"Active, persistent, and careful consideration of any belief or supposed form of knowledge in the light of the grounds that support it and the further conclusion to which it tends"*

The skills related to reflective thinking are:

- identifying the author's conclusion;
- identifying the reasons and the evidence
- identifying vague and ambiguous language
- identifying value assumptions and value conflicts
- identifying descriptive assumptions
- evaluating statistical reasoning
- evaluating sampling and measurements
- evaluating logical reasoning
- identifying omitted information
- articulating one's own values in thoughtful, fair-minded way.

Characteristics of Reflective Thinking

The main characteristics of reflective thinking are as follows:

- It aims at solving complex problems.
- It requires reorganization of all the relevant experiences and the finding of new ways of reacting to a situation or of removing an obstacle instead of a simple association of experiences or ideas.
- There is insightful cognitive approach in reflective thinking.
- It takes all the relevant facts arranged in a logical order into account in order to arrive at a solution of the problem in hand.
- It links the information we possess into tighter network, thus helps to remember the matter better.
- It criticizes what one has learned and tries to expose weaknesses and shortcomings.
- Enhancing decision making requires that we learn from our successes and failures and catalog mentally for future retrieval what has occurred and why.

Lateral Thinking

Lateral thinking is a term coined by Edward de Bono, a Maltese psychologist, physician and writer. It first appeared in the title of his book, *'The Use of Lateral Thinking'*, published in 1967. De Bono defines lateral thinking as *'methods of thinking concerned with changing concepts and perception."* Lateral thinking is about reasoning that is not immediately obvious and about ideas that may not be obtainable by using only traditional step-by-step logic.

De Bono identifies four critical factors associated with lateral thinking: (1) recognize dominant ideas that polarize perception of a problem, (2) searching for different ways of looking at things, (3) relaxation of rigid control of thinking, and (4) use of chance to encourage other ideas.

Characteristics of Lateral Thinking

The main characteristics of lateral thinking are as under:

- Lateral thinking involves discarding the obvious, leaving behind traditional modes of thought, and throwing away preconceptions.
- ***Explanation:*** A person would use lateral thinking when they want to move from one known idea to creating new ideas.

- Lateral thinking can be used to help in solving problems but can also be used for much more.
- With lateral thinking problems can be solved and questions can be answered, as lateral thinkers are able to use their creative skills to change perceptions and come up with new concepts and ideas.
- The lateral thinking technique of 'challenge' is designed to prevent the mind sliding smoothly down the existing patterns.
- Lateral Thinking is the ability to add a slight "twist" to the pattern of logical thinking to produce an unexpected answer.
- Lateral thinking is a way of attacking problems from other angles, as opposed to the more traditional linear and logical ways. De Bono uses the example of chess, where logic normally suffices, if the pieces are a given. Lateral thinking acknowledges that in real life we mostly just assume the pieces are given, when really we need to change those pieces or look beyond them for the most useful solutions.
- Lateral Thinking helps individual to develop skills to: Increase productive idea output, Design the future, Find fresh new solutions to intractable problems, Escape the constraints of routine thinking, Appreciate the diversity of thinking among team members, Plan and lead innovation meetings that deliver powerful results and Find new areas of opportunity.

Creative Thinking

There is no definition of creativity that can be agreed upon because experts in the field have different notions of the mental activity. The following are some definitions of creativity:

1. Torrance (1962) a well-know authority in the area of creativity defined creativity as *"a process of becoming sensitive to problems, deficiencies, gaps in knowledge, missing elements, disharmonies and so on; identifying the difficult, searching for solutions, making guesses or formulating hypotheses about the deficiencies, testing and retesting these hypotheses and possibly modifying and retesting them in; and finally communicating the results"*.
2. Guilford (1991) suggests that *"to be creative one has to think divergently which requires originality (generation of unusual ideas), flexibility (generation of different ideas, sensitivity towards problems; and also to think convergently (equipped with the facts, concepts and principles of the phenomena examined).*
3. Parnes (1967) view "*creativity as a function of imagination and facts, and the ability to find ideas and problems."*
4. Perkins (1984) in a review of various definitions of creativity concluded that "*it is a process of generating unique products by transformation of existing products which could be something tangible or intangible and considered unique and valuable to the person who produced it."*
5. VanGrundy (1991) describes creativity as the "*process for bringing something new, unusual, or original into being which may be a product, a method, a system, or an idea."*

6. Mayesky (1995) defines creativity as *"a way of thinking and acting or making something that is original for the individual and valued by that person or others. What this means is that a new way to solve a problem or to produce a new product, such as a song, a poem, or a new machine, is a creative act. A person does not have to be the first one in the world to produce something in order for it to be considered a creative act".*
7. Khatena (1978) describes creativity as *"fluency which is the ability to produce many ideas for a given task; flexibility which is the ability to show a conceptual shift in thinking relative to a given task; originality which is the ability to produce unusual or clever ideas that not many other people think of; and elaboration which is the ability to add details to the basic idea."*

Many believe that to be creative one has to produce something that has not been produced or done by others and to be the first one to do so. However, this is not altogether true. Creativity could be expressed by adapting or modifying of what is already available. For example, improving on an existing product by making it more efficient, affordable, portable, durable, attractive or whatever is a creative act; sometimes referred to jokingly as being a "creative copycat".

Regardless of how creativity is defined, most people would agree that it is a crucial aspect of a child's development. All the great inventions, discoveries, innovations and artistic expressions known to humankind are the consequences of creative thinking. The advancement of any civilisation or culture depends on the creative abilities of its people or being able to "Think Out of the Box". The ability to think creatively is becoming even more important as nations rapidly transform into technological societies where a strong creative potential will provide the means of coping with the future. It is difficult to predict the nature of future societies but the problem encountered will have to be addressed creatively.

THE CREATIVE PROCESS

How does the creative process operate? Are there specific steps in producing something creative? Onc of the earliest descriptions of the creative process was provided by Wallas in 1926 in which were identified 4 stages: preparation, incubation, illumination and verification (see Figure 26.4).

1. Preparation Stage

At the *preparation stage,* the individual who is confronted with a problem identifies what is to be dome and ways to solve the problem. It is here that information is gathered, ideas manipulated and trying out of ideas to find one that fits or one that feels right.

2. Incubation Stage

If the individual comes to what seems like a dead end or mental block and cannot find the solution, he or she is advised to put the problem aside. This is called the *incubation stage.* By temporarily leaving the problem, the mind "unfreezes" itself of being glued to a particular pattern of thinking. It also

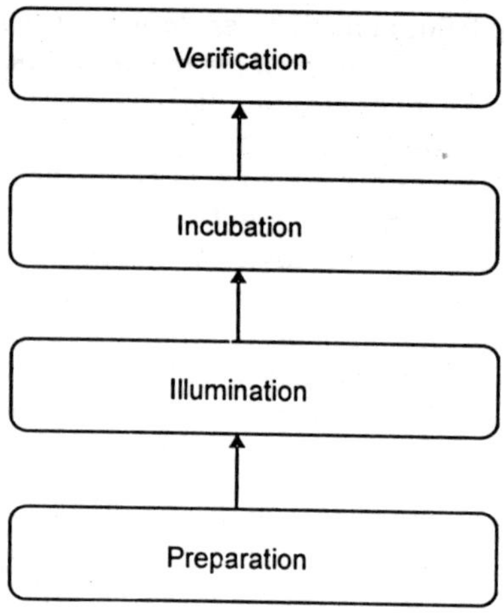

Figure 26.4: Stages in the Creative Process

gives the mind time to recall relevant information from memory which was earlier not available for the solution of the problem.

3. Illumination Stage

After this stage, the chances are that the solution will become apparent at the *illumination stage*. This has been described as the "AHA" phenomenon; the flash-like, unexpected or sudden insight as to the solution of the problem (or *Eureka!* for some). Recognition of the insight usually followed by a positive emotional reaction in the individual such joy, a sense of accomplishment and the desire to share the 'discovery' with others such as parents and teachers.

4. Verification Stage

The verification stage is where the individual checks to determine if the solution to the problem is viable and widely applicable. At times it might be necessary to verify whether the solution is cost-effective, not time consuming and so forth.

Another variant of the creative process is provided by Parnes, Noller and Biondi in 1977 who viewed the process as involving "Three Ss", i.e. sensitivity, synergy and serendipity (see Figure 26..5).

1. *Sensitivity*

Sensitivity is when one uses all the senses (touch, smell, taste, sight and hearing) to investigate the world. It has been suggested that "highly creative people experience the physical world with greater intensity than the rest of us" Halpern, 1984, p. 319). Sensitivity also relates to the ability not only to solve problems but also find problems.

2. *Synergy*

Synergy is the bringing together of seemingly disparate parts into a useful and functioning whole. In other words, Diverse and different bits of information and ideas are synthesised or brought together to form and work as a new entity.

Figure 26.5: Origin of a Creative Idea

3. Serendipity

Serendipity means making discoveries by accident or unexpected discovery that comes about when bits of information are bought together (quite similar to illumination). For example, a new idea is discovered as a result of an accident or mishap. In fact, most inventions and discoveries result from a methodological and systematic process requiring persistence, motivation and sheer hard work. Remember the old saying; "Success is 90 per cent perspiration and 10 per cent inspiration".

Difference between Critical Thinking and Creative Thinking

We have discussed in detail critical and creative thinking. Table 26.3 is a summary of the processes involved in critical and creative thinking.

Table 26.3: Differences in the Processes Involve in Critical and Creative Thinking

Critical Thinking	*Creative Thinking*
Analytic	Generative
Convergent	Divergent
Vertical	Lateral
Probability	Possibility
Judgment Suspended	Judgment
Focused	Diffuse
Objective	Subjective
Answer	An Answer
Left Brain	Right Brain
Verbal	Visual
Linear	Associative
Reasoning	Richness, Novelty
Yes But	Yes And

TOOLS OR INSTRUMENTS OF THINKING

The main tools or instruments of thinking are as under:

Percepts: Percepts stimulate thinking suppose we have seen our friends stealing something. This perception will set our thinking in order to discover ways and means of preventing our friend from this act. Many Other percepts help in Thinking

Images: Images are kind of symbols which include the fault recollection of perceptions. Past experiences of an individual move around in the mind in the form of images. Images may be recalled through a conscious effort but they also flash in the mind involuntary

Concepts: Concepts are indispensable in thinking. Classification of object is done on the bases of concepts. Concepts extend the units of thinking to include both the past and his future

Sign and Symbols: Symbols and sign represent and stand for as substitute for actual subject, experience and activities. Traffic Lights, railway signals, school bells, badges, songs, flags and slogans all stand for the symbolic expression. Concepts are usually represented in thinking by these symbols and signs. Similarly *'Red'* is the symbol which stands for the concepts of readiness.

Language: It services as a tool of thinking. It consists of words and therefore uses symbols. Sometimes instead of words, we use gestures in our language. The showing of thumb; milling or lifting of eyebrows, shrugging of shoulders carries a lot of meaning. Language is the most efficient and developed vehicle for carrying out the process of thinking.

Chapter-27
Concept Formation

Concepts are mental categorizes for object, events or ideas that have a common set of features. Concepts allow us to classify objects and events. In learning a concept we must focus on the relevant features and ignores those that are irrelevant.

MEANING OF CONCEPTS

A concept is the sum total of what we know about the object. It refers to a generalized idea about the objects/persons/events. It stands for a general class and not for a particular object/person/event. It is a common name given on the basis of similarities or commonness found in different objects/persons/ events. There are concepts of objects such as cat, tree, chair etc., concepts of persons such as mother, Indian etc. and concepts of qualities such as honesty, goodness, and obedience. It is a mental disposition that helps in understanding the meaning of the objects or perceived earlier. In one sense, it is general mental image of the objects/persons/events experienced or perceived earlier.

DEFINING CONCEPT

Concepts are one of the key elements of thinking. Concepts represent objects, activities, ideas, or living organisms. They also represent '*properties*' (such as "sour" or "brave"), '*abstractions*' (such as "anger" or "fear") and '*relations*' (such as "smaller than" or "more intelligent than"). Concepts are mental structures which allow us to '*organize knowledge*' in systematic ways. We cannot observe them directly, but we can infer them from behaviour.

We as human beings have the capacity to abstract the essential characteristics of objects, events or whatever we perceive. For example, when we see a Potato we categorize it as 'vegetable', and when we see a towel we categorize it as 'cloth'. Whenever we encounter a new stimulus we tend to treat it as a member of a familiar or remembered category and take the same action toward it and give it the same label.

DEFINITIONS OF CONCEPTS

Some definitions of concept are:

1. "A label for a set of percepts which have essential common attributes."
2. "A phenomenon in a given field which are grouped together for their common characteristics."
3. "Concept is fundamental agent of intellectual works."
4. According to Morgan, "*Concept is a process of representing a common property of objects or events.*"

5. Munn, *"Concept is a process with represents the similarities in otherwise diverse objects, situations or events."*
6. Woodworth, *"Concepts are those thoughts which mention things, incidents, qualities, etc."*
7. Hammerton, *"Concept is the process of discrimination of the common features and relations in the world of events, things and persons."*

NATURE OF CONCEPT

The nature of concept is as below:

- A concept is not static, it is always changing. For example first a child considers even the walls and doors to be living things. Then it understands they are nonliving, considers cars, buses and running objects to be alive. Later, it learns that only animals and plants are living.
- The concept is not common for all, different persons may have different concept about the same object/events.
- Concept is a part of thought process.
- Concept can be formed without the use of language.
- Concert formation is the association of certain stimuli and responses.
- Concept is the process of discrimination of the common features.
- Concepts are very useful in recognizing, naming and identifying the objects/ persons/events.

TYPES OF CONCEPTS

The main types of concepts are as under:

Natural Concepts: These are the concepts that are learnt naturally by the child e.g. concept of food, concept of seasons.

Artificial Concepts: Artificial concepts are those concepts which are not learnt naturally and are taught to the children e.g. Process of Digestion is not known naturally but taught by others to the child, measuring of temperature, Melting and boiling point.

Spontaneous Concepts: These are the concepts which are learnt by the child on his own. Since these concepts are learnt on own they are not well defined concepts e.g. Concepts of Water.

Instructed Concepts: These types of concepts are not learnt by the child on his own, but are taught to him by the elders in family or teacher in through instructions. Since these concepts are learnt through instructions, these concepts are well defined e.g. Concept of Disease.

TYPES OF CONCEPTS ACCORDING TO BRUNER

According to Bruner, the three types of concepts are:

Conjunctive Concepts: They are concrete ideas formed through combining different features or attributes. One or more attributes required to define a concept e.g. Concept of dog, chair, lake etc.

Disjunctive Concepts: These are abstract ideas. They have only one attribute to define a concept e.g. Concept of intelligence, fairness etc.

Relational Concepts: These types of concept always have reference to something or the other in order to be explained. A kind of comparison is made with something in order to be explained e.g. Concept of old, Average etc.

CONCEPT FORMATION

It is a form of thinking that helps us to better understanding the world we live in as well as ourselves

Types of Concept Formation: Three types of concepts are:

Direct Experience: It is the first type of concept formation, in which the learner develops concept through direct experience with the particular objects/persons/events. It is developed during from the early childhood onwards. For example, the concept about cow.

Indirect Experience: Here the learner develops concept through pictures, photos and reading descriptions, hearing from other. For example, the concept about Kangaroo.

Faulty Concepts: The concepts or the general ideas we have about the objects, persons or events, are not always adequate and accurate. Small children have so many concepts that are quite erroneous and inadequate. For example, one's anxiety over the crossing of his way by a cat or one's feeling of hatred towards the person

PROCESS OF CONCEPT FORMATION

The process of concept formation is as follows:

Perception (Experience or Learning): Experience or learning in any form is the starting point of the process of concept formation.

Our perceptions or imaginary experiences, formal or informal learning, provide opportunities for getting mental images of things, persons and events.

Abstraction: The mind Analyses these images and synthesizes what is common to all, neglecting what is merely particular. This process of observing similarities and commonness is named as abstraction.

Generalization: After making such observations in the form of abstraction for a number of times, the child is able to generalize or form a general idea about the common properties of some objects or events. On account of this generalization the child will develop concept of this things and events.

E.g.: Figure of speech – simile and metaphor

Simile- Comparison using words as & like.

Metaphor- Comparison without using as and like.

Therefore any sentences with comparison using words as and like is a simile.

For example, the child perceives a black cow at the first time and is told that it is a cow; he tries to form an idea about it. In the beginning the idea is very particular in nature. Later on, when he perceives a white or red cow he does not at once, call it a cow. He again makes an enquiry and comes to that these are cows. He tries to compare the particular mental image the idea of the previously perceived cow with the images he is having, at present, by perceiving white and red cows. In this way he compares and contrasts the similarities or dissimilarities of his mental images related to all perceived cows. In spite of the differences in colour, appearance etc., they are found to possess so many common properties or characteristics.

LEVELS OF CONCEPT FORMATION

The four levels of concept formation are:

1. *Concrete Level:* At this level the child can discriminate one concept from the other e.g. a small child can identify his mother from others.
2. *Identity Level:* At this level, discrimination is clubbed with generalization e.g. all females become mothers for the child.
3. *Classificatory Level:* The child can identify that this particular lady is my mother e.g. a lady with particular attribute is my mother and rest are not my mothers
4. *Formal Level:* At this level child can compare one concept with from the other e.g. the child knows this is my mother and his friend who is also a child has different mother.

PIAGET'S COGNITIVE DEVELOPMENT

Jean Piaget (1896-1980) was one of the 20th century's most influential researchers in the area of developmental psychology. He was a child prodigy who published his first article at the age of 11. He originally trained in the areas of biology and philosophy and considered himself a "*genetic epistemologist.*"

He was mainly interested in the biological influences on "*how we come to know*". He believed that what distinguishes human beings from other animals is our ability to do "abstract symbolic reasoning."

While working in Binet's test lab in Paris, Piaget became interested in how children think. He noticed that young children's answers were qualitatively than older children. This suggested to him that the younger children were not less knowledgeable but, instead, answered the questions differently than their older peers because they thought differently. This implies that human development is *qualitative* (changes in kind) rather than *quantitative* (changes in amount).

What is Cognition?

- How people think and understand.
- "the act or process of knowing in the broadest sense; specifically, an intellectual process by which knowledge is gained from perception or ideas" (Webster's Dictionary)

What is Cognitive Development?

- The acquisition of the ability to think, reason, and problem solve.
- It is the process by which people's thinking changes across the life span.
- Piaget studied cognitive development by observing children in particular, to examine how their thought processes change with age.
- He pioneered a way of thinking about how children grow psychologically.
- It is the growing apprehension and adaptation to the physical and social environment.

COGNITIVE STRUCTURE

As a biologist, Piaget was interested in how an organism adapts to its

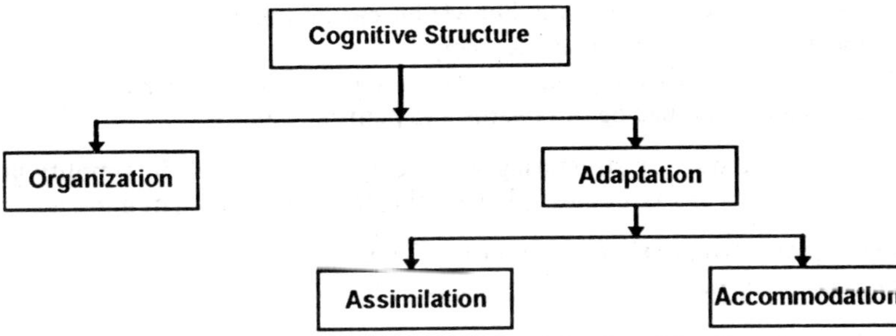

Figure 27.1: Pictorial Representation of the Cognitive Structure

environment (Piaget described this ability as intelligence.). The main elements related to cognitive structure are:

Schema: To know an object one must act upon it either physically or mentally.

Organization: The way cognitive acts are grouped and arranged to form sequences, mental "folders" or *schemata.*

Assimilation: The process of using or transforming the environment so that it can be placed in preexisting cognitive structures. For Example: an infant uses a sucking schema that was developed by sucking on a small bottle when attempting to suck on a larger bottle.

Accommodation: The process of changing cognitive structures in order to accept something from the environment. For Example: the infant modifies a sucking schema developed by sucking on a pacifier to one that would be successful for sucking on a bottle.

Equilibration: This adaptation is driven by a biological drive to obtain balance between schemes and the environment.

BRUNER'S CONSTRUCTIVIST THEORY

A major theme in the theoretical framework of Bruner is that learning is an active process in which learners construct new ideas or concepts based upon their current/past knowledge. The learner selects and transforms information, constructs hypotheses, and makes decisions, relying on a cognitive structure to do so. Cognitive structure (i.e., schema, mental models) provides meaning and organization to experiences and allows the individual to "go beyond the information given".

As far as instruction is concerned, the instructor should try and encourage students to discover principles by themselves. The instructor and student should engage in an active dialog (i.e., Socratic learning). The task of the instructor is to translate information to be learned into a format appropriate to the learner's current state of understanding. Curriculum should be organized in a spiral manner so that the student continually builds upon what they have already learned.

Bruner (1966) states that a theory of instruction should address four major aspects:

- Predisposition towards learning,

- The ways in which a body of knowledge can be structured so that it can be most readily grasped by the learner,
- The most effective sequences in which to present material, and
- The nature and pacing of rewards and punishments.

Good methods for structuring knowledge should result in simplifying, generating new propositions, and increasing the manipulation of information.

Principles of Bruner's Constructivist Theory

The three principles of Bruner's Constructivist Theory are:

- Instruction must be concerned with the experiences and contexts that make the student willing and able to learn (readiness).
- Instruction must be structured so that it can be easily grasped by the student (spiral organization).
- Instruction should be designed to facilitate extrapolation and or fill in the gaps (going beyond the information given).

BRUNER'S MODEL OF CONCEPT LEARNING

J.S. Bruner has suggested a model on concept attainment and structure in teaching. He proposes that economy in thinking and responding requires that we categorize phenomena according to their common attributes. An attribute is a property or characteristic of an object, which differentiates it from the other. Colour, texture, form, size, number of parts, position and sounds are examples of attributes. We categorize objects having common characteristics into one group. For example, we categorize certain animals having four legs, a tail, and a barking voice as dogs. Similarly, we cal also categorize more abstract concepts such as enemy or friend, artisan or professional etc. For teaching about a concept, the teacher must identify such attributes of that concept, which differentiate it from others. For example, dog and cat have four legs and a tail, but cat's voice is different from a dog's.

Bruner studied the strategies people use in acquiring concepts. For this, he used a set of cards, some cards having borders, others without. All the cards have centre figures varying in shape (square, circle or cross), in colour (red, green or black), and in number (single, double or triple). Each card thus combines four attributes: figure shape, figure number, figure colour and presence or absence of borders. Each attribute has three values (variations as listed above). The subject is told that the experimenter has a concept in mind, say red circles, and the subject was to identify that concept. The subject is asked to select a card and then told by the experimenter whether or not the card was an instance of the concept. With these data in mind, the subject would select another card to determine further the attributes of the concepts and would continue doing so till he finds the answer i.e. the card with red circles.

Bruner identified four strategies in concept attainment:

1. Simultaneous Scanning

In this type of strategy, the subject uses each positive instance (each correctly identified card), to deduce which combinations of attribute values are no longer valid. The subject must keep in mind simultaneously all the rejected combinations in order to narrow down the range of subsequent alternatives. This technique is not very efficient since it places a great deal of strain on the subject's memory.

2. Successive Scanning

In this technique, the subject makes an overall estimate of each correct characteristic of the concept and the test, each one by one. This is called successive scanning since the subject tests individual hypothesis about the correct characteristic one at a time in succession. The technique is also inefficient as the subject may choose redundant cards, which give no new information.

3. Conservative Focusing

In this technique, each attribute is tested by selecting a card that is different from a focus card in only one attribute. If the new card is still a positive instance, then the subject knows that the varied attribute is not part of the concept. If, however, the changed attribute yields a negative instance, then the attribute is part of the concept. For example, the concept to be attained is "red circles." Assume that the subject encounters a positive card with three red circles and two borders. This card becomes the focus card and each variable is examined by selecting additional cards. The selection sequence is given below. A plus sign in the parentheses means the card is a positive instance of the concept, a minus sign in parentheses that the card is a negative instance.

Four cards:

> 3 red circles, 2 borders (+) 2 red circles, 2 borders + first decision: eliminate "three figures" as a relevant variable.
> 3 green circles, 2 borders (-) second decision: retain red as relevant attribute value.
> 3 red crosses, 2 borders (-) third decision: retain circle as relevant attribute value.
> 3red circles one border (+) fourth decision: eliminate "two borders" as relevant attribute value.

Conclusion: The concept is "red circle."

This technique is more efficient since the subject uses a correct instance as a point of reference and selects additional cards to test each attribute value individually.

4. Focus Gambling

In this strategy, the subject focuses on a correct card, but varies more than one attribute at a time. This technique can give early result if cards chosen yield a positive instance. If, however, the subject encounters a negative instance, he cannot tell which attribute was essential. In that case he has to revert to simultaneous scanning technique to test hypotheses. This strategy is called gambling since the subject takes a chance varying two attributes at a time.

IMPLICATIONS OF BRUNER'S MODEL OF CONCEPT LEARNING

Bruner's strategies of concepts learning can be applied in science teaching. The use of discovery and enquiry techniques in teaching science provides the pupils with experiences quite similar to the card tasks used by Bruner. For example, if we want the pupils to invent their own system of classification of plants and animals, they can do it by identifying the attribute and putting the plants or animals with common attributes in one group.

Chapter-28
Decision Making

Decision-making is an integral part of modern management. Essentially, Rational or sound decision making is taken as primary function of management. Every manager takes hundreds and hundreds of decisions subconsciously or consciously making it as the key component in the role of a manager. Decisions play important roles as they determine both organizational and managerial activities. A decision can be defined as a course of action purposely chosen from a set of alternatives to achieve organizational or managerial objectives or goals. Decision making process is continuous and indispensable component of managing any organization or business activities. Decisions are made to sustain the activities of all business activities and organizational functioning.

MEANING OF DECISION MAKING

The English word ***'Decision'*** originated from the Latin word '*decisio*' which means "*to cut from.*"

'To decide' means "*to come to a conclusion*" or "*to pass a resolution.*" **Decision making** means to select a course of action from two or more alternatives. It is done to achieve a specific objective or to solve a specific problem. The schematic diagram of decision making process is given in Figure 28.1:

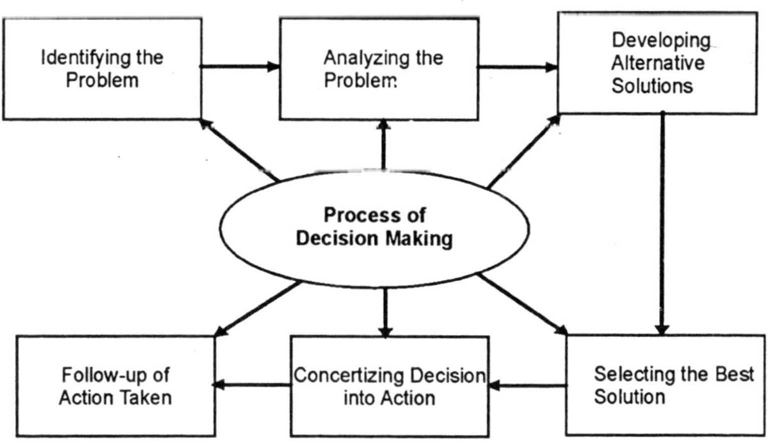

Figure 28.1: Decision Making Process

DEFINITIONS OF DECISION MAKING

1. According to the *Oxford Advanced Learner's Dictionary* the term decision

making means – *'the process of deciding about something important, especially in a group of people or in an organization."*

2. **Trewatha** and **Newport** defines decision making process as follows: *"Decision-making involves the selection of a course of action from among two or more possible alternatives in order to arrive at a solution for a given problem".*
3. According to **James Stoner**, *"Decision making is the process of identifying and selecting a course of action to solve a specific problem."*

As evidenced by the definitions above, decision making process is a consultative affair done by a comity of professionals to drive better functioning of any organization. Thereby, it is a continuous and dynamic activity that pervades all other activities pertaining to the organization. Since it is an ongoing activity, decision making process plays vital importance in the functioning of an organization. Since intellectual minds are involved in the process of decision making, it requires solid scientific knowledge coupled with skills and experience in addition to mental maturity.

Steps Involved in Decision Making Process

Decision-making involves a number of steps which need to be taken in a logical manner. This is treated as a rational or scientific 'decision-making process' which is lengthy and time consuming. Such lengthy process needs to be followed in order to take rational/scientific/result oriented decisions. Decision-making process prescribes some rules and guidelines as to how a decision should be taken/made. This involves many steps logically arranged. The scientific method of decision-making involves the following six steps given in Figure 28.2.

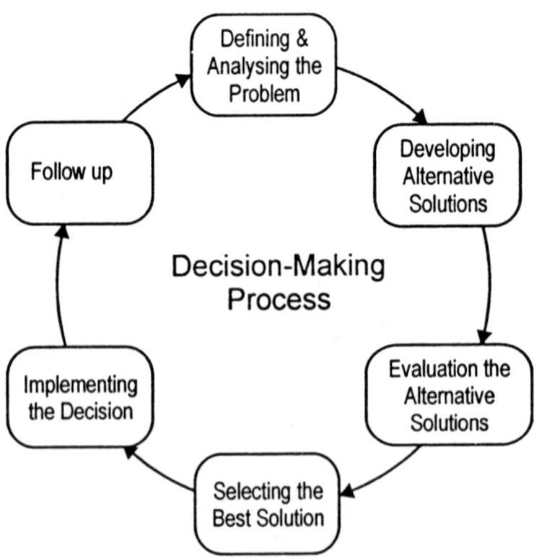

Figure 28.2: Steps Involved in Decision Making Process

1. Defining and Analyzing the Real Problem: The principal/manager should first find out what is the real problem. The problem may be due to bad relations between principal/management and teacher/employees, poor teaching quality, decrease in sales, increase in cost, etc. After finding out the true problem principal/manager must analyze it carefully. He should find out the cause and effect of the problem.

2. Developing Alternative Solutions: After defining and analyzing the real problem, the principal/manager should develop (make) alternative (different) solutions for solving the problem. Only realistic solutions should be considered. Group participation and computers should be used for developing alternative solutions.

3. Evaluating the Alternative Solutions: The principal/manager should carefully evaluate the merits and demerits of each alternative solution. He should compare the cost of each solution. He should compare the risks involved. He should also compare the feasibility of each solution. He should find out which solution will be accepted by the teachers/employees.

4. Selecting the Best Solution: After evaluating all the solutions, the manager/principal should select the best solution. He should select a solution which is less costly and less risky. He should select a solution which is most feasible and which is accepted by the employees/teachers. In short, the principal/manager should select a solution which has the most merits and least demerits. The best solution is called the *"Decision"*.

5. Implementing the Decision: After making the decision, the principal or manager should implement it. That is, he should put the decision into action. He should communicate the decision to the teachers or employees. He should persuade the employees to accept the decision. This can be done by involving them in the decision making process. Then the manager or principal should provide the teachers or employees with all the resources, which are required for implementing the decision. He should also motivate them to implement the decision.

6. Follow Up: After implementing the decision, the administrator/principal/manager must do follow up. That is, he must get the feedback about the decision. He should find out whether the decision was effective or not. This is done by comparing the decision with the action, finding out the deviations (differences) and taking essential steps to remove these deviations. So, follow-up is just like the control function. It helps to improve the quality of future decisions.

MODERN TECHNIQUES FOR MAKING PROGRAMMED DECISIONS

A programmed decision is used to solve routine, repetitive but complex problems. These techniques are also called as *'Quantitative Techniques'*. The teachers, principals and managers working at lower-level of management make these decisions. Various **approaches** or techniques for making programmed decisions are given in Figure 28.3.

Linear Programming: Linear Programming is a quantitative technique. It is used to decide how to distribute the limited resources for achieving the objectives. Here, linear, means the relationship between variables, and programming means taking decisions systematically. Linear programming is used when two or more activities are competing for limited resources.

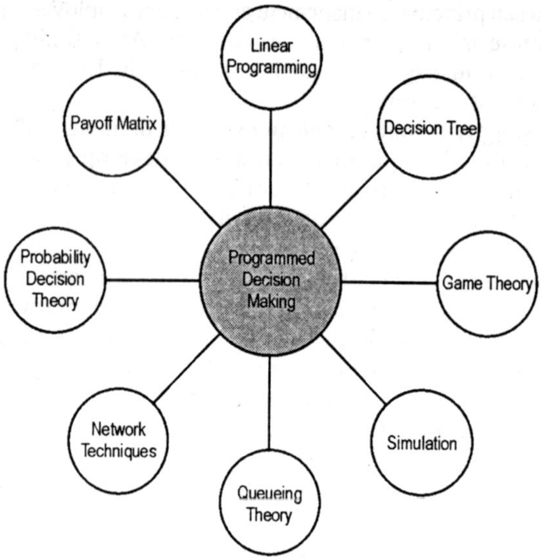

Figure 28.3: Programmed Decision Making Techniques

Decision Tree: A decision tree is a diagram which shows all the possible alternatives of a decision. All this information can be seen at one glance. It is also easy to understand. A decision tree is like a horizontal tree. The base of the tree is called the ***'Decision Point'***. From this point, the different alternatives and sub-alternatives are shown as branches and sub-branches. The manager and teacher must study all the alternatives very carefully and select the best alternative.

Game Theory: A game is a situation involving at least two people. Each person's decision is based on what he expects the other to do. Game theory is used for deciding about competitive pricing. For e.g. A company may increase the price of its product when it feels that the competitor may also increase the price. For example Pepsi will increase its price if it feels that Coca Cola will also increase its price. Here, both decisions- makers adapt to each other's decisions.

Simulation: Simulation technique is used to decide about complex problems. The effect of the decision is observed in a simulated situation and not in a real situation. For e.g. a company can find out the effectiveness of its new advertisement by first showing it to a few people before telecasting it on TV.

Queuing Theory: This technique is used to find solutions to the waiting list problems in case of airline reservations, railway reservations, college admissions, etc. Queuing theory helps to find out the optimum number of service facilities required and the cost of these services. For e.g. a transport company may introduce more vehicles to carry the passengers in the waiting list. This will prevent the passengers from going to the competitor's company.

Network Techniques: Managers use network techniques like PERT (Programme Evaluation Review Technique) and CPM (Critical Path Method) for complex projects, where many activities have to be completed. With the help of these techniques, complex projects can be completed as per the schedule. Network techniques save time and cost.

Probability Decision Theory: Probability decision theory is based on the assumption that the future is uncertain. There is a chance that a certain event may or may not take place. Based on available data and subjective judgment of the manager, various probabilities are assigned (given) to alternative courses of action (decision). The likely/possible outcomes of different alternatives are evaluated, and the most likely alternative is selected.

Payoff Matrix: Payoff matrix is a statistical technique, which helps managers to choose the best alternative. A payoff is the return or reward for selecting the best alternative. The best alternative can be a combination of many alternatives or a single alternative. For e.g. a manager may decide to increase sales and profit by increasing advertising, improving quality of the product, reducing the price, etc. Each alternative or a combination of alternatives may provide an expected reward.

IMPORTANCE OF DECISION MAKING

The importance of decision making is as under:

Better Utilization of Resources: Decision making helps to utilize the available resources for achieving the objectives of the organization. The available resources are the 6 Ms, i.e. Men, Money, Materials, Machines, Methods and Markets. The principal or manager has to make correct decisions for all the 6 Ms. This will result in better utilization of these resources.

Facing Problems and Challenges: Decision making helps the organization to face and tackle new problems and challenges. Quick and correct decisions help to solve problems and to accept new challenges.

Business Growth: Quick and correct decision making results in better utilization of the resources. It helps the organization to face new problems and challenges. It also helps to achieve its objectives. All this results in quick institutional growth. However, wrong, slow or no decisions can result in losses and industrial sickness.

Achieving Objectives: Rational decisions help the organization to achieve all its objectives quickly. This is because rational decisions are made after analyzing and evaluating all the alternatives.

Increases Efficiency: Rational decisions help to increase efficiency. Efficiency is the relation between returns and cost. If the returns are high and the cost is low, then there is efficiency and vice versa. Rational decisions result in higher returns at low cost.

Facilitate Innovation: Rational decisions facilitate innovation. This is because it helps to develop new ideas, new products, new process, etc. This results in innovation. Innovation gives a competitive advantage to the organization.

Motivates Employees: Rational decision results in motivation for the employees. This is because the employees are motivated to implement rational decisions. When the rational decisions are implemented the organization makes high profits. Therefore, it can give financial and non-financial benefits to the employees.

LIMITATIONS OF DECISION MAKING

Time Consuming: A lot of precious time is consumed for decision making. Individual decisions take a lot of time because the principal or manager has to study the merits and demerits of all the alternatives. He also has to take advice from many people before making a decision. All this consumes a lot of time. Group decisions are also time consuming. This is because it involves many meetings and each member has to give his opinion. This results in delayed decisions or no decisions.

Compromised Decisions: In group decisions, there is a difference of opinion. This results in a compromised decision. A compromised decision is made to please all the members. It may not be a correct and bold decision. The quality of this decision is inferior. So, it will not give good results on implementation.

Subjective Decisions: Individual decisions are not objective. They are subjective. This is because the decisions depend on the knowledge, education, experience, perception, beliefs, moral, attitude, etc., of the manager. Subjective decisions are not good decisions.

Biased Decisions: Sometimes decisions are biased. That is, the principal or manager makes decisions, which only benefit himself and his group. These decisions have a bad effect on the teachers, workers, consumer or the society.

Limited Analysis: Before making a decision, the principal, manager must analyze all the alternatives. He must study the merit and demerits of each alternative. Then only he must select the best alternative. However, most managers and principals do not do this because they do not get an accurate date, and they have limited time. Inexperienced researchers and wrong sampling also result in a limited analysis. This limited analysis results in bad decisions.

Uncontrollable Environmental Factors: Environmental factors include political, social, technological and other factors. These factors are dynamic in nature and keep on changing every day. The administrator or manager has no control over environmental factors. If these factors change in the wrong direction, his decisions will also divert and go wrong.

Uncertain Future: Decisions are made for the future. However, the future is very uncertain. Therefore, it is very difficult to take decisions for the future.

Responsibility is Diluted: In an individual decision, only one principal or manager is responsible for the decision. However, in a group decision, all managers are responsible for the decision. That is, everybody's responsibility is nobody's responsibility. So, the responsibility is diluted.

Chapter-29
Intelligence

MEANING OF INTELLIGENCE

Human being is considered to be the most intelligent animal in this world. He is capable of controlling all other beings and many other things in this world. Intelligence has a very important role in day- to-day activities of the individual. The word intelligence has been derived from a Latin verb 'intellegere' means to understand.

DEFINITIONS OF INTELLIGENCE

What is intelligence? There are many answers for this question. The concept of intelligence has been understood by psychologists in different ways. Therefore, there are a number of definitions. The following are some of the important definitions of intelligence:

1. According to Dr. Jean Piaget, *"Intelligence is what you use when you do not know what to do"*.
2. Alfred Binet, *"Intelligence is something which sensory acuity tests or reaction time experiments measure."*
3. Spencer, *"Intelligence is the capacity of the organism to adjust itself to an increasingly complex environment."*
4. Terman, *"Intelligence is the ability to carry on abstract thinking."*
5. Munn, *"It is the capacity for flexible adjustment."*
6. Goddard, *"Intelligence is the degree of availability of one's experiences for the solution of immediate problems and the anticipation of the future ones."*
7. Spearman, *"Intelligence is the capacity for constructive thinking, which involves a discovery of appropriate qualities and relations of the ideas, that are before us and bringing in of other relevant ideas."*
8. According to Stern (1914), *"Intelligence is a general capacity of an individual consciously to adjust his thinking to new requirements. It is the general mental adaptability to new problems and conditions of life."*
9. According to Thorndike (1914), Intelligence may be defined as *"the power of good responses from the point of view of truth or fact"*.
10. Terman (1921), *"An individual is intelligent in the proportion that he is able to carry on abstract thinking."*
11. Wagon (1937), *"Intelligence is the capacity to learn and adjust to relatively new and changing conditions."*
12. Woodworth and Marquis (1948), *"Intelligence means intellect put to use. It is the use of intellectual abilities for handling a situation or accomplishing any task."*

13. Jean Piaget (1952), *"Intelligence is the ability to adapt to one's surroundings."*
14. Ebinghous, *"Intelligence is the capacity to integrate the things."*
15. Ross, *"Intelligence means conscious adaptation to new situation."*
16. Wells, *"Intelligence is the property of recombining our behaviour pattern so as to act better in a novel situation."*
17. Burt, *"Intelligence is the capacity of flexible adjustment."*
18. Colvin, *"Intelligence is the ability to adjust environment."*
19. Spearman, *"Intelligence is the analytic and synthetic ability of mind."*
20. Binet, *"Intelligence is a capacity to think well, to judge well and to be self-critical."*
21. Burt, *"Intelligence is ability to judge well, to comprehend well and to reason well."*
22. Peterson, *"Intelligence is a mechanical means for adjustment and control."*
23. Pinter, *"Intelligence is the capacity of the individual to adapt himself adequately to relatively new situations of life."*
24. Galton, *"Intelligence is the power of recognition and hearing."*
25. Stout, *"Intelligence is the power of attention."*
26. Ausubel and Robinson, *"Intelligence refers to a general level of cognitive functioning as reflective in the ability to understand ideas and to utilize abstract symbols in the solution of intellectual problems."*
27. Heim, *"Intelligent activity consists of grasping the essentials in given situation and responding appropriately to them."*
28. Hollingworth, *"An intelligent person learns how to do and how to get what is wanted."*
29. Rex, *"Intelligence is the ability to discover relevant qualities and relation of the objects and ideas that are before us and provide other ideas."*
30. Stoddard (1943) defined intelligence as *"the ability to undertake activities that are difficult, complex and abstract and which are adaptive to a goal and are done quickly and which have social value and which lead·to the creation of something new and different."*

All these definitions define intelligence in their own way, but they are incomplete, because they give incomplete picture. In view of this problem, many psychologists have accepted a definition by Wechsler. David Wechsler (1944) who devised the intelligence tests for children as well as adults tried to provide a somewhat comprehensive definition: *"Intelligence is the aggregate or global capacity of an individual to think rationally, to act purposefully and to deal effectively with his environment"*.

This definition includes three important processes, viz., to act purposefully means, to act in a determined way without any ambiguity, to think appropriately in a rational way without any prejudices and to deal effectively with the environment or to adjust in a proper way with the environment.

NATURE OF INTELLIGENCE

The nature of intelligence can be best understood by the following points:

- Intelligence is the form of Cognitive ability
- It is the ability to learn
- It is the ability to solve problems
- Ability to deal with abstraction
- Ability to see relevant relationships with object or ideas
- Ability to apply acquired knowledge to new situation
- It as a sort of Mental energy
- Ability to handle environment
- Ability to adapt new situation
- It is the systematic ability of Mind
- Ability to perceive relationships
- Growth of Intelligence is orderly and Cumulative
- Intelligence consist more than one ability
- Intelligence is related to learning
- It is the inborn personal quality
- It distributed as Normal probability curve
- It enhance through Experience
- It is the composite of many abilities

CHARACTERISTICS OF INTELLIGENCE

The main features of Intelligence are the following:

- Intelligence is an innate natural endowment of the child.
- It helps the child in maximum learning in minimum period of time.
- The child is able to foresee the future and plan accordingly.
- The child is able to take advantage of his previous experiences.
- The child faces the future with compliance.
- He develops a sense of discrimination between right or wrong.
- The developmental period of intelligence is from birth to adolescence.
- There is a minor difference in the development of intelligence between boys and girls.
- There are individual differences with regard to the intelligence between boys and girls.
- Intelligence is mostly determined by heredity but a suitable environment necessary to improve it.

THEORIES OF INTELLIGENCE

Psychologists have attempted to understand the structure of intelligence for which they have formulated intelligence theories.

Types of Theories of Intelligence

Intelligence theories can be grouped under two categories, namely, factor theories and cognitive theories of intelligence.

FACTOR THEORIES OF INTELLIGENCE

Factor theories of intelligence attempt to provide a structure of intelligence in terms of its constituents or factors. These theories of intelligence employ factor analysis techniques for identification of factors or common abilities which constitute one's intelligence. These theories exhibit wide variations in terms of the number of factor that they consider important. The range of such factors goes from 1 (Monarchic Theory) to 150 (Guilford's Intellect Model). The main factor theories of intelligence are given below:

Spearman's Two-Factor Theory or Eclectic Theory of Intelligence

The English psychologist, Charles Spearman (1863-1945), in 1904 proposed his theory of intelligence called two-factor theory. The theory was expounded in his book *"The Abilities of Man"*. This book was published in 1927. The essence of his theory in his own words was, *"That all branches of intellectual activity have in common on fundamental- function (or group of functions), whereas remaining or specific elements of the activity seem in every case to be wholly different from that in all the others."* According to him, intellectual abilities are comprised of two factors, namely; the general ability known as G-factor and specific Abilities known as S-factor. The general factor is symbolized by 'g' and the specific factor is symbolized by's'. The performance by the individual is determined by the G-factor and the S-factors. The total intelligence of the individual is the sum total of the G-factor and the S-factors. The performance of a particular task depends on the 'G' factor or general ability and the particular 'S' factor or specific ability.

Here, the 'g' factor is always the same for the same individual and the's' factor varies from the subject to subject according to the nature. But there are differences in general abilities within the different individuals as well as their special abilities. Thus, different individuals differ both in the 'g' as well as's' factors. Different performance requires different amount of 'g' and's'. For instance, an individual who possesses 'g' factor shows better performance in Mathematics and Classics whereas in music and drawing's' factor predominates.

Characteristics of 'G' Factor

The main characteristics of 'G' factor are as follows:

- It is universal inborn ability.
- It is general mental energy.
- It is constant.
- The amount of 'g' differs from individual to individual.
- It is used in every activity of life.
- Greater the 'g' in an individual, greater is his success in life.

Characteristics of 'S' Factor

The main characteristics of 'S' factor are as follows:

- It is learned and acquired in the environment.
- It varies from activity to activity in the same individual.
- Individuals differ in the amount of 'S' ability.

'G' factor represents Native Intelligence, thus when we respond to any situation or perform an intellectual task, our general mental ability or 'G' factor is mainly responsible for it and our specific ability in that particular task is responsible for the rest. There are a large number of specific abilities such as ability to draw inferences, ability to complete sentences, ability to code message etc.

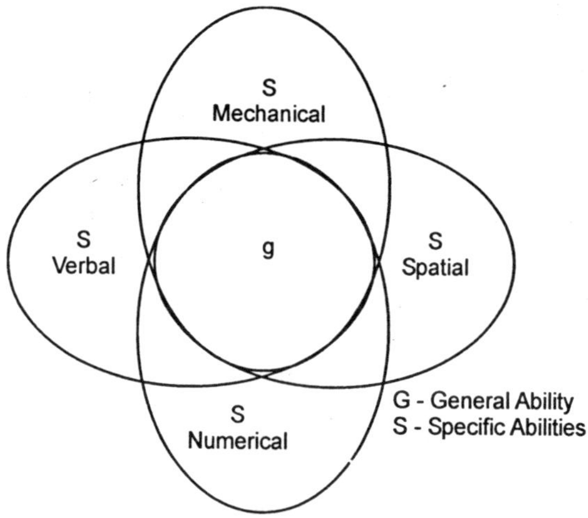

Figure 29.1: Spearman's Two-Factor Theory or Eclectic Theory

Different individuals differed both in their 'G' as well as 'S' factors. For e.g. an individual's performance in literature is partly due to his general intelligence and partly due some specific aptitude for his language, i.e. G+S1. In mathematics his performance may be the result of G+S2. In drawing, it may be due to G+S3 and in social sciences; it may be due to G+S4 and so on. Thus the factor 'G' is present in all specific activities.

Educational Implications and Relevance of Spearman's Two –Factor Theory

The educational implications and relevance of Spearman's Two –Factor Theory is as follows:

- The theory gives a better insight to the teacher about the nature of intelligence.
- The general ability differs from individual to individual.
- The specific abilities also differ from individual to individual.
- 'S' factor varies in degrees. Therefore, it can be modified by learning or habitual training
- A child requires different amounts of 'G' and 'S' factors for achieving success in different Subjects.
- We require a high quality of 'G' factor for our success in life.
- Both 'G' and 'S' have a high correlation.
- This theory could be used to guide, construction of a set of ability test

Thus, we see that spearman did not believe in the concept that mental power as independent of one another. According to him they are unitary.

Spearman's Three Factor Theory of Intelligence

Realizing his error, Spearman added one more factor to his two factor theory, e.g. 'Group Factor". Group factor is less general, wide spread and homogeneous than 'g' and more general, wide spread and homogeneous than's' factor. Thus, the modified theory has got three factors (1) 'g' factor, (2)'s' factor, and (3) group factor.

This theory was criticized by Thorndike. Thorndike considered that there is over simplification of the facts in believing that there is a general factor which is homogeneous. His view was that the intellectual tasks are performed by a complex nervous system which operates in many different total patterns. Those patterns are too complex and varied to be described as mere mixtures of a 'g' and many 's' factors or a 'g' and some group factors and a few 's' factors.

Thorndike's Multiple or Multi-Factor or Atomistic or Anarchic Theory of Intelligence

Prof. Thorndike was the chief exponent of Anarchic theory. After discarding/ criticizing Spearmen's two factor theory of intelligence, E.L. Thorndike, the famous psychologist propounded this multi-factor theory off intelligence. This theory holds that intelligence is the means of undermined independent rudimentary elements or intelligence is the combination of numerous separate elements or the factors of intelligence are independent to each other. These are numerical reasoning, vocabulary, classification and sentence completion etc. This theory believes that every task needs different abilities. Sometimes they may have one or sometimes they may possess 2 or 3 abilities also. Thorndike believes that if a person gets 60 marks in Mathematics and English, it means there may be 2 or 3 factors are present and correlating to each other. He concluded that in every task a group of abilities are manifested and out of which few of them correlates because of their resemblances. Thus, these common abilities may belong to certain faculty and clear that the intelligence is composed of highly particularized and independent faculties.

E.L. Thorndike's multi- factor theory stands in sharp contradiction of Spearman's two-factor theory. According to this theory, intelligence is a name conveniently given to infinite number of specific abilities combined together. It can be stated that intelligence is the sum total of all the specific capacities with regard to every separate act. It also means that E.L. Thorndike denies the existence of a general factor. Intelligence is a host of highly independent factors.

According to this theory, mind is highly particularized and composed of independent faculties. This theory believes that a man may be expert in doing one kind of work; he may not be expert with the same ability to do another kind of work. For example, if a boy is good in literature he may not be equally good in a subject like Chemistry.

E.L. Thorndike has classified intelligence into three categories which are as follows-

- Social Intelligence of ability to understand and deal with persons.
- Concrete Intelligence referring to dealing with things, as in skilled trades and specific appliances.
- Abstract Intelligence or ability to understand and deal with verbal and mathematical symbols

Concrete Intelligence

It is the ability to understand and deal with things as in skilled trades or scientific appliances this is also known as mechanical or motor intelligence. In education concrete intelligence is required in learning dances and participating in games and sports.

Concrete intelligence is also known as mechanical intelligence. It is the intelligence that has the relation with concrete materials. It is the ability of an individual to comprehend actual situations and to react to them adequately. The concrete intelligence is evident from various activities in our daily life. This kind of intelligence is measured by performance tests and picture tests in which an individual is asked to manipulate concrete materials.

Abstract Intelligence

It is the ability to understand words, numbers and letters and to use them effectively abstract intelligence is required in ordinary academic subjects in schools such as reading, writing a solving academic problems. The highest level of abstract intelligence is manifested in the thoughts of poets, philosophers and writers.

Abstract intelligence indicates the ability to respond to words, numbers, formulas, diagram and letters etc. This formula is conspicuously absent in animals. An abstractly intelligent person is able to discover relations among symbols and to solve the various problems with the help of such aids (symbols, formula, diagram, letter etc.)

Social Intelligence

It is the ability of an individual to deal effectively and efficiently with his social and cultural environment. Social intelligence is revealed when a person is able to establish and develop desirable social relations in conformity with his social and cultural norms.

Social intelligence means the ability of an individual to react to social situations of his or her daily life. Social intelligence is possessed by those people who are able to handle people well and also have the ability to make friends easily and understand human relations. Adequate adjustment in social situations is the index of social intelligence.

Attributes of Intelligence According to Thorndike

Thorndike distinguished 4 attributes of intelligence. They are:

Level: This refers to the difficulty of a task that can be solved. If we think of all test items arranged in a sequential order of increasing difficulty, then the height that we can ascend on this ladder of difficulty determines our level of intelligence.

Range: This refers to the number of tasks at any given degree of difficulty that we can solve. Theoretically an individual possessing a given level of intelligence should be able to solve the whole range of task at that level. Range is determined not only by Level but also by the Breadth of experience and by opportunity to learn. In intelligence tests range is represented by items of equal difficulty.

Area: It refers to the total number of situations at each level to which the individual is able to respond. Area is the summation of all the ranges at each level of intelligence processed by an individual.

Speed: This is the rapidity with which an individual can respond to items. Speed and altitude are positively related. Speed is much closely bound up with altitude than are the other attributes. We should not therefore emphasis speed too much in our intelligence test.

In fact, although Thorndike has divided intelligence into three categories, yet in real sense, all types are more or less inter-related. Some people may have more abstract intelligence than the mechanical and social intelligence, or some may have more mechanical intelligence than the abstract and social intelligence.

Thurston's Group Factor Theory of Intelligence

L.L. Thurstone proposed the multiple-factor theory or group factor theory back in 1938. According to him 'Intelligence is a cluster of abilities'. These mental operations then constitute a group. A second group of mental operations has its own unifying Primary factor; a third group has a third Primary factor and so on. Each of them has its own primary factor. Each of these primary factors is said to be relatively independent of others. He pointed out that there were Seven Primary Mental Abilities and later on added two more. They are:

Verbal Comprehension Factor: This factor involves a person's ability to understand verbal material. It is measured by tests such as vocabulary and reading comprehension.

Verbal Fluency Factor: This ability is involved in rapidly producing words, sentences, and other verbal material. It is measured by tests such as one that requires the examinee to produce as many words as possible beginning with a particular letter in a short amount of time.

Numerical Factor: This ability is involved in rapid arithmetic computation and in solving simple arithmetic word problems.

Perceptual Speed Factor: This ability is involved in proofreading and in rapid recognition of letters and numbers. It is measured by tests such as those requiring the crossing out of As in a long string of letters or in tests requiring recognition of which of several pictures at the right is identical to the picture at the left.

Inductive Reasoning Factor: This ability requires generalization—reasoning from the specific to the general. It is measured by tests, such as letter series, number series, and word classifications, in which the examinee must indicate which of several words does not belong with the others.

Spatial Visualization Factor: This ability is involved in visualizing shapes, rotations of objects, and how pieces of a puzzle fit together. An example of a test would be the presentation of a geometric form followed by several other geometric forms. Each of the forms that follow the first is either the same rotated by some rigid transformation or the mirror image of the first form in rotation. The examinee has to indicate which of the forms at the right is a rotated version of the form at the left, rather than a mirror image.

Memory Factor: It means the ability to recall and associate previously learned items effectively or memorize quickly.

Later on other factors were added on like *Deductive Reasoning* (P) – Ability to use the generalized results correctly and *Problem Solving Ability Factor* (PS) -Ability to solve problem independently.

Educational Significance and Implications of Thurston's Group Factor Theory

The educational implications of Thurston's Group Factor Theory of intelligence are as follows:

- Thurston contributed greatly to the measurement of attitudes. In psychology, the 'Thurston scale' developed in 1928 was the first formal techniques for measuring of attitudes.
- Thurston's theory of intelligence was a major influence on later theories of multiple intelligences, such as those of Guilford, Gardner, and Sternberg.
- Thurston has been noted for developing a comparative judgment scaling technique. The rank scale can be used to rank all possible feelings related to an issue and to categorize people expressing an opinion based on the rank of that opinion. It is used today mainly in basic research.
- Thurston held that if the individual wants to perform any particular activity, one or more of these factors or abilities are involved. Some of them are more important than others.

Guildford's Structure of Intelligence (SI) Model or Three Dimensional Theory of Intelligence

J.P. Guilford developed a model of intelligence (1966) using factor analysis. He outlines topography of the structure of intellect, providing an integrated rationale for describing the many dimension of intellectual performance. He suggests that there are three basic parameters along which any intellectual activity takes place. These are:

- Operations – the act of thinking
- Contents – the terms in which we think, and
- Products – the ideas we come up with.

Guilford identified 5 operations, 5 contents and 6 products. Thus the maximum number of factors in terms of the different possible combinations of these dimensions will be 5×5×6 = 150 (see Figure 29.2).

Operations

It consists of five major groups of intellectual abilities.

Cognition: It refers to discovery, rediscovery or recognition.

Memory: Simply remembering what was once known.

Convergent Thinking: This type of thinking, by reasoning, results in useful solution to problems.

Divergent Thinking: This is thinking in different directions, seeking and searching some variety and novelty.

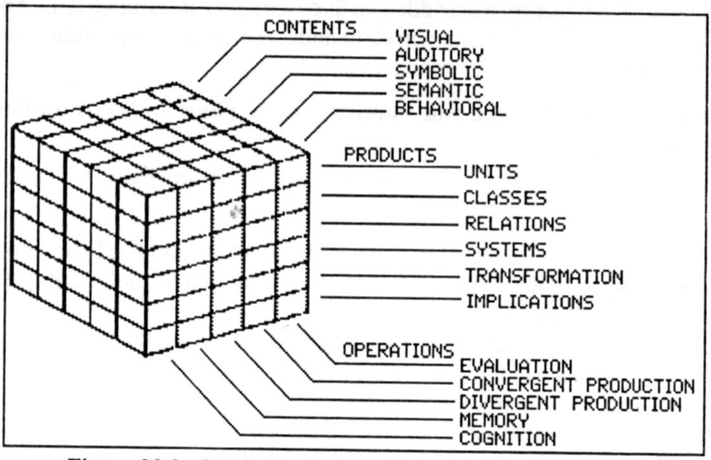

Figure 29.2: Guilford's Model of Structure of Intelligence

Evaluation: It is reaching decisions or making judgments about information.

Content

A Second way of classifying the intellectual factor is according to the kind of material or content involved. It involves five factors:

Visual Content: It is concrete material which is perceived through our senses, i.e. size, form, colour, etc.

Auditory Content: It consists of language, speech, sounds, music and words

Symbolic Content: It is composed of letters, digits, and other conventional signs.

Semantic Content: It is in the forms of verbal meanings or ideas which we get from others.

Behavioural Content: It means social behaviour in society.

Products

When a certain operation is applied to certain kind of content as many as six kinds of products may be involved.

Units: Understanding the meaning of words, visual, auditory and symbolic units.

Classes: It means classification of words and ideas.

Relations: It implies discovering relations of words and ideas.

Systems: The ability to structure objects in space and to structure symbolic elements and to formulate problems.

Transformation: The ability to look into the future lines of development or to suggest changes in the existing situations.

Implications: The ability to utilize present information for future ends.

Educational Implication and Relevance of SI Model

The educational implications and relevance of Guildford's Structure of Intelligence (SI Model) is as follows:

- This theory about the idea that the brain of a child is like a computer, who acquires, stores and uses information.
- It provides knowledge about the specific ability of the students to guide them in the right direction.
- SI Model is useful in finding out the reasons of the unsatisfactory performance of the students in spite of their adequate intelligence.
- This model points out that for understanding higher mental processes like thinking some drastic modifications could be needed in our curriculum or method of instruction.
- This model has explored 150 intellectual abilities and this enables us to find out whether we are paying sufficient attention to each one of them or not and if not how to improve.
- This model guides us to device enrichment programmes for the gifted children.
- It stresses that learning of specific skills should be our focus of attention.
- SI Model is very useful in constructing tests of various types for different age groups.
- This concept of Guildford will prove useful in our future research in the areas of learning, memory, problem-solving etc.
- This model discovered many abilities which were not known before.
- It is very useful for vocational training.

Guildford's theory of Intelligence seems to be the most comprehensive theory as it attempts to take into considerations all possible aspects of intellectual activity.

COGNITIVE THEORIES OF INTELLIGENCE

These theories of intelligence tried to analyze and describe intelligence in terms of certain fundamental cognitive processes. These theories are otherwise called process-oriented theories. They focus on intellectual processes; the patterns of thinking and reasoning in people, used to solve problems. These theories consider intelligence as a process which helps to deal with problems and to find out the answers. They are called cognitive theories because of their focus on fundamental cognitive processes. The important intelligence theories in this category are:

Fluid and Crystallized Intelligence Theory of Raymond Cattell and Horn

The theory of fluid and crystallized intelligence was developed by Raymond Cattell and Horn. They suggests that intelligence is composed of a number of different abilities that interact and work together to produce overall individual intelligence. Cattell's theory is based on two types of intelligences – fluid and crystallized. Fluid abilities *(Gf)* involve abstract thinking/reasoning and problem solving strategies. Crystallized abilities *(Gc)* involve prior knowledge and experiences. *Gf* and *Gc* have been referred to as the mechanics and pragmatics of cognition, respectively.

Crystallized and fluid are types of intelligence that are either lost or increased over time. Fluid and crystallized intelligence are complementary in that some learning tasks can be mastered mainly by exercising either fluid or crystallized intelligence, while some need both to figure out the solution. For example, when taking a psychology exam, you might need to rely of fluid intelligence to come up with a strategy to solve a statistics problem, while you must also employ crystallized intelligence to recall the exact formulas you need to use.

This theory suggests that general intelligence involves a set of non-learning and learning abilities that work together in various ways and to certain degrees over the course of one's lifespan. As one gets older, *Gf* decreases and *Gc* increases.

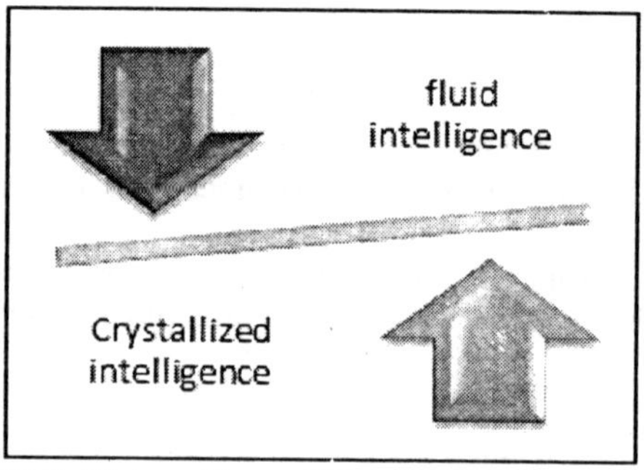

Figure 29.3: Picture Shows Gf Decreases and Gc Increases

Crystallized Intelligence

This intelligence includes information about facts and experiences one gain. This intelligence comes from prior learning and past experiences. Examples include reading comprehension and vocabulary exams. As you age it increases over time.

Fluid Intelligence

Fluid intelligence is described as the ability to perceive relationships independent of previous specific practice or instruction concerning those relationships. This intelligence includes your ability to solve problems quickly and reason abstractly. Examples of this intelligence include solving puzzles and coming up with problem-solving techniques. At about age 20, it peaks and then as you age further it decreases. In a cross-Sectional study researchers tested people of various ages and gave them intelligence tests. They consistently found that older adults gave fewer correct answers than do the younger participants. It concluded that the decline in mental ability with age is a part of the general aging process of an organism (see Figure 29.4).

Gardner's Theory of Multiple Intelligence (MI)

According to Dr. Howard Gardner, *"Intelligence is the ability to find and solve problems and create products of value in one's own culture." "Theory*

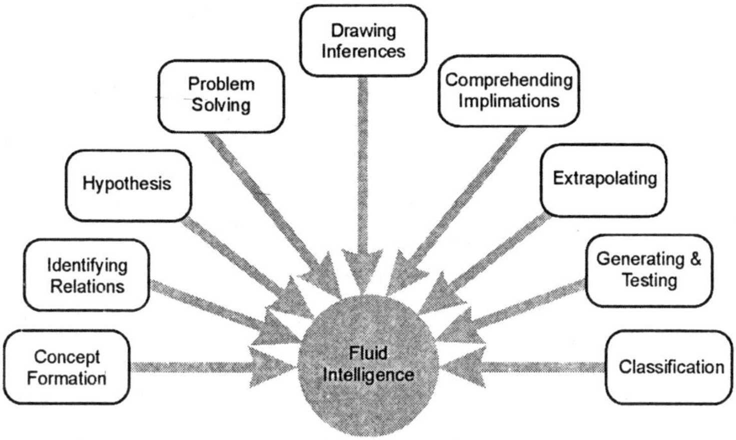

Figure 29.4: Mental Abilities Related to Fluid Intelligence

of Multiple Intelligence" Was proposed by Prof. Howard Gardner of Harvard University in 1983 in his path-breaking book *"Frames of Mind"* to redefine the concept of intelligence. This theory suggests that traditional psychometric views of intelligence are too limited. All people have different kinds of *"Intelligences"*. Gardner proposed that there are eight Intelligences and has suggested the possible addition of a ninth known as "Existentialist Intelligence".

The Theory of Multiple Intelligences posses some simple but powerful questions: Are talented chess players, violinists and athletes *"intelligent"* in their respective disciplines? Why these and other abilities are not accounted for on traditional IQ tests? Why is the term intelligence limited to such a narrow range of human endeavours?

From these questions emerged multiple-intelligences theory. Stated simply, it challenges psychology's definition of intelligence as a general ability that can be measured by a single IQ score. Instead, MI theory describes eight intelligences that people use to solve problems and create products relevant to the societies in which they live.

MI theory asserts that individuals who have a high level of aptitude in one intelligence do not necessarily have a similar aptitude in another intelligence. For example, a young person who demonstrates an impressive level of musical intelligence may be far less skilled when it comes to bodily-kinesthetic or logical-mathematical intelligence. Perhaps that seems obvious, but it is important to recognize that this notion stands in sharp contrast to the traditional (and still dominant) view of intelligence as a general ability that can be measured along a single scale and summarized by a single number.

Difference between Multiple Intelligence (MI) Theory and other Theories of Intelligence

The theory of multiple intelligences has implications for both how intelligence is assessed and how students are taught. While traditional theories of intelligence rely on short-answer tests to evaluate IQ, MI theory holds that such assessments measure memorization and the ability to do well on tests. Some states have developed tests that value the process of problem solving instead of just the answers.

While traditional theories of intelligence hold that people are born with a certain amount of intelligence that remains static over one's lifetime, MI theory posits that humans all have all of the 9 intelligences in their own unique combinations and that all types can be improved.

Type of Intelligences According to Gardner

The 9 different types of intelligences as explained by Dr. Gardner can be briefly described as:

Linguistic/Verbal Intelligence: The Linguistic Intelligence is related with words, spoken or written. It shows the ability to be good at reading, writing, telling stories and memorizing words along with dates. Linguistic Intelligence enables one to learn best by reading, taking notes, listening to lectures and discussion and debate. It also enables one to be skilled at explaining, teaching, creating effective speeches and persuasive speaking. It enables one to learn foreign languages easily as they have high verbal memory and recalling capacities, as well as an ability to understand and manipulate syntax and structure of sentences (see Figure 29.5).

Logical-Mathematical Intelligence: The Logical Intelligence is related with the abilities to naturally excel in mathematics and logical or numerical activities. More accurately speaking, it refers to traditional mathematical ability and more reasoning capabilities, abstract patterns of recognition, scientific thinking and investigation and the ability to perform complex calculations.

Musical Intelligence (Rhythmic Intelligence): The Musical Intelligence denotes rhythm, music and hearing skills. This intelligence induces greater sensitivity to sounds, rhythms, tones and music. It normally enhances good pitch-tone, which enables singing, playing musical instruments and to compose music. Since, there is a strong auditory component to this intelligence; it enables learning best by lectures, audio programmes or louder reading. In addition, the use of songs or rhythms or music playing in the background during learning and memorizing information, can enrich and accelerate the learning process.

Bodily-Kinesthetic Intelligence: The Kinesthetic Intelligence is related with body movements and physiology. Kinesthetic Intelligence enables one to learn better by involving muscular movements. It generally helps one to enhance physical activities, enjoy acting or performing, learning with pacing or rhythmic physical movements, model building, using touch sensations and practically making things.

Visual Intelligence (Spatial Intelligence): The Visual Intelligence is related with vision and spatial judgment. Visual intelligence enables one to be very good at visualizing and mentally manipulating objects, proficient at solving puzzles, a very good sense of direction - speed - distance and considerably good hand-eye coordination. It enhances a strong visual memory and often makes one artistically inclined.

Inter-Personal Intelligence: The Inter-Personal Intelligence is related with social interaction as a whole. Inter-Personal Intelligence enables one to be

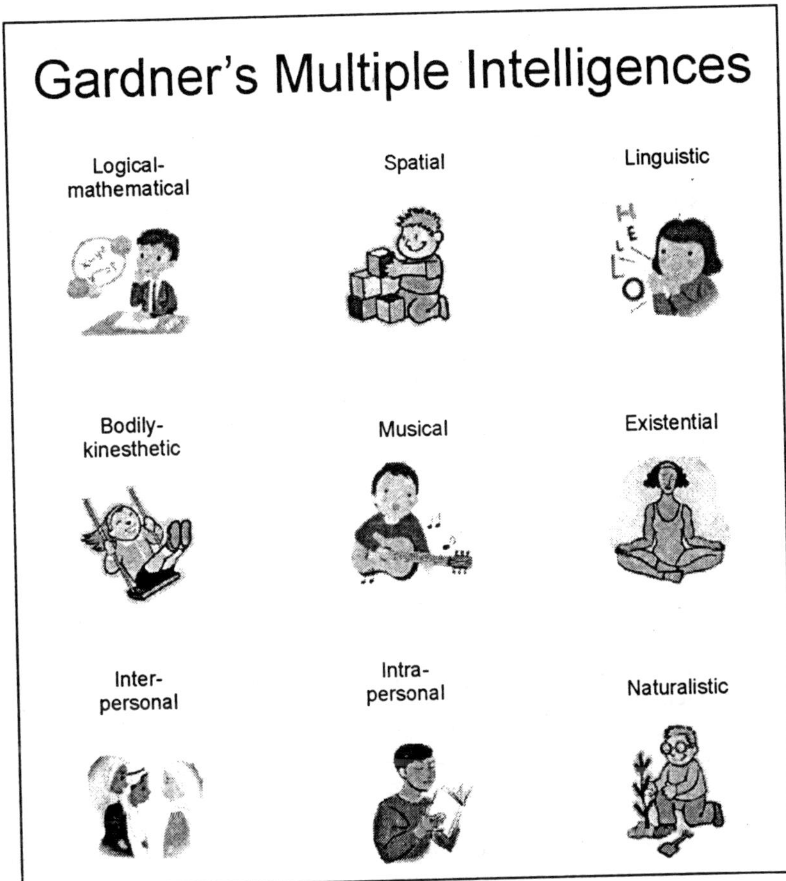

Figure 29.5: Gardner's 9 Types of Intelligences

extrovert, sensitive to others' moods, feelings, temperaments and motivations, and the ability to cooperate in order to work as part of a group. It enhances the capacity to communicate effectively and empathize easily with others. The learning process is best boosted by working with others, discussions and debate.

Intra-Personal Intelligence: The Intra-Personal Intelligence is related with introspective and self-reflective capacities. This intelligence makes one introvert and gives an urge to work alone. It gives high self-awareness and capacity of understanding one's own emotions, goals and motivations. It helps create an affinity for thought-based pursuits such as philosophy. The learning process is best enhanced when by concentrating on the subject by oneself. There is often a high level of perfectionism associated with this intelligence.

Naturalistic Intelligence: The Naturalistic Intelligence relates to greater sensitivity to nature and their place within it, the ability to nurture grow things, and greater ease in caring for taming and interacting with animals. This

Intelligence enables one to learn best when the subject involves collecting and analyzing, or is closely related to something prominent in nature, or while positioning oneself in natural environments.

Existential Intelligence

The Existential Intelligence relates to sensitivity and capacity to tackle deep questions about human existence, such as the meaning of life, why do we die, and how did we get here, etc. It enables one to enhance the philosophical thoughts and theories, exploring the nature of existence and spiritual awareness. It makes one curious about life, death and ultimate realities.

The brief description about the multiple-intelligences is shown in Table 29.1

Classroom Applications of Multiple Intelligence Theory

Although Gardner's MI research is psychological in nature, the biggest impact it has had has been on pedagogy. Educators have benefitted from the theory by being able to tailor instruction to various intelligences and to modify assignments so that students can work to their strengths. Offering a variety of ways in which learning objectives can be met helps students to choose the best way for them to approach as assignment.

Students who may not excel when traditional methods of instructions are used may "tune in" when a visual or kinesthetic teaching method is employed. Rather than teaching a topic or a subject, teachers who embrace the MI theory can structure learning activities around an issue or a question and allow students to approach the assignment in a way that demonstrates their unique understanding of the topic. Students may then become specialists in a particular topic, thereby bolstering their interest in the topic. When students are able to demonstrate and share their strengths, their investment in the learning process increases.

When students begin to understand how they learn and in what way they are intelligent, they are better able to direct their own learning and value their strengths. When teachers understand a student's intelligence, they can create opportunities for students to share their strengths with others. Students may exhibit their learning through portfolios, for instance, versus traditional exams. Students whose individual intelligence compositions are valued go on to become more balanced members of their culture, able to understand questions about notions such as what it means to achieve success or to have a good life.

Teachers should take care not to label students as having one particular type of intelligence. While a student may demonstrate great kinesthetic learning ability in lower elementary, labels can be limiting and counter to the MI theory that we all possess all 9 intelligences in varying degrees and that they can all be nurtured.

THE CONCEPT OF C.A, M.A, B.A. AND I.Q

Some of the basic expressions for the measurement of Intelligence are:

Chronological Age (C.A): This is the physical age of a person counted from the date and time of his birth. It is counted in terms of years, months and hours etc.

Table 29.1: Multiple Intelligences and their Description with Examples

	Intelligence Type	*Description*	*Typical Roles*
1	**Linguistic** (ability to use words & language)	**words and language**, written and spoken; *retention*, interpretation and explanation of ideas and information via language, understands relationship between communication and meaning	Writers, lawyers, journalists, speakers, trainers, copy-writers, English teachers, poets, editors, linguists, translators, PR consultants, media consultants, TV and radio presenters, voice-over artistes
2	**Logical-Mathematical** (ability to use reason, logic & numbers)	**logical thinking**, detecting patterns, scientific reasoning and deduction; analyse problems, perform mathematical calculations, understands relationship between cause and effect towards a tangible outcome or result	Scientists, engineers, computer experts, accountants, statisticians, researchers, analysts, traders, bankers bookmakers, insurance brokers, negotiators, deal-makers, trouble-shooters, directors
3	**Musical** (ability to produce & appreciate music)	**musical ability**, awareness, appreciation and use of sound; recognition of tonal and rhythmic patterns, understands relationship between sound and feeling	Musicians, singers, composers, DJ's, music producers, piano tuners, acoustic engineers, entertainers, party-planners, environment and noise advisors, voice coaches
4	**Bodily-Kinesthetic** (ability to control body movements & handle objects skillfully)	**body movement control**, manual dexterity, physical agility and balance; eye and body coordination	Dancers, demonstrators, actors, athletes, divers, sports-people, soldiers, fire-fighters, PTI's, performance artistes; ergonomists, osteopaths, fishermen, drivers, crafts-people; gardeners, chefs, acupuncturists, healers, adventurers
5	**Spatial-Visual** (ability to perceive the visual)	**visual and spatial perception**, interpretation and creation of visual images; pictorial imagination and expression; understands relationship between images and meanings, and between space and effect	Artists, designers, cartoonists, story-boarders, architects, photographers, sculptors, town-planners, visionaries, inventors, engineers, cosmetics and beauty consultants
6	**Interpersonal** (ability to relate & understand others)	**perception of other people's feelings**; ability to relate to others; interpretation of behaviour and communications; understands the relationships between people and their situations, including other people	Therapists, HR professionals, mediators, leaders, counsellors, politicians, educators, sales-people, clergy, psychologists, teachers, doctors, healers, organisers, carers, advertising professionals, coaches and mentors.

(Contd.)

	Intelligence Type	*Description*	*Typical Roles*
7	**Intrapersonal** (ability to self reflect & be aware of one's inner state of being)	**self-awareness**, personal cognisance, personal objectivity, the capability to understand oneself, one's relationship to others and the world, and one's own need for, and reaction to change	Entrepreneur, consultant, counselor, creative writer, guru, leadership trainer, philosopher, psychologist, spiritual counselor, sage, writer.
8	**Naturalistic** (ability to understanding the world of plants & animals, noticing their characteristics & categorizing them)	**Natural environment** Notices patterns & things from nature easily, has keen senses & observes & remembers things from his environment & surroundings, likes animals & likes to know & remember things about them, really appreciates being outside & doing things like camping, hiking or climbing, makes keen observations about natural changes, interconnections &patterns.	Environmentalist, taxonomist, biologist, meteorologist, palaeontologist, zoo-keeper, animal handler, veterinarian, astronomer, anthropologist.
9	**Existential** (Religion & ultimate issues)	Individuals, who like & enjoy thinking, & questioning, & are curious about life, death & ultimate realities. The ability to be sensitive to, or have the capacity for, conceptualizing or tackling deeper or larger questions about human existence, such as meaning of life, why are we born, why do we die, what is consciousness, or how did we get here.	

Mental Age (M.A): Alfred Binet introduced the concept of Mental Age (M.A.) in year 1908 to measure intelligence. MA merely indicates the level of development which a child has reached at a given age. It shows the mental level but it does not tell us how bright the child is. It gives us an idea whether the child is advanced or retarded or average when compared to normal children of his/her age.

Tests were made for different age levels. This is an index of intelligence rank. A child's mental age can be measured from his performance on an intelligence test. If a test was passed by 60-90 per cent of children of given age, Binet accepted it for that age level. A child who successfully performs all the tasks thus accepted for the five year old child is taken to have a mental age of five, whatever his Chronological Age (C.A.) may be. If he is five years old chronologically too, he is rated as normal or average. A seven year old child having a M.A. of six is considered as mental deficient; but if he has a M.A. of eight then he is said to be above average in intelligence.

The concept of MA has made the interpretation of intelligence easier. If the MA of a child is equal to his chronological age then he is normal. When he is greater than the CA, he is advanced and les than the CA is retarded.

Basal Age (B.A.): Basal age is that age of the child where he or she can solve all questions in a given test. It is the basal age which helps in the calculation of mental age. Suppose a child is 5 years age (CA). He solves all questions in a given test meant for a child of 6 and 7 years and solves only one question out of 6 questions in a test of 8 years and unable to solve any of the questions of 9 years. Thus, his basal age is 7 years 2 months though his CA is % years.

Intelligence Quotient (IQ): Intelligence Quotient (IQ) is the score; one get on an intelligence test. Originally, it was a quotient (a ratio): IQ = MA/CA × 100 [MA is mental age, CA is chronological age]. Today, scores are calibrated against norms of actual population scores (see Figure 29.6).

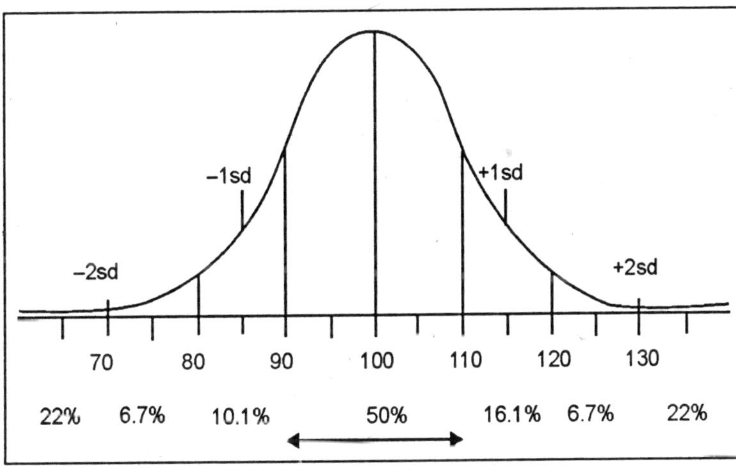

Figure 29.6

Every individual has possessed some amount of intelligence. We may be able to say whether the individual is less intelligent or more intelligent on the basis of his performance in activities. But to know the exact quantity of intelligence possessed by an individual, administration of an intelligence test is essential.

Before the Binet-Simon scale was adopted in America, it was refined in 1912 by the German psychologist William Stern who first proposed the idea of the intelligence quotient (IQ). He suggested that the mental age of a child be divided by the child's chronological age and the result multiplied by 100 to give a measurement he called the IQ. If the two ages were the same, the IQ would be 100 and considered average. If a child had a mental age of 12 and a chronological age of 10, the IQ would be 12/10 × 100 = 120, and above average.

Comparison of chronological and mental age is not suitable beyond childhood, so IQ for adults is calculated by comparison with the average or the normal scores of a large number of people. This is called norm-referencing.

When an intelligence test is administered, we get a score, which may be converted into Mental Age (M A), the concept developed by Alfred Binet. This is an index of his mental ability. But this score does not give us the quantitative measure of his mental ability or intelligence. Hence, in order to know a quantitative measure, a German psychologist by name William Stern proposed a formula, i.e. MA/CA x 100.

The output, we get out of this formula was called as Intelligence Quotient (IQ) by Stern, which is the index of the quantity of intelligence possessed by the person. The Chronological Age (CA) will be the actual or real age of the person.

The resultant product of MA divided by CA may be in decimal point, which does not give a clear picture. Hence, in order to overcome this problem of decimal points, Stern suggested that the product be multiplied by 100. This product will be supposed to be the quantity of intelligence possessed by the individual.

Binet and other psychologists had a firm belief that the IQ remains constant and it will not change though the individual grows chronologically. They believed that the growth of intelligence will be ceased by 16th year in almost all individuals.

Hence, they restricted CA to 16 years-irrespective of the age of individuals after 16 years. That is why the actual CA will be considered, if the age is below 16 years while calculating IQ. But it will be taken as only 16, even if the age of the individual exceeds 16 years.

Examples:

$$
\begin{aligned}
IQ &= MA/CA \times 100 \\
&= 10/10 \times 100 = 100 \\
&= 12/10 \times 100 = 120 \\
&= 8/10 \times 100 = 80
\end{aligned}
$$

It is assumed that IQ scores are normally distributed in a population. This means that most scores are clustered near the mean or average, with fewer very high or very low scores. This produces the typical bell curve of what is known as the 'normal distribution' shown in Figure 29.7. The bell curve shows us that there are many people of average IQ but very few whose IQ is extremely high or extremely low.

The spread of IQ scores is measured by a statistic called the standard deviation (SD). In a normal distribution, 68 per cent of scores lie within one standard deviation (1SD) of the mean. Intelligence tests are designed to produce a mean of 100 and an SD of 16. So having an IQ of 116 (the mean plus 1SD) means that a person has a higher intelligence than 50 + 34 = 84 per cent of the population.

DISTRIBUTION OF INTELLIGENCE

Every individual in a society have some amount of intelligence. But, they differ in the level of intelligence. Some may be very dull, some may be average

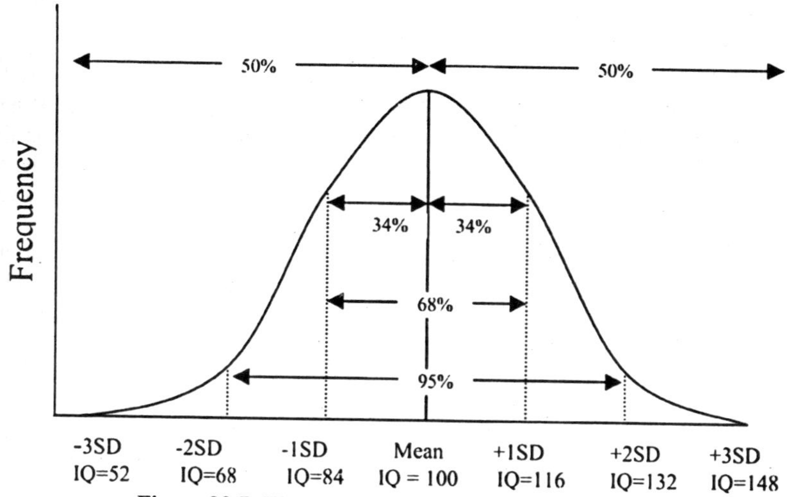

Figure 29.7: The Bell Curve of Normal Distribution

and some other people may be more intelligent. But, how many of them in a group or a society are dull or intelligent or average? The answer to this question lies in knowing the distribution of intelligence in a given population.

If we measure the intelligence of a large number of people and plot the IQ scores of these people on a graph, it assumes the shape of a "Normal Distribution Curve" or otherwise called 'Bell Shaped Curve' (Figure 29.8).

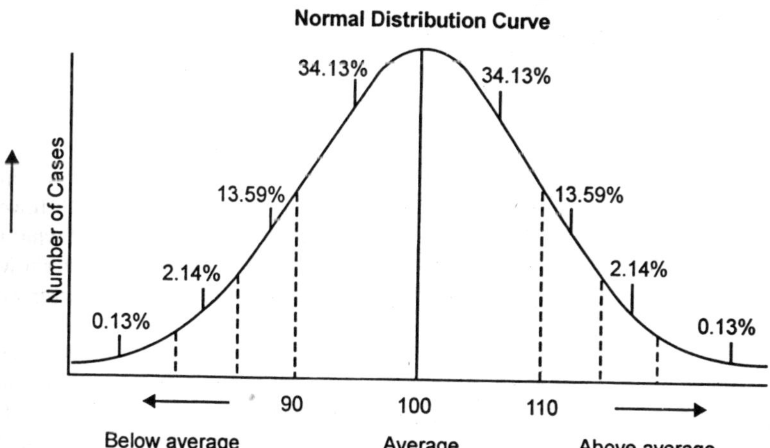

Figure 29.8: Normal Distribution Curve

This curve indicates that, a very few people will be at the lowest score and the equal number will be at the highest level of the IQ. The number gradually increases as we go up from the lowest point till we reach the midpoint or the average. A large number of people in a population will cluster around the mean score.

The number gradually decreases from the midpoint till the highest level is reached wherein there will be very few individuals. The lower side of the curve indicates the people with low intelligence and the higher side indicates people with above average level of intelligence.

Table 29.2 showing the distribution of individuals according to IQ scores and their classification:

Table 29.2: Normal Distribution of IQs

IQ Range	*Classification*	*No. of People (1000)*	*Percentage of Population*
140 and Above	Very Superior/Genius	1	0.13
120-139	Superior	22	2.14
110-119	High Average	136	13.59
90-109	Average	682	68.26
80-89	Low Average	136	13.59
70-79	Border Line Defective	22	2.14
69 and Below	Mentally Retarded	1	0.13

Mentally retarded are divided as follows:
(According to American Association for Mentally Retarded)

Category	*IQ Range*	*Ability*
Mild	50-70	Educable
Moderate	35-49	Trainable
Severe	21-34	Custodial
Profound	0-20	Custodial

Terman and Goddard have classified MR as follows:

- Idiots: IQ: 0-25
- Imbecile: IQ: 26-50
- Moron: IQ: 51-70

MEASUREMENT OF INTELLIGENCE

Intelligence is a person's capacity to (1) acquire knowledge (i.e. learn and understand), (2) apply knowledge (solve problems) and (3) engage in abstract reasoning. It is the power of one's intellect and as such is clearly a very important aspect of one's overall well-being. Psychologists have attempted to measure it for well over a century.

The attempt to measure human intelligence had begun in the 19th century itself. Alfred Binet in collaboration with Theodore Simon developed the first intelligence test in 1905. The Binet - Simon scale contained 30 items. The scale was revised many times by Binet. In 1916, the scale was revised by Lewis M. Terman of Stanford University and is known as Stanford Binet Intelligence Scale.

Another important event in the development of intelligence test was the formation of the Wechsler Adult Intelligence Scale (WAIS) published in 1955 and Wechsler Intelligence Scale for Children (WISC). During the First World War time A.S. Otis developed a group test of intelligence known as Army Alpha Intelligence Examination.

Intelligence being only a concept or an abstraction rather than a substance, it cannot be measured in physical units like a length of cloth or temperature of the body. When we measure an individual's intelligence by means of an intelligence test, we try to interpret his score in terms of the norms set by the author of the test. A piece of cloth may be measured in absolute terms whereas relative measurement or assessment has to be resorted to in the case of intelligence.

The most commonly known intelligence tests fall into three categories. Namely: (1) Individual Tests, (2) Group Tests, and (3) Performance Tests of Intelligence. Intelligence tests may also be classified as Verbal Tests and Non-verbal tests. In verbal tests, the person is asked to read or write. In Non-verbal tests, the person is required to perform some acts or to do some practical work.

VERBAL AND NON-VERBAL INTELLIGENCE TESTS

The description about verbal and non-verbal is as under:

Verbal Intelligence Tests

This denotes tests in which questions are asked oral or in written form of a given language, for which answers also have to be given in oral or written language. These tests are not intended for, and cannot be used in the case of illiterates and small children, since such people lack linguistic ability.

Limitations of Verbal Intelligence Test

The difficulties of the verbal group intelligence tests are fundamentally as follows:

- It is difficult to judge whether the examinee is extending his full cooperation or not.
- It is difficult to determine whether the physical and emotional balance of the examinee is perfect or disturbed.
- It is difficult to ascertain whether examinee is feeling comfortable and free to respond or restrain.
- It is difficult to check cheating and testify whether the person has written the answer himself or copied it from his neighbor.

Non-Verbal Intelligence Tests

These include tests that do not require the use of language but could be manipulated using figures, pictures, blocks or even other objects. Examples of it are Army Beta Intelligence Test, Pidgon's non-verbal tests and Raven's Progressive Matrices. Their advantage is that they can be used for testing subjects who lack language ability.

Features of Non-Verbal Intelligence Tests

The main features of non-verbal intelligence test are as follows:

- The contents of the tests are in the form of material objects.
- What is required of the subject is conveyed by the tester through oral instructions or by pantomime and signs.

- The subject responses are assessed in terms of how he reacts or what he does rather than what he says or writes.
- The comparison between different human groups of various languages and culture can be possible.
- The abilities of illiterate persons are assessed and possibilities of their learning are known.

Difference between Verbal test and Non-verbal Test

The difference between verbal and non-verbal tests is as follows:

Table 29.3: Difference between Verbal and non-Verbal Tests

Verbal Test	*Non-verbal Test*
It makes use of language	It makes use of pictures and designs
The abilities measured are verbal reasoning, memory and numerical reasoning	The abilities measured are spatial ability, speed and induction
It cannot be used for testing individuals who lack language ability	Individuals who lack language ability also can be tests by it.
It is less expensive	It is more expensive
The results of the tests are much affected by schooling	The results of the tests are less affected by schooling
Standardization is easy	Standardization is difficult
Administration and scoring are easy	Administration and scoring are difficult

Individual and Group Intelligence Tests

Individual Tests

These tests are administered to one individual at a time. They include performance tests as well as tests that require linguistic ability. Some examples of these are: Stanford Binet Intelligence Tests, Wechsler Bellevue Intelligence Test, Koh's Block Design Tests, etc. These tests are particularly appropriate for testing individuals but they are not financially feasible as they are expensive. In addition to this they are time consuming. Administration of such tests requires more experts training also.

Group Tests

In this category the tests are administered upon a large number of examinees simultaneously. Such tests are more objective and less expensive. But, in these tests, no rapport between the subject and the examiner is established. Hence, compared to individual tests, they are less useful for solving problems of individuals. Nevertheless, they have proved really useful for the purpose of educational and vocational guidance.

Difference between Individual and Group Intelligence Tests

The difference between individual and group tests is as follows:

Table 29.4: Difference between Individual and Group IntelligenceTests

Individual Test	*Group Test*
Tests intelligence of an individual at a time	Tests intelligence of a group at a time
Useful for children of every age	Not useful for children of lower age groups
Time consuming	Time saving
Uneconomic in terms of money and labour	Economic in terms of money and labour
Administration is not easy	Administration is easy
Interest of the individual is assured	Interest of the individual is not assured
Results can be judged then and there	Results cannot be judged them and there

Performance Tests of Intelligence

These tests measure intelligence through some sort of performance of the individual. The performances are in the form of concrete activities that demand for the ability to see relations and solve problems. For measuring intelligence of persons with language handicap arising out of deafness or speech defect or cultural variations, this type of tests are widely used. Obviously, this is a non-verbal test.

Advantages of Performance Intelligence Tests

Some advantages of Performance Tests are:

- When an individual has limited command over the language, he is handicapped and it is useful in such cases.
- For the study of pre-school children, who have not begun reading and writing, these are suitable tests.
- These tests are useful for clinical purposes for testing feeble minded persons.

Some Performance Intelligence Tests are described below:

The Pinter-Paterson Performance Scale

This has been the first major attempt to develop a standardized series of performance tests. Items in the test were taken from the work of Seguin Form Board, Healy Picture Completion Test, Knox Form Board, Ship test, Cube Test etc. The scale consists of fifteen sub-tests. For most purposes a short scale consisting of ten tests are being employed.

The Arthur Performance Scale

This consists of five tests. They are Know Cube, Seguin Form Board, Porteus Mazes, Healy Picture Completion Test and Arthur Stencil Design Test. This scale is intended for young children.

Bhatia's Performance Test

Koh's Black Design Test, Alexander Pass Along Test, Pattern Drawing Test, Immediate Memory of Sounds and Picture Completion Test are four sub-tests included in this battery. In the first among these, designs printed in 10 cards in increasing difficulty are to be arranged using coloured cubes. Speed is the factor contributing to high score. In the second, graded problems are presented. The coloured boxes are arranged in the reverse order and the individual is to rearrange it to give the shape given in the card. Time is one important factor here also. In the pattern drawing test eight diagrams of increasing order of difficulty are to be drawn without lifting the pencil and repeating the lines. In the memory test, consonants or digits are to be repeated in the same order first and then backwards. Five pictures cut out into 2, 4, 6 or 12 parts are to be assembled in the shortest possible time to gain maximum scores. The total score on the whole test is then determined and it is converted into IQ's using the tables provided in the test manual.

Raven's Progressive Matrices Test

It is a non-verbal test and was developed in the U.K. The test has been designed to evaluate the subject's ability to see the relationship between Geometric figures/designs. It can be administered individually as well as in a group. The test has three forms:

- ***Raven's Standard Progressive Matrices:*** It consists of 60 matrices divided into 5 sets a, b, c, d, e of 12 problems each. These problems are arranged in progressively increasing order of difficulty. The test can be used for persons in the age group of 6 years and 65 years.
- ***Raven's Advanced Progressive Matrices:*** It consists of 36 matrices. It can be administered to one who is average in intellectual capacities. It can be used for person between 111/2 years to 40 years.
- ***Raven's Coloured Progressive Matrices:*** It has 3 sets A, AB, B consisting of 12 matrices in each set (36). It can be used in the age group of 5 ½ yrs. to 11 years and beyond 65 years of age.

Raven's Progressive Matrices Test is most popular and widely used for measuring intelligence. Perceptual and reasoning ability are mainly measured in this type of test.

Wechsler Bellevue Intelligence Scale (WBIS)

This scale, published in 1939, was developed and standardized by David Wechsler of Bellevue Psychiatric Hospital. The test was first revised in 1955 and three different scales come into existence. They are:

- Wechsler Pre-schools and Primary School Scale of Intelligence (WPPSI) – designed for the children belonging to the age group 4 to 6.
- Wechsler Intelligence Scale for Children (WISC) – designed for school children in the age group of 6 to 16 years.
- Wechsler Adult Intelligence Scale (WAIS) – designed for adults in the age group of 16 to 64 years.

Wechsler Adult Intelligence Scale is an individual test which has the unique quality of being simultaneously a verbal as well as a performance scale. The scale consists of eleven sub-tests. Six sub-tests make up the verbal scale and remaining five comprise the performance scale. These tests are listed below in the order in which they are administered.

Verbal Scale:

(a) Test of general information
(b) Test of general comprehension

(c) Test of arithmetic reasoning
(d) Test of distinction between similarities
(e) Test of digit span
(f) Test of vocabulary

Performance Scale:

(a) Block Design Test
(b) Digit Symbol Test
(c) Object Assembling Test
(d) Picture Arrangement Test
(e) Picture Completion Test

The scores on these sub-tests are added together to assess the subject's intelligence.

Advantages of Intelligence Tests

- Intelligence tests are used for the purpose of making selection of suitable candidate for admission to courses that demand different levels of intelligence.
- Intelligence tests help the teacher to classify students into homogeneous groups for providing individualized instruction.
- Scores obtained in intelligence tests can motivate individuals to reach higher levels in the ladder.
- Intelligence tests help in revealing the potentialities of an individual and in this way make possible the prediction of one's success in a particular field.
- Intelligence tests help to detect the exceptional children such as gifted, backward and mentally retarded. This in turn helps the teacher organize appropriate compensatory services.
- Intelligence tests help in the diagnosis of problematic behaviour of the child.
- Intelligence testing has been proved to be very useful in psychological, sociological and educational research.

Limitations of Intelligence Tests

- Intelligence tests label some students as superior and the others as inferior. This type of knowledge may create so many psychological problems.
- A teachers' knowledge of the intelligence of his pupils may result in slackness on his part. He may put the entire responsibility of a pupil's failure on his inferior intelligence, while an intelligent student may be left to work for himself.
- Intelligence tests results have been misused to uphold the theory of royal blood, segregation and sectarian outlook.

Abilities Measured by Intelligence Tests

- Numerical reasoning
- Analogies
- Classification
- Spatial relations
- Logical selection
- Synonyms

- Practical judgment
- Verbal comprehension
- Memory
- Problem solving

Thus, Intelligence Tests have been and or even now being used in education. Intelligence tests are psychological techniques of measurement and their interpretation helps in guidance and intellectual capacities of children.

USES OF INTELLIGENCE TESTS

The following are the important uses of intelligence test:

Understand the Capability of a Child: Intelligence tests are of valuable aid to the educationist as a means of diagnosis of the capacity or efficiency of pupils. The scores of intelligence test reveal the mental age of a child and indicates the readiness of a child for learning.

Homogeneous Grouping: A class consisting of students with widely different abilities is difficult to handle. Thus, homogeneous grouping of pupils can be done on the basis of intelligence test results.

Purpose of Admission/Selection to Various Courses: It has been known that success in school is to a great extent, correlated with intelligence. While admitting pupils it is desirable to consider their MA (Mental Age) rather than CA (Chronological Age). Thus, it is an asset (intelligence test) and help the professionals and students to choose the right institutions and right courses.

Identifying Gifted and Backward Children: Intelligence tests help in classifying individuals according to their mental makeup. On the basis of results, the students can be named as gifted, backward and average and accordingly educational opportunities can be provided.

Educational and Vocational Guidance: The result of intelligence tests helps in providing educational, vocational and personal guidance to students by teachers and guidance personnel. It gives clue in guiding the students into those courses where they have some likelihood of being successful and suggesting a few other courses and careers. These tests are also used as screening devices for selecting suitable candidates from among a large number of applicants and possibility of entering into an occupation in future.

Use in Assessment for Promotion, Reporting to Parents and Degree of Responsibility: The results of intelligence tests along with the achievement tests can be successfully used for promotion of students to next higher grades and help in promotion of people in next higher post. Similarly, intelligence test helps the teacher to sent progress report to the parents about the mental ability and the achievement level of the students. Sometimes the teacher assigns responsibility etc. to students on the basis of intelligence tests.

Raising the Quality of Teaching: Intelligence test helps the teacher to plan his/her teaching-learning activities according to the needs of the child or what the child can learn and how quickly he/she can learnb.

Use in Research Work: Intelligence tests are very much needed for research in the field of education. Mental measurement is a very important aspect in any study whether it aims at survey or comparison. Intelligence test helps us to know the general level of intelligence of a particular country or race.

Chapter-30
Personality

The word personality is derived from the Latin word *'persona'* means mask used by the actors to change their appearance but in Roman period, it was taken to mean the actor. The meaning of the word personality has changed little since classical times. We often say 'fine personality', 'good personality', 'poor personality' etc. on the basis of physical make up, manner of walking, talking, drawing and other similar characteristics of the individual. However, this is a very limited view and the psychological concept of personality goes further and deeper than mere appearance or out ward behaviour.

WHAT IS PERSONALITY?

Personality is the product of social interaction in group life. In society, every person has different traits such as skin, colour, height and weight. They have different types of personalities because individuals are not alike. It refers to the habits, attitudes as well as physical traits of a person which is not same but varies from group to group and society to society. Everyone has personality, which may be good or bad, impressive or unimpressive. It develops during the process of socialization in a culture of a specific group or society. One cannot determine it of an individual exactly because it varies from culture to culture and time to time. For example, a killer is considered criminal in peace time and hero in war. The feeling and actions of an individual during interaction moulds the personality. It is the sum of total behaviours of the individual and covers both overt and covert behaviours, interests, mentality and intelligence. It is the sum of physical and mental abilities and capabilities.

Personality has been derived from the Latin word *"Persona"* which means *"mask"* used by the actors to change their appearance. It is the combination of an individual thoughts, characteristics, behaviours, attitude, ideas and habits.

DEFINITIONS OF PERSONALITY

Some of the important definitions of personality are:

1. Morton Prince (1914) - *"Personality is the sum total of biological innate dispositions, impulses, tendencies, aptitudes and instincts of the individual and the dispositions and tendencies acquired by experience"*
2. Gordon R.G (1928) - *"Personality is a comprehensive term which includes character"*
3. Watson J.B (1924) - *"Personality is the sum of activities that can be discovered by actual observation over a long enough period of time to give reliable information."*
4. G.W. Allport (1937) - *"Personality is the dynamic organization with in*

the individual of those psycho-physical systems that determine his unique adjustment to the environment".

5. R.B. Cattel (1967) - *"Personality is that which permits a prediction of what a person will do in a given situation"*
6. Eysenck H.J. (1947) - *"Personality is the more or less stable and enduring organization of person's character, temperament, intellect and physique, which determine his unique adjustment to the environment".*
7. Guilford J.P (1967) - *"An individual's personality then is his unique pattern of traits"*
8. Lewin, Kurt (1935) - *"Personality is a dynamic totally of systems".*
9. S.R. Maddi (1976) – *"Personality is the stable characteristics and tendencies that determine those commonalities and differences in the psychological behaviour (thoughts, feelings and actions) of people that have continuity in time and that may or may not be easily understood in terms of the social and biological pressures of the immediate situation alone."*
10. Moynihan and Peterson (2001) – *"Personality is the key antecedent of an individual's cognitions and affective states that may influence his/her to and interpersonal or socio-emotional role behaviour."*
11. Macionis define as, *"It is the constant pattern of thinking, feeling and acting."*
12. Ogburn and Nimkoff define it as, *"the totally of sentiments, attitudes, ides, habits, skills and behaviours of an individual."*
13. Brisbane, Holly E. And Eiker, Andrey Palm (1965) observe, *"Personality is the sum total of specific traits (such as shyness or cheerfulness) that are noticeably consistent in an individual's behaviour."*
14. Brown. W. (1946) thinks *"Personality is the total differentiation which the individual makes by incorporating the inherited and acquired powers to stimulate and to activate the imagination of others in art, science and public affairs and also to live in and partake of a super-individual and super temporal word of values."*
15. According to Cronbach. L.J. (1963), *"Character is not really a cumulation of separate habits and ideas. Character is embedded in the total structure of personality."*
16. Deshiell, J.F. (1929) thinks an individual's personality *"as his system of reactions and reaction-possibilities in total as viewed by follow members of society. It is the sum total of behaviour trends manifested in his social adjustments."*
17. Morton Prince, *"Personality is the sum total of all the biological innate dispositions, impulses, tendencies, appetites and instincts of the individual and the dispositions and tendencies acquired by experience."*
18. Warren, *"Personality is the entire mental organization of the human being at any stage of his development. It embraces every phase of human character, intellect, temperament, skills, morality and even attitude."*
19. Woodsworth, *"Personality is the total quality of individual behaviour."*
20. McClelland, *"Personality is the most adequate conceptualization of a person behaviour in all its details."*

FEATURES AND CHARACTERISTICS OF PERSONALITY

Various researchers and observations have led to the identification of the following characteristics of personality:

- Personality is something unique and specific. Every one of us is unique person and different from one another.
- Personality is dynamic and moving force. It is never fixed and rigid. However, it seems to remain stable to a large extent.
- Personality is the sum total of various human qualities. It includes all the behavioural patterns. It includes cognitive, connative, affective domains and covers the conscious, semi-conscious and unconscious activities.
- Personality has a structure. It consists of certain dimensions. It is the combination of inner as well as outer qualities.
- It is not mere physical appearance but it is the study of both physical and psychological factors as an integrated system.
- It is the product of Heredity and environment.
- Personality exhibits self-consciousness as one of its main characteristics. Man is described as a 'person' when the idea of 'self' enter into his consciousness.
- It is subjected to disorganization and disintegration leading to serve personality disorders.
- Learning and acquisition of experiences contributes towards growth and development of personality.
- It can be described and measured.

Thus, it may be said that personality is a complex blend of a constantly evolving and changing pattern of one's unique behaviour, emerged as a result of one's interaction with environment and directed towards some specifications.

FACTORS OF PERSONALITY

Enormously, the following five factors of personality are contributing to the formation and development of human personality:

- Biological Factors
- Social Factors
- Cultural Factors
- Physical Environment
- Situational Factors

Biological Factors of Personality

Biological factors of personality are very important for the formation of human personality. Children are born in a family; inherit many traits and features from their parents. Children get physical and psychological characteristics from their parents, which becomes a part of their personalities. Some of the inherited traits are courage, coward, intelligence, weakness etc.

A normal healthy man has some physical similarities such as two hands, five senses, two eyes and these biological similarities help to explain some of the similarities in the behaviour.

It separates individuals from one another and their various physical characteristics except identical twins having the same physical qualities. So, biological factors of personality are responsible for the development of personality.

Social Factors of Personality

When an individual interact with other persons in his/her group then give and take relationship takes place and it affects the personality of an individual. Social factors of personality are responsible for the formation of personality. When an individual has group experience and contact with others personality of an individual is influenced by others may be bad or good but depends on the association in which he/she keeps. In a society, every person plays a specific role and status.

For example, in our society younger are expected to be respectful for elders. Many other social factors like - environment, group life, family, media with which an individual interact in his/her society daily life, mould their personalities. We can say that whatever comes in contact with an individual's social life affects personality of that individual and develop good or bad personality.

Cultural Factors of Personality

Both material as well as non-material culture affects personality of an individual. An individual living in his/her culture adopts the traits consciously or unconsciously and acts accordingly. Culture of any society determines the behaviours and personality of an individual and he/she is expected to act according to the culture. A person follows all the social norms of a culture which results in the formation of good personality while non-conformity to the cultural rules develops abnormal or bad personality. So, the culture in which an individual seeks satisfaction adjusts himself/herself and develops personality

Physical Environment

Physical environment also determines the personality of an individual. Environmental factors include - land, river, mountains, hills, forests, plain area, atmosphere etc., which affects the personality to be good or bad, healthy or weak. All the feelings, emotions, ideas, attitudes, habits and behaviour as well as body structure are the result of physical environment of to which an individual belongs. For example, body structure, physique, colour and health of the rural people are different from urban people. These people have different environment due to which they develop variety of personalities. The people living in cities have facilities and modern ways of life which creates to develop delicate bodies and minds as compare to the rural people who are deprived of these facilities.

Situational Factors of Personality

Situational factors of personality also have a complete share in the formation of personality of an individual. Situational factors of personality are charging according to the social situations. Every person face may situations in his life which enables him/her to change his/her behaviour. For example, a teacher may be rigid and strict with students but may not with his/her family. An officer may behave with the subordinates differently as compare to his/her friends. Personality is not the result of only one factor but every factor is responsible to give complete share in its formation. A person behave and his/her personality exists when interacts with environment, culture, society, parents, friends and to those who come in contact by chance.

TYPES OF PERSONALITY

Following are the three types of personality:

Extrovert Personality

This type has the tendency to live mostly outside the like to live with others. Those individuals are highly socialized and have contact with outside people in the society. They want to join other groups who are more in number.

Introvert personality

Introvert is opposite to extrovert. Those people are always live alone in their rooms and do not want to go outside. They have their own imaginary world. They are teachers, scientists, thinkers and philosophers.

Ambivert Personality

Between extrovert and introvert personalities, there is a third one type called ambivert. People belonging to this type enjoy both the groups and attend them. They have middle mind and want to live in both parties.

Sometimes they join outside people but sometimes they live in their own rooms.

FACTORS INFLUENCING OR AFFECTING PERSONALITY

Personality is dynamic, growing and different in each person in physical appearance, temperament and motivation. The differences become more pronounced and complex with increasing and maturity due to continuous interaction with the environment and accordingly each one of us develop a personality different from others. Now, the question arises; how does personality develop? What causes these variations? Why do we develop different personalities in spite of basic similarities? All these can be answered, if we examine the various factors, which influence the structure and functions of personality. Thus, the development of personality depends upon the following factors:

1. Physiological and Physical Factors (Genetic or Biological)
2. Environmental or Social Factors
3. Psychological or Mental Factors
4. The Culture Factors.

1. The Physiological and Physical Factors (Genetic or Biological)

The biological factors affecting the development of personality are mainly three. They are:

- Heredity

- Physique
- Chemique
- Nervous System

Heredity

It provides the child with certain endowments to? With- Hereditary factors may be summed as constitutional biological and physiological factors:

Constitutional Factors: The constitution of an individual is an effective factor in determining the type of his Personality. There can be 3 bodily types of personality- (1) short and stout, (2) tall and thin, (3) muscular and well Proportioned. We are always impressed by an individual who has a muscular and a well proportioned body. Height, Weight, physical defects, health and strength affect Personality.

Biological Factors: The working of the nervous system, glands and blood chemistry determines our characteristics and habitual modes of behaviour. These factors form the biological basis of our personality.

Adrenal gland, thyroid gland, pituitary gland and endocrine gland affect personality. Adler points out that personality defects lead to the development of inferiority complex and the mental mechanism of compensation. This aspect also includes the mental ability of the child.

It is this ability which enables him to mould the social environment according to his requirements.

Intelligence: Intelligence is mainly hereditary. Persons who are very intelligent can make better adjustment in home, school and society than those who are less intelligent.

Sex Differences: Sex differences play a vital role in the development of personality of individual. Boys are generally more assertive and vigorous. They prefer adventures. Girls are quieter and more injured by personal, emotional and social problems.

Physique

An individual's personality differ according to his physique. These aspects are - height, weight, body-built, colour appearance and proportion etc, which determine to a large extent the way in which he behaves towards other and how others react towards him. It is seen that in daily life, the fat men are easy going and social, while thin men are self-controlled, irritated and unsocial. Even tall and fair persons enjoy an advantage over their short and ugly associates. Thus, the physical structure has some relation with environment and makes a change in their personality.

Chemique

Chemique is meant the possible effects of the ductless glands on the personality development. Ductless glands called endocrine glands, releases hormones into the blood stream, which carries them to all parts of the body. It brings about changes in physical appearance, motor functioning, intelligence and emotional stability e.g., Pituitary, Thyroid, Adrenal etc. Individuals with profound imbalance of ductless glands are rarely happy or well-adjusted. Glands play an important part in bodily, mental and emotional development.

Nervous System

Nervous system is mainly classified as Central Nervous System (Control of our will) and Autonomous Nervous System (autonomic). The conditions of the body brought by drugs, disease, diet, toxins etc. may also influence one's personality and behaviour. Hence heredity lies at the root of all the possibilities of personality development.

2. The Environmental or Social Factors

Physical and geographical conditions of the environment play an important role in shaping the personality of human beings at every stage of development. The type of home atmosphere, parent-child relationship, financial conditions, types of school and the community or society etc. are some of the factors of environment, which affects the personality.

Environment

The sociologists emphasize that the personality of the individual develops in a social environment. It is in the social environment, that he comes to have moral ideas, social attitudes and interests. This enables him to develop a social 'self which is another term for personality. The important aspects of the environment are as follows:

Physical Environment: It includes the influence of climatic conditions of a particular area or country on man and his living.

Social Environment: In the society, each individual has some peculiar status and roles corresponding to him. It is found that social control is exercised by traditions, myth, legends, customs etc. and determines the style of life of an individual. The individual has to follow rules, regulations, norms and law to govern the individual. Thus, social norms influence even the ways and attitudes of the individual. This ultimately influences his personality.

The child has his birth in the society. He learns and lives there. Hence, the social environment has an important say in the personality development of the child. There are many social factors which influence the development of personality of a child which are as follows:-

Language: Human beings have a distinctive characteristic of communication through language. Language is an important vehicle by which the society is structured and culture of the race transmitted from generation to generation.

The child's personality is shaped by the process of interaction through language with other members of his environment.

Social Role: The child has to play several roles like son, brother student, officer, husband, father, etc., throughout his life at rent stages of his development. Social roles may be described as process by which the co-operative behaviour and communications among the society members are facilitated.

Self Concept: Self concept influences our personality development in two ways-(1) If other people hold high positive "ergative enhances our self and (2) If others hold may us, it creates feelings of worthlessness and to self-defence or withdrawal from social situation.

Identification: Identification is an important mechanism by which we try to imitate the physical, social and mental characteristics of our model. It is a very important relationship with others.

Inter-personal Relations: Inter-personal relations among the members of a society are important means which help in the development of certain social personality characteristics like attraction towards others, concept of friendship, love, sympathy, hostility and also isolation which is a negative orientation.

Home and Family Environment: Besides the role of parents in personality development, the atmosphere in the family is greatly influencing. A peaceful and loving atmosphere results in children being orderly peace-loving and very affectionate and develop mature and pleasant personalities, whereas, in family, where there is tension, constant quarrelling, incompatibility among parents, the child is likely to develop insecurity, inferiority and becomes emotionally confused and unstable. Rigid atmosphere, deprivation, autocratic styles of living, absence of affection and sympathy affect adversely and the child often turns criminal. Thus, the child's personality is a creation of family and its development is fully dependent upon the child's parents and the child himself at home.

Family is the cradle of all social virtues. The first environment, the child moves in, is his home. Here the child comes in contact with his parents and other family member his likes, dislikes, stereotypes about people, expectancies of security and emotional responses all are shaped in early childhood.

The type of training and early childhood experiences received from the family play an important role in the development of personality.

Besides this, economic factors i.e., economic condition of the family and the type of relations between the parents also influence the personality of the child.

Cultural Environment: The cultural environment refers to certain cultural traditions, ideals, and values etc., which are accepted in a particular society. All these factors leave a permanent impression on the child's personality.

School Environment: School plays an important role in moulding the personality of children because a significant part of a child's life is spent in school. In school, the personality and behaviour of the teacher, class fellows and playmates, the richness of the curriculum, co-curricular activities, method of teaching, nature of school organization and discipline that prevails etc. are effecting the child's personality. The child tends tom identify himself with the teachers and tries to imitate his ways and manners. Thus, a good teacher and the congenial atmosphere in the institution develop the child educationally and mentally and helps in formulating balanced personality development otherwise an unethical behaviour could have been found out with children.

3. The Psychological or Mental Factors

The psychological factors like motives, interests, attitudes, character, thinking, intelligence, reasoning, imagination, creativity, habits, mental health etc. developed by the individual also affect their personality to a great extent.

These include our motives, acquired interests, our attitudes, our will and character, our intellectual capacities such as intelligence i.e., the abilities to perceive, to observe, to imagine, to think and to reason

These factors determine our reactions in various situations and thus affect our personality, growth and direction. An individual with a considerable amount of will power will be able to make decisions more quickly than others.

Thus, we see that hereditary, environmental and psychological factors contribute towards the development of personality.

4. The Cultural Factors

Every society is characterized by its cultural heritage, which is transmitted from generation to generation in the form of social heredity. Thus, personality of an individual is gradually shaped by the culture where he is born in. Culture is a way of life. It is a fact that we are able to distinguish one person from other on the basis of effect of his culture over his personality characteristics. Thus, the attributes and values practiced in a culture have a great effect on the personality development of its members.

ASSESSMENT OF PERSONALITY OF AN INDIVIDUAL

Some of the methods to assess the personality of an individual are as follows:

Questionnaire

The word questionnaire refers to a device for securing answers to questions by using a form which the respondent fills in himself. It is a flexible tool for gathering qualitative and quantitative information. It is a form consisting of a series of printed questions. The subject responds to these questions in the space provided. The answers are then examined and the results used for personality measurement. According to Barr and others, the term questionnaire generally refers to systematic compilation of questions that are submitted to a sample of population about which information is desired.

Observation Methods

Observation is a popular method to study the behaviour pattern of an individual in an actual life situation. It is a process in which one or more persons observes what is being occurring in a real-life situations, and classify and record the happenings according to some planned scheme. It is used to evaluate the overt behaviour of individuals in controlled and uncontrolled situations.

The observer decides what personality traits or characteristics needs to be observed and observes the relevant activities in real life situation. There are two types of observations such as Participant observations and Non-participant observation. In participant observation, the observer becomes a more or less part of the group or individual under observation. In non-participant observation the observer takes a position where his presence is least disturbing to the subject and observes every detail of the behaviour of the individual.

These methods are designed to assess outward manifestations through observations. **The different Observational Techniques are given below:**

Observational Techniques

Rating Scales: Rating scale is simply a device for recording the extent to which a person is perceived to have a defined attribute. A rating scale may be self-rating or rating by other observers. Rating scale helps us to know the degree or magnitude of a particular trait of personality present in a given person. Usually the rating scales will be of three points, five points or seven points. For example, to study the sociability trait:

The statement may be, 'I like to be in the company of the people than to be alone' Ans: (a) always, (b) sometimes, (c) never, (3 point scale); (a) strongly agree, (b) agree, (c) indifferent, (d) disagree, (e) strongly disagree, (5 point scale). The subject has to read the question and indicate the degree of the trait in him by marking a tick mark on any one of the answers.

Interview: Interview is a process of communication or interaction in which the subject or interviewee gives the needed information verbally in a face-to-face situation. It is a technique of eliciting information directly from the subject about his personality. Interview may be broadly classified according to the purpose, design, structure, etc.

It is a very popular method of observation. Interview is a situation in which there is a face to face contact between the interviewer and the interviewee. Personality is assessed by asking the questions orally. Generally interview is held as a part of assessment programme. That is to supplement the data collected by other methods. Usually interviews are held to evaluate a person's personality for identifying personality trait. The interviews are of two types: structured and unstructured.

In structured interview the questions to be asked are predetermined according to the need. The interviewer is not supposed to ask any question other than the prepared one. The number of questions to be asked is also predetermined. In unstructured interview the interviewer is at full liberty to ask any question he likes and any number of questions on the issue for which the interview is held.

Behavioural Tests: Several types of behavioural tests are used to assess the personality. In these tests a particular challenging situation is created artificially, but resembles almost the original one. The person will be made to face the situation. Example, the nurse may be asked to face an emergency situation like- taking care of a severe heart attack patient. Depending upon how effectively that situation is faced by the said person, his personality will be assessed. However, these behavioural tests do not assess the personality structure of the individuals, but indicate certain traits possessed by the individual like leadership, initiative, energy level, etc., which are necessary to face critical situations.

Personality Inventories

A personality inventory is essentially a standard set of questions for self-appraisal or self reporting. It consists of statements or questions about personal characteristics, feelings, worries, fears, etc. It is just like a questionnaire in many aspects such as administration, scoring, interpretation, etc.

While it resembles the questionnaire it is different in two ways. Firstly, a personality inventory is specifically designed to seek answers about the person and his personality, while a questionnaire is used for collecting all kinds of information not connected specifically with personality traits or behaviour of the individual. Secondly, the questions set in the questionnaire are generally worded in the second person. While in the personality inventory, they may be worded in the first person. For example:

Questionnaire: *Do you* often feel lonely? Yes/No.

Inventory: *I* often feel lonely Yes/No.

Psychologists have developed many questionnaires, tests, inventories to study personality. The inventories will contain a set of questions or statements meticulously prepared on the problem under study. Each question will have two answers-either yes or no, and the subject has to mark the answer which best suits his nature. This method is easy to administer and to collect data from a large number of people at a time.

The necessary instructions and directions will be available on the face page itself. The subject has to read carefully before answering in order to avoid any confusion. Some of the popular questionnaires/inventories are:

- Minnesota Multiphase Personality Inventory (MMPI)
- Eysenck Personality Inventory (EPI)
- Bell's Adjustment Inventory
- Mysore Personality Inventory
- RB Cattell's 16 Personality Factors Test, etc.

Personal Data Sheet

R.S Woodworth was the first psychologist who designed the first personality inventory in 1919 which he called as the Personal Data Sheet. It consisted of 116 questions that required the subject to answer Yes or No. The questions involved in this are related to feelings, worries, fear and symptoms of mental disorder.

Minnesota Multiphasic Personality Inventory (MMPI)

This is the best known personality inventory developed by J.C. McKinley and S.R. Hathaway. It was developed in the 1930s at Minnesota University as a serious and comprehensive personality test that can be used to detect psychiatric problems. It has ten clinical scales to indicate different psychiatric conditions. The questions included in this inventory are to indicate certain specific personality traits. It consists of 550 items. Each item is printed on a separate card. The subject reads the questions and according to his response put it down as Yes, No or Doubtful in the space provided. With the help of these responses, assessment in terms of the important personality traits can be obtained.

Eysenck Personality Inventory (EPI)

This personality inventory was developed by a British psychologist H.J Eysenck. It is mainly used to assess neurotic tendencies. This inventory has been developed on the assumption that there are only two dimensions of personality, introversion-extraversion and stability-instability.

RB Cattell's 16 Personality Factors Test

This inventory was developed by Raymond B. Cattell and his colleagues. The 16PF (16 Personality Factor) model is probably the most-widely used system for categorizing and defining personality. It is a multiple-choice personality questionnaire specifically designed to discover and measure the fundamental traits of human personality.

The 16 personality factors are: warmth, reasoning, emotional stability, dominance, liveliness, rule consciousness, social boldness, sensitivity, vigilance, abstractedness, privateness, apprehension, openness to change, self-reliance, perfectionism and tension.

A-S Reaction Study

The Ascendance-Submission Reaction Study of G.W Allport was one of the first tool used to measure personality traits. It has been designed to test extroversion-Introversion, sociability-solitariness and ascendance-submission traits of personality.

Projective Techniques

Projection is a compensatory mechanism in which the person reads own thoughts and feelings into others. The projective tests/techniques are based on the principle that the subject reads or projects one's own inner conflicts, frustrations, fears, motives and such other feelings into the unstructured situation. Naturally the responses the subject makes reveal the inner working of his mind. Thus, the projective techniques provide us an insight into the personality of the individual.

As the projective tests are unstructured either in form or in situation, their purpose is disguised. So the chances of giving false information are very less.

A good number of projective tests are available today. Some of the popular projective tests are:

Rorschach's Ink Blot Test

It is developed by Swiss psychiatrist Herman Rorschach (1884-1922) in the year 1921. The test consists of ten symmetrical ink blots (example, see the Figure 30.1). All the cards will be presented one by one in a serial order and in the prescribed position.

The subject will be asked to answer the questions like- what could be the situation? What does he see in the card? All the responses will be recorded by the experimenter. Each response is scored in several ways like-location, determinants, content, popularity and organization.

Set of symbols are used to score the responses. Interpretation of the results will be done on the basis of a number responses scored in a particular way, relative to the total number of responses. However, scoring and interpretation requires special training,

Figure 30.1: Rorschach's Ink Blot Test

Thematic Apperception Test (TAT)

This test was developed by Henry

Murray of Harvard University and psychologist Christina Morgan in 1938. It is a method of revealing the unconscious dominant drives, emotions, sentiments, complexes and conflicts of personality to the trained interpreter. The test contains 19 pictures of different situations of life (example, see the Figure 30.2 given in the box) and one blank card.

Though the figures in the pictures are clear and structured, the vagueness or ambiguity lies in the situation. The subject is asked to write a story on the basis of 4 questions:

Figure 30.2: Thematic Apperception Test (TAT)

- What has led to the event shown in the picture?
- What is happening at the moment?
- What the characters in the picture are feeling and thinking?
- What may be the outcome?

In making up the stories the subject unconsciously projects several characteristics of his own personality and sometimes the narration became an autobiography. As there is no time to think, the stories expresses his own natural life's desires, likes and dislikes, emotions, sentiments, etc. The story is recorded and later interpreted by experts. From this interpretation a competent examiner can learn a lot about the personality of his subject. The test is more useful in knowing the general nature of one's personality rather than diagnostic aspects.

There are many other projective tests, viz., children apperception test, Verbal projection test, sentence completion test, drawing test, etc. Projective tests are often used in clinical practice. Because they are helpful to bring out the unconscious motives, conflicts, anxieties and other problems.

Children Apperception Test (CAT)

The CAT was developed by Leopold Bellak to assess the personality of children between 3-10 years of age. This test consist of 10 cards consisted of pictures of animals instead of human beings. The pictures designed to evoke fantasies relating to child's own experiences, reactions and feelings. The child is asked to tell a story based on the picture and whatever story he makes, he projects his own personality. As per the quality reflected in description, by way of aspects like the theme, nature of anxieties, language used and the time taken for the completion of the test, etc. the child's personality is assessed.

Word Association Test

This test was developed by C.G Jung for diagnosing behaviour disorders. It consisted of a number of selected words related to personality and the subject is asked to write or say associated words with it. Some responses come promptly and others with delay. The examiner records the reply to each word, the reaction time and any unusual behaviour manifestation to the given response. On the basis of this test C.G Jung has divided personality into introvert, extrovert and ambivert.

Sentence Completion Test

This test consists of a list of incomplete sentences, generally open ended, which require completion by the subject in one or more words. The subject is asked to go through the list and answer as quickly as possible without giving a second thought to his answers.

For example:

My hope is ...., My hero is ...., I wish to become a ....

ROLE OF TEACHER IN PERSONALITY DEVELOPMENT OF CHILDREN

Teacher has to play a vital role to ensure favourable environment to foster the development of good personality of children. Teacher can develop a good (balanced) personality among the children by projecting these qualities through his own personality, showing related personalities of eminent persons through audio-visual aids, creating conductive social and emotional climate and environment in the school.

Chapter-31
Creativity

MEANING OF CREATIVITY

Creativity is derived from the word *'creo'* meaning *'to create'* or *'to make'*. Creativity was believed to be a gift of God which was to be found in highly talented people and geniuses. Therefore, the view that the very intelligent or very superior people would also be creative was held. Creativity was regarded as a rare quality of distinguished individuals. A creative person has an inborn talent. The relationship between creativity and intelligence is neither linear nor curvilinear. For a longtime creativity was considered to be associated with artistic individuals who have distinguished in various fields as painters, sculptures or writers, Creativity is distinguished by novelty, originality and is unusually inventive.

Creativity is the power of the mind to form new ideas and thoughts. It helps you imagine something new and special. For example drawing, painting, writing, comes from being able to wonder, appreciate and think about things and be inspired by them. For example if you draw well and you see a beautiful painting, you begin to wonder at its beauty. You ask yourself why you should not paint something as beautiful as the picture you have seen. Next day, you begin to draw or paint something of your own which is more beautiful than that you have seen. This is your creativity. So, creativity brings out something special in you.

DEFINITIONS OF CREATIVITY

Some of the definitions of creativity is given below:.

1. Spearman (1931), *"Creativity is the power of human mind to create new contents by transforming relations and generating new correlates".*
2. Guilford (1959), *"Creativity is the capacity to produce ideas that are both new and useful through divergent thinking".*
3. Drevdhal, J.E. (1956), *"Creativity is the capacity of a person to produce compositions, products or ideas which are essentially new or novel and previously unknown to the producer."*
4. Mc Kinnon, *"Creative is a process extended in time and characterized by original adaptiveness and realization."*
5. Taylor, *"A process is creative when it results in a novel work that is accepted as tenable, useful or satisfying by a group at a point in time."*
6. Torrance, *"Creativity is a process sensing gaps or disturbing missing elements, forming ideas or hypotheses communicating the result, possibly modifying and re-testing hypotheses."*

7. Bronowsky, *"It is distinguished between discovery, invention and creativity by saying that fact is discovered, theory is invented by only a masterpiece is created."*
8. Skinner defined the *"creative thinker is one who explores new ideas and makes new observation, new predictions and new inferences. Thus, creativity is the capacity or ability of an individual to create, discover or produce a new idea or object including the re-arrangement or reshaping of what is already known to him."*
9. Kobie (1958) defined as *"creativity implies invention, the uncovering of new facts or new relationships among new or old data."*
10. Guilford (1960) said that *"creativity refers to abilities that are most characteristics of creative people. Thus, creativity refers to the abilities of individuals to create or produce results of creative nature."*
11. Torrance (1962) defined *"creativity is the process of becoming sensitive to problems, deficiencies, gaps in knowledge, missing elements, disharmonies, and so forth".*
12. Ausubel (1963) defined *"creativity is a generalized constellation of intellectual abilities, personality variables and problem-solving traits".*
13. Thurstone defined *"creativity is an act of the thinker which comes suddenly to him and implies some novelty to him."*
14. Tylor (1964) defined *"a process is creative when it results in a novel work that is accepted as tenable, useful or satisfying by a group at a point in time."*
15. Stein (1974) defined *"creativity is a process which results in novel work that is accepted as tenable or useful or satisfying to a group of people at some point in time."*
16. Willach and Kogan (1965) defined *"creativity lies in producing more associations and in producing more that are unique."*
17. Baker (1962) defined *"creativity as bringing about notable changes in things, thoughts and social structure through action thinking which results in a situation not previously known to us."*
18. Vernon (1967) considers creativity mainly *"as an ability and a form of cognitive activity."*
19. According to Vernon (1967), *"creativity means the abilities and personality characteristics that underline the production of artistic or scientific work which is generally recognized as creative and original."*

If we will analyze the definitions of creativity, it seems to fall under four categories:

- The person who Crates
- Mental processes asserting within the person who creates.
- Cultural and environmental factors working on the creator.
- Products of creativity, i.e. poems, paintings, theories and inventions.

NATURE OF CREATIVITY

The following are the nature of creativity:

- *Creativity is Universal:* Creativity is not confined to any individual, groups of individuals, caste, colour, sex or creed. It has no boundary of age, location or culture. It is applicable to all stages of education and universal in nature.
- *Creativity Abilities are Natural:* It is not surrounded and developed with artificial and forceful situation. It can be nourished and nurtured by training and proper education. It is both innate and acquired.
- *Creative Expressions are New or Novel:* All individuals are creative in diverse ways and in different degrees. It is not restricted to a chosen few. It brings newness or novelty in the system or something new into being. The emphasis is on the newness and lack of previous existence of the idea or product.
- *Creative Expressions are Wider in Scope:* It has no limit or boundaries. It is a kind of adventurous and open thinking. It covers multifarious human accomplishments and all fields of human life.
- *Creative Expressions Carries Ego Involvement:* No one other than the creator can experience the warmth, happiness and satisfaction which he receives through his creation. The creator takes pride in his creation and hence makes ego involved statements like *'it is my idea'* and I have solved this problem, etc.
- Creative abilities are not completely spontaneous rather it requires constant understanding, discipline, hard work and patience to produce something new and unique. It is a kind of adventurous thinking and a departure from the closed thinking.
- Creativity is the ability to go beyond the immediate solution, redefine the problem or some part of it and unusual ideas and new approach to the problem. It involves many abilities like fluency, flexibility, originality and elaboration.

CHARACTERISTICS OF CREATIVITY

All the definitions reveal the following nature and characteristics of creativity:

- It is universal (individual, cast, colour, creed, age, location, culture)
- It is innate as well as acquired
- It produces something new or novel
- It is adventurous and open thinking (It encourages complete freedom to accept and express the multiplicity of responses)
- It carries ego involvement
- It has a wide scope
- No positive correlation between Creativity and Intelligence
- It rests more on divergent thinking than on convergent thinking
- It cannot be separated from intelligence
- Creativity and school achievement are not correlated
- Sociability and creativity are negatively correlated
- Creativity and anxiety often go together
- Creativity is the resultant of some interaction.
- Creativity is the ability to synthesize ideas or objects.
- It is a ability to create new ideas, theories or objects.

- It is a ability to develop something original.
- It is a process as well as a product.
- It is a complex and dynamic process.
- It knows no special medium, place, person or time.
- It is the capacity to accept challenges.
- It is readiness to change self and environment.

Torrence has compiled a list of eighty four characteristics of a creative person. Some of these are:

- A creative person is very adventurous.
- He is flexible in his thinking, feeling and doing.
- He is very keen to explore and invent.
- He is intuitive, self disciplined, visionary and willing to take risk.

On the whole, creative children are constantly probing, discovering, imagining, asking questions, guessing and wondering. Therefore, they should be encouraged to ask unusual questions, to explore new ways of thinking, to try novel approaches to problem solving, to play with ideas and material etc.

DIMENSIONS OR ELEMENTS OF CREATIVITY

According to Guilford, there are four creative thinking abilities: fluency, flexibility, originality and elaboration. The intellectual operation for these abilities is divergent and it can apply to all content areas. Generally creativity test (verbal or non-verbal) measure all the above dimensions of creativity. The description of five dimensions of creativity is given below:

1. Fluency

Fluency is the ability to think well and effortlessly in order to generate a quantity of ideas, responses, solutions or questions. (Brainstorming builds fluency). *Ex: List all things you can think of that are blue or have the word "blue" in them (Butterfly, sea, sky, blueberry)*

Researches in the field of creativity have revealed that highly creative persons are thought to be more fluent in their thinking and able to generate alternative ideas in great variety and large quantity. The three types of fluency are:

Ideational Fluency: Examples of this competency include writing large number of acceptable plot titles for untitled literary works and imagining many consequences of a change in the environment or in the conditions of life (e.g. suppose the world's supply of oil would dry up; list as many consequences as you can imagine). This is called *ideational fluency* because it denotes skills in generating quantities of ideas in a language context.

Associational Fluency: *Associational fluency* is the ability to produce many relationship or meaningful associations with a given idea. It is evident by the quantity of synonyms a person can attach to any familiar word that has many meanings or it characterizes thinking by analogy.

Expressional Fluency: *Expressional fluency* refers to skills in juxtaposing words to meet sentence structure requirements. It is the production of alternative organized thoughts. A sequence of words in a sentence represents a thought system.

2. Flexibility

Flexibility is the ability to easily abandon old ways of thinking, adopt new ones, and produce ideas, responses, questions or solutions in a variety of categories. Flexibility generates a variety of ideas. *Ex: Write many uses of paper?*

The skill of being to able discontinue an existing pattern of thought and shift to new patterns or shifts from one set of assumption or approach to another is called flexibility. The two types of flexibility are:

Spontaneous Flexibility: Spontaneous flexibility deals with changes in direction of thinking when a person is not instructed to do so. For example, in listing the various uses of a brick, the flexible individual tends to produce ideas relating not only to the weight of the object but also to its size, colour, shape, texture and so on.

Adaptive Flexibility: Adaptive flexibility deals with changes in direction of thinking to solve problems. In this case, content is figural, such as geometric forms which the persons use to make as many objects as possible.

3. Originality

It is the ability to develop ideas that are statistically unusual, novel or unique. *Ex: Invent a machine to help you clean your room. Be sure to write down details on how the machine works, what it uses, and what it is made of. Draw a picture of your new invention and give it a creative title.*

The process of originality is on products that are unexpected and sometimes amusing. It is found out that divergent production is the generation of logical alternatives to fit the needs of given information and that logical alternatives depend upon the original ideas of the person concerned. Thus, creativity is the process of originality, uniqueness and even sometimes idiosyncratic ways of doing things or showing problems.

4. Elaboration

Elaboration is the ability to add details in order to modify or expand upon an idea or a general scheme.

Elaboration is seen in facility in giving details to round out a complex innovation, such as an organized plan or how much skilled in planning and organization. For example, a person demonstrates the ability to fill in all of the various details necessary to make a briefly outlined project depends upon the elaboration.

5. Sensitivity

It is the ability to notice and perceive the problems before others notice it or see it again.

STAGES OF CREATIVE THINKING

Graham Wallas, one of the leading psychologists of early twentieth century stated that there are five stages of creative thinking. These are *Preparation, incubation, illumination, evaluation,* and *revision.* The briefly discuss of these five steps of creative thinking is given below:

1. Preparation: This is the first stage in which the thinker formulates the problem and collects facts and materials necessary for the solution. He/she finds that the problem cannot be solved after days, weeks, or months of concentrated effort. Unable to solve the problem the thinker deliberately or involuntarily turns away from the problem, initiating stage two i.e. incubation. At this stage of problem solving, it is important to overcome negative consequences of mental set and any kind of mental set or bias.

2. Incubation: This is a stage of no solution and involves a number of emotional and cognitive complexities. However, the negative effects of mental set, functional fixedness, and other ideas that interfere with the solution tend to fade. Perhaps, fatigue and too much of concern with the problem also mount up during this period. Further, the unconscious thought processes involved in creative thinking are at work during this stage.

3. Illumination: In this stage a potential solution to the problem seems to be realized as if from nowhere. It is about having the insight about the possible solution. Illumination occurs with its *"aha"* experience when a sudden idea or solution appears into consciousness.

4. Evaluation: In this stage the obtained solution is verified or tested to see if it works. Frequently, the insight may turn out to be unsatisfactory, and may need some modification in the strategy of approaching the problem.

5. Revision: Revision is required in the case a solution which is not satisfactory.

It has been found that creative people are generally talented (e.g. artists, musicians, mathematicians etc.), and have specific abilities. Creative people have been found to have some specific personality characteristics such as they are independent in their judgments, self-assertive, dominant, impulsive, prefer complexity, etc.

CREATIVITY AS A PRODUCT

Creativity in terms of product refers to the capacity of individual by which something new is produced, i.e., an idea or an object including a new form or arrangement of old elements.

CREATIVITY AS A PROCESS

Creativity in terms of process refers to the act of mind that calls into play, motivation, perception, learning and thinking. According to Rogers *"the creative process is the emergence in action of a novel relational product growing out of the uniqueness of the individual on the one-hand and materials, events, people or circumstances of his life on the other"*.

CHARACTERISTICS OF A CREATIVE PERSON

According to Tylor, the characteristics of a Creative Person are the following:

- Strong memory powers and full of new ideas about things;
- Tendency to evaluate the ideas and actions of self and others;
- Flexible and open minded;
- All the four qualities like originality, fluency, flexibility and power of elaboration;

- Sensitivity to problems, openness to new ideas and experiences;
- Curiosity and having intellectual persistence;
- Tendency to seek challenges and manipulative ideas;
- Preferring complex ideas and tolerance for ambiguity;
- Commitment to work and inclination to take risk;
- Resourceful, adventurous and extrovert; and
- More perseverance and less traditional-bound.

Torrance indicated that a creative person is a:

- divergent thinker;
- forming ideas or hypothesis—concerning problem;
- testing these hypothesis and communicating the results;
- capable of modifying and retesting the hypothesis;
- original, useful and socially accepted abilities and
- development of novel approach to solve problems.

The researchers in their findings concluded the following behavioural characteristics of a creative person:

- Flexible and open minded
- Suggest better ways of doing a job
- Originality of ideas and expression
- Ability to use material, words or ideas in new ways
- Bold and emotionally sensitive, resourceful, radical or a sense of adventure and curious nature
- A high degree of awareness, enthusiasm and concentration
- Self-discipline and capacity to integrate things
- Respect for the opinions of others
- Humorous, playful, dominant and self-assertive
- Lack of rigidity, high values, intolerant for injustice, enjoy strange ideas, rich imagination and expressive
- Need for autonomy and- have high aspirations
- Sense of self-confidence and reserve and
- Venturesome and pursuit of self-chosen interests

TECHNIQUES FOR FOSTERING CREATIVITY

Some special techniques for fostering creativity in students are:

Brainstorming

It was developed by Osborn in 1957. It is the strategy or technique for allowing a group to explore ideas without judgment or censure. The children may be asked to sit in a group for solving a problem and attacking it without any inhibition from many angles.

Lateral thinking

It is solving problems through an indirect and creative approach, using reasoning that is not immediately obvious and involving ideas. The term was coined in 1967 by Edward de Bono. It is sometimes referred to in business, to use your inspiration and imagination to solve problems by looking at them from unexpected perspectives. Lateral thinking involves discarding the obvious, leaving behind traditional modes of thought, and throwing away preconceptions.

Synectics

It is derived from the Latin word *'Synetikos'* meaning *'hold together'*. Synectics is a problem solving methodology that stimulates thought processes of which the subject may be unaware. This method was developed by George M. Prince and William J.J. Gordon in 1961.

ROLE OF TEACHER IN FOSTERING STUDENT'S CREATIVITY

The role of teacher in fostering student's creativity is as under:

- Freedom to respond
- Opportunity for ego involvement
- Encouraging originality and flexibility
- Removal of hesitation and fear
- Providing appropriate opportunities and atmosphere for creative expression.
- Developing health habits among children
- Using the creative resources of the community
- Avoidance of blocks to creative thinking
- Proper organization of the curriculum
- Reform in the evaluation system
- Use special techniques for fostering creativity.
- Teaching by example

EDUCATIONAL IMPLICATIONS OF CREATIVITY

If anything you will prepare, you must think how this can be used. Here you know that how creativity can be identified and you also have prepared a creativity test. So you should use it. Before using it, you should know how you can use it.

You know that creativity is a natural endowment. It needs stimulation and nourishment. Most creative talent, if not given proper training, education and opportunity for creativity expression, results in wastage. Moreover, creativity is universal. It is not the monopoly of a few geniuses only. Every one of us to certain degree possesses creative abilities. In a democratic set up like owners, it is not only the geniuses who are needed to create, manifest and produce, others whether mediocre or below averages are also required to think, to construct and to creative.

Creativity tests are useful in finding the nature and amount of creativity among the children. This also helps us to provide proper environment and guidance to develop the originality of the individual in a fully fledged way. We can organize various activities and situations to develop creativity among children according to their abilities. These are:

Freedom to Respond: Adequate freedom should be given to children in responding to a situation. They should be encouraged to think about as many ideas as they may for the solution of a problem.

Opportunity for Involvement: The feelings like *'It is my creation', 'I have solved'* give much satisfaction to children. Therefore opportunity should be provided to them to derive satisfaction from creating.

Encouraging Originality and Flexibility: Originality on the part of children in any form should be encouraged. They should also be asked to solve problems. They should essentially be encouraged to do it.

Removal of Hesitation and Fear: The cause of hesitation and fear for doing any work should be discovered and removed as far as possible.

Providing Appropriate Opportunities and Atmosphere: A healthy favourable atmosphere for creative thinking and expression is an essential condition for the stimulation and nourishment of creativity among children.

Developing Healthy Habits among Children: Industriousness, persistence, reliance and self confidence are some of the qualities that are helpful in creative output. Therefore children should be helped to imbibe these qualities.

Using the Creative Resources of the Community: Children should be made to visit the centers of creative art or scientific and industrial creative work. Occasionally, the creative artists, scientists or creative persons from other fields may also invited to schools to help enhance the span of knowledge of children and kindly the spark of creativity among them.

Avoidance of Blocks to Creative Thinking: Factors like conservatism, faulty methods of teaching, rigid habits of work, unsympathetic treatment should be avoided.

Proper Organization of the Curriculum: Curriculum should reflect what it desires from the creative children in terms of fluency, flexibility, originality, divergent thinking, inventiveness and elaboration etc.

Use of Special Techniques: Besides these uses, special techniques also should be used to foster creativity, Researchers have suggested some special techniques like. Brain Storming: It is a technique which emphasizes the important of divergent thinking. It involves generating ideas in response to some problems in a group. It allows children to attack and solve a problem without any inhibition or restriction.

Providing the Self Examples and Ideals: Self example is better than precept.' Children are very imitative. Therefore the presents, teachers and elders should try to develop the habit of creative thinking among themselves.

Besides these, gaming techniques, encouraging debates, discussions, providing activities like drama, dance music etc. should be arranged for the children to develop their creativity.

After identifying creative children, adequate and appropriate provisions should be made for their education and training, because the future of mankind depends upon the development of their creative potential.

MEASUREMENT OF CREATIVITY

To measure creativity, there are many standardized tests available in India and abroad. These are:

- Minnesota Tests of Creative Thinking
- Guilford Divergent Thinking Instruments
- Wallach and Kogan Creativity Instruments
- Torrance Tests of Creative Thinking

- Baquer Medhi's Test of Creative Thinking
- Passi's Test of Creativity
- Sharma's Divergent Production Abilities Test
- Acharyulu's Think Creativity

On the basis of these tests, the creative abilities of several dimensions of one's behaviour can be measured.

TORRANCE TESTS OF CREATIVE THINKING

The Torrance test of creative thinking is one such test which can be used in primary and secondary schools. This test consists of verbal and figural activities and measures fluency, flexibility, originality and elaboration. Some of the tasks in this test are given below. The figural forms as a non-verbal testing device make use of tasks that require drawing and picturization. The activities required in the non-verbal subtests are the following:

1. Figural or Picture Completion Tests or Incomplete Figures

In this subtest, there are some incomplete figures. The subject is asked to complete these figures by adding new dimensions or lines for providing new ideas. Further he/she is asked to give suitable titles for the completed figures or pictures.

2. Picture Construction Test

In this subtest, the subject is provided with a piece of coloured paper cut in curved shape and asked to think of a figure or picture of which this piece of paper may be a part. He/She is asked to provide a suitable title for this picture.

3. Parallel Lines Test or Repeated Figures

In this subtest, there are several parts of straight lines and circles. The subject is required to draw as many objects or pictures by using each pair and circle. He/She is asked to provide a title for each of his/her drawings.

Similarly, the verbal forms incorporate tasks, which require the use of language. The subject is required to provide written responses to the questions put to him/her. The tasks in this form are the following:

4. Ask and Guess Type

In the asking type of activities, the subject is encouraged to show his ability in such a way so that normal human being cannot perceive it. Here, the subject is asked questions needed to know exactly what is happening in the drawing. Similarly, in the guessing aspect, he/she is asked to guess as many causes as possible in the picture and its consequences of what is taking place in the picture.

5. Product Improvement Type

Here the subject is asked to suggest ways and means of improving a toy, a machine or some other such product to make it interesting and useful as far as possible.

6. Unusual Uses Type

Here the subject is asked to think about the number of ways in which a product may be used. He/She is to enumerate as many interesting and unusual uses he/she can think of an object like card board box, knife or brick be used.

7. Unusual Question Type
Here the subject is asked as many unusual questions as he/she can put about a picture, scene or verbal description of phenomena.

8. Just Suppose Type
Here the respondent is asked to guess what would happen if a certain situation occurred? It means he/she is to predict the outcomes of unusual situations like what would have happened if you had been selected as Prime Minister of India?

Thus, combining both verbal and figural forms, Torrance test of creativity evaluate the creative abilities of an individual.

Thus, for creativity there is no correct response. It is new or original and unique. It is the capacity or ability of an individual to create, discover or produce a new idea or object including the rearrangement or reshaping of what is already known to him.

The creative person is a divergent thinker. He discovers or offers uncommon thoughts or ideas, unexpected suggestions and unconventional views. Andrews (1961) defines a creative person has a positive self-integrating force, a process of self-actualization and expression of being.

Chapter-32
Impact of Media on Growing Children and Adolescents

Education today has a far greater responsibility than it had ever before. It has to meet the demands of a dynamic world which change its character every day. Contemporary education has to be more comprehensive and complete than it was ever before. The role of the various agencies of education like home, society, community etc. has consequently increased, so has the role of the mass media like television, radio, cinema, newspaper increased. So now-a-day, press, radio, cinema, television, etc. are becoming more and more important in an individual's life.

MEANING OF MEDIA

Media is a term referring to those organized means of dissemination of fact, opinion, entertainment and other information, such as newspapers, magazines, out-of- home advertising, cinema films, radio, television, the World Wide Web, books, CDs, DVDs, videocassettes, video games and other forms of publishing. Academic programmes for the study of mass media are usually referred to as mass communication programmes.

MEANING MEDIA OR MASS-MEDIA

Mass Media refers to the means of public communication reaching a large audience. When members of the general public refer to *"the media"* they are usually referring to the mass media, or to the news media, which is a section of the mass media. Sometimes mass media are referred to as the *"corporate media"*.

In its word meaning, the term mass-media stands for the media (means and mode of communication) for the masses. It can thus represent all channels, means and modes that can be used for conveying information, messages or appeal simultaneously to a number of people breaking the barrier of location, places and timings. It can exist in audio, video or multi sensory forms and thus may appeal a number of senses for producing lasting effects or impressions on the minds and hearts of the individual.

CLASSIFICATION OF MASS MEDIA

Media refers to any kind of format used to convey information. Mass Media refers to those types of media that are designed to reach large numbers of people. The various types of mass media are:

- Television (cable, network, satellite, etc.)
- Radio

- Film & Video
- Print (newspapers, magazines, direct mail, etc.)
- Photography
- Electronic (E-mail, the Web, etc.)
- News papers and magazines
- Books (Printed and e-form)
- Advertisement
- Radio Broadcast
- Telecasts
- Films and Movies
- Internet and Web material
- The modern communication means like messages and audio-video material loaded on smart phones, face book, Blogs, Twitter etc.

All media produce a variety of genres, which refers to a particular type of style or content. Mass media genres can be divided into four basic types:

- *Informative media*- such as news shows, newspapers, informative Web sites, etc.
- *Educational media*- such as books, educational video, or educational software programmes.
- *Persuasive media*- such as all types of advertising, television infomercials, newspaper editorials, or Web sites that attempt to persuade.
- *Entertainment media*- such as entertainment magazines, movies, novels or entertainment related Web sites.

IMPORTANCE OF MASS MEDIA

- Mass Media provide information to the mass within a less time.
- It takes a wide coverage of information regarding anything that is happening in any comer of the world.
- It brings the entire world to the individual or to the classroom. Children spend hours together sitting in front of the television and can visualize, hear and acquire knowledge about the world.
- These media easily reach groups, allow repeated use, give more reality, influence attitudes, show cause and effect relationships and ultimately motivate the audience.
- It sends information to remote places and helps in distant learning.
- It helps in modification of attitudes, inculcation of desirable values and acquaintance with cultural heritage.
- Mass media acts as an agency of social change.
- Mass media are useful for reinforcing group dynamics and interpersonal communication.
- Mass media as means of communication make ideas clear to children and help them to acquire correct knowledge. They help in simplifying and in giving vividness to explanation.
- Mass Media make the instruction concrete and stimulate interest and excite curiosity in things.

IMPACT OF MASS MEDIA ON GROWING CHILDREN AND ADOLESCENTS

Mass media play a quite dominant role in influencing behaviour and development of the children and adolescents in a number of ways and forms. What they read, listen and watch through the mass media appeal to their senses and goes deeply in the minds and hearts in a great way and as a result they may learn and imbibe so many things in their habits, ways of behaving and doing that may go to shape the events of their life in a particular way. The impact of Mass Media on Growing Children and Adolescents can be best understand with the following points (Mangal, 2015):

- When the children and adolescents read about the things and events in newspapers, pamphlets, magazines and books etc., it may catch their attention and get them acquainted with so many things-positive as well as negative.
- It can add to broaden their mental horizon and learn so many things.
- Learning as we know can result in the desirable or undesirable developments of interests, attitudes, habits, temperament and so many other personality traits. It happens also in the case of the children's exposure to reading material. They may not only get acquainted with the goods and evils, virtues and vices but also consciously and unconsciously try to imbibe them in their behaviour.
- The audio-visual and multi-media means like radio and television, films and movies and what is available to them on their computer and mobiles screen, exercise much greater influences in shaping their behaviour and personality then their verbal comprehension of the material available in the newspapers, magazines and books.
- The learning takes place in a more organized way. It is multi-sensory and observational learning much superior to the verbal. When a child observes his most liked actor or actress to perform or do certain types of acts or behaviour, he can't resist the desire to get it copied in his behaviour. It is nothing but hero worships that in most common among children and especially in adolescents.
- As a part of social learning as advocated by Bandura (1977), all such observations of their part are imitated, practiced and assimilated in their behaviour on the part of children and adolescents who get exposed to such type of mass media experiences.
- The easy and unlimited availability of such multimedia exposure to the youngsters through the developed electronic and computer means has almost revolutionized such type of social learning. As a result, we may find tremendous changes in the interests, attitudes, ways of thinking, feeling and behaving of the youngsters-affecting the task of shaping and developing their personality in a positive or negative way.
- The exposure to available mass media resources has resulted in increasing awareness towards the things and events concerning one's environment.
- The children and adolescents of today have much opportunity to get exposed to their physical, social and cultural environment-local, regional national and international in comparison to a few decades ago. Hence, much credit

for the development in the cognitive behaviour of the children goes the mass-media.

- Mass media is also credited for bringing rapid changes in social, emotional, language, communication and aesthetic development of the youngsters. Mass media have given them enough opportunities for getting acquainted with the social and cultural life of their own and others. They may know how people behave and live in their own region country, or other parts of the Globe. It has thus contributed in understanding the people living on this earth, developing global understanding, cooperation and collaboration.
- Mass media in also credited for removing a number of social barriers, stereotypes, social evils, discriminations, marginalization and misunderstandings among the members of a community, regions and nations.
- Children and youths of today are proceeding towards a global society or community, having less rigidity and bondage of caste, colour, religion, language, nationality etc. They are having inter-caste, inter-religion and international relationships, friendships and marriages. It is all happening with the services of the developed mass media platforms and related technologies.

DECONSTRUCTION OF SIGNIFICANT EVENTS THAT MEDIA HIGHLIGHTS AND CREATES

Media has a strong appeal to influence the behaviour and development of children and adolescents. Deconstruction is process of analyzing or breaking down a thing into its components or elements in order to understand its nature and characteristics in a better way. In this way, when a news items, story or television episode appears before the children, they must be helped in making its analysis for learning or picking up the inherent meanings. In our day to day language by the term deconstruction we mean a process of reconstructing a structure. It refers to a process of falling walls, only to build them again for sorting our requirements in the desirable way.

Deconstruction provides one a way to have an objective assessment of the things conveyed through media. It helps in bringing and picking up positive messages from tin[1] things conveyed and displayed over media. Through deconstruction, we can replace or give more weight age to the things which leave more positive results and impressions on the minds and hearts of the children in terms of their wellbeing and progress. Similarly, deconstruction of the events portrayed by media, should be made in such a way as to help in developing necessary social values, democratic virtues, ethical norms and humanity among the developing children. They must be helped in getting rid of social evils, stereotypes and marginalization practices prevalent in the society. As illustration of such desirable deconstruction of media events we can cite the things like below (Mangal, 2015):

- In working over deconstructing news or events related to communal riots occurring at some place in the country, the emphasis should be in highlighting the role of somebody (individual, group, organization) who helped the victims of riots by risking his or her life with no consideration of caste or religion.

- In the deconstruction of the reporting and display the terrorist activities by the media, while terrorism should he-condemned as a most inhuman, uncivilized and cowardice act, due care should be taken not to brand and portrait all the people belonging to a particular community, race or caste as the villains, bad guys or terrorists.
- The reports and displays in the newspaper, TV channels, movies or other electronic media should be presented before children in such a manner or children should be helped in deriving purposeful meaning and lessons from them as to inculcate among them the habits and attitudes related to:
  - love for animals and birds.
  - pollution free environment.
  - cleanliness and tree-plantation
  - freedom from superstitions, misbeliefs, prejudices and stereotypes,
  - faith in democracy and democratic values including secularism, equity, equality, liberty, peaceful coexistence and universal brotherhood,
  - opposition to any type of discrimination injustice, oppression and marginalization on one or the other accounts.
  - love for nature, adventurism, creativity and invention.
  - Self-confidence, Self-efficacy, Self-learning and Self-esteem.
  - Striving for integrated wholesome development of their personality.
  - Loyalty and contribution towards the progress of the society and nation.
- In reporting and display of the media it should be so featured or de-constructed as to provide the masses including children a clear message that in a democratic society wedded to equity, equality, liberty and secularism, all have equal opportunities to get ahead on the path of their development and progress irrespective of their gender, caste, race, language or religion.
- The achievements of the girls and women in academic, sport, vocational, political and social field should be acknowledged, and appreciated.
- The rise of the children from poverty ridden environment, rural and tribal belts, socially and culturally deprived families to extra ordinary positions.
- The incidence of providing due opportunities and encouragement for education and development of the girl child on the part of parents, families, societies and communities should be highlighted and produced.

Chapter-33
Mental Health and Mental Hygiene

One of the most important aims of education is to help the individual in making adjustment with the changing environment. It is the mental health which helps the person to adjust in the environment. Mental health stands for the health of the mind Carter V. Good in the Dictionary of Education (1959 P. 263) has termed it as "The wholesomeness of the mind".

It is a state or condition on which an individual feels a sense of well being. This condition also provides an individual the capacity to be resilient to the stresses her / meets and to respond to these challenges without having to compromise his well being. This also makes him productive and fruitful for himself and his community.

MEANING OF MENTAL HEALTH

The concept of mental health is as old as human beings. Our ancient scriptures are full of references to mental diseases. But this concept is comparatively new even in the West. Burmham who emphasizes the importance of integration or wholeness of personality said "*a mentally healthy person is one who has a balanced personality, free from schism and inconsistencies, emotional and nervous tension, discords and conflicts. a well adjusted person can deal with his potentialities as well as he can accept his limitations.*"

Health is often used to refer to a state of physical, mental, social and spiritual wellbeing of the individual. Thus, mental health is one of the components of the broad concept of health. It is concerned with an optimum level of emotional and behavioural adjustment of the individual. It is a state of maintaining harmony or balance between the needs, desires, aspirations and attitudes of the individual with respect to the prevailing conditions in the external environment.

In order to understand mental health in a better way you are also required to know the meaning of mental ill-health and mental illness.

MENTAL ILL-HEALTH

Mental ill-health is defined as the absence of the qualities of positive mental health in the individual. For example if someone among you often displays negative feelings and attitudes about others, you can assume that this person is displaying the characteristics of mental ill-health.

MENTAL ILLNESS

Mental illness is a broad term which includes almost all the disorders of behaviour which are caused by faulty perception, emotion, thinking and attitude. Such individuals have problems in making adjustment with others in the society. We will discuss the categories of mental illness in lesson.

DIFFERENCE BETWEEN MENTAL HEALTHY AND MENTAL UNHEALTHY

From the above discussion we can easily distinguish between the mentally healthy and unhealthy person in the following ways:

Table 33.1: Difference between Mental Healthy and Mental Unhealthy

Mental Healthy	*Mental Unhealthy*
1. Aware about their self and have some respect for others	1. Not aware about their own self and have no respect for others
2. Understand one's own limitation and also can tolerate others limitation.	2. Can't understand one's own limitation and can't tolerate others limitation.
3. They can understand that all behaviour is causal.	3. They can't understand the cause of behaviour.
4. They can understand the basic needs that motivate behaviour.	4. They can't understand the basic needs which motivate behaviour.

Mental health is, thus, a condition of psychological maturity. It is a condition of personal and social functioning with a maximum of effectiveness and satisfaction. A mentally healthy person is responsible, self reliant and has a true sense of individuality. He has a realistic life goal as well as philosophy of life and values. He can differentiate between the right and the wrong.

DEFINITIONS OF MENTAL HEALTH

1. WHO (2001) defines mental health as, *"A state of complete physical, mental and social well being and not merely the absence of disease or infirmity."*
2. *"A state of emotional and psychological well being in which an individual is able to use his or her cognitive and emotional capabilities function in society, and meet the ordinary demands of everyday life."*

CHARACTERISTICS OF MENTAL HEALTH

On the basis of the above discussion, the following are the main characteristics of mental health:

- Concept of mental health is subjective
- Mental health is depending on sound physical health.
- Measurement of mental health is difficult as we don't have any standard.
- Mental health depends on many factors.
- Criteria of mental health may be different from country to country.
- Mental health is synonymous to balance personality.
- Mental health is also related with stress and strain of life.
- Nothing called perfect mental health – No person is with perfect mental health rather it is optimum mental health.
- Mental health is a dynamic concept: Mental health denotes a state of balance or equilibrium of our mind, this balance is not static, it is quite dynamic.
- Mental health can't be achieved without physical health. For achieving an optimal level of mental health one has to first acquire adequate physical health.

- Mental health and efficiency is not the same thing – One may be quite efficient and successful at his work or profession but he could be most unhappy, full of anxiety etc.
- Mental health and social ability is not the same thing- A mentally healthy person is sociable. It is not necessary for a sociable or socially adaptable person to be healthy minded.
- Mental health differs from ethical standards – Morality does not guarantee mental health.

IMPORTANCE OF MENTAL HEALTH

Mental health has much wider scope than physical health as it aims for the development of wholesome balanced and integrated personality. Mental health is very important because of following things:

Helps in the Development of Desirable Personality: Mental health helps in the development of a wholesome, well-balanced and integrated personality.

Helps in Proper Emotional Development: The individuals who enjoy good mental health are supposed to demonstrate proper emotional maturity in their behaviour. On the other side, those who are tense, disintegrated and mentally unhealthy demonstrate sudden emotional outburst.

Helps in Proper Social Development: One's mental health helps one in becoming sociable and establishing proper social relationships in the society.

Helps in Proper Moral Development: The individuals who enjoy sound mental health are usually found to behave as men of integrity and character by following the ethical standards of the society.

Helps in Proper Aesthetic Development: Proper mental health helps the individual in the development of appropriate aesthetic sense, artistic taste and refined temperament.

Helps in Seeking Proper Adjustment: A mentally healthy individual is an adjusted person. He is able to adjust his needs as per the demands of the situation and well being of the society.

Helps in Seeking Goals of Life: Optimum mental health always helps the individuals to divert his energies in full capacity for the realization of the goals.

Helps in Progress of the Society: Mental health helps the individual to develop as well balanced useful citizens who are conscious not only of their rights but also of their responsibilities.

Helps in Prevention of Mental Illness: A sound mental health and balanced personality has enough resistance to fight against the odds of life and bear the accidental stresses and strains of life in comparison to those with impaired mental health.

INDICATORS/SIGNS OF POOR MENTAL HEALTH

As human beings we are required to maintain sound mental health. However, we develop certain behaviours and habits which can lead to a poor state of mental health. Such behaviours range from mild irritation to severe forms of anxiety and depression. The main behaviours which indicate poor mental health are as follows:

- Haphazard and disorganized daily life routine.
- Short-tempered and irritating behaviour.
- Anger and aggressive behaviour.
- Restlessness.
- Increased or poor appetite and indigestion.
- Irregular sleeping pattern such as insomnia, disturbed sleep, or narcolepsy (excess sleep).
- Poor interpersonal relationships.
- Anxiety and worry.
- Negative attitude toward self and others.
- Withdrawing from relationships.
- Irregular and abnormal physiological conditions (e.g., blood pressure, heart palpitation, and pulse rate).
- Excessive use of drugs (e.g., alcohol, tranquillizers, and hallucinogens).
- Cigarette smoking and use of tobacco in other forms.

The above may cause threat to mental health. If an individual is frequently involved in such behaviours or remains in a particular state for a long period then it is more likely that (s)he may develop various kinds of mental disorders.

FACTORS AFFECTING MENTAL HEALTH

Mental health plays a crucial role in the development of the personality but there are many factors which help in developing positive or negative development of mental health. Mental ill health is caused by different factors which have been described by different authors in different ways. Here we are presenting some of the models which explain the causes of mental ill health. These are:

Socio Cultural Model: Socio Cultural Model emphasizes the role of social condition, such as poverty discrimination, casteism, violence etc. as the basic causes of poor mental health.

Medical Model: Medical Model emphasizes the role of various organic conditions that affect our brain functioning.

Psycho Analytical Model: Psycho Analytical model emphasizes the stress situations that involve a threat to the individual's psyche. It gives importance to early childhood experiences as a major factor for mental ill health.

Behaviouristic Model: Behaviouristic model gives importance to faulty learning such as the failure to learn necessary adaptive behaviour.

The Interpersonal Model emphasizes the unsatisfactory interpersonal relationship among human beings.

Besides these models, different authors have given some more causes to understand the factors responsible for ill mental health. These are:

Primary Cause: The primary cause is the condition without which the mental ill health would have not occurred.

Predisposing Cause: A predisposing cause is a condition that comes before and paves the way for later maladjustment For example: if a child is very much rejected in his early childhood, he may develop some mental disorder.

Precipitating Cause: A precipitating cause is a condition that proves too much to bear for the individual and triggers maladaptive behaviour. For example, the sudden death of one's father may cause mental disorder for that reason.

Reinforcing Cause: A reinforcing cause is a condition that tends to maintain the maladaptive behaviour already present such as playing a 'sick role' and relieved from unwanted responsibility say for family.

MEANING OF MENTAL HYGIENE

Mental hygiene is a Science which deals with the process of attaining mental health and preserving mental health in the society. The term mental health is closely related with the term mental hygiene as the main objective of mental hygiene is to attain mental health. In other words, mental hygiene is a means of mental health. That is why we can say that mental hygiene is the means and mental health is the end.

DEFINITIONS OF MENTAL HYGIENE

There are many definitions of the term mental hygiene. Some of the definitions are mentioned below:

According to Klien, *"Mental hygiene is an endeavour to aid people to ward off trouble as well as to furnish ways of handling trouble in intelligent fashion when it cannot be warded off."* To him, these troubles may be:

- Illness
- Finances
- Social Position
- Religion
- Sex
- Economic Security
- Old Age
- Inadequate Shelter etc.

According to Rivillin, mental hygiene:

- Means the application of a body of hygiene information and technique.
- It is taken from the sciences of Psychology, Child psychology, Education, Sociology, Psychiatry, Medicine and Biology.
- It cares for the purpose of the preservation and improvement of mental health of the individual and community.
- It is meant for prevention and cure of minor and major mental diseases and defects of mental, educational and social maladjustment.

The History of mental hygiene is old as our civilization. In India, Ayurveda successfully developed a full fledged system for treating the mentally ill people long back. But, in the West the mental hygiene movement started in the first decade of the 20th century. Clifford Beers, a graduate of Yale University can be regarded as the father of mental hygiene. He being frustrated with his life once attempted to commit suicide in the year 1908. But, luckily he was saved and treated for his mental illness. After recovery he wrote a book entitled *"A Mind That Found Itself"*, where he described about his illness and the type of treatment he had received. This book created a revolution among the general public for the necessity of mental hygiene. Gradually many Institute of Mental

Hygiene were established in India as well as in many other parts of the World to train personnel in the field of mental hygiene.

OBJECTIVES OF MENTAL HYGIENE

Mental Hygiene is a science. The main objective of mental hygiene is to build up one's ego rather than tearing down another's ego. It tries to develop the power of tolerance and praise and discourages the habit of blaming others. Hence, we can say that the approach of mental hygiene is positive rather than negative. The main objectives of the mental hygiene can be summarized as shown below:

To Help to Realizes One's Potentiality: Every individual possess certain potentialities. Mental hygiene tries to help each individual to develop his/her potentialities.

To Develop Self-respect and Respect for Others: Loss of self-respect is one of the factors for the great majorities of emotional disorders. A person who likes himself can like others and one who dislikes himself cannot like anybody. Hence, the main aim of mental hygiene is to help one to respect oneself.

To Understand One's Limitations and Tolerate the Limitations of Others: Mental hygiene helps one to understand his own limitations as well as to tolerate others' limitations.

To Cause Harmonious Development: Mental hygiene aims at the harmonious development of the physical mental and spiritual capacities of the individual so that he can adjust himself in the environment.

To Create Happiness: Another objective of mental hygiene is to develop a positive attitude towards life so as to create a sense of happiness in a person who can live happily in this world.

To Enable One to Make Effective Adjustment: Mental hygiene also prepares an individual for effective adjustment in all sphere of life and all situations such as in school, home, society work and also with self.

To Enable One to Know His or Her Self: Many of us do not know our own self. We are not at all aware about our potentialities, weaknesses, limitations etc. for which many individuals suffer from different types of confusion. Mental Hygiene helps an individual to know himself.

FUNCTIONS OF MENTAL HYGIENE

Mental hygiene has four important functions. These are:

Prevention or Preventive: The most important function of mental hygiene is to prevent mental health problems by developing some programmes.

Creative: Another function of mental illness is to develop programme like counseling, psychotherapy to treat an individual or a group or to treat a mental patient.

Preservative: Not all people are mentally ill; rather of them possess sound mental health. So the third function is to develop programme through education for preserving mental health.

Training: Another function of mental hygiene is to train a set of personnel who can help the people with psychological problem by trying to understand their problems and then helping them to meet their needs.

PRINCIPLES OF MENTAL HYGIENE

To formulate general principles of mental hygiene is a really difficult task as there is a wide range of differences among the individuals. Some of the reasons for this are:

- Human beings have multiple needs which grow in the course of development. These needs are contradictory in nature.
- There is no single, also absolute standard to judge human behaviour or action. However, in spite of these difficulties, we can formulate some general principles. These are:

Adjustment in Home: Every child should develop such type of behaviour at home so that he can adjust himself in any type of situation. Parents should take utmost care because the behaviour patterns that develop in early childhood leave permanent impression on the child. Parents should try to develop the desirable traits in their children and develop competence, security, adequacy, self esteem and discipline by catering to their basic needs.

Adjustment in School: After home, school plays an important role in the development of personality. The school through its various activities can go a long way in creating an environment for the children to preserve and develop their mental health.

Adjustment to Society: Man is a social animal and he has to adjust himself with the society. Without proper social interaction, harmonious development of personality cannot occur. Hence, parent's, teacher and society must provide socially acceptable channels for the release of pent up emotional feeling so that the children and adolescents develop healthy personality.

Adjustment to Work: According to Freud, one is mentally healthy, if one can work successfully. School through its programme, should develop the proper mental state towards work in child.

MENTAL HYGIENE STRATEGIES FOR GOOD MENTAL HEALTH

The term *mental hygiene* is closely related to mental health. We use the term hygiene to refer to keeping oneself and one's living and working areas neat and clean in order to prevent illness and disease. When we extend this concept to the domain of mind it stands for the art of developing, maintaining and promoting necessary behavioural, emotional and social skills to sustain good, effective and efficient mental health. One can achieve this by following some basic strategies at mental and behavioural levels in one's daily life. These are as follows:

Reality Contact: In order to maintain good and sound mental health it is important to have a realistic appraisal of one's own reactions, emotions, and abilities. If you are in touch with reality you may be able to avoid a number of disappointments and frustrations in your daily life.

Impulse Control: A person with healthy adjustment would have good control over his/her behaviours and impulses. So in order to maintain good mental health it is necessary that you should be in complete control over your impulsive behaviours.

Self-Esteem: The awareness about oneself is called self-concept. It includes all the statements about "I" or "me" expressed in terms of feelings, beliefs and values. Thus self-concept is sum total of all that a person is aware about his or her own self. Self-esteem is the evaluative component of self. The personal evaluation of self could be either positive or negative. A sense of personal adequacy or positive self-concept is essential for mental health.

Positive Thoughts: The quality of mental health depends on whether we direct our thoughts in positive or negative ways. Negative thoughts generate negative emotions such as anger, hate, jealousy, fear, and despair. The effect of such negative emotions on our mind is unhealthy. They also harm the endocrine system. Therefore in order to maintain good mental health, we need to develop the power of positive thinking which generates positive emotions such as love, joy, happiness, hope, compassion, empathy, and optimism in us. Such emotions strengthen our capacity to cope with various life challenges.

LIMITATIONS OF MENTAL HYGIENE

Though mental hygiene is an important aspect in our educational system, yet there are many limitations in implementing the principles of mental hygiene. Some of these are:

- Majority of our parents are not aware about mental hygiene. Hence they do not give importance how to keep their children's mental health preserved and un- impaired.
- Teachers in our school system are so overloaded with work that they cannot devote time to organize different types of programmes which help the students in helping their mental health intact.
- There is also a dearth of trained personnel to deal with the mental health problems of our population.

Chapter-34
Life Skills and ARSH Skills

Adolescence, a vital stage of growth and development, marks the period of transition from childhood to adulthood. It is characterized by rapid physiological changes and psychosocial maturation. Adolescence is also the stage when young people extend their relationships beyond parents and family and are intensely influenced by their peers and the outside world in general. As adolescents mature cognitively, their mental process becomes more analytical. They are now capable of abstract thinking, better articulation and of developing an independent ideology. These are truly the years of creativity, idealism, buoyancy and a spirit of adventure. But these are also the years of experimentation and risk-taking, of giving in to negative peer pressure, of taking uninformed decisions on crucial issues, especially relating to their bodies and their sexuality. Adolescence is thus a turning point in one's life, a period of increased potential but also one of greater vulnerability.

WHAT IS A SKILL?

A skill is the learned capacity to carry out pre-determined results often with the minimum outlay of time, energy or both. Skills can often be divided into domain-general and domain-specific skills. For example, in the domain of work, some general skills would include time management, teamwork and leadership, self motivation and others, whereas domain-specific skills would be useful only for a certain job. Skills usually require certain environmental stimuli and situations to assess the level of skill being shown and used.

WHAT ARE LIFE SKILLS?

Life skills are behaviours that enable individuals to adapt to and deal effectively with the demands and challenges of life. There are many such skills, but core life skills include the ability to:

- Make decisions, solve problems, and think critically and creatively
- Clarify and analyze values
- Communicate, including listen, build empathy, be assertive, and negotiate
- Cope with emotions and stress
- Feel empathy with others and be self-aware.

UNDERSTANDING LIFE SKILLS

Life skills have been defined as *"the abilities for adaptive and positive behaviour that enable individuals to deal effectively with the demands and challenges of everyday life" (WHO)*. *'Adaptive'* means that a person is flexible in approach and is able to adjust in different circumstances. *'Positive behaviour'* implies that a person is forward looking and even in difficult situations, can find a ray of hope and opportunities to find solutions.

The terms *'Livelihood skills'* or occupational/vocational skills refer to capabilities, resources and opportunities to pursue individual and household economic goals and relate to income generation. Thus, Life skills are distinct from livelihood skills.

KEY LIFE SKILLS

Life skills include psychosocial competencies and interpersonal skills that help people make informed decisions, solve problems, think critically and creatively, communicate effectively, build healthy relationships, empathize with others, and cope with managing their lives in a healthy and productive manner. Essentially, there are two kinds of skills - those related to thinking termed as *"thinking skills"*; and skills related to dealing with others termed as *"social skills"*. While thinking skills relate to reflection at a personal level, social skills include interpersonal skills and do not necessarily depend on logical thinking. It is the combination of these two types of skills that are needed for achieving assertive behaviour and negotiating effectively. "*Emotional*" can be perceived as a skill not only in making rational decisions but also in being able to make others agree to one's point of view. To do that, coming to terms first with oneself is important. Thus, selfmanagement is an important skill including managing/coping with feelings, emotions, stress and resisting peer and family pressure. Young people as advocates need both thinking and social skills for consensus building and advocacy on issues of concern (see Figure 34.1).

The description of key life-skills is given below:

Self Awareness: Self-awareness includes recognition of 'self', our character, our strengths and weaknesses, desires and dislikes. Developing self-awareness can help us to recognize when we are stressed or feel under pressure. It is often a prerequisite to effective communication and interpersonal relations, as well as for developing empathy with others.

Empathy: To have a successful relationship with our loved ones and society at large, we need to understand and care about other peoples' needs, desires and feelings. Empathy is the ability to imagine what life is like for another person. Without empathy, our communication with others will amount to one-way traffic. Worst, we will be acting and behaving according to our self-interest and are bound to run into problems. No man is an island, no woman either! We grow up in relationships with many people – parents, brothers and sisters, cousins, uncles and aunts, classmates, friends and neighbours.

When we understand ourselves as well as others, we are better prepared to communicate our needs and desires. We will be more equipped to say what we want people to know, present our thoughts and ideas and tackle delicate issues without offending other people. At the same time, we will be able to elicit support from others, and win their understanding.

Empathy can help us to accept others, who may be very different from ourselves. This can improve social interactions, especially, in situations of ethnic or cultural diversity.

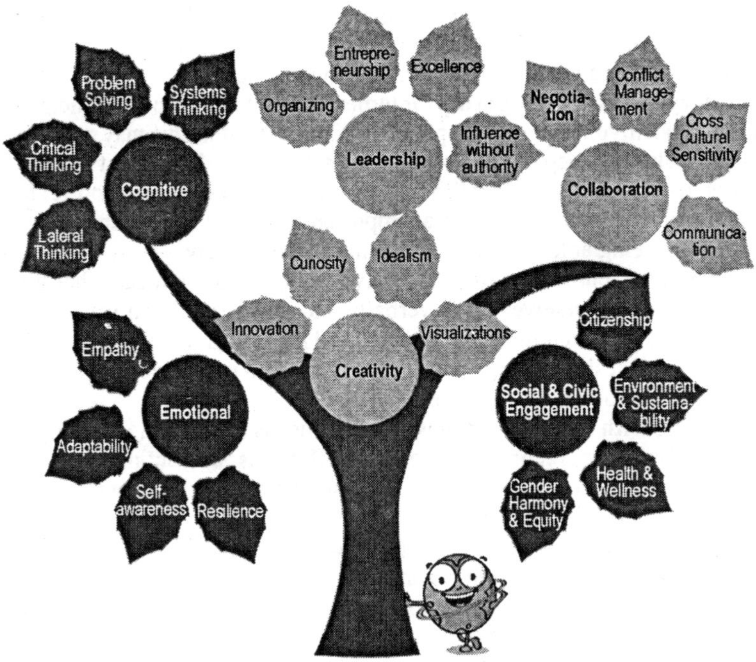

Figure 34.1: 21st Century Life Skills Framework

Empathy can also help to encourage nurturing behaviour towards people in need of care and assistance, or tolerance, as is the case with AIDS sufferers, or people with mental disorders, who may be stigmatized and ostracized by the very people they depend upon for support.

Critical Thinking: Critical thinking is an ability to analyze information and experiences in an objective manner. Critical thinking can contribute to health by helping us to recognize and assess the factors that influence attitudes and behaviour, such as values, peer pressure and the media.

Creative Thinking: Creative thinking is a novel way of seeing or doing things that is characteristic of four components – fluency (generating new ideas), flexibility (shifting perspective easily), originality (conceiving of something new), and elaboration (building on other ideas).

Creative thinking contributes to both decision making and problem solving by enabling us to explore the available alternatives and various consequences of our actions or non-action. It helps us to look beyond our direct experience, and even if no problem is identified, or no decision is to be made, creative thinking can help us to respond adaptively and with flexibility to the situations of our daily lives.

Decision Making: Decision making helps us to deal constructively with decisions about our lives. This can have consequences for health. It can teach people how to actively make decisions about their actions in relation to healthy assessment of different options and, what effects these different decisions are likely to have.

Problem Solving: Problem solving helps us to deal constructively with problems in our lives. Significant problems that are left unresolved can cause mental stress and give rise to accompanying physical strain.

Interpersonal Relationship: Interpersonal relationship skills help us to relate in positive ways with the people we interact with. This may mean being able to make and keep friendly relationships, which can be of great importance to our mental and social well-being. It may mean keeping, good relations with family members, which are an important source of social support. It may also mean being able to end relationships constructively.

Effective Communication: Effective communication means that we are able to express ourselves, both verbally and non-verbally, in ways that are appropriate to our cultures and situations. This means being able to express opinions and desires, and also needs and fears. And it may mean being able to ask for advice and help in a time of need.

Coping with Stress: Coping with stress means recognizing the sources of stress in our lives, recognizing how this affects us, and acting in ways that help us control our levels of stress, by changing our environment or lifestyle and learning how to relax.

Coping with Emotions: Coping with emotions means involving recognizing emotions within us and others, being aware of how emotions influence behaviour and being able to respond to emotions appropriately. Intense emotions like anger or sadness can have negative effects on our health if we do not respond appropriately.

WHO NEEDS LIFE SKILLS?

The Life Skills programme is a school based programme where Life Skills are imparted in a supportive learning environment. They are applicable for all ages of children and adolescents in school. However, the age group targeted is mainly 10-18, adolescent years, since young people of this age group seem to be most vulnerable to behaviour related health problems. The programme is for the promotion of health and well being and targeted group is all children.

HOW LIFE SKILLS ARE IMPARTED

The method used in teaching of Life Skills builds upon the social learning theory and on what we know of how young people learn from their environment; from observing how others behave and what consequences arise from behaviour.

It involves the process of Participatory learning using 4 basic components:

- Practical activities
- Feedback and reflections
- Consolidation and reinforcement
- Practical application to day to day life challenges

METHODS FOR LIFE SKILLS

The following methods can be used to enhance life skills in students

- Class discussions
- Brainstorming

- Demonstration and guided practice
- Role plays
- Audio and visual activities, e.g., arts, music, theatre, dance
- Small groups
- Educational games and simulations
- Case studies
- Story telling
- Debates
- Decision mapping or problem trees

LIFE SKILLS EDUCATION

Life skills education enhances the well being of a society and promotes positive outlook and healthy behaviour. In particular, it enables the individual to:

- translate knowledge, attitude, skills and values into action;
- behave responsibly and this leads to healthy living;
- develop positive attitude towards themselves and others;
- develop full potential;
- promote the state of mental well being as this motivates them and others;
- promote risk free behaviour;
- communicate effectively;
- develop negotiation skills;
- improve self perception by:
  - building self confidence
  - building self esteem
  - building self worth

BENEFITS OF LIFE SKILLS EDUCATION

Life Skills Education has long term benefits to the society. These include educational, social, health, cultural and economic benefits.

Educational Benefits

- Strengthens teacher pupil relationship
- Leads to desirable behaviour change
- Improves discipline in schools
- Reduces learner problems such as truancy, absenteeism drug and substance abuse and teenage pregnancies
- Helps learners to improve their performance

Social Benefits

- Improves the socialization process among learners such as relating to others in a friendly way
- Enables learners to choose good and reliable friends
- Helps learners to use their leisure time properly
- assists learners to recognize and avoid risky situations
- Bring about meaningful interaction among learners, teachers and the school community
- Helps in character building.

Health Benefits

- Leads to prevention and control of diseases such as STIs, HIV and AIDS
- Contributes to a person's general well being (physical, mental, emotional and social)
- Leads to less strain on health facilities
- Helps people to be responsible for their own and other people's health

Cultural Benefits

- Enables people to adopt and maintain meaningful cultural practices and avoid practices that may put self and others at risk
- Promotes harmonious interaction between people of different cultures
- Helps in the clarification of values in the society

Economic Benefits

- It leads to high productivity due to a motivated, strong and energetic labour force
- Savings are increased as money used e.g. on management and control of HIV and AIDS can be invested elsewhere. Resources such as time and money are saved as learners acquire skills to manage themselves and their environment.
    - ➢ rehabilitation of drug and substance abuses
    - ➢ repair of damaged property
    - ➢ buy teaching learning resources

ADOLESCENT REPRODUCTIVE AND SEXUAL HEALTH (ARSH)

Adolescence (10-19 Years) is a vital stage of growth and development. It is a period of transition from childhood to adulthood and is marked by rapid physical, physiological and psychological changes. This period results in sexual, psychological and behavioural maturation. Adolescents are a diverse group and are in varying situations of risk, status and environments. For example, they could be married or unmarried, in-school or out-of-school, living in urban or rural areas or have a different sexual orientation. Some young people are especially vulnerable. For example, street children, those engaged in sex work, and/or affected by disaster. Each of these groups has varying concerns and need to be appreciated as distinct segments of the population.

During adolescence, hormonal changes lead to onset of puberty, sudden and rapid physical growth and development of secondary sexual characteristics. Psychological and emotional changes like assertion of self identity and independence, sex drive, and attraction towards the opposite sex take place simultaneously. Adolescents begin extending their relationships beyond the family. They feel an inclination for distancing themselves from parents and expanding their social circle to carve an important place amongst peers.

If young people are not well informed or guided, they are likely to make decisions that could harm them. Adolescents are particularly inclined to try out new ideas. While this is a positive trait, lack of abilities, particularly life skills to assimilate multiple stimuli from media and peers, could encourage them to experiment with risky behaviours. They could engage in smoking, substance abuse, consumption of alcohol, unprotected sex, and while these behaviours may start on an exploratory note, many young people get trapped for a lifetime, and are not able to realize their potential.

ARSH SKILLS

Life Skills Approach appears to cover all aspects of human life. But skill development in adolescence education relates only to adolescent reproductive and sexual health concerns. It, therefore, may be known as Adolescent Reproductive and Sexual Health Skills (ARSH Skills) and may be conceptualized as follows:

"Adolescent Reproductive and Sexual Health (ARSH) Skills are abilities and competencies that help promote physical, mental and social well-being in respect of reproductive and sexual health among adolescents and youth, empowering them to take positive actions, to protect themselves from risky situations and to promote healthy social relationship".

EDUCATION IN ARSH SKILLS

All educational efforts particularly those in school education inter alia focus on skill related objectives. The content and process of school education are expected to influence this process and develop skills related to all the subject areas and other concerns that are incorporated in the school curriculum. However, it is commonly felt that the curriculum transaction process being adopted in school education has not been able to lay the desired emphasis on skill building. The existing teaching-learning methods focus mainly on transmission of information and imparting of knowledge to learners. In recent years, some efforts have been made sporadically to bring about the needed change in the teaching methods and make them activity-oriented and joyful. But, specific pedagogical methods to actualize skill building among the learners still remain a lively subject of intellectual discussion and are yet to assume their rightful place in the teaching-learning process. There is an urgent need to ensure that education in schools lays greater emphasis on the development of skill, more so on ARSH skills, mainly because of the following reasons:

- Education in skills is necessary because skills in relation to everyday life may form the foundation among people for promotion of mental well-being and highly interaction and behaviour. It is expected to enable individuals to translate knowledge, attitude and valued into actual abilities i.e. "what to do and how to do".
- It can influence the way individuals feel about themselves and others and also the way they think they are perceived by others. It may contribute to developing among them proper perceptions of self-efficacy, self-confidence and self-esteem.
- Education and skill development are the areas that are most often confused. It is believed that a person who is educated is equipped with the needed skills or abilities. But, in reality this does not happen. Knowing what needs to be done will enable the learners to actually do the job. But, knowing what needs to be changed does not mean that they automatically know how to make the changes. Skill development provides the 'know how' and the tools to implement changes.

- Individuals quite often lack necessary skills to deal effectively with various situations, even though they are educated and know the application of certain skills in some situations. This is particularly true in respect of adolescent reproductive and sexual health (ARSH) concerns. There is an urgent need, therefore, to enhance the copying resources and personal and social abilities among adolescents.
- As is evident from different kinds of emerging health and reproductive health problems, young people are not adequately equipped with skills to deal with the increased demands and stresses they experience. It is necessary to enhance their ability to take greater responsibility for their own lives by making healthy choices, gaining greater resistance to negative pressures and avoiding risky behaviours.
- Developing ARSH skills among adolescents are needed also because the influence of traditional mechanisms, family and other cultural factors that extended their support to individuals in managing the demands and challenges of everyday life is waning particularly because of changing cultures and life styles. The support is no longer adequate considering the influences that young people experience.
- The rapid social change, consequent upon modernization, urbanization, globalization and the media boom, has made the lives of young people, their expectations, values and outlook very different from those of older generations. This is more so regarding reproductive and sexual health concerns, in respect of which young people are not sufficiently equipped with skills to help them deal with the increased demands and pressures. The threat of AIDS pandemic and the fast growing risk of drug abuse among adolescent and the youth demand urgent efforts for skill development among them.

TYPES OF ARSH SKILLS

A set of life skill, described as generic life skills for psychological competence, was identified by WHO as core life skills applicable across a wide range of contexts in daily life and risk situations. Based on the definition of life skills by WHO, a reference of core life skills has been made as "the five foundation life skills areas: These are:

- Decision Making — Problem Solving
- Creative Thinking — Critical Thinking
- Communication — Interpersonal Skills
- Self-Awareness — Empathy
- Coping with Emotions — Coping with Stress

SKILLS FOR TEACHERS RELATED TO ARSH

Skill development among students has been an important objective of the school curriculum since long, but very little has been done to realize this objective. Teacher themselves need to develop skills to realize the objective of skill building among students is yet to receive adequate attention of the teacher preparation process. This is more so for a curricular area like adolescence education that is focused on adolescent reproductive and sexual health concerns, a substantial number of which are culturally very sensitive. In order to ensure effective curriculum transaction for skill building in the area of adolescent reproductive and sexual health, the teacher has to be equipped with the following three core skills:

- Communication Skills
- Non-Judgmental Skills
- Empathic Skills

Communication Skills

Communication is used in a number of ways-to inform, educate, persuade, motivate, help, reinforce or advocate. It is the ability as well as a process to express and convey information, ideas and experiences, both verbally and non-verbally. There are many channels of communication that aim at achieving these objectives and every channel employs specific set of skills to make communication effective. Teachers need interpersonal communication skills to help adolescent students develop skills related to adolescence reproductive and sexual health. Interpersonal communication is a "person-to-person, two-way, verbal and non-verbal communication between two or more people". As such, it can be one-to-one or group communication. It may be very effective in communicating technical or non-technical information and also the emotional or executive component, so important in interpersonal interaction.

The communication skills related to ARSH for teachers have certain crucial sub-skills, such as rapport building, listening, attending, speaking, questioning. These skills are commonly used by every individual, but quite often not in an effective way. Particularly, when teachers are to interact with students on adolescent reproductive and sexual health issues, it is necessary to understand the following sub-skills that make communication effective:

Rapport Building

Teachers are expected to equip themselves with skills that facilitate the establishment of a spontaneous relationship between them and students based on respect and mutual trust. These skills help in creating a congenial environment free from apprehensions and inhibition.

Active Listening

The teacher has to develop listening skills consciously. For active listening, it is necessary to listen to the speaker (s) what he/she says and also how he/she says it. The speaker is not to be interrupted or cut in to describe teacher's own experience. The teacher is expected to avoid distracting movements and not to pay attention to outside disruptions.

Attending

Students need focused attention of the teacher while interacting with them. The teacher is expected to make students feel comfortable and respond to them with interest. He/she needs to win the confidence of students through attentive listening. Students are not to be criticized or put down. The teacher has to encourage students to speak.

Speaking

While speaking, the teacher has to maintain his/her voice at an appropriate pitch, neither loud nor too soft. The teacher should not dominate the conversation and express that he/she feels, not only what he/she thinks.

Questioning

When students are speaking, the teacher has to ask questions. But, questions should be asked to show interest in what speaker is saying, to encourage the speaker and not to find out his/her ignorance or to embarrass him/her.

Non-Judgmental Skills

While teaching any value-laden area, it is essential for the teacher to be non-judgmental. He/she is not expected to impose his/her own values and beliefs. This is more so in respect of adolescence education concerns. It is possible only when the teacher develops the needed skills to observe the following:

Dos:

- First of all the teacher has to be convinced about the need for skill building in respect of adolescent reproductive and sexual health among students.
- He/she has to avoid conveying personal values, especially while discussing value laden issues.
- He/she has to respect the diversity of background of the learners, their values and beliefs.
- He/she has to convince students that no idea or opinion is absurd or unwarranted.

Don'ts

- The teacher need not be prescriptive, as experiences prove abundantly that preaching is counter-productive.
- He/she is not to make value judgment either of students of their views, as education is more effective when varied views are expressed and discussed.
- In any situation, the teacher is not expected to treat students as problems, but as individuals who need compassion and care.
- He/she need not comment on things that cannot be changed.
- He/she need not reject or ridicule any point of view expressed by students, even though it may not be accept able to him/her or may be against the social norms.

Empathic Skills

Being empathic may not be considered as a skill or a set of skills in itself, but skills are required to understand the situation of a particular student with whom the teacher is interacting. Empathy is the ability to feel and appreciate the situation in which another person is placed, even though one is not familiar with the situation. It enables the individual to experience fully the feelings and concerns of another person. The needed skills foe empathy may help the individual to understand and accept others who may be placed in a very different situation. These skills also help in encouraging individuals to be compassionate towards other who is in need of care and attention. To help adolescents manage their problems well, teachers need these skills to see beyond stereotypes and appreciate how the world of adolescent work. It is necessary that the teacher understands how a particular student feels in a specific situation and what is his/her point of view.

SKILLS FOR STUDENTS

The main objective of educational intervention for skill building is to develop necessary skills among students with a view to enhancing their coping resources and personal and social competencies to manage ARSH issues and problems. Adolescent students need to develop the following skills

Thinking Skills

All human beings think. Thinking is a process of gathering information, understanding issues and problems, examining the alternatives, making decisions, solving problems and doing many other things. But, without inculcating certain specific skills, such as critical and creative thinking, self-awareness, social-awareness, problem-solving and decision making, thinking does not contribute effectively to respond to various challenges of life. In the context of ARSH issues also, adolescents and young people have to develop the ability:

- To gather, analyze, interpret, assess and use the information effectively
- To determine the authenticity, accuracy and value of information and perceive the situation in totality
- To examine the alternatives, seek reasons and change views based on evidence
- To look at pros and cons of the decision they are making and refrain from making hasty, unplanned decisions

Communication Skills

Human beings express and share among themselves the information, their thoughts, experiences, feelings and attitudes through a language or any other tool. This is communication. The most significant quality of communication is that it connects one individual with another individual or a group of individuals. Communication is key to human relationships. But, to make it effective individuals need to develop certain skills. These skills are much more needed for communicating in respect of a subject like reproductive and sexual health which has been the least discussed area in almost all social settings. It is essential particularly for adolescents and young people to acquire skills for effective interpersonal communication and also to negotiate well with others to manage their problems with greater responsibility and confidence and avoid risky situations.

Interpersonal

Interpersonal communication is essential for human relationship, as it permits and encourages the development of a relationship between communicators. Adolescents need interpersonal communication skills to maintain both their independence and relationships. During the process of growing up, adolescents experience changing relationships with their parents, peer group and the opposite sex. While interacting with their parents or the peer group or the opposite sex, they quite often experience a conflict between their independence and relationships. They are in a dilemma whether to accept or reject what his/her parents or the peer group or the opposite sex are suggesting even though it means compromising their independence for relationships and vice versa. By using interpersonal communication skills, they may manage the ARSH related issues well and properly respond to the increasing demands and pressures on them.

Negotiation

Negotiation skills are at the heart of the skills based initiatives in reproductive and sexual health for adolescents and young people. The initiatives that will make efforts to develop various kinds of skills among them will contribute to enhancing their coping resources to negotiate ARSH issues and concerns. It is true that without even realizing it, negotiation is something we do all the time to solve our problems or resolve conflicts. To negotiate means to deal or bargain with another person or group to confer for mutual agreement, to manage or to cope with certain situation successfully. Adolescents require negotiation skills in respect of reproductive and sexual health to manage their concerns while interacting with parents and adults, the peer group and the opposite sex. These skills may help them in maintaining a healthy and happy life and importantly overcoming the peer pressure. They have to develop skills for understanding the point of view of others, being firm on one's values and beliefs and being assertive rather than aggressive. They have to negotiate not only with others but also with self in order to cope with emotions and stress, withstand peer pressure and say 'no' to harmful behaviour.

Chapter-35
Stress and Its Management

MEANING OF STRESS

Stress is a very common problem being faced today. Every individual will experience stress in one or the other time. Stress is an internal reaction to events and circumstances that challenge us to make changes in our lives. There are both external and internal causes of stress.

DEFINITIONS OF STRESS

Some definitions of stress are:

Lazarus and Folkman (1984) have defined stress as *"an internal state which can be caused by physical demands of body or by environmental and social situations, which are evaluated as potentially harmful, uncontrollable, or exceeding our resources for coping".*

According to David Fontana *"stress is a demand made upon the adaptive capacities of the mind and body".*

These definitions indicate that stress represents those conditions under which individuals have demand made upon them, that they cannot physically or psychologically meet, leading to breakdown at one or other of these levels.

Stress is usually thought of in negative terms. But, it can manifest itself in both positive and negative way. It is said to be positive when the situation offers an opportunity for one, to gain something. Eustress (the Greek word 'eu' means good) is the term used to describe positive stress. It is often viewed as motivator, since in its absence the individual lacks the spirit necessary for peak performance. Distress is the term used to indicate negative stress.

CATEGORIES OF STRESS

Selye identified two types of stress: *eustress*, also known as Positive Stress and *distress* also known as Negative Stress. The difference between the experience of positive stress and negative stress lies in the nature (real or imagined) of the stressor, the duration of the stressor and our ability to cope with the stressor.

Two categories of stress are given below:

Positive Stress

Positive Stress is experienced when a stressor leads to an improvement in our overall performance and productivity. Positive stress is usually the outcome of a positive attitude towards a stressor (being proactive), good time management practices and effective prioritising of one's activities (putting first things first). Good news, or an unexpected benefit, can also cause a positive stress experience. Experiencing positive stress leads to several benefits which include:

Increased Creativity: Not only are we able to make or develop things, we are also able to think of new or more effective methods for completing tasks.

Higher Productivity: We are able to complete more tasks at work and participate in more activities in our personal life.

Improved Self-Esteem: We generally feel good about yourself and happy with the life that you are leading.

Better Health: Positive stress stimulates our immune system to operate optimally, meaning that we are less likely to become ill.

Negative Stress

Negative Stress will impair and eventually incapacitate our ability to perform. Negative stress is usually the outcome of a poor attitude towards a stressor (being reactive), poor time management practices, and failing to prioritise one's activities. Sometimes, traumatic events can also lead to the experience of negative stress.

TYPES OF STRESS

Three types of stress are given below:

Acute Stress

The first type of stress is called acute stress. This is the most common form of stress and normally comes from demands and pressures of the past and future. This kind of stress tends to be short term. For example, suppose you have a busy day. You have to drop your niece and nephew at school, stop by the post office, go to class, take a quiz, get an oil change, pick your niece and nephew up from school, drive home through traffic and make dinner. A busy day such as this can create stress but it is short term, because perhaps tomorrow you are less busy or are looking forward to the weekend where you don't have as much to do. Every person experiences this kind of stress. Acute stress is a laundry list of the things we must do or a list of the things that didn't go right. For example, if your car breaks down on the way to the post office, this creates a certain amount of acute stress, but once the car is fixed there is no stress associated with it.

The most common symptoms of acute stress are:

- *Emotional distress:* some combination of anger or irritability, anxiety and depression, the three stress emotions.
- *Muscular problems* including tension headache, back pain, jaw pain and the muscular tensions that lead to pulled muscles and tendon and ligament problems.
- *Stomach, gut and bowel problems* such as heartburn, acid stomach, flatulence, diarrhea, constipation and irritable bowel syndrome.
- *Transient over arousal* leads to elevation in blood pressure, rapid heartbeat, sweaty palms, heart palpitations, dizziness, migraine headaches, cold hands or feet, shortness of breath and chest pain.

Acute stress can crop up in anyone's life and it is highly treatable and manageable.

Episodic Acute Stress

Episodic acute stress is a more serious form of acute stress. In this type of stress, the person feels stress on a daily basis and rarely gets relief. Unlike acute stress, where there may be one or two busy, stressful days, episodic acute stress happens on a daily basis. The person who suffers from episodic acute stress feels stressed constantly with little relief. You have probably met these people. They may constantly complain about how much work they have and may be constantly late or always in a rush and may be anxious and irritable on a regular basis. Often, a person who suffers from this type of stress may have taken on too much and created self-imposed demands.

Chronic Stress

Chronic stress is the type of stress that happens month after month, year after year. This is long-term stress where people see little way out of a situation. Sometimes, chronic stress begins with traumatic experiences such as Post Traumatic Stress Disorder (PTSD) or childhood experiences. In others, chronic stress can occur in response to everyday stressors that are ignored or not managed well. For example, someone may have episodic acute stress but over a long period of time, this can become chronic stress. With this type of stress, the person has given up looking for solutions to the stress and tends to just live with it. For example, consider a couple who is very unhappy in their relationship. While at one point in time in their relationship they may have experienced acute stress when arguing, this could have turned into episodic acute stress as the arguing occurred more frequently. Then when that type of stress was unrelieved for a long time, it became chronic stress. It becomes chronic because the couple took no steps to repair their relationship.

While acute stress can be thrilling and exciting, chronic stress is not. This is the grinding stress that wears people away day after day, year after year. Chronic stress destroys bodies, minds and lives. It wreaks havoc through long-term attrition. It is the stress of poverty, of dysfunctional families, of being trapped in an unhappy marriage or in a despised job or career.

Chronic stress comes when a person never sees a way out of a miserable situation. It's the stress of unrelenting demands and pressures for seemingly interminable periods of time. With no hope, the individual gives up searching for solutions.

SYMPTOMS OF STRESS

Stress symptoms are not always recognizable and they can take over when we least expect them. Stress often affects sleep patterns, energy levels, appetite and sex drive but can also have less obvious symptoms.

Our moods and emotions are also affected by stress. If we are put under too much pressure either at work or at home, we can react by being angry most of the time, becoming overly emotional, and even showing restlessness and agitation. On the other hand, stress can also cause a person to shut down completely and freeze under pressure, some people describe the feeling as being paralyzed on the outside but exploding on the inside.

Table 35.1: Symptoms of Stress

STRESS WARNING SIGNS AND SYMPTOMS	
Cognitive Symptoms	**Emotional Symptoms**
• Memory problems	• Moodiness
• Inability to concentrate	• Irritability or short temper
• Poor judgment	• Agitation, inability to relax
• Seeing only the negative	• Feeling overwhelmed
• Anxious or racing thoughts	• Sense of loneliness and isolation
• Constant worrying	• Depression or general unhappiness
Physical Symptoms	**Behavioral Symptoms**
• Aches and pains	• Eating more or less
• Diarrhea or constipation	• Sleeping too much or too little
• Nausea, dizziness	• solating yourself from others
• Chest pain, rapid heartbeat	• Procrastinating or neglecting responsibilities
• Loss of sex drive	• Using alcohol, cigarettes, or drugs to relax
• Frequent colds	• Nervous habits (e.g. nail biting, pacing)

CAUSES OF STRESS

The major causes of stress at work place are given in Figure 35.1.

Career Concern: If an employee feels that he is very much behind in the corporate ladder, then he may experience stress. If he seems that there are no opportunities for self-growth, he may experience stress. Hence, unfulfilled career expectations are the significant source of stress.

Role Ambiguity: It occurs when the person does not know what he is supposed to do, on the job. His tasks and responsibilities are not clear. The employee is not sure what he is expected to do. It creates confusion in the minds of the worker and results in stress.

Rotating Work Shifts: Stress may occur in those individuals who work on different work shifts. Employees may be expected to work on day shift for some days and then on the night shift. That may create problems in adjusting to the shift timings, and it can affect not only personal life but also family life of the employee.

Role Conflict: It takes place when people have different expectations from the person performing a particular role. It can also occur if the job is not as per expectation, or when a job demands a certain type of behaviour that is against the person's moral values.

Occupational Demands: Some jobs are more demanding than others. Jobs that involve risk, and danger are more stressful. Research findings indicate, job that cause stress needs constant monitoring of equipments and devices, unpleasant physical conditions, making decisions, etc.

Lack of Participation in Decision-making: Many experienced employees feel that management should consult them on matters affecting their jobs. In

Figure 35.1: Major Causes of Stress

reality, the superiors hardly ask the concerned employees before taking a decision. That develops a feeling of being neglected, which may lead to stress.

Work Overload: Excessive workload leads to stress as it puts a person under tremendous pressure. Work overload may take two different forms:

- *Qualitative work overload* implies performing a job that is complicated or beyond the employee's capacity.
- *Quantitative work overload* is a result of many activities performed in a prescribed time.

Work Underload: In this, case, too little work or very easy work is expected on the part of the employee. Doing less work or jobs of routine and simple nature would lead to monotony and boredom, which can lead to stress.

Poor Working Conditions: Employees may be subject to poor working conditions. It would include bad lighting and ventilation, unhygienic sanitation facilities, excessive noise, and dust, presence of toxic gasses and fumes, inadequate safety measures, etc. All these unpleasant conditions create physiological and psychological imbalance in humans thereby causing stress.

Lack of Group Cohesiveness: Every group is characterized by its cohesiveness, although they differ widely in its degree. Individuals experience stress when there is no unity among work group members. There are mistrust, jealousy, frequent quarrels, etc., in groups and this lead to stress to employees.

Interpersonal and Intergroup Conflict: These conflicts take place due to differences in perceptions, attitudes, values and beliefs between two or more individuals and groups. Such conflicts can be a source of stress for group members.

Organizational Changes: When changes occur, people have to adapt to those changes, and this may cause stress. Stress is higher when changes are significant or unusual like transfer or adoption of new technology.

Lack of Social Support: When individuals believe that they have the friendship and support of others at work, their ability to cope with the effects of stress increases. If this kind of social support is not available, then an employee experiences more stress.

Certain factors outside the scope of an organization also cause stress. The main causes of stress outside work or organization:

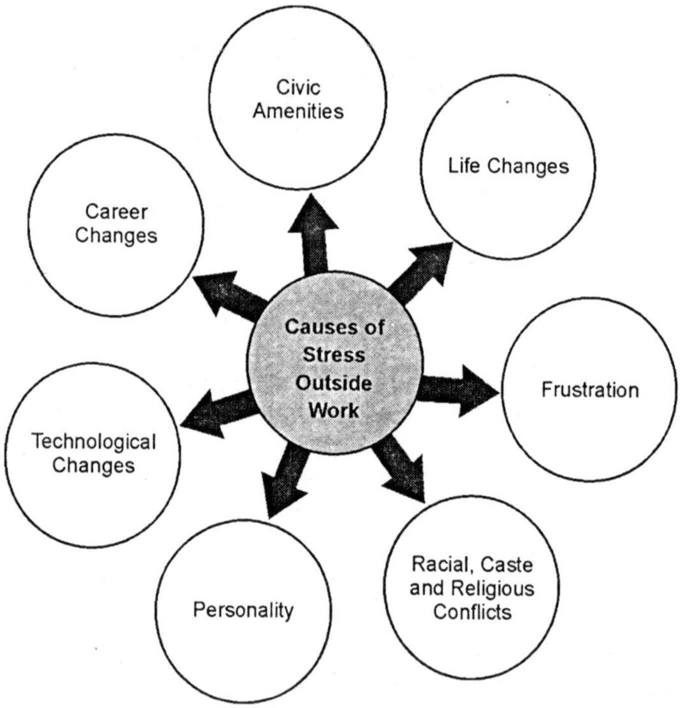

Figure 35.2: Causes of Stress Outside Work

Civic Amenities: Poor civic amenities in the area in which one lives can be a cause of stress. Inadequate or lack of public facilities like improper water supply, excessive noise or air pollution, lack of proper transport facility can be quite stressful.

Life Changes: Life changes can bring stress to a person. Life changes can be slow or sudden. Gradual life changes include getting older, and abrupt life changes include death or accident of a loved one. Sudden life changes are highly stressful and very difficult to cope.

Frustration: Frustration is another cause of stress. It arises when goal-directed behaviour gets blocked. Management should attempt to remove barriers and help the employees to reach their goals.

Racial, Caste and Religious Conflicts: Employees living in areas, which are often prone to conflicts among people based on differences seen in their race, caste and religion do suffer more from stress. In the case of a religion, the minorities and lower-caste people (especially in India) are subject to more stress.

Personality: We can classify people as 'Type A' and 'Type B'.

The 'Type A' people:

- They feel guilty while relaxing.
- They get irritated by minor mistakes of self and others.
- They feel impatient and dislike waiting.
- They also multitask and prefer to do several things at one time.

The 'Type B' people are exactly opposite and hence are less affected by stress due to the above factors.

Technological Changes: When there are any changes in technical fields, employees are under the constant fear of losing jobs or need to adjust to new technologies. It can be a source of stress.

Career Changes: When a person suddenly switches to another job, he is under stress to shoulder new responsibilities adequately. Under-promotion, over-promotion, demotion and transfers can also cause stress.

EFFECTS OF STRESS

Stress is not always harmful. In fact, it is recognized that low levels of stress can even helps for better performance. For example, a student can prepare well for forthcoming examination only if he has some stress. However, excess level of stress is undoubtedly harmful.

The effects of stress are divided into three categories:

Physiological Effects: Commonly appearing stress related bodily disorders are-peptic ulcers, hypertension, chronic fatigue, hormonal changes, increased heart rate, difficulty in breathing, numbness of limbs, heart disease and reduction in immunity, etc.

Psychological Effects: Anxiety, depression, hopelessness, helplessness, anger, nervousness, irritability, tension and boredom may be experienced.

Behavioural Changes: Decreasing efficiency, making mistakes, inability to take decisions, under eating or overeating, sleeplessness, increased smoking, develop addiction to alcohol and drugs, forgetfulness, hypersensitivity or passiveness, accident proneness and interpersonal difficulties are seen.

Stress is linked to disorders such as cancer and heart disorders. There are several mediating variables that determine whether stress becomes dangerous or not. For example, good coping mechanisms which can help to reduce stress, having good social support, often help in reducing stress.

Perception of stress or how a person views stress is also very important.

For example, a person may not perceive a situation as stressful whereas the same situation may be perceived as highly stressful by some other person. People with personality type 'A' are more prone to be affected by stress related disorders like cardiovascular diseases. Personality character like hardiness or emotional stability helps to withstand effects of stress.

Hans Selye, a renowned biological scientist defines stress as the nonspecific response of the body to any demand upon it. He termed the body's response to stressors the *"General Adaptation Syndrome" (GAS)*. The GAS consists of 3 stages:

Alarm Reaction: It is an emergency response of the body. In this stage prompt responses of the body, many of them mediated by the sympathetic nervous system, prepare us to cope with the stressor here and now.

Stage of Resistance: If the stressor continues to be present, the stage of resistance begins, wherein the body resists the effects of the continuous stressor. During this stage certain hormonal responses of the body are an important line of defense in resisting the effects of stressors.

Stage of Exhaustion: In this stage, the body's capacity to respond to both continuous and new stressors has been seriously compromised. The person will no longer be able to face stressor and he will finally succumb to it. The person may develop psychosomatic illness. The stress leads to many psychosomatic diseases. Treatment for such diseases involves medical help for the physical problems and, at the same time, attention to the psychological factors producing the stress.

COPING WITH STRESS

There are different ways of coping with stress such as: confronting (facing), distancing (remoteness), self-control, seeking social support, accepting responsibility, escape or avoid (from the stressor), plan a problem solving strategy and positive reappraisal.

Usually two broad type of coping types are seen- Instrumental coping and Emotional coping. In instrumental coping, a person focuses on the problem and tries to solve it. In emotional coping, the focus is more on the feelings generated by the problem. However, some specific techniques to eliminate or to manage more effectively the inevitable, prolonged stress are as follows:

Exercise

Good physical exercise like walking, jogging, swimming, riding bicycle, playing soft ball, tennis are necessary to cope with stress.

Relaxation

Whether a person simply takes it easy once in a while or uses specific relaxation techniques such as bio-feedback, or meditation, the intent is to eliminate the immediately stressful situation or manage a prolonged stressful situation more effectively. Taking it easy may mean curling up with a good book on an easy chair or watching some light programme on television or listening to a light music. Meditation is scientifically proved to be very useful, both physically and mentally to cope with stress.

Behavioural Self-control

By deliberately managing the antecedents and the consequence of their own behaviour, people can achieve self-control. Besides managing their own behaviour to reduce stress, people can also become more aware of their limits and of 'red flags' that signal trouble ahead. They can avoid people or situations that they know will put them under stress.

Maladaptive strategies, rigid strategies or relying on one type of coping method lead to increase in the stress. Social support helps reduce the effect of stress. People may provide help, advice, material support or moral support that helps to reduce stress.

In addition to the above, psychotherapy (Beck's cognitive therapy, Ellis's rational emotive therapy and Meichenbaum's stress- inoculation training), skill training, environmental changes, Bio-feedback (control of physical signs such as Blood pressure, headache, etc), family therapy, group therapy, hypnosis, yoga, are found to be very useful. Finally, uses of drugs are some of the other strategies adopted in coping with stress.

STRESS MANAGEMENT

Stress is a part of life but the healthier you are; the better able you are to manage stress when it happens. Chronic stress can impact human immune system, which lowers resistance to getting sick. Approaching stress management from a wellness lifestyle approach can give oneself *"money in the bank"* when it comes to preventing stress, and can give the energy one need to handle stress when it happens. The following components are part of a wellness lifestyle approach.

Attitude: Attitude is everything. What does that mean? The way you think about things can make all the difference in how you react to events. We can change the way we think in order to reduce stress.

Healthy Eating: Good nutrition and healthy eating habits can help from stressful times. Eating well will increase physical, mental and emotional stamina. Fueling with nutrient dense foods can boost immune system, help maintain a healthy weight and help feel better.

Physical Activity: Physical activity provides immediate stress relief as well as long-term stress management. Just 20-30 minutes of walking a day, for example, can give more energy, help put things in perspective, improve sleep, sharpen mental productivity and boost self-confidence. Our bodies are made to move and everyone can find some type of activity that is enjoyable.

Relaxing Mind and Body: There are a number of relaxation techniques that can help to manage stress and also improve concentration, productivity and overall well-being.

Sleep: Consistent sleep is critical for a healthy life. Although we all need varying amounts of sleep, if we do not get enough sleep, everything from our immune system to our ability to learn and remember information will be negatively affected. Sleep is as important as nutrition and exercise when preparing for peak performance.

Healthy Relationships: Changes in relationships can be a source of stress for many students, as can feeling socially isolated. At the same time, talking with a supportive friend or family member can be helpful in coping with stress.

Time Management: Sometimes all the things we have to do can seem overwhelming and impossible to accomplish. Learning how to be a good time manager is a skill that one can use throughout his life, which can make work, play and studying more manageable, more productive and less stressful.

Alcohol and Other Drugs: Alcohol and other drug use can lead to many problems that can add stress to lives. High-risk use can lead to poor decision-making, impaired abstract thinking, injury and legal problems. By understanding overall risks, one can make healthier choices.

Tobacco: Tobacco can impact sleep, ability to fight infection and overall health. These issues can create stressful situations. Tobacco use by some, however, is seen as a stress reducer. In order to achieve a healthy lifestyle, it is important to learn strategies to deal with stressors and to understand that quitting tobacco use takes time and practice.

Spirituality: Spirituality means finding personal meaning in life; it doesn't mean just following a particular religious dogma.

THE 4 AS TECHNIQUE FOR REDUCING OR COPING WITH STRESS

We all experience stress at one time or another. However, we can take action to assess and relieve the stress in our life. First, we do some self-analysis to determine the stressors in our life and how we handle it. This emotional intelligence skill (self-awareness) allows us to see what we need to improve upon. Then, we can apply self-management tools to help us manage the stress in our lives. The benefit of this identification and management is that it allows us to relate better to others both in our work life and personal life. Once we do some self-analysis, we can use a method called the four As. The four As gives us four choices for dealing with a stressor (see Figure 35.3).

Avoid the Stressor: We can try to avoid situations that stress us out. If watching certain television programmes causes stress, stop watching them. Spend time with people who help you relax. We can also look at saying no more often, if we do not have the time necessary to complete everything we are doing.

Alter the Stressor: Another option in dealing with stress is to try to alter it, if you cannot avoid it. When changing a situation, you can be more assertive, manage time better and communicate your own needs and wants better. For example, Mohan can look at the things causing her stress, such as her home and school commitments; while he cannot change the workload, he can examine ways to avoid a heavy workload in the future. If Mohan is stressed about the amount of homework he has and the fact that he needs to clean the house, asking for help from roommates, for example, can help alter the stressor. Often this involves the ability to communicate well.

Adapt to the Stressor: If you are unable to avoid or change the stressor, getting comfortable with the stressor is a way to handle it. Creating your own coping mechanisms for the stress and learning to handle it can be an effective way to handle the stress. For example, we can try looking at stressful situations in a positive light, consider how important the stressor is in the long run, and adjust our standards of perfectionism.

Accept the Stressor: Some stressors are unavoidable. We all have to go to work and manage our home life. So, learning to handle the things we cannot

Avoid the Stressor	Look at the Stressor. Try to put the stressor in a positive light. Consider the stressor and the long-term impact. Will this be a stressor in three months or one year?
Alter the Stressor	Learn to say no to things that may cause stress. Change the way you are working with the stressor. Communicate needs and wants.
Adapt to the Stressor	Change your opinion of the stressor. Look at how the stressor can be positive, for example "I have a lot of work but if I do well, it might mean a promotion."
Accept the Stressor	Find other outlets to handles the stressor. Develop a tolerance to the stressor. Let go of things you cannot control.

Figure 35.3: The Four As for Dealing with Stress

change by forgiving, developing tolerances, and letting going of those things we cannot control is also a way to deal with a stressor. For example, if your mother-in-law's yearly visits and criticisms cause stress, obviously you are not able to avoid or alter the stress, but you can adapt to it and accept it. Since we cannot control another person, accepting the stressor and finding ways of dealing with it can help minimize some negative effects of the stress we may experience.

Researchers have found the following activities cut stress significantly:

- Meditating
- Listening to music
- Getting enough sleep
- Drinking black tea
- Spending time with a funny friend
- Pampering, such as a massage
- Doing something spiritual
- Chewing gum
- Exercising
- Developing good time management skills
- Eating a healthy diet
- Organization such as keeping workspace organized
- Picturing yourself relaxed
- Breathing deeply
- Social interaction such as spending time with family and friends
- Positive thinking

Chapter-36
Games and Group Dynamics

MEANING OF GAME

A game is structured form of play, usually undertaken for enjoyment and sometimes used as an educational tool. Games are distinct from work, which is usually carried out for remuneration, and from art, which is more often an expression of aesthetic or ideological elements. However, the distinction is not clear-cut and many games are also considered to be work (such as professional players of spectator sports or games) or art (such as jigsaw puzzles or games involving an artistic layout such as Mahjong, solitaire, or some video games).

Key components of games are goals, rules, challenge, and interaction. Games generally involve mental or physical stimulation, and often both. Many games help develop practical skills, serve as a form of exercise, or otherwise perform an educational, simulational, or psychological role.

DEFINITIONS OF GAME

Some important definitions of game are:

1. According to Katie Salen and Eric Zimmerman, *"A game is a system in which players engage in an artificial conflict, defined by rules, that results in a quantifiable outcome."*
2. Greg Costikyan, *"A game is a form of art in which participants, termed players, make decisions in order to manage resources through game tokens in the pursuit of a goal."*
3. Clark C. Abt, *"A game is an activity among two or more independent decision-makers seeking to achieve their objectives in some limiting context."*
4. Elliot Avedon and Brian Sutton-Smith, *"At its most elementary level then we can define game as an exercise of voluntary control systems in which there is an opposition between forces, confined by a procedure and rules in order to produce a disequilibrial outcome."*
5. Kevin J. Maroney, *"A game is a form of play with goals and structure."*
6. Bernard Suits, *"to play a game is to engage in activity directed toward bringing about a speciûc state of affairs, using only means permitted by speciûc rules, where the means permitted by the rules are more limited in scope than they would be in the absence of the rules, and where the sole reason for accepting such limitation is to make possible such activity."*
7. Jane McGonigal, *"When you strip away the genre differences and the technological complexities, all games share four defining traits: a goal, rules, a feedback system, and voluntary participation."*

MEANING OF GROUP DYNAMICS

Group dynamics is the study, analysis and understanding of the behaviours and psychology surrounding group interactions. The field typically differentiates between interactions within a social group (intragroup dynamics) and between social groups (intergroup dynamics). The field is based on a belief that the whole is more complex than the sum of the parts and that an understanding of how groups operate has a fundamental effect on the organization of society and public policy. For businesses, a greater understanding of what motivates teams, what type of people make up successful teams and what inhibits team success can fuel HR decision-making and help the company create a more successful, happy workforce.

Group dynamics deals with the attitudes and behavioural patterns of a group. Group dynamics concern how groups are formed, what is their structure and which processes are followed in their functioning. Thus, it is concerned with the interactions and forces operating between groups.

The history of group dynamics has its roots in experimental psychology and sociology. Wilhelm Wundt, known as the founder of experimental psychology, expressed a view that communities possessed unique qualities of language and customs that could not be ascertained through a study of the individual alone.

EDUCATIONAL IMPLICATIONS OF GROUP DYNAMICS

Dynamics mean change and group dynamics means the change of behaviour through interaction in the group. As we know that students live in groups in school as their classroom, group of playmates, hobby club, science club, library etc.

It is natural that students interact with each other in groups to perform their needs, get information's, provide messages etc. As we know that human behaviour is not static, so when students interact in their group/groups with other members then the behaviour of members who constantly, interact, undergoes continuous changes. This kind of changing in behaviour of students due to their interaction in group with group members is called group dynamics.

Every group demands reciprocity among its members. Every group influences, to a great extent, the behaviour of its members. Students interact with the environment for their development. This development depends on social interaction. A teacher should study group dynamics to deal with various groups of students.

The following are the main educational implications of group dynamics:

Provide Appropriate Guidance to Students for their Adjustment

If teacher has basic knowledge of group dynamics then he/she can provide appropriate guidance to his/her students for their adjustment. As we know that education aims to make socially adjustable citizen of the country, we want that our students should have positive adjustment with their friends, classmates, playmates and others.

Sometimes students can face certain problems regarding their process of adjustment. If teacher is well-equipped with the basic knowledge of group dynamics, if teacher knows how a student should interact with other members of his/her group positively then he/she (teacher) can provide proper guidance to students about their adjustment.

Improve the Emotional and Social Climate of the Class

As we know that we cannot even imagine organizing participative, effective and armful teaching-learning process in the class which does not have proper emotional and social climate.

If the students of the class have negative attitudes about each other, if they act unsociably as enemies, if they do not care emotions, needs, expectations of others then we cannot expect a successful transaction of teaching-learning process in that kind of class.

Through the study of group dynamics, a teacher can guide his/her students for making proper adjustment and healthy interaction with each other. Teacher can improve the emotional and social climate of the class.

Improve Group Relations in the Class

We can see some particular patterns of relationship among the students of the class as-stars, isolates, mutual pairs, chains etc. If teacher has basic knowledge of group dynamics then he/she can provide a leadership role. The role of the leader is now shifting from authoritarian to a democratic and participatory one.

Teacher should try to encourage participation of students in all the school activities. If teacher has studied about group dynamics, then he/she can improve the climate of the students of his class by taking them into confidence.

Teacher can take his/her decisions democratically. By studying group dynamics, he/she can motivate students to participate in learning activities. Since group relation has an important role in teaching-learning process so a teacher should improve group relation in the class. For this improvement he/she should have knowledge of group dynamics.

Deal Effectively with Social Groups

Teacher has to organize various activities in various groups. To deal efficiently with social groups in classroom, in playground, in laboratory, in co-curricular activities, teacher should have study about group dynamics.

Thorough Knowledge of the Interaction Process

As we know that in a class we cannot find all the students of same qualities, needs, interests etc. They may be of different socio-economic background.

Teacher should try to ascertain positive interaction among these students. For this teacher should have a complete knowledge of group dynamics and the interaction process.

Remove Conflicts and Stresses in the Group

As we know that conflicts and stresses in the group, disturb the learning climate of the class. A teacher should try to remove these. For this a teacher should have study the group dynamic process.

MEANING OF CONFLICT

Conflict refers to some form of friction, disagreement or discord arising within a group when the beliefs or actions of one or more members of the group are either resisted by or unacceptable to one or more members of another group. Conflict can arise between members of the same group, known as intragroup conflict or it can occur between members of two or more groups and involve violence, interpersonal discord and psychological tension, known as intergroup conflict. Conflict in groups often follows a specific course. *Routine group interaction* is first disrupted by an *initial conflict*, often caused by differences of opinion, disagreements between members, or scarcity of resources. At this point, the group is no longer united, and may split into coalitions. This period of *conflict escalation* in some cases gives way to a *conflict resolution stage*, after which the group can eventually return to *routine group interaction* once again.

Conflict Resolution

Conflict resolution is the process of trying to find a solution to a conflict. Ideally conflict resolution is collaborative problem-solving, a cooperative talking-together process that leads to choosing a plan of action that both of you can feel good about.

Conflict resolution is the process of resolving a dispute or a conflict by meeting at least some of each side's needs and addressing their interests. Conflict resolution sometimes requires both a power-based and an interest-based approach, such as the simultaneous pursuit of litigation (the use of legal power) and negotiation (attempts to reconcile each party's interests). There are a number of powerful strategies for conflict resolution.

A conflict is resolved when the inconsistency between wishes and actions of parties is resolved. Negotiation is an important part of conflict resolution and any design of a process which tries to incorporate positive conflict from the start needs to be cautious not to let it degenerate into the negative types of conflict.

Structured Process of Conflict Resolution

Conflict resolution is based on a structured problem-solving process that uses the following steps: (1) set the stage, (2) gather perspectives, (3) identify interests, (4) create options, (5) evaluate options, and (6) generate agreement. Each of the following strategies is amenable to this process:

- ***Negotiation*** occurs when two disputing parties work together, unassisted, to resolve their dispute.
- ***Mediation*** occurs when two disputing parties work together, assisted by a neutral third party called the mediator, to resolve their dispute.
- ***Consensus decision making*** is a group problem-solving strategy in which all parties affected by the conflict collaborate to craft a plan of action, with or without the assistance of a neutral party.

FIVE STYLES OF CONFLICT RESOLUTION

Conflicts can arise at any time. How you utilize conflict resolution strategies depends on both your conflict style and your conflict resolution skills. There are many different ways to respond to conflict situations; some conflict styles involve a considerate or cooperative approach while others involve either a competitive or passive approach. The five styles of conflict include:

Accommodating: Accommodation involves having to deal with the problem with an element of self-sacrifice; an individual sets aside his own concerns to maintain peace in the situation. Thus, the person yields to what the other wants, displaying a form of selflessness. It might come as an immediate solution to the issue; however it also brings about a false manner of dealing with the problem. This can be disruptive if there is a need to come up with a more sound and creative way out of the problem. This behaviour will be most efficient if the individual is in the wrong as it can come as a form of conciliation.

Avoiding: In this approach, there is withdrawal from the conflict. The problem is being dealt with through a passive attitude. Avoiding is mostly used when the perceived negative end outweighs the positive outcome. In employing this, individuals end up ignoring the problem, thinking that the conflict will resolve itself. It might be applicable in certain situations but not in all. Avoidance would mean that you neglect the responsibility that comes with it. The other individuals involved might think that you are neglecting the problem. Thus, it is better to confront the problem before it gets worse.

Collaborating: Collaborating aims to find a solution to the conflict through cooperating with other parties involved. Hence, communication is an important part of this strategy. In this mechanism, effort is exerted in digging into the issue to identify the needs of the individuals concerned without removing their respective interests from the picture. Collaborating individuals aim to come up with a successful resolution creatively, without compromising their own satisfactions.

Competing: Competition involves authoritative and assertive behaviours. In this style, the aggressive individual aims to instil pressure on the other parties to achieve a goal. It includes the use of whatever means to attain what the individual thinks is right. It may be appropriate in some situations but it shouldn't come to a point wherein the aggressor becomes too unreasonable. Dealing with the conflict with an open mind is vital for a resolution to be met.

Compromising: Compromising is about coming up with a resolution that would be acceptable to the parties involved. Thus, one party is willing to sacrifice their own sets of goals as long as the others will do the same. Hence, it can be viewed as a mutual give-and-take scenario where the parties submit the same amount of investment for the problem to be solved. A disadvantage of this strategy is the fact that since these parties find an easy way around the problem, the possibility of coming up with more creative ways for a solution would be neglected.

MEANING OF NEGOTIATION

Negotiation is a strategic discussion that resolves an issue in a way that both parties find acceptable. In a negotiation, each party tries to persuade the other to agree with his or her point of view. Negotiation is a process of discussion between two or more disputants, who seek to find out a common solution for a common problem, one that meets their needs and of interests. During negotiations, parties involved must feel comfortable with what has been agreed so that they can move forward and develop an ongoing relationship. Either parties can take the process of negotiation themselves or they can take help of any professional negotiator.

LEVELS OF NEGOTIATION

Negotiation is a means to an end. There are three basic levels of negotiation:

Power: Negotiations that rely on power often involve threats and coercion. This is not a long-term strategy as it has a negative impact on the future of the relationship between parties.

Rights: This type of negotiation is based on contracts and precedent and often leads to legal action, which can be expensive and time consuming.

Interest: Interest-based negotiations are what you should strive for. They often involve good communication and collaboration, resulting in win-win situations for both parties.

BENEFITS OF TEACHING CONFLICT RESOLUTION TO YOUNG CHILDREN

Learning to handle conflicts in productive ways is an important social skill that children will use throughout their lives. When child care providers help preschoolers practice resolving conflicts, they become more sensitive to the needs and feelings of others. Children also develop self-confidence when they learn how to solve their problems in a positive and assertive way. Conflict resolution involves *good communication, real listening*, and *searching for solutions* that children can agree to. This kind of problem solving teaches children how to think creatively and to evaluate solutions.

STEPS IN RESOLVING CONFLICTS THROUGH NEGOTIATION

Teachers can begin teaching children to negotiate and solve disagreements by guiding them through some simple steps. Remember that children need repeated practice to resolve conflicts. Child care providers will need to lead children through the steps at first. With repeated practice, preschoolers and school-age children can learn to work through these steps by themselves.

Find Quiet Place to Talk: Before helping children resolve the conflict, child care providers need to remove children from the place where the conflict occurred. Find a quiet place in the room where everyone can sit and discuss the situation without interruptions.

Set Ground Rules: Conflicts raise strong emotions in most children. Ground rules will help ensure that children discuss the situation rationally and arrive at a solution that all children are willing to try. Common ground rules for children resolving conflicts include:

- Everyone gets a say.
- Everyone listens without interrupting.
- Everyone gets to propose a solution.
- All solutions must be discussed.
- The group must choose the best solution together.

Give Each Person Say: Go around the circle and ask each child to tell her side of the story. Use questions like "Amy, what happened?" and "Beth, what happened?" to allow each child to share. Remind children to listen without interrupting. Be sure everyone has the chance to speak about the problem.

State the Problem Clearly: Based on the information that all children shared, summarize the problem in a few words. You might say something like, "Amy and Beth, it sounds like you both want to be the mother in dramatic play. Is that right?"

Ask Each Person to Suggest a Solution: Go around the circle again and ask each person, "What do you think we should do to solve this problem?" Again, remind children to listen without interrupting. Encourage each child to suggest a solution, even if the suggestion is the same as the one proposed by another child.

Help the Group Choose a Solution: Guide the children in discussing the pros and cons of each solution. Ask them to think about how they would feel about that solution, and encourage them to consider how the solution would affect others as well as themselves. For example, you might say, "Amy has suggested that both of you get to be the mother and take care of your own babies. Beth, how would you feel about that solution? Are there any problems with this idea?"

Put the Solution into Effect: Congratulate the children on coming up with a solution together. Go with the children as they begin trying out their solution. Remind them of the agreement if children are not following the solution chosen.

Observe and Check in if Needed: Watch the children interact for a little while. Watch the ways that they are playing together, and pay attention to any problems that still seem to be happening. If the solution is not working, or children are unhappy with the solution, bring the group back together to renegotiate a better solution.

CONFLICT RESOLUTION THROUGH NEGOTIATION

It's wise to deal with conflict if the issue is important and causing problems. Sometimes, if it is a minor issue, you could just let it go, but if you are feeling unhappy, see if you can work it out.

The most effective way to deal with conflict is to negotiate with the other person involved. Getting angry or aggressive often makes the situation much worse. Much conflict can be resolved if you use a positive and respectful approach - but sometimes this can be very difficult, especially if you or the other person are used to getting what you want by becoming angry, or used to just giving in.

Win-Win Approach: One of the most effective ideas is the win-win approach.

- This approach is about both people being satisfied with the outcome.
- It's about finding out what you both want and where there are areas that you can both agree on, then working towards them.
- It's about working together as partners trying to solve a problem, not as opponents trying to win against each other.
- It's about working together on a basis of mutual respect to find a satisfying solution.

Chapter-37
Play and Child Development

MEANING OF PLAY

Play is a way of 'doing things'. Play is the work of children. It consists of those activities performed for self-amusement that have behavioural, social, and psychomotor rewards. It is child-directed, and the rewards come from within the individual child; it is enjoyable and spontaneous. Play is an important part of the childhood development. Through play children learn about shapes, colours, cause and effect, and themselves. Besides cognitive thinking, play helps the child learn social and psychomotor skills. It is a way of communicating joy, fear , sorrow, and anxiety .

DEFINITIONS OF PLAY

Some definitions of play are as follows:

1. According to Stern, *"Play is a kind of voluntary self-constrained activity."*
2. According to Hurlock, *"Play relates to any activity engaged in for the enjoyment it gives, without consideration of the end result."*
3. According to Crow and Crow, *"Play can be defined as the activity which a person engages when he is free to do what he wants to do."*
4. According to Ross, *"Play is joyful, spontaneous, creative activity in which man finds his fullest self-expression."*

TYPES OF PLAYS

Some of the main types of plays are:

Creative Play: Creative play involves children exploring and using their bodies and materials to make and do things and to share their feelings, ideas and thoughts. They enjoy being creative by dancing, painting, playing with junk and recycled materials, working with play-dough and clay, and using their imaginations.

Games with Rules: Another type of play involves games with rules. Even babies and toddlers can partake in these, as *peek-a-boo* and turn-taking games have rules. In the beginning children often play by their own rather flexible rules! In time they also partake in more conventional games with 'external' rules. Language is an important part of games with rules as children explain, question and negotiate the rules. Rules are often an important part of pretend play where children negotiate rules about what can and can't be done.

Language Play: Language play involves children playing with sounds and words. It includes unrehearsed and spontaneous manipulation of these, often with rhythmic and repetitive elements. Children like playing with language – enjoying patterns, sounds and nonsense words. They also love jokes and funny stories.

Physical Play: Physical play involves children developing, practising and refining bodily movements and control. It includes whole body and limb movements, co-ordination and balance. These activities involve physical movements for their own sake and enjoyment. Children gain control over their gross motor skills first before refining their fine motor skills.

Exploratory Play: Exploratory play involves children using physical skills and their senses to find out what things feel like and what can be done with them. Children explore their own bodies and then they explore the things in their environment.

Manipulative Play: Manipulative play involves practising and refining motor skills. This type of play enhances physical dexterity and hand-eye co-ordination. Over time children need to experience a range of different levels of manipulation if they are to refine their motor skills. This type of play includes manipulating objects and materials.

Constructive Play: Constructive play involves building something using natural and manufactured materials. As children develop, this type of play can become more complex and intricate.

Pretend: Pretend, dramatic, make-believe, role, and fantasy play involves children using their imaginations. It includes pretending with objects, actions and situations. As children grow, their imaginations and their play become increasingly complex. Children use their developing language to move from thinking in the concrete to thinking in the abstract. They make up stories and scenarios. Children act out real events and they also take part in fantasy play about things that are not real, such as fairies or super heroes. Children try out roles, occupations and experiences in their pretend play.

Small World Play: Small world play involves children using small-scale representations of real things like animals, people, cars, and train sets as play props.

Socio-dramatic Play: Socio-dramatic play involves children playing with other children and/or adults. It provides opportunities for children to make friends, to negotiate with others, and to develop their communication skills. This play helps extend language. The ability to write stories also has its roots in socio-dramatic play.

Solitary Play: In such play activities, a child may be found to play all alone with his toys, blocks, ball or even with the objects like sticks, stones etc. or get involved in activities like jumping, climbing, racing etc. all alone.

Spectator Play: The child watches others playing without joining in.

Parallel Play: The child plays side by side with another child, often with similar materials, but without interacting.

Associative/Partnership Play: Children begin to play together, developing interactions through doing the same activities or playing with similar equipment or by imitating.

Co-operative Play: Children interact, take turns, share and decide how and what to play. They collaborate, develop, and negotiate ideas for their play.

CHARACTERISTICS OF PLAY

Some of the characteristics of play are listed below:

Active: Children use their bodies and minds in their play. They interact with the environment, with materials and with other people.

Adventurous and Risky: Play helps children to explore the unknown. The pretend element offers a safety net that encourages children to take risks.

Communicative: Children share information and knowledge through their play. Their communication can be verbal or non-verbal, simple or complex.

Enjoyable: Play is fun and exciting, and involves a sense of humour.

Involved: Children become deeply absorbed and focused in their play, concentrating and thinking about what they are doing.

Meaningful: Children play about what they have seen and heard, and what they know. Play helps them to build and extend their knowledge, understanding and skills in a way that makes sense to them.

Sociable and Interactive: Children play alongside or with others. Sometimes they also like and need to play alone.

Symbolic: Children imagine and pretend when they are playing. They try out ideas, feelings and roles. They re-enact the past and rehearse the future. This can involve them 'reading' and 'writing' long before they develop these skills.

Therapeutic: Play helps children to express and work through emotions and experiences.

Voluntary: Children choose to play. Their play is spontaneous. They shape it as they go, changing the characters, events, objects, and locations.

PLAY AND CHILDREN

In young children, play is frequently associated with cognitive development and socialization. Play that promotes learning and recreation often incorporates toys, props, tools or other playmates. Play can consist of an amusing, pretend or imaginary activity alone or with another. Some forms of play are rehearsals or trials for later life events, such as "play fighting", pretend social encounters (such as parties with dolls), or flirting. Modern findings in neuroscience suggest that play promotes flexibility of mind, including adaptive practices such as discovering multiple ways to achieve a desired result, or creative ways to improve or reorganize a given situation

PLAY AND CHILD DEVELOPMENT

Play is essential to development because it contributes to the cognitive, physical, social and emotional well-being of children and youth. Play also offers an ideal opportunity for parents to engage fully with their children. Despite the benefits derived from play for both children and parents, time for free play has been markedly reduced. Children today receive less support for play than did previous generations in part because of a more hurried lifestyle, changes in family structure, and increased attention to academics and enrichment activities at the expense of recess or free play.

What are the benefits of play in a child's life? A child who has been allowed to develop play resources receives many enduring advantages.

Emotional-Behavioural Benefits of Play

- Play reduces fear, anxiety, stress, irritability

- Creates joy, intimacy, self-esteem and mastery not based on other's loss of esteem
- Improves emotional flexibility and openness
- Increases calmness, resilience and adaptability and ability to deal with surprise and change
- Play can heal emotional pain.

Social benefits of Play

- Increases empathy, compassion, and sharing
- Creates options and choices
- Models relationships based on inclusion rather than exclusion
- Improves nonverbal skills
- Increases attention and attachment

Physical Benefits of Play

- Positive emotions increase the efficiency of immune, endocrine, and cardiovascular systems
- Decreases stress, fatigue, injury, and depression
- Increases range of motion, agility, coordination, balance, flexibility, and fine and gross motor exploration

FUNCTIONS OF PLAY IN CHILD'S GROWTH AND DEVELOPMENT

Play reinforces the child's growth and development. Some of the more common functions of play are to facilitate physical, emotional, cognitive, social, and moral development.

Physical Development

Play aids in developing both fine and gross motor skills. Children repeat certain body movements purely for pleasure, and these movements develop body control. For example, an infant will first hit at a toy, then will try to grasp it, and eventually will be able to pick it up. Next, the infant will shake the rattle or perhaps bring it to the mouth. In these ways, the infant moves from simple to more complex gestures.

Emotional Development

Children who are anxious may be helped by role playing. Role playing is a way of coping with emotional conflict. Children may escape through play into a fantasy world in order to make sense out of the real one. Also, a child's self-awareness deepens as he explores an event through role-playing or symbolic play.

When a parent or sibling plays a board game with a child, shares a bike ride, plays baseball, or reads a story, the child learns self-importance. The child's self-esteem gets a boost. Parents send positive messages to their child when they communicate pleasure in providing him or her with daily care. From these early interactions, children develop a vision of the world and gain a sense of their place in it.

Cognitive Development

Children gain knowledge through their play. They exercise their abilities to think, remember, and solve problems. They develop cognitively as they have a chance to test their beliefs about the world.

Children increase their problem-solving abilities through games and puzzles. Children involved in make-believe play can stimulate several types of learning. Language is strengthened as the children model others and organize their thoughts to communicate. Children playing house create elaborate narratives concerning their roles and the nature of daily living.

Children also increase their understanding of size, shape, and texture through play. They begin to understand relationships as they try to put a square object in a round opening or a large object in a small space. Books, videos, and educational toys that show pictures and matching words also increase a child's vocabulary while increasing the child's concept of the world.

Social Development

A newborn cannot distinguish itself from others and is completely self-absorbed. As the infant begins to play with others and with objects, a realization of self as separate from others begins to develop. The infant begins to experience joy from contact with others and engages in behaviour that involves others. The infant discovers that when he coos or laughs, mother coos back. The child soon expects this response and repeats it for fun, playing with his mother.

As children grow, they enjoy playful interaction with other children. Children learn about boundaries, taking turns, teamwork, and competition. Children also learn to negotiate with different personalities and the feelings associated with winning and losing. They learn to share, wait, and be patient.

Moral Development

When children engage in play with their peers and families, they begin to learn some behaviours are acceptable while others are unacceptable. Parents start these lessons early in the child's life by teaching the child to control aggressive behaviour. Parents can develop morals while reading to children by stressing the moral implications in stories. Children can identify with the moral fictional characters without assuming their roles. With peers they quickly learn that taking turns is rewarding and cheating is not. Group play helps the child appreciate teamwork and share and respect others' feelings. The child learns how to be

References

Anderson, J.R. (1983). *The Architecture of Cognition.* Cambridge, MA: Harvard University Press.

Anderson, J.R. (2000). *Cognitive Psychology and Its Implications.* New York, NY: Worth Publishers.

Aziz Ghefaili. (2003). Cognitive Apprenticeship, Technology, and the Contextualization of Learning Environments. *Journal of Educational Computing, Design & Online Learning*, Vol. 4, Fall, 2003. A copy on apan.org

Bandura, A. (1969). *Principles of Behavior Modification.* New York: Holt, Rinehart & Winston.

Bandura, A. (1973). *Aggression: A Social Learning Analysis.* Englewood Cliffs, NJ: Prentice-Hall.

Bandura, A. (1977). *Social Learning Theory.* New York: General Learning Press.

Bandura, A. (1986). *Social Foundations of Thought and Action.* Englewood Cliffs, NJ: Prentice-Hall.

Bandura, A. (1997). *Self-efficacy: The Exercise of Control.* New York: W.H. Freeman.

Bandura, A. (1997). *Social Learning Theory.* Englewood Cliffs, NJ: Prentice-Hall.

Bandura, A. and Walters, R. (1963). *Social Learning and Personality Development.* New York: Holt, Rinehart & Winston.

Behar-Horenstein, Linda S.; Gail S. Mitchell; Netta Notzer; Randy Penfield, Ilana Eli (2006). Teaching Style Beliefs among U.S. and Israeli Faculty, *Journal of Dental Education.* http:www.jdentaled.org/cgi/reprint/70/8/851.pdf PDF Reprint.

Belknap, R.A. (2000). One Woman's Life Viewed through the Interpretive Lens of Gilligan's Theory. *Violence Against Women*, 6, 586-605.

Bettina Lankard Brown (2003). Teaching Style vs. Learning Style: Myths and Realities. *ERIC*, No. 26.

Brown, B. (2003). Teaching Style vs. Learning Style. *Educational Resources Information Center.* http://www.calpro-online.org/eric/docs/mr41.pdf

Brown, J.S., Collins, A., and Duguid, P. (1989). Situated Cognition and the Culture of Learning. *Educational Researcher*, 18, 32-42.

Bruner, J (1986). *Actual Minds, Possible Worlds.* Cambridge/London: Harvard University Press.

Bruner, J. (1974). *Beyond the Information Given.* London: George Allen & Unwin Ltd.

Bruner, J. (1990). *Acts of Meaning.* Cambridge/ London: Harvard University Press.

Bruner, J. S. (1961). "The Act of Discovery." *Harvard Educational Review* 31: 21-32.

Bruner, J.(1996). *The Culture of Education.* Cambridge/ London: Harvard University Press.

Bruner, J., Oliver, R., Greenfield, P., *et al.* (1966). *Studies in Cognitive Growth* New York: John Wiley & Sons.

Cannon, W.B. (1927) The James-Lange Theory of Emotion: A Critical Examination and an Alternative Theory. *American Journal of Psychology*, 39, 10-124.

Caudron, S. (2000). Learners Speak Out. What Actual Learners Actually Think of Actual Training. *Training and Development,* 54, no. 4: 52-57.

Claxton, C. (2003). *Learning Styles*. http://www.ntlf.com/html/lib/bib/88dig.htm

Cognition and Technology Group at Vanderbilt (March 1993). Anchored Instruction and Situated Cognition Revisited. *Educational Technology*, 33(3), 52-70.

Coles, Robert (1997). *The Moral Intelligence of Children: How to Raise a Moral Child.* New York: Random House.

Collins, A., Brown, J. S., and Newman, S. E. (1987). Cognitive Apprenticeship: Teaching the Craft of Reading, Writing and Mathematics (Technical Report No. 403). BBN Laboratories, Cambridge, MA. Centre for the Study of Reading, University of Illinois. January

Crittenden, Paul (1990). *Learning to be Moral: Philosophical Thoughts About Moral Development.* Atlantic Highlands, NJ: Humanities Press International, 1990.

Delahoussaye, M. (2002). The Perfect Learner: An Expert Debate on Learning Styles. *Training* 39, no. 5: 28-36.

Doherty, Jonathan (2003). Teaching Styles in Physical Education and Mosston's Spectrum, *Sports Media,* August 2007 (MEST).

Eggen, P and Kauchak, D. (2007). *Educational Psychology Windows on Classrooms.* 7th ed. New Jersey: Prentice Hall.

Felder, R (2007). Learning Styles. http://www4.ncsu.edu/unity/lockers/users/f/felder/public/Learning_Styles.html

Feldman, R. S. (2005). *Understanding Psychology*. 7th ed. Boston: McGraw Hill.

Fetsco, T. and McClure, J. (2005). *Educational Psychology: An Integrated Approach to Classroom Decisions*. Boston: Allyn and Bacon.

Gilligan, C., and Attanucci, J. (1988). Two Moral Orientations: Gender Differences and Similarities. *Merrill-Palmer Quarterly*, 34, 223-237.

Gilligan, Carol (1982). *In a Different Voice: Psychological Theory and Women's Development.* Cambridge: Harvard University Press.

Glenn, J. M. (2000). Teaching the Net Generation. *Business Education Forum,* 54, no. 3: 6-8, 10, 12-14.

Grasha and Grasha (1996). *Teaching with Style*. Pittsburgh, PA: Alliance Publishers.

Grasha, Anthony F. (1996). *Teaching with Style: A Practical Guide to Enhancing Learning by Understanding Teaching and Learning Styles*. Pittsburgh: Alliance Publishers.

Hayes, J., and Allinson, C. W. (1997). Learning Styles and Training and Development in Work Settings: Lessons from Educational Research. *Educational Psychology,* 17, nos. 1-2: 185-193.

Heider, F. (1958). *The Psychology of Interpersonal Relations.* New York: Wiley.

Heimlich, J. E., and Norland, E. (2002). Teaching Style: Where Are We Now? *New Directions for Adult and Continuing Education,* no. 93: 17-25.

Huxley, Ronald (1998). *Love and Limits: Achieving a Balance in Parenting.* San Diego: Singular Publishing Group, Inc.

James, W. (1884). What is Emotion?, *Mind*, 9, 188-205.

Johnson, S.D. (1992). A Framework for Technology Education Curricula which Emphasizes Intellectual Processes. *Journal of Technology Education*, 3; 1-11.

Kohlberg, Lawrence (1981). *Essays on Moral Development, I: The Philosophy of Moral Development: Moral Stages and the Idea of Justice.* San Francisco: Harper & Row, 1981.

Kohlberg, Lawrence *(1984). Essays on Moral Development, II: The Psychology of Moral Development.* San Francisco: Harper & Row.

Kurtines, William M., and Jacob L. Gewirtz, eds. (1995). *Moral Development: An Introduction.* Boston: Allyn and Bacon.

Ladd, P., and Ruby, R., Jr. (1999). Learning Style and Adjustment Issues of International Students. *Journal of Education for Business,* 74, no.: 363-367.

Lahey, B.B.(2004). *Psychology: An Introduction.* 8th ed. Boston: McGraw Hill.

Langlois, J. (May, 2001). Teaching and Learning Styles in the Clinical Setting. *Family Medicine.* http://www.stfm.org/fmhub/fm2001/may01/ftobtofm.pdf

Lave, J. (1988). *Cognition in Practice: Mind, Mathematics and Culture in Everyday Life.* Cambridge, UK: Cambridge University Press.

Lave, J., and Wenger, E. (1990). *Situated Learning: Legitimate Peripheral Participation.* Cambridge, UK: Cambridge University Press.

Lefrancois, G.R. (2000) 4th ed. *Theories of Human Learning.* The University of Alberta: Wadsworth.

Lefton, L.A. (2000). *Child Development. In Psychology,* (7th ed.) pp. 350-351, Allyn & Bacon publishing.

Mangal, S.K. (2015). *Childhood and Growing Up,* Tandon Publications, Ludhiana

McLellan, H. (1994). Situated Learning: Continuing the Conversation. *Educational Technology* 34, 7- 8.

McLellan, H. (1995). *Situated Learning Perspectives.* Englewood Cliffs, NJ: Educational Technology Publications.

Mearns, P., and Thorne, B. (1988). *Person-Centred Counselling in Action (Counselling in Action series).* London: SAGE Publications Ltd.

Miller, N. and Dollard, J. (1941). *Social Learning and Imitation.* New Haven, NJ: Yale University Press.

Miller, P. (2001). Learning Styles: The Multimedia of the Mind. *Research Report.* (ED 451 140)

Mosston, M. and Ashworth, S. (1986). *Teaching Physical Education.* Columbus, OH: Merrill.

Nuckles, C.R. (2000). Student-Centered Teaching: Making It Work. *Adult Learning,* 11, no. 4: 5-6.

Ormrod, J.E. (2006). *Educational Psychology: Developing Learners.* 5th ed. New Jersey: Prentice Hall.

Papalia, D.E., Olds, S.W., and Feldma R.D. (2007). *Human Development.* 10th ed. Boston: McGraw Hill.

Piaget, J. ((1965). *The Moral Judgment of the Child.* New York: The Free Press.

Pithers, B. (2001). An Aspect of Vocational Teachers. Cognitive Style: Field Dependence-Field Independence. *Australian and New Zealand Journal of Vocational Education Research,* 9, no. 2: 47-60.

Pithers, R.T. (2002). Cognitive Learning Style: A Review of the Field Dependent-Field Independent Approach. *Journal of Vocational Education and Training,* 54, no. 1: 117-132.

Power, F.C., *et al.* (1989). *Lawrence Kohlberg's Approach to Moral Education: A Study of Three Democratic High Schools.* New York: Columbia University Press.

Pratt, D.D. (2002). Good Teaching: One Size Fits All?. *New Directions for Adult and Continuing Education,* no. 93: 5-15.

Rogers, C. (1951). *Client-centered Therapy: Its Current Practice, Implications and Theory.* London: Constable.

Rogers, C. (1959). A Theory of Therapy, Personality and Interpersonal Relationships as Developed in the Client-centered Framework. In (ed.) S. Koch, *Psychology: A Study of a Science. Vol. 3: Formulations of the Person and the Social Context.* New York: McGraw Hill.

Rogers, C. (1975). Empathic: An unappreciated way of being. *The Counseling Psychologist,* 5(2), 2-10.

Rogers, C. (1986). Carl Rogers on the Development of the Person-Centered Approach. *Person-Centered Review*, 1(3), 257-259.

Rotter, J.B. (1966). Generalized Expectancies for Internal Versus External Control of Reinforcement. *Psychological Monographs* 80 (1, Whole No. 609).

Rown, J.S., Collins, A. and Duguid, S. (1989). Situated cognition and the culture of learning. *Educational Researcher*, 18(1), 32-42.

Santrock, J.W. (2008). *Educational Psychology*. 3rd ed. Boston: McGraw-Hill.

Schachter, S. and Singer, J. E. (1962). Cognitive, Social and Physiological Determinants of Emotional State. *Psychological Review*, 69, 379-399.

Schulman, Michael and Eva Mekler. (1994). *Bringing Up a Moral Child: A New Approach for Teaching Your Child to Be Kind, Just, and Responsible.* rev. ed. New York: Main Street Books/Doubleday.

Schunk, D.H. (2012). *Learning Theories: An Educational Perspective*, 6th ed. Boston, MA: Pearson Education.

Solomon, R.L. and Corbit, J.D. (1974). An Opponent-Process Theory of Motivation: I. Temporal Dynamics of Affect. *Psychological Review*, 81, 119-145.

Spoon, J.C., and Schell, J.W. (1998). Aligning Student Learning Styles with Instructor Teaching Styles. *Journal of Industrial Teacher Education,* 35, no. 2: 41-56.

Stitt-Gohdes, W.L. (2001). Business Education Students. Preferred Learning Styles and Their Teachers. Preferred Instructional Styles: Do They Match? *Delta Pi Epsilon Journal,* 43, no. 3: 137- 151.

Stitt-Gohdes, W.L. (2003). Student Teachers and Their Students: Do Their Instructional and Learning Preferences Match? *Business Education Forum,* 57, no. 4: 22-27.

Stitt-Gohdes, W.L.; Crews, T.B. and McCannon, M. (1999). Business Teachers: Learning and Instructional Styles. *Delta Pi Epsilon Journal*, 41, no. 2: 71-88.

Suchman, L. (1988). Plans and Situated Actions: The Problem of Human/Machine Communication. Cambridge, UK: Cambridge University Press.

Tan O.S., Parsons, R.D., Hinson, S.L. and Sardo-Brown, D. (2003) *Educational Psychology. A Practitioner-Researcher Approach.* Australia: Thomson.

Vygotsky, L.S. (1962). *Thought and Language*. Cambridge, MA: MIT Press.

Vygotsky, L.S. (1978). *Mind and Society: The Development of Higher Mental Processes*. Cambridge, MA: Harvard University Press.

Weiner, B. (1979). A Theory of Motivation for Some Classroom Experiences. *Psychological Review* 71:3–25.

Weiner, B. (2004). Attribution Theory Revisited: Transforming Cultural Plurality into Theoretical Unity. In *Big Theories Revisited*, edited by D. M. McInerney & S. Van Etten, 13–29). Greenwich, CT: Information Age Publishing.

Weiner, B., I.H. Frieze, A. Kukla, L. Reed, S. Rest, and F.M. Rosenbaum. (1971). *Perceiving the Causes of Success and Failure.* Morristown, NJ: General Learning Press.

Wertsch, J.V. (1985). *Cultural, Communication, and Cognition: Vygotskian Perspectives*. Cambridge University Press.

Woolfolk, A. (2007). *Educational Psychology.* 10th ed. Boston: Pearson.